# Encountering Islam

## Joseph Pitts: An English Slave in 17th-century Algiers and Mecca

A FAITHFUL

# ACCOUNT

OF THE

## Religion and Manners

OF THE

# 𝕸𝖆𝖍𝖔𝖒𝖊𝖙𝖆𝖓𝖘.

In which is a particular
RELATION of their *Pilgrimage* to
*Mecca*, the Place of MAHOMET'S
Birth; and a Defcription of *Medina*,
and of his Tomb there: As likewife
of *Algier*, and the Country adjacent;
and of *Alexandria*, *Grand Cairo*, &c.
With an Account of the Author's
being taken Captive; the *Turks* Cruelty to him; and of his Efcape. In
which are many Things never publifh'd by any Hiftorian before.

By *JOSEPH PITTS*, of *Exon*.

The THIRD EDITION, *Corrected, with Additions.* To
this Edition is added a Map of Mecca, and a Cut of
the Geftures of the Mahometans *in their Worfhip*.

LONDON,
Printed for J. Osborn *and* T. Longman, *at the* Ship *in*
Pater-nofter-row; *and* R. Hett, *at the* Bible *and*
Crown *in the* Poultry. M.DCC.XXXI.

Title page, at actual size, of *A Faithful Account of the
Religion and Manners of the Mahometans*, 1731

# Encountering Islam

### Joseph Pitts: An English Slave in 17th-century Algiers and Mecca

A critical edition, with biographical
introduction and notes, of
Joseph Pitts of Exeter's
*A Faithful Account of the Religion and Manners
of the Mahometans*, 1731

## Paul Auchterlonie

Arabian Publishing

Encountering Islam: Joseph Pitts: An English Slave
in 17th-century Algiers and Mecca.
A critical edition of Joseph Pitts of Exeter's *A Faithful Account of the Religion and Manners of the Mahometans*, 1731
By Paul Auchterlonie

© Arabian Publishing Ltd 2012

Produced and published in 2012 by Arabian Publishing Ltd
4 Bloomsbury Place, London WC2A 2QA
Email: arabian.publishing@arabia.uk.com

Edited by William Facey

**BFSA**
British Foundation
for the Study of Arabia
المؤسسة البريطانية لدراسة الجزيرة العربية
Published in association with the BFSA

A catalogue card for this book is available from the British Library

ISBN: 978-0-9558894-9-3

Typesetting and digital artwork by Jamie Crocker, Artista-Design, UK
Printed and bound by TJ International, Cornwall, UK

# CONTENTS

# ACKNOWLEDGEMENTS

Many people have helped me with this work. I would like to thank in particular Wafa Iskander, Professor Sajjad Rizvi and Dr Clémence-Yucel of the Institute of Arab and Islamic Studies, University of Exeter, and Sara Yontan Musnik of the Bibliothèque Nationale de France, for assistance on linguistic issues. I am grateful too to Dr Gareth Cole and Dr Christine Faunch of Exeter University Library for advice on bibliographical matters. In particular, I would like to thank the director of Arabian Publishing, William Facey, who commissioned this book, and whose editorial expertise and attention to detail immeasurably improved the quality of the whole work. Special thanks go also to Mrs Lindy Ayubi, who produced the excellent transcription of Pitts's text and whose skill in copy-editing greatly enhanced the Introduction, and to Peter Colvin, who generously deciphered Pitts's often opaque transcriptions of 17th-century Turkish for me. Above all, I owe a great debt to my wife, Mitzi, who has shared my interest in Joseph Pitts and given the project constant support and encouragement.

Paul Auchterlonie

Exeter, January 2012

# NOTE ON TRANSLITERATION AND TRANSCRIPTION

## System of transliteration

Well-known Arabic and Turkish names and technical terms have been left in their familiar English form, for example Algiers, Oran, Cairo, Mecca, Medina, Janissary, Pasha, Agha. Arabic names and terms have been transliterated according to the system adopted by Arabian Publishing, which is based on that used in *New Arabian Studies*. Turkish names and terms have been rendered according to the norms of modern Turkish orthography. All quotations from the Bible in the notes to the text are from the King James version, since that is the one Joseph Pitts would have been familiar with.

## Transcription of Pitts's text (Part II)

The text forming Part II is a faithful reproduction of the 1731 edition, and mirrors Pitts's spelling, his use of capital letters and of italics. The only exceptions are Pitts's own notes: in the 1731 edition, shorter notes are generally placed within the text, longer notes at the foot of the page. In this 2012 edition, the author's notes are introduced and closed by double square brackets and are inserted into the text at the most appropriate place. Editorial additions are placed within single square brackets. The pagination of the original 1731 edition is shown by page numbers in bold, and all references in the text and notes of Part I refer to the relevant page in the 1731 edition, unless indicated otherwise.

# LIST OF MAPS AND ILLUSTRATIONS

## Maps

## Illustrations

# Maps and Illustrations

MAPS

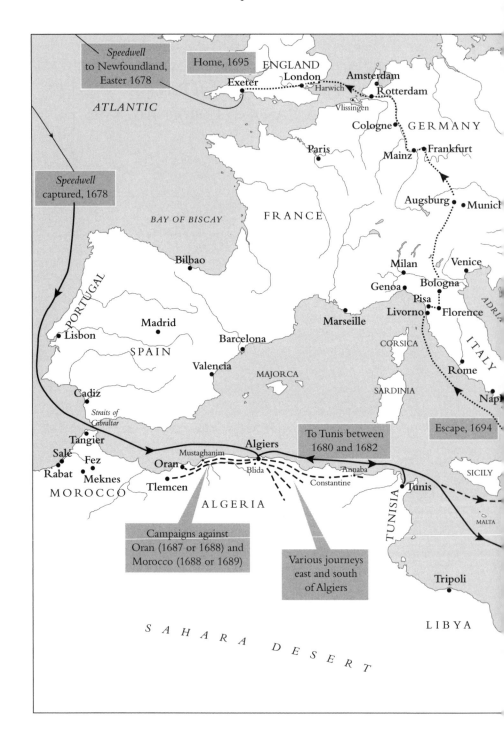

Speedwell
to Newfoundland,
Easter 1678

Home, 1695  ENGLAND

London  Amsterdam

Exeter  Harwich

Rotterdam

Vlissingen

ATLANTIC

Cologne  GERMANY

Paris

Mainz  Frankfurt

Speedwell
captured, 1678

Augsburg  Munich

BAY OF BISCAY  FRANCE

Milan  Venice

Genoa  Bologna

Pisa

Bilbao

Livorno  Florence

PORTUGAL

Marseille  CORSICA

Madrid  Barcelona

Lisbon  SPAIN

Valencia  MAJORCA

Rome

SARDINIA  Nap

Cadiz

Escape, 1694

Straits of
Gibraltar

Tangier  Mustaghanim  Algiers  To Tunis between
1680 and 1682

Salé  Oran

Fez  Blida

Rabat  Meknes  Annaba  SICILY

MOROCCO  Tlemcen  Constantine  Tunis

ALGERIA  MALTA

Campaigns against
Oran (1687 or 1688) and
Morocco (1688 or 1689)

Various journeys
east and south
of Algiers

Tripoli

LIBYA

S A H A R A   D E S E R T

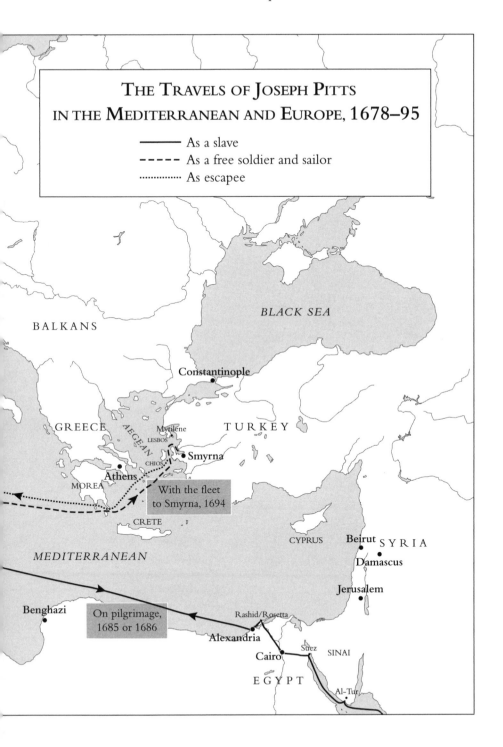

THE TRAVELS OF JOSEPH PITTS
IN THE MEDITERRANEAN AND EUROPE, 1678–95

——— As a slave
– – – – As a free soldier and sailor
·············· As escapee

BALKANS

BLACK SEA

Constantinople

GREECE    AEGEAN    TURKEY

Mytilene
LESBOS
CHIOS    Smyrna
Athens
MOREA

With the fleet
to Smyrna, 1694

CRETE

CYPRUS    Beirut    SYRIA
Damascus

MEDITERRANEAN

Jerusalem

Benghazi

On pilgrimage,
1685 or 1686

Rashid/Rosetta
Alexandria
Cairo    Suez    SINAI
EGYPT

Al-Tur

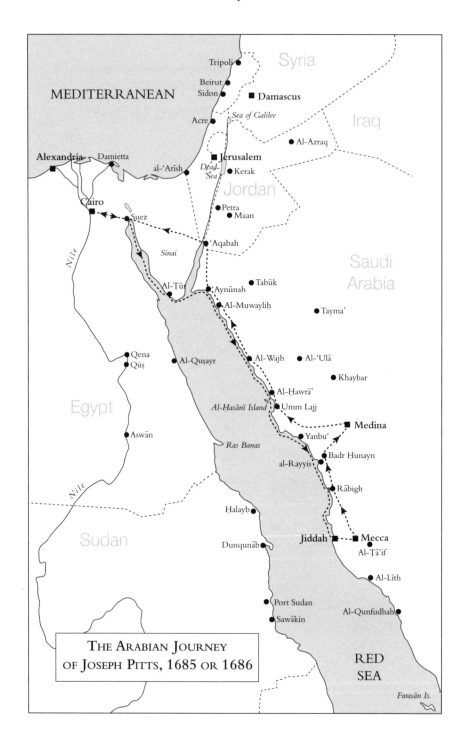

MEDITERRANEAN

Tripoli

Beirut
Sidon
■ Damascus

Syria

Iraq

Acre *Sea of Galilee*

Alexandria Damietta

al-'Arīsh

■ Jerusalem
*Dead-
Sea* ●Kerak

Jordan

● Al-Azraq

Cairo
● Suez

●Petra
●Maan

Saudi
Arabia

*Nile*

*Sinai*

●'Aqabah

Al-Ṭūr ●Aynūnah ● Tabūk

●Al-Muwayliḥ

●Tayma'

Qena
Qūṣ

Al-Quṣayr

●Al-Wajh ●Al-'Ulā

●Khaybar

Egypt

*Al-Ḥasānī Island*

Al-Ḥawrā'

Umm Lajj

■ Medina

Aswān

*Ras Banas*

Yanbu'

*Nile*

al-Rayyis

Badr Ḥunayn

Rābigh

Ḥalayb

Sudan

Dunqunāb

Jiddah ■ Mecca
Al-Ṭā'if

●Al-Līth

Port Sudan

Sawākin

●Al-Qunfudhah

THE ARABIAN JOURNEY
OF JOSEPH PITTS, 1685 OR 1686

RED
SEA

*Farasān Is.*

# PART I

## JOSEPH PITTS: SAILOR, SLAVE, TRAVELLER, PILGRIM

By Paul Auchterlonie

# INTRODUCTION

*A* *FAITHFUL ACCOUNT* of the Religion and Manners of the Mahometans[1] by Joseph Pitts is an intriguing and, as far as is known, unique combination of three distinct genres: captivity narrative, travel account, and description of Islam. There are 17th- and 18th-century English books combining two of these three elements but, on the face of it, no author other than Pitts combines all three strands within a single work.

To fully evaluate and appreciate these aspects, it is important to place the book in the context of what is known about Pitts's life and personality, and the milieu in which he grew up. Vital as background too are the history of the Barbary States, how they were created, how they became economically dependent on slavery and ransom, how they were governed, and how they interacted with Christian Europe. Also needed is an understanding of what it was like to be a slave in Algiers, Tripoli or Tunis, how slaves were treated, what their relationship was to their masters, and what happened if a slave renounced Christianity and "turned Turk". From the point of view of travel, it is necessary to discover how Pitts's description of the places he visited relates to previous and subsequent travellers, whether he was accurate, and how much he knew about earlier travel accounts. Crucial to understanding Pitts's account of Islam, and his view of Barbary society, are the way Islam was viewed in contemporary England and the extent of awareness of the actual rites and practices of the religion. A judgement can then be made as to whether Pitts adds anything to the knowledge of the time. Is he still worth reading for the information he imparts, for the *Zeitgeist* he embodies, for the adventurous tale he tells, or for a combination of all three? Did he give the 18th-century English-speaking public new facts and insights about being a slave, about Algerian society, about Islam and about the Middle East in general, or did he just tell a good story, set against the background of commonly held beliefs and information? In short, was his book really ground-breaking and unique in its time?

Captivity narratives were an interesting sub-genre of literature between

1589,[2] the date of publication of the first such account, and the first quarter of the 19th century, when the last of the memoirs of North African slavery was published.[3] Few of the early narratives[4] "achieved any of the breadth, the historical and ethnographical detail, or the geographical variety of the post-1640 accounts",[5] and were concerned mostly with the authors' "personal ordeals, their faith and their commitment to their religious and national identity",[6] whereas accounts from the second half of the 17th century onwards tended to be much longer and offered much more narrative detail, local colour and informative excursuses. An indication of the 18th-century interest in the genre is shown by the number of editions published within the space of a few years: Pitts's book itself was published five times between 1704 and 1738 (including two pirated editions), while the tale of Thomas Pellow (b. 1703 or 1704) entitled *The History of the Long Captivity and Adventures of Thomas Pellow in South Barbary* was published four times between 1739 and 1752, variously in London, Bath and Dublin. This was the period when the staple literary fare of most non-aristocratic Britons consisted of the Bible, *Pilgrim's Progress*, and *Robinson Crusoe*,[7] and the providentialist adventures of Britons escaping from "infidel" slavery in North Africa fitted into this category very neatly.

During the 19th century and the first half of the 20th, English captivity narratives were all but forgotten. A few were republished as adventures,[8] or as a contribution to family history,[9] or as part of a miscellany of voyages,[10] but in general interest in the genre stagnated until after the Second World War. To some extent, the same can be said of histories of the Barbary corsairs, especially of the relations between the regencies of Tripoli, Tunis and Algiers (and the independent state of Morocco) and European states. After the conquest of Algiers in 1830, the French began to publish works on North Africa,[11] and produced some important editions of early travellers there,[12] but before 1950 almost the sole significant monograph in English on the subject of the Barbary corsairs was that by Stanley Lane-Poole in the *Story of the Nations* series,[13] which is now hardly cited at all ("It adds nothing to the story except that it is in English"[14]). However, the situation slowly began to change after the Second World War, and not only were critical histories of the Barbary corsairs written,[15] but works using captivity narratives as source material also appeared.[16]

The real transformation in captivity studies, however, came about with the publication of Nabil Matar's trilogy,[17] and, in a companion volume, a modern edition of seven captivity narratives edited by Daniel Vitkus, which also included a major survey of the genre by Nabil Matar, and an evaluation of these narratives as sources of information, identity and attitude.[18] Matar's books use a very wide range of sources, including not just captivity narratives (although he was the first to see them in a new postmodern light), but also British state papers and contemporary English works of theology, travel, literature and history. Matar traces the influence of Islam (in the form of the Ottoman Empire as well as the North African states) through English writings about the figure of the renegade on the stage as well as in religious books; he looks at how certain 17th-century English Protestants utilized Islamic theological concepts in their writings on eschatology; he examines the presence of Muslims in Britain, as both captives and ambassadors, and how the British state and private individuals responded to the challenge of ransoming Britons held captive in North Africa; he analyses the stories of the captives themselves through the prism of their (auto)biographies and finds interesting correlations between captivity narratives from North Africa and North America; he studies the British colony of Tangier and its effect on Anglo-Moroccan relations, and scrutinizes the common accusation made by captives and travellers that Muslims openly practised homosexuality; he traces the evolution of Islamic studies in 16th- and 17th-century England; and he even considers the relationship between Barbary and British women. In short, Matar has revolutionized the way in which the relations between Islam (and more especially North Africa) and Britain have evolved, by looking at the subject in as wide a perspective as possible, by drawing critically on a huge range of sources, and by taking account of recent challenges to the Eurocentric way in which Islam had been portrayed by earlier writers.[19] His three monographs (plus his extensive range of articles on the subject) have provoked a dramatic response: captivity studies and the whole question of European–North African relations have been the subject of a great array of new books and articles, some historical,[20] others from a more literary or cultural perspective,[21] while the subject itself has recently engaged the popular imagination,[22] spawning several websites and an online collection of papers.[23]

While captivity narratives in general languished in unwarranted neglect for almost 200 years until this extraordinary efflorescence of activity towards the end of the 20th century, Pitts by contrast has always maintained a presence in historical surveys of Arabian exploration, due to his achievement as the first recorded Englishman to visit Mecca and to write about it. Pitts's account of his visit to the Muslim Holy Places occupies a significant place in the classic work by Sir Richard Burton (1821–90), *Personal Narrative of a Pilgrimage to Al Madinah and Meccah*,[24] and he is usually accorded a short chapter in most of the 20th-century books on Arabian travel or visits to Mecca, for example those of Hogarth, Ralli, Kiernan, Bidwell, Brent, Freeth and Winstone, and Simmons,[25] and even in those written in French and German.[26] However, most of these accounts, even the most substantial of them by Freeth and Winstone, are little more than extracts from the Arabian part of Pitts's book, while the chapter on him in Sabine Baring Gould's (1908) *Devonshire Characters and Strange Events*[27] is merely a recapitulation in Pitts's own words of his time in Algiers and his escape through Europe, stripped of all his observations on Islam and his journey to Mecca and Medina. Probably the only significant 20th-century contribution to our knowledge of Pitts as a traveller is the critical and well-annotated edition of his visit to Egypt, Mecca and Medina by Sir William Foster for the Hakluyt Society,[28] since this edition includes detailed geographical, linguistic and other notes, which help to clarify precisely where Pitts went and what he did.

Although Pitts has always been appreciated as an Arabian traveller and his book is now much studied as a captivity narrative, very little consideration has been given to his contribution to our understanding of Islam, which is the third facet of his book. Although this work was entitled *A Faithful Account of the Religion and Manners of the Mahometans*, his name is scarcely mentioned in many of the recent monographs on the history of Islamic studies in early modern England.[29] The few times his name does crop up in connection with Islam, it tends to be in a derogatory context,[30] and a re-examination of the Islamic content of his book (as well as his observations on Algerian society) is long overdue.

# 1

## ALGIERS: A CORSAIR STATE

### Algiers and the Ottoman Empire

FROM THE MIDDLE of the 9th century until the beginning of the 16th, North Africa, from Libya to Morocco, had operated more or less independently of the central caliphal authority based initially in Baghdad under the Abbasids till AD 1258 and then in Cairo under the Mamluks. However, the rise of the Ottoman Empire in the 15th century changed the balance of power. Initially the Ottomans focused their military strength on the Balkans and Anatolia, but once they had conquered Constantinople in 1453 and consolidated their power in the Balkans, they looked both southwards and westwards in order to extend their territory. At the beginning of the 16th century, they built a substantial navy in order to compete with Venice in the eastern Mediterranean. However, as Palmira Brummett explains, it is important to understand the Ottoman concept of a navy:

> The term "navy" invokes an image of armed vessels engaging in battle on the open sea: a seaborne version of an army. In the eastern Mediterranean, sea warfare was not the primary function of navies. Rather, naval functions were transport, defense of commerce, support of sieges and land campaigns, and protection against piracy.[1]

Indeed, most of the activities of the Ottoman navy in the early 16th century were directed against pirates, both Muslim ones, such as Kara Durmuş, and Christian ones, such as the Knights of St John, while conversely, in times of actual war, "what was possible and cost-effective in terms of fighting ships was the incorporation of corsair fleets into state naval operations either on a permanent or a temporary basis".[2] There was a fine line between state-sanctioned activity and private enterprise, and some Muslim jurists in the pre-

The brothers Oruç and Hayreddin Barbarossa, founders of Algiers as a corsair power, in a 17th-century Dutch engraving graphically conveying the terror they inspired in the European imagination.

Ottoman age had "codified piracy as a form of *jihād*, licit as long as it was carried out according to the principles governing war with *dār al-ḥarb*",[3] and such nice distinctions were evident in the careers of the two most famous Ottoman admirals, the brothers Oruç and Hayreddin (Khayr al-Dīn) Barbarossa. The Ottomans entered the western Mediterranean through the semi-independent activities of Kemal Reis, who made contact with the Hispano-Muslims of Granada in 1487, and subsequently used North African ports such as Bougie (Bijāyah) to harass Christian shipping, until, in 1495, he returned to Istanbul and formally entered the service of Bayazid II's navy.[4] The experiences of Kemal Reis seem to have acted as a spur to both Oruç and Hayreddin Barbarossa. Born in the town of Mytilene on the Aegean island of Lesbos to a Turkish father and a Greek mother probably between 1465 and 1475, the brothers began operating in the eastern Mediterranean but, falling out of favour at court in 1512, "the Barbarossa brothers fled westward toward Tunis, rather than face the penalties a sultan as fierce as Selim the Grim applied to those who backed the wrong candidate".[5] Oruç and his brother were initially very successful and captured a number of important prizes, and by 1514 they had re-established themselves in the Sultan's favour by sending the nephew of Kemal Reis, the famous geographer Piri Reis, to Istanbul with gifts for the Sultan, who responded by sending them two war galleys. As Andrew Hess explains:

> Transcending the immediate importance of the new equipment, the mission of Piri Reis wedded the Maghribian privateers to an urban center, where the corsairs could obtain powder technology, trained footsoldiers, and the support of an empire with a celebrated reputation for the prosecution of the holy war.[6]

After failing twice to take Bougie, in 1516 Oruç answered an appeal from the inhabitants of Algiers to rid them of the Spaniards who had established a fort on Peñón, just outside the harbour. Oruç was unable to eject the Spaniards, but took possession of the town of Algiers and installed a force there of about twelve ships and a thousand Turkish troops;[7] Oruç also conquered the port of Cherchel (Shirshāl), but was killed in the autumn of 1518, while attempting to wrest control of the former Algerian capital of Tlemcen (Ṭilimsān) from its Arab rulers, who paid tribute to the Spanish.

Hayreddin Barbarossa, who had succeeded his brother as ruler of Algiers, sent another envoy to the Sultan in 1519 and asked for Algiers to be included within the Sultan's dominions. In return for swearing allegiance to the Ottoman Sultan, he received 2,000 troops directly with another 4,000 as volunteers, as well as the title of *beylerbey*. In the following decade, Hayreddin consolidated his power by subduing (at least temporarily) the tribes of the interior, and in 1529 he finally forced the Spanish to abandon their fort on Peñón. This conquest, as well as the construction of a large breakwater to protect the harbour, enabled him to turn Algiers into the Ottomans' principal naval port in their struggle for supremacy in the western Mediterranean against the Spanish. After Barbarossa's death in 1546, the Ottoman Sultan continued to appoint the *beylerbey*, who although he was based in Algiers had control of all Ottoman North Africa, including Tripoli (conquered in 1551) and Tunis (conquered in 1574). During the 1580s, however, the Ottomans reviewed their naval strategy in the light of their defeat at Lepanto in 1571 and the truce which they had signed with Spain in 1580. As Ellen Friedman remarks:

> The age of the crusades was over. Philip II was occupied with European concerns. Faced with the threat of Protestant-inspired revolts in the Netherlands and France, the notion of a crusade against Islam lost much of its force. At the same time, the Turks, too, were drawn away from the western Mediterranean. For them, the center of gravity shifted eastwards, to internal conflicts within their own empire.[8]

As a result of these strategic changes, in 1587 the *beylerbey* in overall control of Ottoman North Africa was replaced by three pashas, one for each of the territories of Tripoli, Tunis and Algiers, all of whom were appointed directly from Istanbul for a fixed term of three years. However, the pashas were unable to compete with the janissaries,[9] the Turkish-speaking military elite, in any of the three regencies, and in Algiers Hızır Paşa (Khiḍr Pasha, died *ca.* 1605), the only Ottoman-appointed official to challenge the authority of the soldiers (known collectively as the *ocak*[10]), failed to hold on to power.[11] In the 17th century, the point was reached "when the pashas ceased to exercise any check on janissaries and *ra'īses*[12] except to make their own fortune while time permitted".[13] As Francis Knight (dates unknown), a slave in Algiers in the 1630s, explained to his readers, "in fine, the Bashaw is but a figure",[14] and in 1659 the ruling council in Algiers, the *dīwān*,[15] decided to "abolish the pasha's last remaining prerogatives – issue of pay, appointment of *qā'id*s [regional sub-governors] and jurisdiction over the *Baldi*s [native Algerians]",[16] and the pasha's prerogatives were duly transferred to the de facto ruler of Algiers, who was the head of the *dīwān* and known as the *bey*. However, the destruction of much of the Algerian fleet by a squadron of British ships under the command of Sir

Edward Spragge (*ca.* 1629–73)[17] in 1671 caused the vanquished corporation of sea-captains, the *ṭā'ifah*,[18] to rebel and take control of the *dīwān* themselves, by electing the head of the *dīwān* and renaming him the *dey*. Then, in 1689, this situation was reversed again, when the janissary corps reasserted its right to nominate the ruler of the regency and head of the *dīwān*.[19] Finally, in 1711, "the tenth dey, Ali Çavuş ('Alī Shāwush), declined to receive the envoy of the Porte and persuaded the Sultan to grant him the title of Pasha",[20] thus ending any remaining direct connection between Algiers and Istanbul, although the Regency remained nominally suzerain to the Sultan until the French invasion of 1830 finally put an end to more than three hundred years of Turkish rule in Algiers.[21]

## The political and social organization of Algiers

LIKE THE OTHER regencies of Tunis and Tripoli, Algiers was a mixture of a number of groups, at the apex of which were the Turkish-speaking military forces, often called janissaries. Janissaries in many parts of the Ottoman Empire were the product of the *devşirme* tradition, whereby Christian children from the Balkans or the Caucasus were taken from their families, brought up as Muslims and trained in the military arts,[22] although they were sometimes young Christian men captured in war who converted to Islam.[23] Pitts was aware of this tradition and describes the make-up of the soldiery in the main Ottoman Empire:

> Indeed, in the *Grand Turk's Country* [i.e. Turkey], in *Egypt*, and the Parts thereabout, where those Sorts of *Christians* are which are taken by the *Tartars*, coming out of the country of the *Russians*, *Georgians*, *Circassians*, &c. these being a very *ignorant Sort of Christians*, and especially the *Younger of them*, are no sooner taken Slaves, and sold, but they are immediately clothed with the *Turkish Habit*, put to School and brought up in the *Mahometan* way.[24]

However, in Algiers, the situation was different and as Tal Shuval has shown:

> The uniqueness of the Algerian corps lies not in its avoidance of hereditary status but in its ability to maintain the system long after the janissary corps of the imperial center had abandoned it. This was reflected in three practices: the militia's recruiting policy

11

(concentrated in the empire's heartland, mainly in Anatolia); the restrictive marriage practices of the janissary corps; and the policy regarding the integration of elite members' sons into the militia.[25]

In Algiers, Turkish volunteers, rather than the *devşirme* tradition of converted captives were the mainstay of the army (the soldiers themselves called each other *yoldaş* or comrade).[26] They were an efficient and disciplined military force, who undertook campaigns on land against the native Arabs and Berbers, against the neighbouring territories of Morocco and Tunis and also against the Spanish enclave of Oran (which they finally captured in 1792), and they were usually the dominant element in the ruling council or *dīwān* under their commander, the agha.[27] From the 1560s they also went to sea, where they were used not only to capture other vessels, but often to go on raids to Italy, Spain and France, capturing and enslaving whatever local Christians they could find on the coast. The janissaries tried "to preserve the exclusively Turkish character of their group,"[28] so much so that if a janissary married a local Algerian woman, their offspring (named *kuloğlu*) were hardly ever admitted to the ranks of the elite.[29] As Paul Rycaut (1629–1700), a seasoned contemporary observer of Ottoman society, remarked:[30]

> The government [of Algiers] … fearing lest the power should at last become subject to the natives, have made it a law that no son of a Turk born in that country [i.e. Algiers], whom they call Cololies [*kuloğlu*] can be capable of office in their commonwealth, but only such, who having been born Christians, are perverted to the Turkish religion, or else such who come from parts of the Turkish dominions to be members of their *république*.[31]

The other main element of the *ocak*, or the group in overall command of Algiers, was the *ṭā'ifah*, which controlled the Algerian naval forces. Initially dominated by the army, by the 16th century the *ṭā'ifah* had become a distinct group,[32] whose members were much more mixed ethnically, because the *ṭā'ifah* allowed former slaves to serve as captains, owners or officers on board the ships, provided they had converted to Islam. Many Europeans sailors who were captured had special skills which the Algerians and other regencies found valuable,[33] and as a consequence many of the famous sea-captains (sing. *ra'īs*) were Europeans who had converted. An example was the Dutch renegade, Murad Bey, who led the attack on Baltimore in Ireland in 1631.[34] Similarly, the captain of the ship which captured Joseph Pitts was "a *Dutch Renegado* and able

12

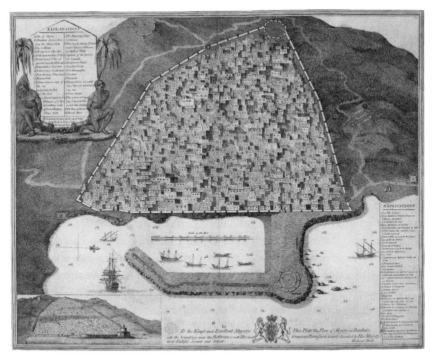

This British plan of Algiers by Richard Ball, published in 1776, shows how developed and well defended the city and port had become by the mid-18th century.

Another British view of Algiers, drawn by Charles Rumker and published in 1816.

to speak *English*".[35] In his edition of the diary of Thomas Baker (dates unknown; Baker was English Consul in Tripoli 1677–85 and later consul in Algiers 1691–94), C. R. Pennell shows that of the "thirteen raises listed by Baker in 1679, five were renegades, six were Turks, one was a Kulughli and one a 'Moor'".[36]

The Moriscos, who made up a significant element of the population after their expulsion from Spain between 1609 and 1614, were another powerful group in Algiers, Morocco and Tunis. They brought skills with them as well as knowledge of the Spanish coastline and of Spanish,[37] and, in addition, an intense desire for revenge.[38] In contrast, the Moors or ethnic Arabs who made up the urban workforce within the city of Algiers, as well as the majority of the population outside the city, were excluded from public office along with the Kabyles or Berbers.[39] Pitts did not have a high opinion of the Moors, calling them "of *small* Courage"[40] and "much given to *Sloth*,"[41] but considered the Kabyles "a very rugged sort of People [who] care not to pay the *Tribute* demanded of them by the *Bay*."[42] However, the religious and legal system was dominated by Arabs, and included the *muftīs*,[43] who were at the apex of the Islamic system of justice, and who often played a significant role in the power struggles between the janissaries and the *ṭā'ifah*.[44] There were two *muftīs* in Algiers itself (as in Tunis and Tripoli), one to serve the Mālikī *madhhab*, to which the majority of the inhabitants of North Africa belonged, and one for the Turks, who chiefly followed the Ḥanafī *madhhab*. Baber Johansen estimates that Algiers supported fourteen Ḥanafī and ninety Mālikī mosques towards the end of the 18th century, while 120 religious functionaries were paid in some way by the state.[45] The Jews comprised another constituency within Algiers and were extremely important in commerce, eventually coming to dominate Algiers' overseas trade with Europe, especially Livorno (known at that time as Leghorn).[46]

It is difficult to estimate the population of Algiers at the time of Pitts. The only accurate figures we have are those for the number of janissaries in Algiers in the 18th century, based on data taken from pay registers by Jean Deny;[47] this suggests that there were around 12,000 for the first half of that century. Various visitors made their own estimates, including Pitts who claimed that "there are about twelve thousand janizaries in Algier, including the invalids who have half pay."[48] The English consul, Samuel Martin (dates unknown), reckoned the population of Algiers in 1675 "to be some 32,800 families (including Kulughlis, Jews, Arabs, Jerbans [from the island of Djerba off the Tunisian coast] and others) and another 31,000 individuals (Christian slaves, Turks and Berbers)."[49] Using the figures given by Père Pierre Dan (1580?–1649), Emanuel d'Aranda (1602–

1686), Laurent d'Arvieux (1625–1702) and Laugier de Tassy (dates unknown),[50] J. B. Wolf calculates that "seventeenth-century Algiers maintained its population at a reasonably stable figure of one hundred to one hundred twenty-five thousand freemen and slaves".[51] Julien[52] and Abun-Nasr[53] agree that 100,000 inhabitants was a reasonable estimate of the total population of Algiers at that time, plus a slave population of around 25,000, while Davis suggests that slaves made up a quarter of the population, and that Turks constituted twelve percent and renegade Christians eight percent.[54]

This very mixed population in Algiers (as in Tripoli and Tunis) was governed by the *dīwān*, or ruling council, which was made up of Janissaries, who were all Turkish-speaking, and the *ṭā'ifah* of *ra'īses*, the more mixed ethnic group of sea captains. In Algiers, the *dīwān* was initially presided over jointly by the head of the janissaries (the agha) and the pasha,[55] but as noted above, the army took over the *dīwān* in 1659, and although they lost control in 1671, they soon reasserted their authority and retained it until the regency disappeared in the wake of the French invasion in 1830. The *dīwān* consisted of 40 people according to Emanuel d'Aranda,[56] and met twice a week.[57] Former captive Francis Knight has given us an interesting eyewitness account of the *dīwān*'s activities:

> They have two great duana [Diwan] days weekly, Saturday in the Alcassaba and Sunday morning in the Bashaw's house, however, they sit every day in council; if a Christian hath any matter of importance, it must be treated in the Alcassaba, yet is no Christian permitted to enter that place, but must stand at the door, send in his demands by the Trugman or interpreter, who is a renegade, by whom they return their answer; nor is any Christian permitted to speak publicly in the Duana, nor will they have any matters delivered to them, but in the Turkish tongue, and by a Trugman.[58]

During Joseph Pitts's residence there, Algiers was governed by the head of the *dīwān*, the *dey*, who was assisted by the agha, or the head of the army (who was also in charge of the city of Algiers and the surrounding country), together with the *khaznajī*, or state treasurer, and both agha and *khaznajī*[59] were always *ex officio* members of the *dīwān*. For administrative purposes, the regency was divided into three regional *beyliks*, an Eastern, a Western and a Southern one. Each *beylik* was governed by an official appointed by the *bey* (later the *dey*) who tended to choose the person who promised the largest sum of money, and the appointee had more or less free rein within his *beylik*. His main duties were to maintain the land in cultivation, collect taxes and keep the Arab and Berber inhabitants in order, which was no easy task. Joseph Pitts was very familiar with the military expeditions which went out annually and which seem to have involved most of the able-bodied men amongst the Turks and renegades.[60] He describes how:

> The *Algerines*, in the Month of *April*, have *three* several *Camps* go forth: one to the *East*, another to the *West*, and a third to the *South*; of which the *first* is the greatest, and consists of about an Hundred Tents, each Tent containing *twenty* men … Each of these Divisions hath a *Bay*, or *General*, who gives so many Thousand *Pieces of Eight* Monthly for his Place to the *Dey* or *Governour* of *Algier*.[61]

Pitts continues:

> The Reason and Intent of the *Algerines* setting forth these *Camps*, is to *overawe* the *Moors*, and to cause them to hasten in their Tribute to the *Bay*; which whether they do or no, I say, the *Soldiers* will not stay in the *Camp* beyond their *stated* time.[62]

Apart from maintaining internal order, the *dey* had also a duty to protect the regency against external enemies. Pitts participated in several of these campaigns too; for example, he fought against the Spanish who held the enclave of Oran, probably in 1686, which was the "first Camp I made after I was thus for myself [i.e. after he had returned to Algiers from Mecca and been given his freedom]" since the Spanish garrison was "a great Eye-sore to the *Algerines*, and proves oftentimes no small Damage to the Country about them".[63] He describes how the *dey* besieged Oran with "Bombs also, and several pieces of Cannon" as well as "3 or 4000 Men".[64] In the following year Pitts took part in the Algerian campaign against the kingdom of Morocco.[65] Occasionally the *dey* also went to the assistance of his nominal suzerain in Istanbul, and Pitts's escape in 1694 came about because "there came a Messenger from the *Grand Turk* [i.e. the Ottoman Sultan] to *Algier* to bespeak some of the *Algerines* Ships to assist him; which was granted", and Pitts was able to exchange his military duties for naval ones with a colleague.[66]

As well as repulsing enemies from without, like many soldier-dominated regimes the regencies were subject to endless coups, both successful and unsuccessful, and to regular insurrections by the heavily taxed Arabs and Berbers. Magali Morsy has calculated that "of the 28 deys who succeeded each other as rulers of Algiers between 1671 and 1830, fourteen came to power as the result of the assassination of their predecessors",[67] while C. R. Pennell has shown that the situation was no better in Tripoli, where there were no fewer than seventeen *deys* between 1603 and 1684.[68] Pitts himself witnessed the death of his patron in a failed attempt at a coup,[69] and describes the murder in 1682 of Baba Hasan[70] by Hacı Hüseyin (Ḥajjī Ḥusayn, usually known, because of his sickly appearance, as Medio Morto or Mezzo-Morto, i.e. Half-Dead).[71] As Pitts himself remarked: "And indeed it's a rare thing for a *Dey* of *Algier* to die a *Natural* Death."[72]

## The economic organization of Algiers and the development of privateering

ABUN-NASR ASSERTS that "of the economic life of Algeria during the Ottoman period very little is known", and in the wider sense this is true.[73] However, we know from many European observers that the Arabs and Berbers lived mainly by agriculture and animal husbandry. Pitts mentions agriculture, and fruit in particular, several times, remarking for example that:

> About ten Miles off *Algier*, to the *Westward* also, is a pretty little Town called *Bleda*, accommodated with *fine Gardens, full of all manner of Fruits, and plenty of Water,* insomuch, that there are upon the River *Grist Mills*, which is such a Rarity as I seldom, or never saw in any other Part of that Country.[74]

Pitts adds that near Bleda (al-Bulaydah) there is "this *Mateeja*, or Plain ... [which] is *very fruitful*, and abounds with many *handsom [sic] Farmhouses*",[75] a fact confirmed by Abun-Nasr who comments that the Mitījah plain "was, and still is, one of Algeria's most important agricultural areas."[76] Pitts also launches into a long description of the Moors' cultivation of wheat and barley,[77] and explains that when the Kabyles do not submit to paying tribute, the army seizes their cattle, destroys their corn and ruins their vineyards.[78] Some cities such as Constantine (Qusanṭīnah) and Tlemcen (Ṭilimsān) also thrived on the caravan trade. But the chief economic activity in Algiers, and the one which sustained the janissaries and the seamen, indeed the inhabitants of the whole city, was privateering and the associated ransoming of slaves.

Algiers began as a privateering or corsair port under Hayreddin Barbarossa in the early 16th century and remained so until 1830, probably because, as

Lucette Valensi has suggested, the Algerians, like the other regencies, were unable to adapt their fleet from a war to a commercial footing as the Venetians did. As a consequence, their ships were denied access to European ports and were constantly harassed by the naval vessels belonging to the Knights of St John (who, having been expelled from Rhodes in 1522, were now based in Malta).[79] The size of the Algerian fleet and its success fluctuated over time. Its most successful period was probably from 1580 to the 1640s, when it may have comprised as many as fifty to sixty ships,[80] although Abun-Nasr suggests that about seventy-five ships were active at the beginning of the 17th century,[81] while d'Aranda observed in the summer of 1641 "that the sixty-five pirate ships and the four gallies which were at sea ... were most of them manned by soldiers of the garrison".[82] At its weakest point, in the mid- to late 18th century, the fleet was reduced to about twenty vessels, although successes were scored even as late as the beginning of the 19th century, when the European powers were engaged in the Napoleonic wars and the United States had not yet built up a substantial navy.[83]

Up till about 1615, the Algerian fleet consisted mainly of galleys, manned by slaves (as were many of the other Mediterranean fleets[84]). Muslim galleys were faster under oars than those of any other nation, except the Republic of Venice. As Guilmartin explains: "Under oars alone, any Muslim galley in halfway decent shape, let alone a *galiot* or a *fusta*, could outrun a Spanish galley hands down."[85] The Muslim galleys were also slightly more seaworthy, particularly if the sea was calm; furthermore, even if they carried less armament than the Spanish galleys, they possessed a very strong upward-pointing prow designed to ram the side of their adversary's ship, not only damaging it, but allowing the janissaries to storm aboard.[86] As with all galleys, their range was limited by the need to provide water for the sailors, soldiers and rowers (a typical Mediterranean galley might have 144 oarsmen, plus 30 to 40 soldiers, sailors and officers aboard),[87] and by the complex tidal currents prevailing in North European waters, which meant that the galley's normal speed of around three knots or so would have been too slow to make headway in these seas.[88]

Nevertheless, in their home waters, Algerian galleys were more than a match for armed European merchantmen and the galleys of other navies,[89] and from the middle of the 16th century the Algerians were extremely active in the western Mediterranean. Much of their time was spent raiding the southern shores of Christian Europe. Sicilian archives show that "the island was attacked at least 136 times between 1570 and 1601, sometimes in sorties that penetrated ten or even twenty miles inland",[90] while in August 1566 on the east coast of Italy from Abruzzo to Puglia, in the only major campaign involving co-

*Barbaryjsche Galeyen.*

This Dutch engraving, published in 1684, shows in striking detail how Barbary galleys were equipped and manned by soldiers and slave rowers.

operation between the corsair fleets and the Ottoman army:

> An army of 6,000 Turks and corsairs sailed up the Adriatic and
> disembarked at Francavilla … The corsairs found themselves in
> possession of an immense stretch of coast, which they had gained
> without encountering the slightest resistance. Unimpeded, the Turks
> had all the time they needed to work their way inland and south as
> far as Serracapriola, over 60 miles down coast, enjoying their pick
> of the loot from over 500 square miles of abandoned towns and
> villages.[91]

It was not only Italy that suffered. France and especially Spain had long
stretches of deserted coasts, and "by the late sixteenth century the entire
Murcian coast, except for Marazón and Cartagena, was unpopulated; empty
stretches were common in Valencia as well".[92] Neither did raids on Christian
territory preclude numerous and persistent attacks on Christian shipping too.
Between 1575 and 1589, according to Ellen Friedman, more than thirty percent
of Spanish captives were captured on or near the Spanish coast, while twenty-
one percent were captured on the high seas.[93] English slaves were not nearly as
numerous as Spanish ones in the 16th century, particularly since Queen
Elizabeth had signed a treaty with the Ottoman Empire in 1583, but they could
still end up as rowers in North African galleys. For example Richard Hasleton
(dates unknown), who published his captivity narrative in 1595, described how
he was captured in 1582 off the Spanish coast while his ship was bound for
Patras in Greece.[94]

On the other hand, life in Barbary could seem attractive to English
privateers, especially after James I made peace with Spain in 1603 and
prohibited his subjects from attacking Spanish vessels, by proclaiming:

> No man of war be furnished or set out to sea by any of his Majesty's
> subjects, under pain of death and confiscation of lands and goods,
> not only to the captains and mariners, but also to the owners and
> victuallers, if the company of the said ship shall commit any piracy,
> depredation or murder at the sea, upon any of his Majesty's friends.[95]

As a result, several naval captains, among them John Ward (1553?–1623?),
Robert Walsingham (dates unknown), Sir Henry Mainwaring (1586/7–1653;
he claimed that Algerian ships were "manned out by the Turks, after the
proportion of 150 Turks to 20 English, yet the English in their persons are well

used and duly paid their shares"[96]), Sir Francis Verney (1584–1615), John Nutt (dates unknown) and Ambrose Sayer (dates unknown),[97] all transferred their winter operations to Tunis or Algiers during the first two decades of the 17th century.[98] In the summer they operated from the south coast of Ireland.[99] Indeed, Ward and Verney became Muslims and Ward ended his days in Tunis living in "a faire palace, beautified with rich marble and alabaster stones".[100]

The English and other privateers like the Fleming Simon Dansker (*ca.* 1579– *ca.* 1611)[101] are credited with introducing the Algerians and the other states in North Africa to the techniques required for deep-water sailing in the Atlantic,[102] although David Hebb suggests that the North Africans may have learnt their navigational and sailing skills by trial and error, or from the Moriscos who were expelled from Spain between 1609 and 1614, rather than from renegade captains.[103] What is certain is that notwithstanding the continued usefulness of the galley for close-shore work and as a floating gun platform, the North African navies began to turn their attention to building broad-sail ships from the beginning of the 17th century. Hebb claims that the Barbary states were taking "70–80 Christian ships a year between 1592 and 1609"[104] using tall ships, and Alexander de Groot calculates that "the Algiers squadron [consisted of] 50 sail in 1617 and 80 in 1625, other estimates going up to 120", based on the calculations of Wynant de Keyser van Bollandt (dates unknown), the first Dutch Consul in Algiers.[105] Whatever the causes of the transformation, the change to broad-sail ships meant that there was no longer a need for the 10,000 to 15,000 slave rowers required by the galley fleets at the height of their activities.[106] However there was still a great need for trained seamen to operate these vessels. Both Guilmartin[107] and Brummett[108] highlight the chronic shortage of seamen even during the heyday of the galleys, and how the change to tall ships led to a great increase in the number of renegade captains, that is Christians who had renounced their faith and turned Turk, as well as renegade and slave sailors.[109]

The sailing ships of the Algerian corsairs soon branched out into the Atlantic, together with those operating from the Atlantic coast of Morocco, particularly from the ports of Ma'mūrah during the first fifteen years of the 17th century,[110] and Salé (Salā) during the 1620s and 1630s when it was dominated by the Hornacheros, a Morisco group.[111] Among the Algerian pirates' most famous exploits are the sacking of Baltimore in Ireland in 1631 when they took more than a hundred people captive,[112] and the attack on Iceland in 1627 when several hundred were enslaved,[113] but throughout the 17th century in the whole of the North Atlantic their attacks on merchant shipping were regular and persistent. In the early part of the 17th century, Algeria had a fleet larger than any in Europe according to Nicholas Rodger, who asserts: "Between 1613 and

1621 the Algerines brought in 447 Dutch, 193 French, 120 Spanish, 60 English and 50 German prizes, not counting those sunk."[114] In addition, many Christians were still captured from dry land in this period; for example, Friedman shows that from 1570 to 1609 only one in thirty of all Spaniards captured was seized from the Atlantic coasts, while by 1630–39 the percentage of Spaniards captured from Atlantic coasts was roughly the same as those captured from the Mediterranean coasts, and "during the second half of the seventeenth century, between sixteen percent and twenty-three percent of all Spanish captives surveyed were captured in the Atlantic".[115] Although Spanish captives outnumbered those of any other nationality, North African vessels were also regularly seen off the south coast of England as well as elsewhere in the Atlantic. Hebb has calculated that between 1616 and 1642, "English losses to the Barbary pirates come to a staggering total of approximately 400 ships and above 8,000 persons",[116] and that the bulk of the losses came from London and the ports of the South-West. The cost of these losses was huge, amounting to at least one million pounds,[117] of which Todd Gray calculates that "the counties of Devon and Cornwall as a whole had lost £100,000 in eight years".[118] The situation became so bad that regular petitions were sent from the West Country to London requesting help in ransoming the captives and for the support of the wives and children left behind, while many of the South-West fishing fleets hardly dared to leave port. The Royal Navy under James I was so starved of money that it was unable to protect Britain's southern shores and "the Irish Sea was so dangerous that it became acutely difficult to send money to Dublin to pay the King's little squadron there".[119] As Sir John Eliot (1592–1632) lamented in 1625:[120]

> The boldness and insolence of those pirates was beyond all comparison, nor former times having been exampled with the like. Their adventure formerly on those seas was rare, almost unheard of, which made their coming more strange.[121]

One reason for the success of the corsairs was their close attention to seaworthiness and navigation. As the famous sailor Sir William Monson (1568?–1643)[122] said in 1636:

> You must understand that all the Turkish pirate ships are vessels of Christians, taken from them by violence, which, when the Turks are possessed of, they use all art and industry to make better sailers than all other ships. To this purpose they first cut down their half decks

and all other weighty things over head which make them wind-tight and burthensome ... They never regard the strength of their ships more than for one voyage, for they want not continual prizes which they take of Christians and then use. Every fortnight or three weeks, they grave their ships and make them clean to go better; they carry no weight over head, or in hold, but victuals, by means whereof and all these things considered, no ship is equal to them in going.[123]

Pitts confirms the Algerians' attention to detail:

The first Thing the *Algerines* do when any Ship comes home from Cruising, is with all Expedition to take every Thing out, Ballast and all; and then careen again, and tallow all under Water to the very Keel.[124]

In other words, the corsairs sacrificed strength and durability for speed and manoeuverability. Time and time again, captives bemoaned their ships' inability to outrun the corsairs, for example William Okeley (dates unknown) in 1639,[125] Thomas Phelps (d. 1695) in 1684,[126] Edward Coxere (1633?–1694) in 1657,[127] and Joseph Pitts in 1678.[128] Gradually, however, as the 17th century drew on, improvements to the armoury of European naval vessels meant that they were able to outgun their Barbary counterparts in open combat.[129] Nevertheless, the Algerians were canny enough not to provoke a massed battle at sea, and, as a consequence, the Europeans were limited to shows of strength and bombardments of Algerian ports. For instance, although the attack by Sir Edward Spragge on the Algerian fleet in Bougie (Bijāyah) in 1671 did sink several vessels (as recorded by Pitts[130]) and brought about a renewed peace treaty, the expedition of Sir Robert Mansell (1570/71–1652) against Algiers in 1620 was ineffective,[131] the expedition of Robert Blake (1598?–1657) against Tunis in 1655 indecisive,[132] and the bombardment of Algiers by French squadrons in 1682, 1683 and 1688, while inflicting considerable damage, achieved no major strategic object for the French.[133] In the aftermath of the 1682 attack, Admiral Arthur Herbert (1648–1716) was able to negotiate a peace treaty between Algiers and Britain which lasted until 1816[134] but, as Julien shows, at a price, since "the Dutch in 1680 and the English in 1682, had to agree to supply rigging, spars and arms in return for the right to export grain".[135] Pitts describes the 1688 attack:

*An English Ship in Action with Barbary Corsairs, ca.* 1685:
oil painting by Willem van de Velde, the Younger.

A third Time the *French* came, with a Squadron under the
Command of *Mareschal d'Estree*, who fired 10000 *Bombs* into the
Town ….These … were design'd for the Ships that were in the
*Mole*, but they did no great Execution upon them; for, to the best of
my remembrance, they lost not one *Privateer*, only some Prizes
which lay then in the Harbour; …

'Tis true, the *City* was so much beaten down, that you could not
distinguish one Street or Lane from another, and 'twas several Years
before the Damage was quite repair'd.[136]

Given the increasingly uneven balance of naval power in the Mediterranean
from the mid-17th century onwards, the Algerians could not afford to be at
war with all the European powers, but, conversely, neither could they afford to
be at peace with all their potential enemies, if they were to maintain a steady
income from privateering. Julien expresses it succinctly:

A state of war, with all its risks, but also with its profits, was still a
worth-while proposition. At the very least, and when driven by

necessity, Algiers would negotiate with only one power and increase the fury of its attacks on the rest. The peace entered into with [the Dutch admiral] de Ruyter in 1663 was marked by a recrudescence of privateering attacks against French vessels. The treaty with Louis XIV in 1670 involved a rupture with the English and the Dutch; and the treaty with the English in 1681 was followed by a declaration of war against France.[137]

At the same time, Pitts records:

"They [the Algerians] dread much our *English Men of War*, and when we have War with them, will seldom venture in or out the *Straights-mouth* [Gibraltar] by Day .... But if they have Peace with *Us*, tho' they have War with all *Christendom* besides, they will then not scruple to pass the *Straight's-mouth* by Day, more than by Night."[138]

Another reason for Algeria's playing off one hostile power against another was the logistical problems faced by the regency in acquiring the requisite raw and manufactured materials for shipbuilding. The Algerians' greatest difficulty lay in procuring masts, as trees of the most appropriate type did not grow in North African forests, but cordage, tar, canvas, and guns often had to be imported as well.[139] The two solutions adopted by the Barbary States were to utilize captured boats (either refitting them to suit their own purpose or cannibalizing them for their constituent parts,[140]), or to acquire the necessary equipment by treaty. By the late 17th century the Algerians were inserting clauses in their treaties which "provided for 'gifts' of masts, sail, cannon balls, cannons, cordage and such other merchandise in return for immunity from attack".[141]

Nabil Matar's view is that "by the third quarter of the 17th century, Britons were becoming the most formidable power in the Western Mediterranean",[142] and that by the 18th century the Barbary States had become:

The consumers of services and products manufactured, transported and sold by the Europeans. They also became so dependent on British naval protection that they started treating London as the locus of their maritime activity and the metropolis for petitions, financial assistance, restitution and mediation.[143]

He also notes: "Britain and France did not so much retaliate against the seizure of their ships: they pursued a strategy to eliminate the regencies as a maritime power."[144] The Algerian fleet and those of the other Barbary regencies did indeed decline in the 18th century, but never to the point of complete insignificance. Despite hostile powers having larger navies with bigger ships, in the 18th century the Algerians and the other North African states still managed to maintain a significant presence on their local seas, by dint of seamanship, diplomacy and determination, and, even as late as the 1780s, many of the Great Powers were still paying Algiers large sums to prevent attacks on their shipping.[145] Pitts was critical of the Algerians' naval qualities, but his claim goes against the evidence:

> The *Algerines* are a very *timorous* sort of People, *willing to sleep in a whole Skin* [i.e. not wishing to be hurt], and therefore care not how little they fight; but shew themselves *wondrously* Valiant upon *poor small* Merchant-men. But many times they have made some Attempts on *great* Merchant-men, and have come off with Shame and broken Bones. And this is not much to be admired at, because they have *no Order* in their Engagements, neither is there *any Punishment* for such of the Inferiour Soldiers as fight not.[146]

As against this, the British Consul in Tripoli, Thomas Baker, describes in his diary how the flagship of the Tripolitanian privateer, the Mallorcan renegade Şaban Reis (Sha'bān Ra'īs), was "new, excellently well manned and a prime sayler",[147] and that Şaban Reis was easily able to take large merchantmen such as the *Three Kings of Marseilles*, despite the latter being armed with twelve guns and the fact that the merchantmen's crew "manfully defended themselves".[148] In a similar vein, Joseph Morgan (dates unknown), the 18th-century historian, pours scorn on the claim that the "Algerines [are] but a crew of cowardly skulking pyrates"[149] and goes on to observe that:

> Algiers is very well known to be a powerful government, which has stood its ground for more than two centuries against several vigorous attacks made upon it; nor does it seem in much danger of not continuing to do so still. The Algerians must be allowed to be a martial people, whose amity is sought after, nay courted by the first potentates of Europe.[150]

Nicholas Rodger asserts likewise that:

The best policy for a Christian trading power was to make itself sufficiently annoying as an enemy, and sufficiently attractive as a friend to be elected as an ally of the Barbary states, and equally important, to preserve these alliances by a faithful observance of their terms. Then, the presence of the Barbary cruisers against the other Christian states with which they remained at war, would become a tax on England's trading competitors. This simple realisation was to become one of the essentials bases of British commercial and naval operations in the Mediterranean throughout the eighteenth and well into the nineteenth century.[151]

All this shows that the naval forces of Algiers and the other Barbary regencies were a significant force in the Western Mediterranean until the end of the Napoleonic wars, forces which the European powers could not afford to ignore despite their eventual overwhelming superiority of ships, armaments and power.

## The corsair economy

THE ECONOMY OF Algiers and its fellow Barbary regencies was heavily predicated on the success of its privateering forces and the wealth they created. There are very few available figures, but Alonso Cano, a Trinitarian, calculated that sixty-two percent of the Algerian state's revenues came from tributes and taxes levied in the provinces, while thirty-eight percent came from the city of Algiers itself, with ransoms contributing fourteen percent.[152] These figures date from 1768–69, a time when privateering income was at one of its lowest points, and one can make a reasonable assumption that in the late 16th and much of the 17th century, privateering supplied a much greater share of the state's revenues than thirty-eight percent. Essentially, the revenues of the state and the income of the inhabitants of the city depended on three factors: how many slaves were captured; how much booty was taken; and what use could be made of the ships which fell into the hands of the corsairs.

Investment in corsair voyages was a major commercial activity in the cities of Algiers, Tunis and Tripoli. Since in this case goods did not need to be bought for trading, the ship's owner only needed enough money to outfit, arm and provision his vessel. As Robert Davis explains:

> Everyone from the *armadores* [investors] to the *re'is* [captain], the soldiers, their officers, the crew and even the galley slaves themselves

This engraving, published in 1684, shows Dutch ships in Algiers harbour carrying out revenge punishment of 125 captured corsairs in full sight of the city. The prisoners were hanged from the yardarm or bound back-to-back before being thrown into the sea.

... was allotted a set number of shares, appropriate to his rank, or (in the case of the *armadores*), proportionate to the amount he had put up, of any prizes that might be taken. The polity of Algiers itself, in the person of the pasha [later the *dey*] received an eighth of the take, as well as 'the naked shells' – the stripped, captured vessels.[153]

Pitts observed the system in action: "The *Gunners* have *two Parts* or Shares of what is taken; and the *Soldiers* the same; the *Slaves* that labour, some *two*, some *three*, and some *four*, but it goes to their *Patroons* [owners]; and all the rest have *one Part*,"[154] while the "*Governor* may have the *Pengick*; i.e. The One Eighth."[155] John Rawlins (dates unknown) confirmed that the "bashaw had the overseeing of all prisoners ... so chose one out of every eight for a present or fee for himself",[156] despite William Okeley's contention that "the viceroy or bashaw ... according to the custom and his own right, is to have the tenth man for his dividend of the slaves".[157]

The best analysis of the returns available from investments in voyages is probably that from Consul Baker in Tripoli in the 1670s and 1680s. He shows that Şaban Reis "brought in big prizes on every trip he made from 1683 onwards",[158] and that between 1679 and 1685 Tripoli took more than a million Spanish dollars in prizes (seventy-five ships and their cargoes), and that more than a thousand men were enslaved to a value of almost a quarter of a million dollars. Davis, commenting on the underlying economics of Şaban Reis's privateering in Tripoli, has calculated that "captives represented a fairly small proportion of the overall value of the profit the corsairs could realise from a prize and its cargo – somewhat between a fifth and a quarter, or about $6,500 worth of slaves per prize",[159] [but that] "such a figure is considerably skewed, however, by the five very lucrative prizes taken during [Consul] Baker's tenure", and that "if one were to focus on the more modest but also more typical prizes ... the 665 captives taken on these vessels were worth, in Baker's estimation, around $150,000, or very nearly as much as the prizes themselves."[160] Şaban Reis's most profitable exploits included the capture off the coast of Crete of the *Three Kings of Marseilles*, which was "the richest prize that was ever brought into this place by a single ship, being really worth dollars 120,000",[161] while other ships contained "fine Spanish wool, some cochineal and other rich goods from Venice",[162] and "103 bales of silk and other goods esteemed worth one hundred thousand crownes".[163] Empty ships were worth between 300 dollars ("a small French vessel empty") and 2,500 dollars ("an empty Venetian ship"[164]), always assuming that these ships could not be used for corsairing or had no useful material on board which could be recycled by the local shipwrights (two ships out of Şaban Reis's squadron were converted from captured ships[165]).

However, it was also possible to return from a long voyage with nothing. Joseph Morgan comments that "this cruising trade of theirs was a perfect lottery (more especially while they used only row-vessels) and has brought many to ruin, as it has others to immense opulency",[166] and "this hiring of rowers was extremely expensive, and one or two unsuccessful cruises have broken the backs of many a corsair".[167] Poor returns on investment were not only common in the days of the galleys (when rowers often had to be hired), but could affect corsairs whatever form of ship they were using. William Okeley explains that in the 1640s his master lost all his fortune by investing in a failed voyage and that he had to sell all his slaves as a result,[168] while Consul Baker quotes Mustapha Caddi (Muṣṭafā Qāḍī/Mustafa Kadi) who undertook thirteen voyages out of Tripoli without success in the 1680s.[169]

Nevertheless, despite occasional failures, North African corsairs were more often successful than not, as Consul Baker's figures show. Algiers, with a bigger fleet, a larger body of soldiers and the capacity to capture slaves on land and at sea both in the Mediterranean and the Atlantic, was probably less reliant on ships and their cargoes than on slaves and ransoming. This does not mean that the Algerian corsairs did not score notable successes in taking booty. For example their capture of the London ship *Rebecca* in 1640, which was carrying more than £260,000 in silver, was so damaging to the English economy that the pound slumped.[170] However, while corsairs from Tripoli found it worthwhile taking home empty vessels, Joseph Pitts's Algerian captors did otherwise: "After they had taken out of her [Pitts's ship] what they thought fit, and necessary for their use, they sunk her; for being laden with *Fish*, they thought it not worth while to carry or send her home to *Algier*."[171] They were also prepared to sink three other small English ships laden with fish and a Dutch vessel with pipe staves on board and to make a profit just by selling the crews as slaves or for ransom. Although we do not know exactly how many slaves there were in Algiers at any one time, all the estimates point to around 25,000 being a reasonable figure for the 17th century. In his chapter devoted to how many slaves there were in the Barbary States, Davis comes to the conclusion that "the figures of 35,000 that we have arrived at can be taken as an averaged-out white slave count for Barbary, roughly how many captives were held at any given time between 1580 and 1680" – figures which show that Algiers, by possessing around 25,000 slaves at any one time, took the lion's share when it came to income from ransoms.[172]

The value of slaves was twofold: first, slaves could be used for labour in galleys, in agriculture, mining, construction, industry and domestic service.

Second, slaves could be sold to another owner, or ransomed for profit. We have a considerable amount of information on the cost of ransoming slaves. Robert Davis has looked at Italian redemptions, where "each Italian state operated its slave ransoming though a confraternity".[173] In Rome, for example, the Gonfalone in the late 16th century collected money throughout the Papal States in order to redeem as many slaves at the same time as possible. Davis observes how:

> Everyone on the Christian side agreed that the greed of the slave owners was not easily put off, especially because masters generally understood that ransomers were under considerable pressure to free a conspicuous quantity of slaves, and that to do so in a timely fashion they necessarily had to come to Barbary laden with cash. Big redemptions required massive amounts of money to pull off: sometimes, 50,000 or even 100,000 scudi, zecchini or pieces of eight, all in coins had to be physically transported to Barbary.[174]

This system was so expensive that many Italian states tried to decide on a specific price for each slave, but even then they could often be forced to pay more than they intended. Francis Knight tells the story of a French Embassy to Algiers which tried to negotiate with the pasha, but every time the French made an offer, the *dīwān* raised the price, so that in the end the embassy was forced to pay the Algerians for leave to depart without having ransomed a single slave, adding that they were now "derided of all nations".[175] Often, families of Italian captives were forced to sell almost all their possession or to pawn their daughters' dowries to redeem their relatives.[176]

For Catholic countries in general, there were two major religious orders, the Mercedarians and the Trinitarians,[177] as well as several smaller ones, which sought to redeem captives, while under Philip II the Spanish state began to provide considerable support as well.[178] Friedman provides a table showing that between half and three-quarters of a million silver reales were collected annually for the redemption of Barbary captives between 1648 and 1669,[179] while "in the sixteenth and seventeenth centuries, the price for a typical captive ranged from about 1,000 to 2,000 reales".[180] Indeed, by examining more than eighty record books belonging to the redemptionist orders and dating from 1562 to 1769, she demonstrates conclusively that "not only was the redemption welcome in Algiers, it was eagerly courted".[181] Davis calculates that "the Spanish Trinitarians alone carried out no fewer than 72 redemptions in 77 years during the 1600s, liberating 15,573 slaves in the process, or an average of 220 slaves per trip".[182]

In Britain, there were neither religious orders nor much state help in the 17th century to assist with the redemption of captives. James I sent an ineffectual naval squadron in 1621,[183] and the continual depredations of the Barbary corsairs during the reign of his son, Charles I, caused much distress particularly among those living in London and on the south and south-west coasts of England. In 1640, Francis Knight in his book implored the King to rescue the 16,000 "Christians who lie groaning under the yoke of Turkish tyranny",[184] and eventually Parliament decided to take a hand in the matter, passing an act in 1642 for the *Relief of Captives taken by Turkish, Moorish and other Pirates*, which enforced a one percent tax on all goods shipped into or out of England. This was followed in 1649 by an *Act for the Redemption of Captives*.[185] Parliament also sent expeditions on two occasions to Algiers under Sir Edmund Cason (dates unknown), once in 1645 when Cason's ship sank, and again in 1646. Cason's own version of the events declares:

> The greatest part of the inhabitants had rather keep their slaves than permit them to be freed: they come to so much more per head than I expected, the reason is here be many women and children which cost £50 per head and might sell them for an £100. Besides them there are divers which are masters of ships and carpenters, caulkers, coopers, sailmakers, chirurgions and others which are here highly esteemed so that they do come £32 per man.[186]

Cason ended up paying between "£7 for one Edmond Francis of Dorset and well over £80 for Elizabeth Alwin of London, the average price [being] just over £30 per captive, which was the usual rate for ransoming ordinary mariners and boys".[187] In addition, Cason had to pay various dues to the pasha, Turkish officials, janissaries and translators, all of which amounted to a six percent surcharge of the ransom fee per person.[188] Other calculations suggest that in England in the first half of the 17th century "nationally the average cost of redeeming individual captives was £45".[189]

Cason was probably lucky to pay only six percent in surcharges. In 1622 expenses for the redemption of a Dutch slave were 1,636 Spanish doubloons of which only 1,000 went to the slave owner, 259 went on surcharges, and 377 doubloons, or around 30 percent of the slave's ransom, were required for the costs involved in realizing the bill of exchange.[190] Particularly valuable were slaves with rich relatives. The Dartmouth merchant John Newman (dates unknown) had to pay £200 for his freedom,[191] while the Fleming Emanuel d'Aranda and his two Flemish companions were exchanged for five Turks held in Flanders, but on top of that they also had to pay a substantial sum themselves for the privilege of their freedom.[192] Joseph Pitts himself recounts that when his master took him to Tunis, he met the English consul there and asked whether he and the other English merchants there could ransom him:

> They ask'd him [Joseph's master] what Price he put upon me. He told them Five hundred *Dollars*, which was, I suppose, Three hundred more than he bought me for. They offered Two hundred. He made a slight of that, and laugh'd at them. They advanced to Two hundred and fifty *Dollars*. He still made a *Pish* of it. They at length came up to Three hundred *Dollars*, which is near sixty Pounds *Sterling*, but my *Patroon* plainly told them, he would not abate one *Asper* (*i.e.* about *five Farthings*) of his Demands. At which the *Consul* told me that I must have Patience, for *an Hundred* Pounds was a considerable Sum to be contributed by three only ...[193]

Even as late as the 1670s, the Algerians were able to inflict considerable damage on northern European shipping. An anonymous four-page list published in London in 1682 shows that "between 1677 and 1680, 153 British ships were taken by the corsairs of Algiers" – including the *Speedwell* of Topsham, the very ship that Joseph Pitts sailed in[194] – and that most of the passengers and crew were ransomed at a cost of around £100 per sailor, with up to £1,000 being paid for the most important passengers.[195] From these examples (which represent a tiny proportion of the information we have about the redemption costs of European captives in North Africa), it can be seen how central an element the ransoming of slaves was in the economy of Algiers and the other Barbary states.

### The condition of slavery

ISLAM DEFINES SLAVERY with two different terms, *asr* (captivity) and *'ubūdiyyah* (slavery). *'Ubūdiyyah* means captives (*'abīd*), "who had to spend the rest of their lives in captivity",[196] while *asr*, on the other hand, was "slavery that could be prevented or determined by mutual agreement" and also "an exchange and commodification of soldiers and sailors, traders and travelers, men, women and children for the purposes of gaining ransom payments, exchanging them with captive coreligionists, or utilizing their skills".[197] It was thus under the conditions of *asr* that so many Christians were incorporated, sometimes temporarily, but often for life, in the Barbary state.

When Christians were captured in the 16th century by a Barbary corsair, they were often put to work straightaway by the corsair captain as rowers on the galley.[198] When sail took over in the 17th century, new captives were usually confined below decks while the corsair continued to sail on and seek new prizes, until the ship's home port was reached. As Pitts recounts:

> … we were near thirty *new-taken* Slaves, besides between twenty and thirty *old* Slaves brought with the *Pirate* out of *Algier. For such they usually bring to sail the Vessel, and to do all the Ship's work for them, while the* new *Slaves are put into Irons in the Hold, and for a Month's time not able to stand on their Legs, nor suffered to come upon Deck, being confin'd either to sit or lie down, without the least provision of Bedding to ease themselves.*[199]

While on board, the captured men and women had technically no master, since most voyages were financed by a multitude of investors, all of whom had a stake in profiting from the cruise. Once on land, the ruler claimed his *pencik* or eighth share (which could be twelve and half percent of all captives, or just several captives of rank, who could be expected to bring in high ransoms), and the rest were paraded in the *badistan*, or slave market, described by Pitts thus:

> After which [i.e. the *dey* had made his choice of slaves] we were all driven from thence [the *dey's* palace] to the *Battistan*, or *Market-place*, where *Christians* are wont to be sold: There we stand from eight of the Clock in the Morning, until two in the Afternoon (which is the limited time for the Sale of *Christians*) and have not the least bit of Bread allow'd us during our Stay there. Many Persons are curious to come and take a view of us, while we stand exposed to sale; and others, who intend to buy, to see whether we be *sound* and *healthy*, and *fit for Service.* The *taken Slaves* are sold by way of Auction, and the *Cryer* endeavours to make the most he can of them; and when the *Bidders* are at a stand, he makes use of his Rhetorick, *Behold what a* strong Man *this is! What limbs he has! He is fit for any* Work. *And, see what a* pretty Boy *this is! No doubt his parents are very* rich, *and able to* redeem *him with a* great Ransom. And with many such like fair Speeches does he strive to raise the Price. After the *Bidders* have done bidding, the Slaves are all driven again to the *Dey's* House, where any that have a mind to advance above what was bidden at

the *Battistan*, may; but then whatsoever exceeds the Bidding at that Place, belongs not to the *Pickaroons*, or *Pirates*, but goes to the *Dey*.[200]

Such experiences are related in most captivity narratives, and a similar tale is told by John Rawlins of his sale in Algiers in the 1620s:

> And so the soldiers hurried us, like dogs, into the market, where as men sell hackneys [horses] in England, we were tossed up and down to see who would give the most for us. And although we had heavy hearts and looked with sad countenances, yet many came to look at us, sometimes taking us by the hand, sometimes feeling our brawns [muscles] and naked arms, and so beholding our prices written in our breasts, they bargained for us accordingly, and at last we were all sold, and the soldiers returned with their money to their captains.[201]

Another account by William Okeley explains how prospective buyers checked the captives' teeth ("a good, strong entire set of grinders will advance the price considerably"[202]), and especially their hands:

> For if they be callous and brawny, they will shrewdly guess that they have been inured to labour; if delicate and tender, they will suspect some gentleman or merchant, and then the hopes of a good price of redemption makes him saleable.[203]

Once purchased, slaves were divided into those from whom the owner expected to make an immediate return, i.e. captives who, by their dress or bearing, appeared to have the funds to purchase a ransom, and those who were needed for work. Davis estimates that during the 16th and early 17th centuries around three-quarters of all slaves would have been the slaves of work, and that it was only "when charitable ransoming expeditions became regular events in the later 1600s, that there would be much hope of selling slaves as poor as these".[204] However, after 1650 or so, many slave owners like the renowned Ali Pichilin[205] saw slaves as a commodity to be traded for profit, and Pichilin is quoted as saying: "I have bought my slaves to make some advantage of them."[206] Davis suggests that investors expected a return of ten to twelve percent on their investment.[207] On the other hand, even after 1650 many Algerians still bought slaves exclusively for work (including the *dey*, other officials and many members of the *ṭā'ifah* of *ra'ī̄s*es), since Algiers and the other North African regencies suffered from a constant shortage of manpower caused by recurrent episodes

"The Going into Slavery at Algiers": an English drawing of *ca*. 1700 shows European slaves being hustled ashore at Algiers.

of plague. Ten per cent of the population of Algiers are said to have died in the plagues of 1647–48, and up to one-third in the plague of 1654,[208] while "when plague broke out in Algiers' overcrowded slave pens in 1662, some said that it carried off 10,000 (others claimed 20,000) of the city's 30,000 captives; in 1699 it cut the already reduced slave count in that city by a further quarter".[209] Joseph Pitts himself caught the plague while returning from the pilgrimage to Mecca with his master:

> The *Plague* was hot in *Alexandria* at this time; and some Persons infected with it being taken on board our Ship, which was bound for *Algier*, the *Plague* reigned amongst us: Insomuch that besides those that recovered, we threw twenty Persons overboard, who died of it.[210]

It was not only the plague that killed the seventeen percent of slaves who died in captivity.[211] Many were sent to the galleys in the 16th century. This was a very arduous existence and many must not have survived, if we are to believe the testimony of former galley-slaves such as Francis Knight:

For a drop of water, they would pawn their souls and often are constrained to drink of the salt oceans. Their repast at best but bread and water and for want of sleep are in continual ecstasies, the strokes of the oar is dolourous ... The scorching heat now penetrates their brains, their flesh is burned off their bodies, when anon they are much pinched with cold, strong fetters are their nearest consorts from which they are never exempted ... their repose when they have any is sitting ... not having so much room as to stretch their legs, their sleep when they have any is an hour in twelve ...[212]

Similarly, Edward Webbe (b. 1553 or 1554) reported that the food they ate "was very black, far worse than horsebread, and our drink was stinking water", and that if they fell ill the slaves would sometimes be beaten to death.[213] It should be pointed out that conditions were little better for free Muslims who chose to act as rowers, and were just as bad, if not worse, in Christian galleys. A Spanish doctor reported how on two Spanish galleys docked in Barcelona in 1719

... 156 of the rowers were extremely ill and that 8 had already died as a result of exposure to a long spell of wet and cold weather. The report added that all of the rowers were considerably weakened as a result of poor diet and exposure.[214]

Once galleys were replaced by broad-sail ships, conditions on board improved, but many slaves still had to undertake hard labour, particularly in winter when the corsair fleet spent much of its time in harbour. Francis Knight explains how in Algiers some slaves were "set to hailing the cart in lew of horses ... to chop the vineyard and others to build houses",[215] and that the famous slave-owner Ali Pichilin forced many to work on "sumptuous architectures or edifices for the lodging of soldiers" which "caused a languishing dejection in all of us his slaves, as none of us [was] exempted from those toils, which was to us an interminable vexation".[216] Emanuel d'Aranda explains how, when building a house for their master in the upper part of Algiers city, all "the materials were ... carried up on men's backs or in their arms", since the road leading to the house was "so steepy to get up to, that a mule could not go up it with any load".[217] Many Algerian captives also laboured in mines and quarries, usually in chain gangs, while working on repairing the harbour was considered especially arduous. Friedman describes how in 1736 a group of nineteen Spanish captives complained that:

*Mannier Hoe de Gevange Kristen*

fol: 384.

tot Algiers verkoft worden.

I. Luyken, invent. et fecit.

"How captured Christian slaves were sold in Algiers":
a Dutch engraving published in 1684.

in the three and one-half years that they had been captives in Algiers, they had never gone without very heavy chains and that during this period they had worked daily on the reinforcement of the mole, making four trips each day pulling the carts filled with stone from the quarry to the port [which was] four leagues [distant].[218]

Agriculture was another area of slave employment. Emanuel d'Aranda, like Francis Knight above, had to "delve in the vineyard … which was a very hard work",[219] while William Okeley worked on his master's farm about twelve miles from Algiers.[220] However, if the captive possessed skills of use to the Algerians, especially anything to do with shipbuilding or gunnery, then he might escape hard labour, and almost certainly would have fetched a much higher value on the market.[221] Richard Hasleton explains how his skills as a carpenter enabled him to become chief master of works and that "by this means I had more liberty than before and was very well entreated", but this was not always the case.[222] Although Edward Coxere, having been captured by a Tunisian corsair in 1657, was appointed to be "boatswain over the Christians in the *Rear Admiral* to go into the Great Turk's service to fight against the Venetians",[223] he still had to work all day with an iron shackle on his leg, while at night:

> Our lodging was a dark room in a castle [at Porto Farina near Tunis], where we could not see in the daytime without a lamp burning. When we left work, we were put in chains, two and two together, sometime forty couple of us thronged into this hole, where we lay without beds … In the middle of the room, was two great tubs amongst us, where we eased ourselves, and no air but what came into the door, and that was shut all night, and an exceedingly hot country.[224]

Beatings were not infrequent. William Okeley gives vivid descriptions of his punishment for straying too far outside the city,[225] and of how a Dutch slave was punished for drawing his knife at his patron.[226] Okeley considered that "all [punishment] is arbitrary and unlimited; if a patron shall kill his slave, for aught I could perceive, he suffers no more for it than he should kill his horse",[227] and this was Joseph Pitts's experience also:

> Within eight and forty Hours after I was sold, I *tasted* of their *Barbarity*; for I had my tender Feet tied up, and beaten twenty, or thirty Blows for a *beginning*: And thus was I beat for a *considerable*

time, every two or three Days, besides Blows now and then, *forty*, *fifty*, *sixty*, at a time. My *Executioner* would fill his Pipe, and then give me *ten*, or *twenty* Blows, then stop, and smoak his Pipe for a while, and then he would at me again, and when weary stop again; and *thus cruelly* would he handle me till his Pipe was out.[228]

One might have expected some assistance from one's fellow nationals. However, there are numerous examples in the captivity narratives of how Englishmen could be just as nasty to their fellows as to any other ethnic group. When discussing the habits of the various national groups of slaves held in Ali Pichilin's *bagno*, Emanuel d'Aranda considered that "the English [are] not so shiftful as others, and it seems also that they have no great kindness for one another".[229] Thomas Phelps found that fellow slave William Robinson "professed himself a Christian in words, but indeed we found more civility from the Moors than him".[230] T. S., of *The Adventures of TS,* complained of a faithless and apostate Cornishman who tried to "worm secrets out of new captives",[231] while Joseph Pitts's encounters with James Grey of Weymouth left much to be desired.[232] William Okeley seems to have had the worst experience, saying, "I could relate a passage during our captivity in Algiers that had more of bitterness in it than in all our slavery, and yet they were Christians, not Algerines, Protestants not Papists, Englishmen, not strangers that were the cause of it".[233]

However, not every aspect of slavery was as negative as those described above. If a slave was lucky he might be assigned to household duties, which were not arduous, and which allowed the male slave a considerable amount of freedom. Joseph Pitts says of his third master, "an old Batchelor":

My Work with him was to look after his House, dress his Meat, wash the Clothes; and, in short, to do all those Things that are look'd on as a Servant-Maid's Work in *England.* ...

I must own, I wanted nothing with him; Meat, Drink, Clothes, and Money, I had enough.[234]

---

*Following page, left* "The pitiful tortures inflicted on the slaves by the Turks." This Dutch engraving of 1684 depicts some of the standard slave punishments – disembowelling, burning and crucifixion.

*Following page, right* An untitled Dutch engraving of 1684 depicting more slave punishments: beating, hanging by the feet, and the bastinado.

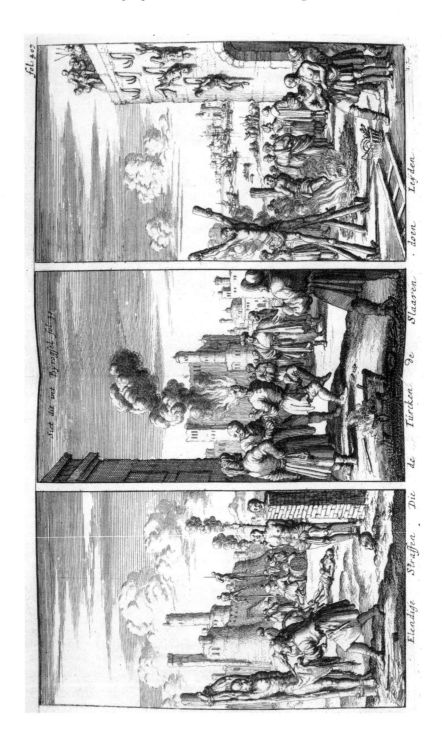

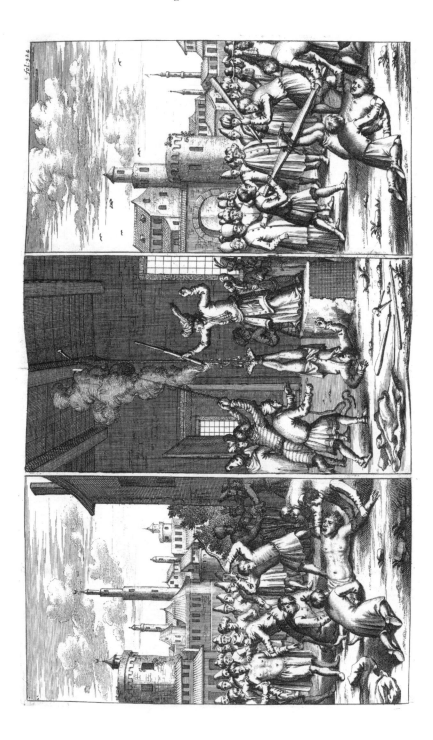

*Hoe de Slaaven Met de Keetenen aen haer beenen gaen*

"How slaves walked with their legs shackled": a Dutch engraving of 1684.

Even those who were not as fortunate as Pitts and did not live in their master's household could derive some comfort and even profit from their captivity. Most captives had to spend their evening and nights confined in the *bagni* (slave pens, also known as *bains*, *banhos* and *baños)*, which had been specially constructed to house the public slaves (i.e. those belonging to the ruler and members of the *dīwān)*. The first *bagno*, the *bagno beyliç*, built in Algiers in 1531, was said by Joseph Morgan to hold as many as 2,000 captives,[235] while a century later there were six *bagni* in Algiers and nine in Tunis. Numbers fluctuated between eight and four in Algiers during the rest of the 17th century.[236] Stephen Clissold called the *bagno* "a cross between a Nazi concentration camp [in that persons were confined there by virtue of their status without any judicial process], an English debtors' prison [in that the *bagni* were integrated into urban public life and were open for all to enter] and a Soviet labour camp [in that the inhabitants faced a life of hard labour]".[237] Each *bagno* was a large enclosure with a multitude of small rooms in which the captives were locked up at night, but by the 17th century the activities of the Redemptionist fathers had enabled conditions to improve for those of all faiths, which meant that many slaves had considerable freedom of movement. William Okeley recounts how, when his master was short of cash, he was sent ashore and expected to find employment so that he could pay his master two dollars a month. He tried to find work with another English slave, a tailor, but when the latter changed his mind about employing him, he borrowed a "pittance" from another slave, an Englishman who had "a little shop" and went into partnership with him. Okeley recounts how:

> that very night I went and bought a parcel of tobacco. The next morning we dressed it, cut it, and fitted it for sale, and the world seem to smile on us wonderfully. In this way of partnership, we continued some time, and what we got clear, we divided every week according to the proportion of our respective stocks. In a while, finding the world come in upon us, we ventured no less than a whole butt of wine.[238]

Indeed, despite Islam's prohibition of alcohol, taverns and wine shops were quite common. The *British State Papers* quote an anonymous ex-captive in 1675 as saying that captives in Algiers "for the most part are better trated then any slaves in all the grand Signors dominions, having the benefit to keep shopps, taverns, to worke upon their hand craft trade ... many thousand captives obtayned their liberty by theer own industry".[239] And Edward Coxere talks of buying the local alcoholic drink *rakı* in Tunis.[240] Even Pitts talks about working in a shop, and how "a *Taverner* ... brought Wine and Victuals for his master", who had "brought a *Madam* with him".[241]

Friedman describes how *bagni* "were also social centers and a great source of pleasure for all captives, whether or not they resided in the *baños*",[242] and notes that the tax levied on tavern keepers helped to maintain the churches and chapels in the *bagni*[243] where captives were able to find religious solace. William Okeley describes how Devereux Spratt, an English "minister of the gospels", prayed and preached to as many as eighty captives three times a week "yet we never had the least disturbance from the Turks or Moors",[244] while the *dey* of Tunis "once remarked that he would not give up Father Gracián [a Spanish priest captured in 1592] for any amount of money because 'he makes my Christians obedient'".[245] It was not only the captives' spiritual welfare which was looked after. Friedman spends a whole chapter discussing the hospitals created in the *bagni* of Algiers by the Trinitarians in the second half of the 17th century,[246] while Joseph Pitts describes how he was able to visit an English doctor for an eye infection.[247]

Many of the captives often had reasonable freedom to go where they wanted. Pitts was able to visit the English consul in Tunis quite openly while a slave,[248] and later he explains that household slaves were often treated in a similar way to servants in Britain:

> ... such [Algerians] as have occasion for Servants, do buy *Slaves*, and bring them up to their Houshold [*sic*] Work, as our *Servant-Maids* are here in *England*; who, as soon as they have done up all their Work in the House, are usually allow'd the liberty to go abroad, and visit their Countrymen.[249]

Earlier in the 17th century, William Okeley describes how he was allowed "to walk out of the town to take the fresh air, a liberty which for somewhat above a mile is indulged to the slaves",[250] and how "the freedom I found in servitude, the liberty I enjoyed in my bonds was so great, that it took off much of the edge of my desire to obtain, and almost blunted it from any vigorous attempt after liberty".[251] Indeed, he and his fellow slaves had so much freedom from their masters that they were able to build a boat in a cellar in the *bagno* in Algiers and carry it in bits to the seaside, pretending firstly that their makeshift sails were clothes they were washing in the sea, and then disguising the keel and ribs of the boat as a coffin which they were carrying to a funeral.[252] (Joseph Pitts explains that while slaves were now buried in a Christian cemetery purchased with funds provided by the King of Spain, "formerly [the Algerians] would not permit such [slaves] to be interr'd, but threw their dead Bodies into the Sea".[253]). In Algiers, slaves were constantly meeting captives from different countries, ranging from Muscovy to Brasil, and were able to form transnational friendships. John Fox (dates unknown) counted sixteen different nationalities among the 268 Christians in prison in Alexandria in 1577,[254] while Francis Knight listed as his companions in their escape from Algiers "four Englishmen, one Welch man, one Gersie man, two French men, one Spaniard, one Marjorcine, a Neapolitan and a boy of Malta".[255] Lisa Voigt quotes Diego de Haëdo (dates unknown) as listing "Indios de la Indias de Portugal, del Brasil y de la Nueva España" – Indians from the Indies of Portugal, of Brasil and of New Spain – among the long list of renegades in Algiers, which represents virtually every nationality in Christendom.[256] These slaves were often able to collaborate across linguistic boundaries because of the existence of *lingua franca*, a mixture of Spanish, Portuguese, Italian and French which was spoken almost universally in the port cities of the Mediterranean and which was used by the Turks of the Barbary regencies as their primary language of communication with their slaves.[257]

Just as not all slaves were in chains, or forced to undertake hard labour on a daily basis, so not all captives had to endure insults and beatings. Many were treated well and some even built up quite close personal relationships with their masters. One Algerian captive wrote that "many privately owned slaves were very highly regarded by their masters and lived as though they were free.[258] Francis Knight said of his master that he was "an honest moral man".[259] William Okeley remarked that:

> If I should be silent here, I should be the most ungrateful wretch living. I found not only pity and compassion, but love and friendship from my new patron. Had I been his son, I could not have met with more respect nor been treated with more tenderness.[260]

This was a sentiment also expressed by Pitts:

> He [his master] would say to me, *Though I was never married my self, yet you shall in a little Time, and then your Children shall be mine.* [i.e. Pitts's children would inherit his master's fortune] ... Many more Kindnesses, of this my last *Patroon*, I could relate; for which I cannot but say, I had a great Love for him, even as a Father.[261]

The most striking example of friendship between a Muslim and a Christian slave is probably that shown to Francis Brooks (dates unknown) by a Moor whom he met in Morocco. The Moor helped Brooks to escape, but as a punishment for aiding a Christian he was "taken and burnt", for which Brooks "was much grieved, knowing the Moor's true-heartedness towards us in bringing and directing us on our journey, when we made our escape from Macqueness [Meknes/Miknās]".[262]

So, although many slaves suffered terrible hardships from their masters, from working in the galleys, or the mines, or at other forms of hard labour, the situation seems to have improved gradually from the middle of the 17th century, brought about mainly by the numerous missions of the Redemptionist fathers and by the peace treaties signed by the regencies with European nations. Nobody would ever have willingly been a captive in Algiers or elsewhere in North Africa, but the captivity narratives often show us a world of more complex relations than one might have imagined, in which a limited form of freedom was allowed many of the slaves. Pitts's apprehension when captured was that he would be eaten,[263] and similar fears must initially have been felt by many captives, but it emerges from the evidence that for many slaves these fears gradually metamorphosed into a semi-acceptance of life in Algiers and the other regencies.

# 2

# JOSEPH PITTS: THE MAN AND HIS BACKGROUND

"THE CITY OF EXETER was one of the largest and wealthiest of English towns during the 16th and 17th centuries."[1] So begins the foreword by W. G. Hoskins (himself another famous son of Exeter) to W. B. Stephens's economic study of the Exeter of Pitts's time, *Seventeenth-Century Exeter: a Study of Industrial and Commercial Development, 1625–1688* (Exeter, 1958). Indeed, if one includes Topsham,[2] Exeter in the early 17th century was consistently the busiest trading port in the provinces after Hull.[3] It may be difficult now to think of Exeter as a major industrial and trading centre, but before the industrial revolution the towns in the Exe and Culm valleys produced large quantities of serge,[4] principally for export not only to France (where production had been damaged by the flight of many Huguenots), but also to many other countries in Europe, including Spain, Italy, Germany and the Netherlands. Most visitors to Exeter remarked on this thriving trade. For example Count Lorenzo Magalotti (1637–1712) remarked in 1669 on how Exeter depended on

> ... bays[5] and different sorts of light cloth [which] is sold to all parts, being sent to the West Indies, Spain, France and Italy; but the greater part goes to the Levant. The very best cloth is also made, both for home consumption and for exportation; but the trade in this is not considerable, in comparison with the other.[6]

In 1698, Celia Fiennes (1662–1741) considered Exeter "a town very well built ... spacious noble streetes, and a vast trade is carryd on ... [in] serges – there is an incredible quantity of them made and sold in the town",[7] while Daniel Defoe (1661?–1731) observed that Exeter "was full of gentry and good company, and yet full of trade and manufactures also", that it was "large, rich, beautiful [and] populous", and that:

This city drives a very great correspondence with Holland, as also
directly to Portugal, Spain and Italy; shipping off vast quantities of
the woollen-manufactures, especially, to Holland, the Dutch giving
very large commissions here for the buying of serges, perpetuan's[8]
and such goods.[9]

Apart from exporting cloth, Exeter and Topsham in the late 17th century
also imported timber, pitch, hemp, flax and minerals from Scandinavia and
Germany, sugar from the Canaries, Azores and Madeira, olive oil and dried fruit
from Spain and other Mediterranean countries, and a wide variety of other
products from France, Spain and the Netherlands; it also sustained an extensive
coastal trade, exporting cloth and cider, and importing coal, wool, corn, timber,
malt and general goods from other ports in England, Wales and Ireland.[10] A
particularly important Devonian business in the 17th and 18th centuries was
fishing for cod off Newfoundland and New England. Once caught, the cod
would be salted and sold either in England or, more often, on the Continent,
where dried fish was a staple of the winter diet for many Mediterranean
countries. Almost seventy percent of the fishing fleet setting out for
Newfoundland in 1675, for example, consisted of boats from Devon,[11] and
while Dartmouth, Plymouth and North Devon ports dominated the Devon
contingent, Exeter is known to have sent five boats to Newfoundland in 1676,
sixteen in 1683 and thirteen in 1690.[12]

Given the importance of maritime trade to Exeter, it is not surprising that
Pitts tells us that "when I was about fourteen or fifteen Years of Age, my *Genius*
led me to be a Sailor",[13] and that after a few short voyages he set sail from
Lympstone[14] aboard the *Speedwell* "bound to the *Western Islands* [probably
Ireland], from thence to *Newfoundland*, from thence to *Bilboa* [Bilbao], from
thence to the *Canaries*, and so home, had God permitted".[15] The boat he sailed
on sounds like a typical member of the English fishing fleet, being small with
a crew of five or six and which fished off Newfoundland or New England for
cod or herring, which would then be salted or pickled and sold in Spain or
farther south. Indeed, the corsairs who captured his boat also took three more
English boats, all with crews of five or six and all carrying fish.[16] Pitts's narrative
talks about English ships on several occasions, the most notable being when his
father uses George Taylor, master of the *Speedwell*, to carry a letter to Algiers,[17]
and the encounter in Alexandria with Mr Bear of Topsham, which furnishes
us with the only evidence we have that Exeter ships travelled as far east as Egypt
in the 17th century.[18]

If Exeter's dependence on maritime trade was a major influence on Pitts's

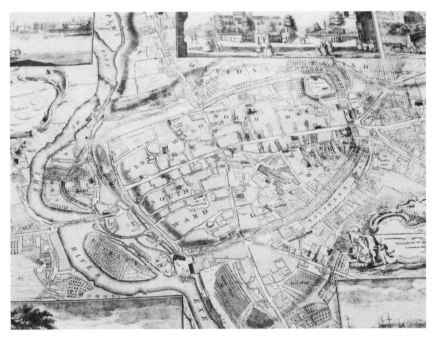

Portion of the map of Exeter by John Rocque,
published in 1744 as *Plan de la ville et faubourgs d'Exeter*.

choice of career, then the strength of Protestant belief in Devon, and the Puritan tradition in particular, determined his whole attitude to life and was the bedrock of his identity. Devon had become "one of the most fiercely Protestant counties in England",[19] and many Devonians enthusiastically welcomed the Commonwealth, which was declared in May 1649. In Devon:

> When Puritanism gained the upper hand during the Civil War and Commonwealth and set out to eliminate episcopacy, about one-third of the of the clergy of Devon were ejected from their livings, mostly from the rural parishes … [but] the return of Charles II [in 1660] ended the last hopes – or fears – of Puritan rule. The *Act of Uniformity* (1662) forced the Puritan clergy from the retention of their livings. Of the 2,000 clergy who resigned as a result of this Act, 132 were to be found in Devon … the Presbyterians were cast out of the national church, and went to swell the ranks of nonconformity outside it.[20]

In fact, ten clergymen in office in Exeter during the latter years of the

Commonwealth were either Presbyterians or independents, and only one of these conformed, i.e. returned to the Church of England, when the *Act of Uniformity* was passed in 1662.[21] The rest became Nonconformists and, although subject to many civil disabilities, particularly after the passing of the first and second *Conventicle Acts* in 1664 and 1670, Nonconformists continued to be strong in Exeter, and "by the Sessions records, we know that Conventicles [gatherings of Nonconformists] continued to be held, despite the penalties attached, attended by more than 200 people at one time".[22] It is not known to which Presbyterian assembly[23] Joseph Pitts belonged, but it is possible to trace the career of two of the three ministers who were consulted by Joseph's father, John Pitts, when he received his son's letter confessing his renunciation of his Christian faith.[24] Both John Hopping and Joseph Hallett were well-known Presbyterians in Exeter, John Hopping (d. 1705) being a minister of the Bow Meeting, while Joseph Hallett (the elder) was a minister of James' Meeting and died in 1689. (Of Mr Collings, the third minister mentioned in Pitts's book, we know nothing).[25] Joseph Hallett's son, also called Joseph Hallett (1656–1722), and his grandson, yet another Joseph Hallett (*ca.* 1691–1744), were involved in a major controversy between 1716 and 1719 which centred on the doctrine of the Trinity. The Halletts were said to have introduced Arian[26] views into their academy, which resulted in their being asked to publicly to declare their belief in the Trinity, and, although they did so, their commitment was seen as lacklustre and so their academy was closed down in 1719. It has been argued that this controversy had a significant effect on Pitts.[27] This is debatable, but what we can be sure of is that he received a thorough Christian education. His father John Pitts may not have been wealthy (we know nothing of his socio-economic status), but, as was common in most Nonconformist families, he ensured that his son Joseph was able to read and write.

Almost all that is known about Joseph Pitts is what is contained in the autobiographical sections of his book. As far as can be deduced, he was born around 1663, and set sail from Devon on Easter Tuesday 1678,[28] although even this date can be contested since *A list of ships taken since July, 1677 from his Majesties subjects, by the corsairs of Algier, with their names, masters names, and places to which they belong'd, and time of taking, with a modest estimate of the loss,* claimed that the *Speedwell* was captured in 1679[29] and not 1678, as recorded by Pitts. However, it would be an extraordinary coincidence were Pitts's father, the various Presbyterian ministers consulted, and Exeter port records, as well as other seamen to have mistaken the date of the *Speedwell's* departure, and therefore, on the balance of probability, 1678 must be assumed to be the correct date for Pitts's departure from England. Pitts claimed that he "remain'd several

Years a slave"; he goes on to mention that he lived with his first master Mustapha (Muṣṭafā) "two or three Months" before undertaking a two-month voyage on a corsair vessel prior to being sold to Dilberre Ibrahim (Dilber Ibrahim), an event which probably took place at the end of 1678 or the beginning of 1679.[30] Dilber Ibrahim took Pitts on two occasions to Tunis, where he met Consul Francis Baker, who is known to have been in post there until 1683.[31] During his time with Dilber Ibrahim, Pitts was forced to convert to Islam,[32] at some point between the time when he sent his first letter to his father which he did "about two or three Months, as near as I can guess, after I was taken a Slave"[33] (so probably towards the end of 1678), and the receipt of his father's reply, which reached Pitts "some Days after I had, through my *Patroon's* Barbarity to me, *turn'd* from my *Religion*".[34] It is impossible to know exactly when Pitts became a Muslim, but Dilber Ibrahim lost his life in an attempt to become *dey* in the aftermath of the second French bombardment of 1683,[35] so Pitts must have converted between 1679 and 1683. It can be further argued that it was most probably in 1683, since Pitts says that he had lived with his third master for about a year before he accompanied him to Mecca,[36] and, furthermore, the third edition of his book includes a quotation from a letter written by George Taylor, master of the *Speedwell,* and dated 22 October 1682, in which he says of Pitts:"I have not seen him these thirteen or fourteen Months; but do hear by all that come in Company of him, that he hath still a *Christian* Heart, which I hope will continue with him to the End of his Days."[37]

After Dilber Ibrahim's abortive coup, Pitts was sold to his third and final master, Eumer (Ömer/'Umar), an "old Batchelor"[38] who took him on the pilgrimage and who gave Pitts his freedom at Mecca.[39] There is some debate about the date of Pitts's pilgrimage, with various scholars suggesting years ranging from 1680 to 1686.[40] The evidence from Pitts's own text is conflicting. If Pitts is correct in stating that he lived with his third master for about a year before accompanying him on the pilgrimage, then he probably made his *hajj* in 1684 since we know that Dilber Ibrahim died in 1683. On the other hand, Pitts describes how during the first year of his freedom, "the *French* came a third time to bombard *Algier, Anno* 1688";[41] so, again if Pitts is correct, he cannot have undertaken the pilgrimage earlier than 1686. In the most detailed analysis of the matter, Charles Beckingham used a combination of Arabic and Western sources to arrive at the conclusion that Pitts spent August to November 1685 in Mecca and Medina,[42] but the internal evidence of Pitts's book (mainly his military campaigns in Oran and Morocco) would suggest that he went on the pilgrimage the following year, 1686, from July to October, but even 1687 is possible. Unfortunately, given the conflicting evidence, the exact date of Pitts's journey to Mecca may never be known, but it is almost certain that 1694 was the year Pitts effected his escape, since he cites verbatim a letter of recommendation from Consul Baker in Algiers to Consul Ray (also spelled Raye) in Smyrna dated 14 June 1694.[43]

What little information there is about Pitts's life in Algiers after he was freed would indicate that he was a soldier. Pitts describes how, when a Christian turns Turk, the new renegade "is immediately entred [*sic*] into Pay, and directed to the Place where he shall quarter, with some of his Fellow-Soldiers",[44] and states that this is exactly what happened to him – "Being now at liberty from my *Patroon* (who gave me my *Letter of Freedom* at *Mecca*) and enter'd into Pay ...".[45] Pitts goes on describe campaigns he undertook once he had been freed, in his first year against the Spanish enclave of Oran,[46] and in his second year against Morocco.[47] Pitts supplies further evidence of his military career, by describing how he undertook cruises with the corsairs, participated in the camps, i.e. in the summer campaigns against the Arab and Berber inhabitants in the regions, and how, in the year he escaped, he "made an Exchange with one, who agreed to go in my room [place] to the *Camp*, and I was to go to his room in the *Ship*".[48] Domestically, Pitts seems to have continued living with his third master even after his freedom,[49] probably in a court or *funduck*[50] "where lived none but *Batchelors*",[51] so it would appear that he lived a single life and never took a wife while in Algiers.

Pitts tells his readers that he was tempted to remain in Algiers because of his comfortable situation, his love for his third master, his expectations of preferment, and for fear of being "put to death after the most cruel, and exemplary manner"[52] if he was caught trying to escape. However, this is balanced by Pitts's constant claim that he was never a Muslim at heart. He asserts that during his nine or so years as a renegade escape was never far from his mind, telling his readers that he made "two or three Voyages, hoping to be *retaken* ... but *Providence* did not order it that way".[53] However, he did not pluck up the courage to plan his actual escape in detail until he was encouraged to do so by an English merchant, Mr Butler, and by John Thomas of Bristol, "whom I had a long Time before let into my *Secrets*".[54] The latter introduced him to the British Consul Thomas Baker (Consul in Algiers from 1691 to 1694) who, once he heard of Pitts's plan of "going with the ships of *Algier* up to the *Levant*"[55] and then making his escape far from the watchful gaze of his fellow Algerians, gave him a letter of introduction to the English Consul in Smyrna (now Izmir).[56] In total, as far as can be ascertained, Pitts spent up to seventeen years away from Exeter, made up by six months at sea before he was captured,[57] fifteen years in Algiers (of which about five or six were spent as a slave, and probably eleven or twelve as a Muslim), and a year on the journey back to England.[58]

Of Joseph Pitts's life after his return to Exeter very little is known. From the preface to the third edition it can be deduced that he spent some time in London,[59] and that he was acquainted with some of the more famous men of the day, such as William Lowndes (1652–1724), Secretary to the Treasury from 1695 until his death,[60] and Peter, Lord King, Baron Ockham (1669–1734),[61] an Exeter man probably educated by the Joseph Hallett to whom Pitts's father turned, and who as Lord High Chancellor between 1725 and 1733 was tolerant of dissenting opinion (and to whom the third edition of Pitts's book is dedicated). The standard article on Pitts's life, outside the information supplied by his book, was published as long ago as 1920 by Cecily Radford,[62] and is based on surviving records held in Exeter and elsewhere. Joseph Pitts's father was called John as is known from the text,[63] and he was "probably the John Pitts who signed the petition of a church in Exeter to King Charles II".[64] Radford assumes that Pitts belonged to James' Meeting (of which all records prior to 1707 have been lost) and that he was buried in the Free Cemetery at Friernhay in Exeter (again there are no burial records before 1800), probably in 1739, since a will of a Joseph Pitts was proved in Exeter in that year. This will is undated and gives no indication of the testator's station in life or place of residence, but leaves £100 to his daughter Elizabeth Skutt to be paid on his wife Hannah's death, with "the effects at her death to be divided among the children as their circumstances shall require and behaviour deserve". Radford surmises that "his social status was not high, or he would have appeared as Mr Joseph Pitts in the notice of probate",[65] and it is at this point that he disappears from history.

# 3

## *A Faithful Account of the Religion and Manners of the Mahometans*

### A captivity narrative

DANIEL VITKUS GIVES bibliographical details of twenty-seven English North African captivity narratives dated between 1589 and 1704 as an appendix to his edition of seven of the most significant of them,[1] while as an introduction to these edited texts, Nabil Matar supplies a seminal essay identifying the main characteristics of this mode of writing.[2] In this, Matar explores how the personal core of these narratives is nearly always a justification of the captives' Protestant beliefs, and an apologia explaining how the captives' faith remained intact despite the many trials and tribulations they had to face at the hands of their masters. All returning captives were subjected to what Nabil Matar calls "identity insecurity", since to have been a slave in North Africa meant that the captive's "English/British/Christian identity ... had been tested and there was no foregone conclusion that it would have passed the test successfully".[3] Gerald Maclean outlines three major issues confronting all those Christians who came into contact with the Ottoman Empire: first, admiration for Ottoman wealth and power (very evident in the works of Rycaut and many other contemporary travellers and diplomats, and usefully termed by Maclean "imperial envy"[4]); second, the fact that "life in the Islamic Mediterranean offered an enormously attractive alternative to life in the British Isles [and elsewhere in Europe, particularly during periods of war and religious persecution]"; and, third, that "for those who came back, the experience of going [to the Islamic world] had changed what it meant to be English".[5]

In general, captives react with shame and anger to the trauma of being held captive, which is often magnified when the captors' culture is radically different from their own. This sense of loss of identity was something shared by most of the North African captivity narratives, since each individual had been uprooted from his native soil, forced to speak a new language, eat unusual food, dress in a different way and undertake arduous and unfamiliar tasks, all the time uncertain as to whether he would ever return home. As Francis Brooks explained it:

> I shall offer nothing but truths which ten years sufferings have made me too long acquainted with. We were not only banished from our native country (being English-men and myself born in the Ratcliff parish of Bristol), but from all the spiritual as well as temporal comforts. We were confined amongst those whose religion was composed of cruelty, whose customs were extravagant, and whose usages almost intolerable …[6]

Similarly, Joseph Pitts declared that when two of his master's servants tried to make him wear "the *Turkish* Garb", he kept crying and told his master that "although he had changed my *Habit* [clothes], yet he could never change my *Heart*".[7]

Almost all the narratives seek some sort of self-justification for having been captured and explain how the narrators and their fellow Englishmen were men of courage who fought against great odds to prevent capture. John Fox is typical in his description of the battle against the Turks, boasting how "the Englishmen showed themselves men indeed, in working manfully with their brown bills and halberds",[8] while Richard Hasleton, despite being "sore hurt with a musket shot", still fought against the boarders with his knife until forced to jump overboard.[9] Joseph Pitts's crew was unable to avoid being taken, and although they were determined to try to overcome the Turkish soldiers on board, they failed because of a lack of courage shown by their Dutch fellow-captives. Pitts describes this incident in detail:

> The first Adviser of an Insurrection was one Mr. *James Goodridge*, now of *Exon* [Exeter], who was one of the *old* Slaves and a Cabin-Servant; and in order to it, brought down two naked Swords, and a pair of Pincers to loose the Iron Bar on which we were shackled. All this while none of the *Spaniards*, or Slaves of other Nations, knew any thing of our Design; and we so order'd it, for fear we should be discovered by them, that only the *English* and *Dutch* were privy to it. The Night being come when we were resolved to rise … the Heart of the *Dutch* Master flagg'd, and so a Stop was put to our Design; whereas, had we been all unanimous, the Thing might, and

in all probability would have been accomplish'd with a great deal of *Honour* and *Profit*.[10]

In his book, Pitts accuses the Algerians of being "timorous",[11] of being sailors who "dread much the *English Men of War*",[12] who "are *wondrously* Valiant against a weak Enemy"[13] but "if at any time they see a Ship preparing to *fight* them, their Courage is apt to be very soon daunted".[14] He concludes his second chapter by declaring that "the *Algerines* are not in truth such daring Sparks as they are thought to be. And I verily believe that many Ships, much unequal to them in Strength, might escape being taken, if they would but *appear brave*, and look them *boldly* in the Face."[15] To characterize their captors as cowards is to devalue whatever claims Englishmen might make to valour in the face of enslavement, leaving them little to boast about. It is possible that Pitts's abiding feelings of guilt and shame blinded him to this, and that he cannot restrain himself from making such comments out of a simple prejudice that Englishmen, however much subjected to humiliation, are nevertheless braver than their oppressors and enemies.

Once in Algiers (or Tunis, Tripoli or Morocco), the narrators usually described the miseries and shame of slavery, and how they suffered both physically and mentally. The anonymous T. S. complains that one master "with a cudgel made me understand a trade I never knew before [and] I endured much with him",[16] while his next master was "an Italian renegade named Ishmael Reiz, who was not kinder to me than my former masters; my work was painful, my diet mean and my rewards the blows of a hard cudgel".[17] Adam Elliot (1645/6–1700) was beaten about the head by his master, who "was so transported with passion, he showered down a whole torrent of blows upon me, and lighting unluckily upon a stick, he broke my head in several places and never ceased till he had made me all in a gore-blood".[18]

Apart from attacks on their own persons, many narrators also take delight in describing "barbarian cruelty". Thomas Phelps seems to enjoy exposing the extreme behaviour of "Muley Ishmael, emperor of Morocco and Fez, etc."[19] who, in comparison with "Sicilian tyrants and Roman emperors" is a "monster of Africk, a composition of gore and dust, whom nothing can atone but human sacrifices".[20] T. S. describes with relish punishments such as driving a stake into convicted thieves so that "it enters in between their legs and appears again at their mouth," while adulterers "are cast headlong down a precipice, at the bottom whereof sharp stakes are erected to welcome them", while anyone who dishonours Muhammad's name has boiling lead poured down their throats.[21] The fact that some of T. S.'s descriptions may be fabrications serves to underline rather than invalidate the general principle that captivity narratives are designed to show that the Turks and Moors are less civilized than Englishmen. Joseph Pitts describes the apparently random cruelty he suffered from his first master,[22] the punishment inflicted on schoolchildren and soldiers,[23] (which, though severe, was hardly excessive by contemporary European standards), and paints a vivid picture of the attempts by his second master to force him to turn Turk, emphasizing his own stubborn but ultimately futile resistance.[24]

Another constant in captivity narratives is the attempt to buttress the author's identity by constant mention of either his Englishness or his faith in God, or both. This anxiety is not surprising given how many captives must have been greeted on their return with the suspicion that their Christian faith might have been tainted by their enforced residence in Islamic lands. One of the collects for Good Friday in the Anglican Book of Service exemplifies the fear and anxiety faced by Christians encountering the world of Islam and is quoted by Pitts at the end of the first edition of his book:

> O Merciful GOD, who hast made all *Men*, and hatest nothing that thou hast made; nor wouldest the Death of a Sinner, but rather that he should be Converted & live; have Mercy upon all *Jews*, *Turks*, *Infidels*, and *Hereticks*; and take from them all Ignorance, Hardness of Heart, and Contempt of thy Word; and so fetch them home, Blessed Lord, to thy Flock …[25]

The concern for God's mercy is most obvious in William Okeley's account, which is the most sustained of captivity narratives in its attachment of the divine presence, devoting more than a dozen pages at the beginning of the book (including a substantial poem) to God's providence and the need to trust in Him. Okeley's narrative is full of Biblical quotations and references to deliverance from bondage (which may also signify the author's strong anti-Catholic bias), but like Pitts he was unable to maintain his opposition to his master in the face of compulsion, even when this meant going against his conscience. In Okeley's case, he was ordered to act as a member of the crew of his master's man-of-war when it went out raiding Christian shipping ("here a case of conscience offered itself, whether I might without sin in any case fight against Christians on the part of the common enemy of all Christianity"[26]), but, like Pitts above, Okeley felt that he had no choice in the face of his master's authority but to comply. Other narrators too talked in similarly providentialist terms about God. John Rawlins introduced his narrative thus:

Hearken then, I pray you, to this following relation, and learn thereby, as I said, both to give God the praise of all deliverances, and to instruct one another in the absolute duties of Christianity. By the one, the power and the providence, with all the attributes belonging to so immense a deity, shall be made manifest; by the other, the weak brother shall be comforted, the strong confirmed, the wavering reduced, the faint-hearted erected, and the presumptuous moderated.[27]

The benefits of being English were also stressed by many narrators, none more so than Thomas Phelps, who wrote that:

Here [in England] the government secures every man in the possession and enjoyment of what God's blessing and his own industry has allowed. Here even the poor and needy, the impotent and those who the hand of God has touched have a comfortable subsistence and plentiful provision against all extremities. Here the industrious mechanic or country farmer can sit down at his table better provided than many barons of German, marquises in France, and knights in Spain. In a word, slavery is so strange a condition to England, that to touch its soil is ipso facto manumission, and the generality of the people have but little heard and less understood the miserable state which the most part of world is now subject to, so that the plenty and great liberty of the English subjects is no great happiness to them, because they never weigh their condition with the lot of other nations.[28]

The big identity challenge confronting many captives who stayed any length of time in the Barbary states was conversion to Islam. Almost all captivity narratives mention converts, who are always referred to as renegades, often in conjunction with the worldly success these converts enjoyed. Edward Kellett (1583–1641), in a sermon preached in 1627 and entitled *A Return from Argier*, enumerates the reasons for conversion, which include weakness and lack of faith, torture ("the misusage of poor captive-Christians by the barbarous tyranny of savage Mahumetans"), the sight of the freedom enjoyed by other renegades and, above all, "the enticements of pleasure and worldly preferment".[29] John Rawlins complained that the Turks beat new slaves to make them convert but acknowledged that some needed little persuasion: "Others, I must confess, who never knew any god but their own sensual lusts and pleasures, thought that any religion would serve their turns and so for preferment of wealth very voluntarily renounced their faith and became renegadoes."[30] Edward Coxere was told that if he converted he might become captain of the ship on which he was working,[31] while Francis Knight lamented: "How facile doe these [former shipmates] profess the new religion, priding themselves in Turkish ceremonies, and in a faith once execrable unto them."[32] The traveller and merchant Henry Blount (1602–82)[33] found that while some renegades had been forced to convert, others "left our cause for the Turkish as the more thriving in the world and fuller of preferment".[34]

As far as identity crises went, Pitts was tested as severely as any captives before him. In the first place, as noted above, he had been captured when very young and immature ("When I was about fourteen or fifteen Years of Age, my *Genius* led me to be a sailor and to see *foreign* Countries; much contrary to my Mother's Mind ..."[35]), which meant that by the time he was an adult he had become acclimatized to life in North Africa. In addition, his conversion to Islam gave him status, privileges and expectations not accorded to other slaves, and he admits on several occasions that he was very tempted to remain in Algiers. Indeed, by the time of his escape he had been a renegade for probably eleven or twelve years, and there is every reason to believe that he published his book on his return not only because, as he says in the preface to the first edition of 1704, he was "importun'd" by many of his friends to give an account of his experiences and adventures, but also because he wished to "make some manner (at least) of *Restitution* and *Reparation* for my past *Defection*".[36] This clearly remained a sensitive issue with Pitts, since he devoted a whole paragraph in the preface to the third edition of 1731 to the fact that "I have often been reflected on for my *Apostasy*".[37] He mentions with some bitterness that it was not persons of "Learning or Piety" who still censured him but that they were "for the most part, ignorant or vile Persons". He concludes:

> I do not pretend to excuse what I did; but whether it was *voluntarily*, or I was a true *Mussulman*, let any judge, when they have considered what Hazard I ran in making my Escape. I was in a much fairer Way for *Honour* and *Preferment* in *Algier*, than I could expect ever to have been in *England*.[38]

Pitts's book is not as full of Biblical quotations and theological asides as Okeley's, nor of protestations of Englishness as Phelps' narrative, but there are constant assurances to the reader by Pitts that he never became a Turk at heart. He gives a detailed description of his forced conversion (almost literally a blow-by-blow account),[39] and mentions that although his master's brother made him "large Offers", "it was not out of Choice, or Inclination, or Perswasion, or any Temporal Advantage that I became a *Mahometan*; for I abhorred the Thoughts of such an *Apostasy*".[40] Indeed, he argues that although it is reported that "when any *Christians* are taken by the *Algerines*, they are put to the *extremest Tortures*, that so they may be thereby brought over to the *Mahometan Faith*", such reports are false, since the Turks "*very seldom* use any such Severities on that account … They do not use to *force* any *Christian* to renounce his *Religion*",[41] and that therefore his case was an unusual one. He offers the cruel and unusual brutality that he was subjected to as his exoneration.

Pitts writes movingly of his despair, just after he had converted, at receiving a letter from his father, not only because he had betrayed his religion and his parents, but also because "if the Letter had come to my Hands before I had turn'd *Turk*, my *Patroon* would rather have accepted of the promis'd *Ransom* for me, than that I should become a *Mahometan*."[42] He wrote back to his father that he had been forced to convert; had his father not replied, or replied disowning him, it is entirely possible that Pitts would have accepted his fate, and remained in North Africa. However his father, although devastated by the news, had sought the opinion of "several *Ministers*, who unanimously concurred in their Opinion, that I had not sinned the *unpardonable Sin*",[43] and wrote to his son of God's "boundless Mercies", and that "*what thou hast done with thy* Mouth, *was not with thy* Heart", and that "*I will promise thee as* welcome *to me* upon thy Return *and* Repentance, *as though thou hadst never done it*". Not surprisingly, this strengthened Joseph's resolve to maintain his Christian faith and he describes how he "would often go into some By-corner, or under some Hedge of a Garden, to read it"[44] and thereby sustain himself. He also tries to persuade the reader of his continuing Christian faith by explaining how his second master treated him with less kindness after he had converted "because he thought that I was no true *Mussulman* in my Heart; for he observ'd me to be far from being *zealous* in the *Mahometan* way",[45] a reproach also made by fellow renegade James Grey.[46]

However, this is not to say that Pitts did not struggle to retain his Christian faith. Although he makes a point of his second master's criticism of his lack of zeal for Islam, he admits that his third master did not doubt that Pitts was "a true Mussulman".[47] Having been a renegade himself, he sometimes writes about Christians abjuring their faith without outright condemnation. On the one hand, he censures some Spanish renegades who escaped back to Spain but without ascribing their escape to God's providence,[48] which is surprising since almost all Christian captives who escaped back to their homelands saw their return in terms of divine intervention and as examples of God's mercy. On the other hand, he tells three separate stories about renegades who rejected the opportunity to reconvert back to Christianity, and expresses disapproval only about the first case, which was of an Englishman who was ransomed and went back to England, only to return voluntarily to Algiers and re-embrace Islam. The second example was a gun-smith (a valued trade, and one leading to a potentially lucrative career), who had been ransomed and was awaiting a ship home to England, but "chose rather to be a *Mahometan*, than to return to *England*".[49] The third was an Irish renegade who had spent thirty years in the Spanish and French galleys, but who had been redeemed by the Algerians and "was look'd on as a very pious Man, and a great *Zealot*, by the *Turks*, for his not turning from the Mahometan Faith, notwithstanding the great *Temptations* he had so to do."[50] In the latter two cases, Pitts utters no word of censure.

Indeed there is evidence that Pitts was tempted to follow the examples of these renegades. He describes how his master encouraged him to improve his reading and writing, and admits that:

> I could strike the *Turkish* Character beyond their Expectation; and all in the School admir'd me for it. But I began to consider with my self [*sic*], that I should soon be *Master* of writing, as well as a pretty good *Accountant*, and my *Patroon* being related to the then *Dey*, could easily get me promoted, as such usually are; and for this very Reason I laid aside my Writing, fearing what the Consequence might be ... Had I been prevailed with to alter my Condition there, I tremble to think what the Issue might have been.[51]

Even when he had decided to escape and was awaiting a ship from the island of Chios, Pitts was still in two minds, as he describes:

> Now the *Devil* was very busy with me, tempting me to lay aside all thoughts of *escaping*, but to return to *Algier*, and continue a *Mussulman* ... But here the *Goodness* of God was manifested to me in such a measure, that I at last surmounted all the Temptations and Fears that so furiously beset me, which were indeed very great: For it was suggested to me, first, That it was a very difficult, if not *desperate* Attempt, to endeavour to make my *Escape*; and that if I were discovered in it, I should be put to death after the most cruel, and exemplary manner: And also, in the next place, the Loss that I should sustain thereby, in several respects, *viz.* The loss of the profitable Returns which I might make of what Money I had, to *Algier*, and

of receiving eight Months Pay due to me there, and the frustrating my Hopes and Expectations which I had from my *Patroon*, who made me large Promises of leaving me considerable Substance at his Death. ... This was also a great Temptation to me to return to *Algier*.

In the midst of all, I would pray to *God* for his Assistance, and found it.[52]

Despite such wavering, Pitts never leaves the reader in doubt that at bottom he never ceased to believe in the Christian God. Even when discoursing on his love for his third master, he makes it plain that Algiers "was not *England*, and I wanted to be at *home*",[53] and in another section of the book he states that the chief reason for his escaping was "That I might worship God as I ought",[54] while the text of the third edition ends with a paean to Christianity and to "the *wonderful* Goodness of the Lord towards me, whose blessed Name I shall desire to glorify *in the Sight of all Men*".[55]

Pitts's captivity narrative is as effective in describing the psychological and physical trauma of loss of identity as any that preceded or succeeded it. Indeed, it is all the more credible since Pitts does not present himself as just a "hardworking Briton who had endured years of slavery and labor among the Muslims in order to preserve the integrity of his religious and national identity",[56] which is how Matar characterizes most works in this genre. Pitts does indeed conform to this norm by emphasizing the fortitude and determination it took to retain his Christian identity, and much of the narrative can be read as that of a plain-speaking, honest Englishman, but he continually subverts this picture of himself by his capacity for self-inspection: he is able to admit how he was constantly assailed by overwhelming feelings of fear, loneliness, guilt and shame. He is determined to prove how, in the face of coercion and enticements, he never lost his Christian faith, and his narrative can be read as an apologia for his sins, one which seeks to explain if not excuse his recantation. He is honest enough to admit his susceptibility to the temptations he faced, and the centrality of his father's second letter for his mental and spiritual health cannot be exaggerated. While Pitts's escape is a rare example of courage in that he journeyed on his own for a whole year, mostly on foot, before reaching England, it is his episodes of doubt and despair while in Algiers, and his understanding of, and even identification with, an alien culture which makes his narrative both believable and sympathetic.

## A travel account

JOSEPH PITTS IS JUSTLY celebrated for his description of the Muslim Holy Places and the pilgrimage ceremonies, but this has almost completely overshadowed his contribution to our knowledge of North African society. Pitts's description of the *hajj* will be discussed in the next section, which looks at Pitts's views of and attitude towards Islam; this section will try instead to analyse his observations on Algerian and North African society and will only cover the Arabian Peninsula part of his travels in passing.

There were remarkably few accurate and detailed English-language descriptions of North Africa published either before or during Pitts's lifetime. There are several reasons for this. One is that some travellers showed little interest in contemporary Muslim society. Two typical examples of this approach are the Anglican clergyman Thomas Shaw (1694–1751),[57] whose *Travels and Observations Relating to Several Parts of Barbary and the Levant* (Oxford, 1738) evinces the author's "permanent concern with the classical past of the Maghreb, which eclipses frequently his awareness of the present",[58] and Joseph Morgan, whose supposedly comprehensive *History of Algiers* (London, 1728) hardly extends beyond the 16th century and offers no observations on the structure or culture of 17th-century Algerian society.

In addition to such works, there were travel and captivity narratives, some of which undoubtedly incorporated fabrications. Concerning *The Totall Discourse of the Rare Adventures and Painfull Peregrinations* (London, 1623) by William Lithgow (1582–1645?), Edmund Bosworth remarks that "the whole of Lithgow's journey to Fez, his stay in the city and above all his journey back through the interior of North Africa, raise acute questions of its authenticity".[59] Gerald Maclean considers *The Adventures of Mr. T. S. Taken Prisoner by the Turks of Argiers and Carried into the Inland Countries of Africa* (London, 1670) "most likely to be historically based fiction of the kind associated with Aphra Behn and Daniel Defoe".[60] Linda Colley is equally sceptical of the veracity of some of *The History of the Long Captivity* (London, *ca.* 1739) by Thomas Pellow (b. 1703 or 1704), praising Magali Morsy's critical translation of the narrative into French for separating "its authorial wheat from its editorial chaff".[61] Indeed, Colley's view of the whole genre is that "highly factual and invaluable material in Barbary and other captivity narratives is sometimes intercut with fictional or pirated passages. Political, religious, cultural and racial bias is combined with reportage that can be substantially verified; and terrible ignorance is exhibited side by side with rare perceptiveness and serious insights".[62] Colley does, however, continue her argument by defending captivity narratives as historical sources, which admittedly have to be "sampled and sieved", but which are ultimately not merely "revealing only about the observers and never of the observed",[63] but which contain valid data for the historian. She likens captives to ethnographers,[64] quoting anthropologist Mary Louise Pratt's approval of captives' capacity for "learning indigenous languages and lifeways with a proficiency any ethnographer would envy, and often producing accounts that are indeed full, rich and accurate by ethnography's own standards",[65] even though captives suffered from the same problems that fieldworkers do such as "the sense of dependency, lack of control, the vulnerability to being isolated completely or never left alone".[66] This is a point taken up by Nabil Matar, who emphasizes that captives gained an intimate view about life in North Africa, and because they lived within the society they were not, unlike travellers, merely passing through, and for this reason "their knowledge of the world of Islam was unparalleled in the early modern period of European geographical expansion".[67] As Joe Snader points out, "the captivity narrative places a premium on empirical inclusiveness, on capturing a broad range of experience, everything that the captive can remember, everything he or she witnessed or heard reported from other captives, and, further, on shaping that material as the full truth about an alien, allegedly archaic people".[68]

However, in a different publication, Snader criticizes captivity narratives from the Saidian orientalist standpoint by suggesting that the "very alienation and insularity that the captives experience as unwilling travellers reinforce their adoption of distant observational, scientific positions in relation to the Orient".[69] He goes further and claims: "At least partly driven by colonial imperatives, the Barbary captivity narrative adopted the aggressively antagonistic and totalizing epistemological stance characteristic of orientalism."[70] In addition, he criticizes Pitts for devoting more time to describing the society in which he lived than his own "personal sufferings", since Pitts "continually digests Algeria and Arabia into an easily managed anatomical structure, cataloguing towns along the African coast, shrines along the pilgrimage to Mecca, and the schedule of Muslim daily prayer."[71]

There is no doubt that captivity narratives are examples of the supposed triumph of Protestant Christianity over an alien culture, that they exhibit many features of perceived cultural superiority, and that they often emphasize negative features about the culture of the captors, dwelling on stereotypical examples of cruelty, cowardice and superstition. However, it is also true that some captives were able to produce a subtle and complex view of Ottoman and North African society, since their often lengthy exposure to Islamic society enabled them to differentiate between good and bad and to empathize in some way with their captors. According to Nabil Matar, they were not always "aggressively antagonistic" and, as he notes, "intentionally or not, the captives' accounts showed the Muslims as 'round' characters" so that "although they were captives, they grew to like their captors and were not unwilling to recall the humor in cross-cultural misunderstandings between themselves and the Muslims".[72]

Nor were captivity narratives always driven by the "colonial imperative". Matar suggests that before the 18th century, Britain and other Western countries recognized the power of the Ottoman Empire and its allies, and that descriptions of Muslim countries in contemporary Western writings emphasized the splendour and military might of Islam as an equal player on the world stage. He cites such works as *The Generall Historie of the Turkes* (London, 1603 and many subsequent editions)[73] by Richard Knolles (1550?–1610), and points out the failure of England to hold on to the enclave of Tangier (an English outpost from 1661 to 1684) as an example of how "the lands of Islam were beyond colonization and domination".[74] Indeed, the permanent presence of renegades in captivity narratives testifies to the power and attraction of the "Other", as does Pitts's own description of how tempted he was to remain in Algiers. Snader's final point about the imperialist need for knowledge would imply that any pre-20th-century writing about foreign cultures is *ipso facto* orientalist. However, most captivity narratives are neither "scientific" nor "catalogues" designed to "appropriate" the Orient. In fact they are often quite difficult to use as historical, geographical or linguistic sources. Gerald Maclean comments that he was "unable to find any evidence confirming or disproving the historicity of many events"[75] in T. S.'s *Adventures,* while d'Aranda's captivity narrative, though extensive, is also among the most disorganized of historical accounts. Moreover the episodes in Pitts's text dealing with the history of the rulers of Algiers mostly lack dates or any sense of historical perspective. The transliteration of geographical names is usually unscientific, e.g. Tremesen for Ṭilimsān, Mustagollem for Mustaghanim,[76] and some transcriptions even render places unidentifiable;[77] in addition, some of the Arabic or Turkish phrases found in the narratives are seriously corrupted, for example *ashhadu an lā ilāh illā-Llāh* is rendered by Pitts in his first edition as "ashhead wa la e la he il allah".[78] All of this combines to suggest that the narratives are neither scientific nor systematic and are less harbingers of imperialist ambitions than personal tales designed to show the author's resolution, courage and fortitude in the face of superior odds and to describe the conditions in which he spent his captivity. As Linda Colley says:

> It is emphatically not the case, as has sometimes been suggested, that

captivity narratives were comprehensively safe texts that only corroborated pre-existing and dismissive European viewpoints about other societies. Read scrupulously, indeed, they usefully disrupt the notion that there was ever a single identifiable British, still less European perspective on the non-European world.[79]

Pitts emphasizes the first-hand veracity of his narrative several times, for example in the prefaces to both the first and the third editions:

> I have hinted at some Mistakes in *Authors*, who are Persons of great *Learning* and Worth, and whose Names I acknowledge my self unworthy so much as to mention, were it not for the sake of *Truth*, which ought to be the dearest Thing in the World to every Man; and upon that account alone I have made bold to mention some Things, in which I am sure they have been misinform'd. What I speak I *know* to be true; nor have I recited Things meerly [*sic*] upon *Hearsay*.[80]

His interest in the world into which so many of his countrymen had been absorbed against their will is keen, and he gives many, if often somewhat disconnected, descriptions of Algerian, particularly Turkish Algerian culture. Some of his motifs are common to other captivity narratives, for example, how slaves were sold in the market,[81] methods of torture and punishment,[82] the layout of the city of Algiers,[83] the names and locations of other towns in Algeria,[84] and the internal organization of the Turkish civil and military government,[85] although he often gives much more detail than other authors. For example, he gives a detailed description of military expeditions:

> In their *March* they move but *two* in a breast, each Rank keeping at a considerable distance; so that a *Thousand* Men make a great *Shew*, and a very long *Train*. The *Cayah-Beulick*, or *Lieutenant*, rides in the Van of the Army, with two *Hoages*, or *Clerks*, each of them bearing a *Flag*. The *Sergeants* follow on foot: And then comes the *Aga*; and him follows the *Bay* with Trumpets, Drums, Pipes, Kettle-Drums, and such like Warlike Musick. They have a pretty odd way of *beating* their drums, *viz*. The *Drummer* beats with a Drum-stick knobb'd at the end in his Right-hand, upon the *Head* of the Drum; and the *bottom* of it, he at the same time strikes with a small Wand, which he holds in his *Left-hand*.[86]

The reader can often feel that Pitts is drawing on his own personal experiences, as for example when he describes how soldiers going on a route march into hostile territory, on the way out "do not travel very *hard*", while on the way home "they travel from *Morning* to *Night*".[87]

Pitts is also a keen ethnographic observer of domestic matters such as marriage, burial, children, dress, food, even wrestling.[88] His descriptions are fuller than most other captivity narratives and appear to be accurate in that they are rarely contradicted by accounts found in travellers from a later period or describing another region of the Muslim world. His description of marriage and divorce,[89] for instance, accords well with the much fuller one in *The Policie of the Turkish Empire* (1597)[90] by Giles Fletcher (1546?–1611), while his explanation of how to make and eat couscous (or, as he terms it, *cuska seu*)[91] is very similar to that supplied by the 18th-century French traveller Philémon de La Motte (dates unknown). (Indeed, La Motte's recipe is so similar that one suspects that it might even be based on Pitts's).[92] Some areas that Pitts ventures into are seldom found in other narratives of the period, for example "the compendious Method which they (*i.e.* the *Moors*) take to teach their *Children* to *read* and *write*",[93] salutations among Muslims,[94] or the nature of domestic housing.[95] Pitts often illustrates his descriptions with a personal anecdote, which gives his narrative a strong flavour of verisimilitude, as demonstrated in the following passage:

> As for the Men, they never visit one another at their Houses; nay, it is not esteem'd civil, or decent for one *married Man* to enquire for another at his House. Nay, what is more, it is thought rude to ask of any Person, *Sir, Where is your House?* Or, *Where do you live?* I my self [*sic*] once spake innocently to one when in *Egypt*, saying, *Whereabouts is your House in* Algier? And he took me up somewhat roughly, and said, *Why do you ask that question? My* Shop *is in such a place of the Town.*"[96]

One issue that almost all contemporary travellers to Islamic lands and most captivity narratives mention is sodomy. Nabil Matar's survey of 16th- and 17th-century English writings shows that "the link between sodomy and 'Islam' was deeply entrenched in English minds",[97] while Stephen Murray has demonstrated how it was felt to be particularly prevalent among regimes dominated by slave soldiers such as the Mamluks of Egypt and the Janissaries of the Barbary regencies.[98] Pitts was no different to the other writers of his time in succumbing to stereotyping, observing:

... the *Soldiery* [are] apt to drink, and are abominably rude, insomuch that it is very dangerous for *Women* to walk in any By-place, but more for *Boys*; for they are extremely given to *Sodomy* ... And yet this horrible sin of *Sodomy* is so far from being punish'd amongst them, that it is part of their ordinary Discourse to boast of their detestable Actions of that kind. 'Tis common for Men there to fall in Love with Boys, as 'tis here in *England* to be in Love with Women: And I have seen many, when they have been drunk, give themselves deep Gashes on their Arms with a Knife, saying, *'Tis for the* Love *they bear to such a* Boy.[99]

Yet Pitts, despite his long immersion in Muslim culture, seems to have remained under a misapprehension as to the nature of homosexuality. Sexual intercourse between men is clearly prohibited by Islamic law,[100] but there is ample evidence in the Arabic literature from the 17th century, when Pitts was living in Algiers, that homosexual love was common, was viewed sympathetically, and that it did not necessarily extend to sodomy.[101] Khaled El-Rouayheb's important recent study shows that Paul Rycaut's intuitive belief that "Platonick love" was the basis of much Islamic "homosexuality"[102] was fundamentally correct. As El-Rouayheb argues:

It may seem natural for modern historians to gloss over the distinction between committing sodomy and expressing passionate love for a youth, and to describe both activities as manifestations of "homosexuality." But this only goes to show that the term is anachronistic and unhelpful in this particular context. Islamic religious scholars of the period were committed to the precept that sodomy (*liwāṭ*) was one of the most abominable sins a man could commit. However, many of them clearly did not believe that falling in love with a boy or expressing this love in verse was therefore also illicit. Indeed, many religious scholars indulged openly in such activity.[103]

El-Rouayheb goes on to show that the courting of boys by men extended to all classes (including soldiers),[104] and that in many cases "falling in love with a boy was widely considered an involuntary act, and as such, outside the scope of religious condemnation".[105] It may well be that Pitts, who mentions sodomy only once, and never in the context of his own experience or that of fellow captives, may have misunderstood the nature of homosexual love in the Islamic world and confused it with actual intercourse. Certainly, the distinction between the two appears to have escaped nearly all observers of Islam and the Middle East until recent times.

While Pitts's understanding of Algerian domestic and military life was profound, he was not a particularly acute or perceptive traveller on the occasions when he ventured outside Algiers – excepting his unique observations on the *ḥajj*. Tunis, Tlemcen and Oran feature only as backgrounds to his experiences and we learn almost nothing of any significance about any of these three cities from his book. Indeed, where Pitts does stray out of the zone of primary experience (i.e. Algiers and its immediate hinterland), he is prone to error.[106] Although not given to fanciful stories based on hearsay, he does occasionally repeat them, such as when he claims (correctly in this case) that when he was near Bône ('Annābah) he passed through a river "*the Water of which was so hot, I could scarce suffer it*", continuing, "*and I was credibly* inform'd, *that a little farther up in the River the Water was* hot *enough to* boil *an* Egg".[107] Almost certainly without a classical training, Pitts also shows almost no interest in Greek or Roman history, and he rarely refers to other travellers or scholars.[108] Indeed he apologizes for his observations on Alexandria since "*Historians*, undoubtedly, have given a far more satisfactory Account of this Place than I can pretend to",[109] and spends almost as long describing a game in which blindfolded Muslims try to touch a pillar as he does discussing Pompey's Pillar or the Mosque of a Thousand Pillars (named by Pitts as Bingbeer Drake[110] – Bin bir direk in modern Turkish). He shows no interest in the history of Cairo or its government, focusing instead on everyday issues (weather, dress, food, transport, fuel, illnesses, lodgings, agriculture and animal husbandry), with digressions on the moral failings of the Egyptians (lewdness, rudeness and cheating). Indeed, he betrays the typical interests of an intelligent and observant tourist rather than those of a serious traveller, and certainly not those of an incipient Saidian imperialist. Almost the only time he makes reference to current affairs is when he considers the condition of slaves in Egypt, where they come from and how they are treated, thereby displaying a natural desire to compare experiences.[111] Even when Pitts recounts his escape, the towns and countries he mentions feature only insofar as they form the background to the narrative – almost no details are given of their history or distinguishing features.

Pitts therefore does not display the standard attributes of a travel writer, understood as someone who has read up on his subject, quotes previous writers on it, and puts the places he visits into historical, architectural or archaeological perspective, often embellishing the narrative with stories acquired from native informants. Rather, he describes the society in which he lived for fifteen years in a very personal way and from his own first-hand experience, particularly those domestic and military features with which he was best acquainted, often interspersing his story with his own memories and illustrating it with mundane (and therefore all the more believable) anecdotes. His style is simple and he makes few claims on the reader's credulity, but he remains both proud and modest,[112] offering his book as just his "poor *Memoirs*".[113] As he says in the preface to the third edition:

> I do not pretend to give an exact and methodical *Account* of what I
> have observ'd; for I am sensible that I have not the Abilities which
> are required in a Person that writes such an *History*: Only, I beg leave
> to say plainly, I have the *most valuable Qualification* of an *Historian* on
> my side, i.e. *Truth*.[114]

## A description of Islam

ALTHOUGH NABIL MATAR and other scholars have demonstrated conclusively that there were numerous and varied contacts between Europe and the Middle East in the 16th and 17th centuries, it is remarkable how little was known about the history, beliefs, structures and practices of Islam during this period. However, in the mediaeval period, the situation was even worse, as G. J. Toomer observes:

> In general, the picture of Islam and especially of its Prophet,
> derivable from medieval Latin texts, is an unedifying farrago of myth
> and invective leavened with a few facts and historical events. Western
> knowledge of the history of the Arabs, even during the time of
> Muhammad, was extremely defective and indeed there was no
> interest in it except for the purposes of polemic.[115]

Fortunately, this situation began to change in the 16th century as European nations established trade and diplomatic links with the Ottoman Empire. France was the first Western country to negotiate with the Ottomans, when François I signed a treaty with them in 1536. England followed suit in 1580, while the English Levant Company was founded in 1581.[116] Religion soon followed trade and after the establishment of diplomatic links with the Ottomans, both Catholics and Protestants attempted to make contact with the Eastern Churches, thus stimulating an academic interest in both Arabic and Islam. In addition, it was felt by scholars that knowledge of Arabic, the most widespread of the Semitic languages, would assist in understanding the Hebrew Bible and this impulse, allied to the existing diplomatic and commercial interests, led to the study of Arabic becoming much more systematic and widespread, particularly in Protestant countries. The University of Leiden in the Netherlands, founded in 1575, soon became "the centre of Dutch Orientalism and of academic life more generally; indeed, it was the leading Protestant university in Europe and the place swarmed with British, German and Huguenot students".[117] In Britain, Thomas Adams, a wealthy draper, founded a Chair of Arabic at the University of Cambridge in 1632, for "the enlarging of the borders of the Church and propagation of Christian religion to them who now sitt in darkness",[118] while Archbishop Laud founded a similar Chair at Oxford in 1636. Laud "believed that close study of the original Hebrew of the Old Testament would provide vital support for the Church of England in its doctrinal struggle with the Roman Catholics".[119]

However, while the increased number of English scholars working with Arabic may have led to a greater understanding of Islam, it did not necessarily lead to any greater sympathy with it, and the 16th- and 17th-century literature of Islamic studies in Britain is full of anti-Islamic rhetoric, especially regarding the Prophet Muhammad. Among the first English scholars of Arabic in this period was William Bedwell (1563–1632),[120] one of whose published works was *Mohammedis imposturae: that is, Discovery of the Manifold Forgeries, Falsehoods and Horrible Impieties of the Blasphemous Seducer Mohammed* (London, 1615), the title of which is sufficient guide to its contents.[121] Abraham Wheelocke (*ca.* 1593–1653)[122] was the first Professor of Arabic at Cambridge, and had a similar attitude to Islam, as is made clear in a surviving letter of his in which he talks about publishing on the Qur'an:

> I would not set out the Alcoran only to tell the Latin Church …
> but by the help of our merchants I would have the method of
> confutinge it, and the discoverie of the plaine falacies thereof, be …
> communicated to some well minded Christians at Aleppo &ce and
> in Persia …[123]

Other scholars of the same period were equally critical of Islam and Muhammad. The Frenchman André du Ryer (*ca.* 1580–*ca.* 1660)[124] published a translation of the Qur'an into French in 1647 of which an English translation was published in 1649 and republished in 1688, this latter edition being prefaced by a life of Muhammad. In this biography of the Prophet, du Ryer propagated the commonly held, and scurrilous, view that Muhammad used sorcery to overawe his followers, who were "fugitives and vagabonds", that he concocted the Qur'an with the help of the Nestorian monk Sergius,[125] that when a pigeon used to fly and nibble his ear, it was God telling him what to say, and so on.[126] Indeed, in a postscript by Alexander Ross (1591–1654),[127] who may have translated du Ryer's French version of the Qur'an into English, the reader is warned "that the great Arabian imposter, now at last, after a thousand years, is by way of France arrived in England and his Alcoran or gallimaufry of errors (a brat as deformed as the parent, and as full of heresies as his scald head was full of scurf) hath learned to speak English".[128] Edward Pococke (1604–91),[129] who has been called "perhaps the greatest Orientalist of the 17th century",[130] was also entirely hostile to Islam, although "his was a kind of hostility that was conducive to sound scholarship, as he was particularly concerned to discredit Western folklore and crude polemical lies about the Prophet and Muslim doctrine in order that Islam's real errors could be exposed".[131] Even those authors whose treatment of Islam were examples of the "early Enlightenment",[132] and who represented the best scholarship of the early 18th century, like Adriaan Reeland (1676–1718),[133] considered Muhammad a false prophet:

> This account which I have given of the Great Imposter's life and actions is of itself a sufficient confutation of his pretences to divine revelation and the delivering of a general and most perfect rule of law to all mankind. Besides this, I suppose all my readers too well instructed to need any antidote against this poison.[134]

Indeed, historians and travellers with a historical bent like Giles Fletcher, Henry Marsh (dates unknown), George Sandys (1578–1644)[135] and William Lithgow were often as defamatory as the scholars. Giles Fletcher began his *Policie of the Turkish empire: the First Booke Concerning the State and Summe of the Turkes Religion*, by stating "that the religion of the Turkes was first forged and invented by the false prophet Mahomet: and that the Saracens and Arabians his own people and countrymen were the first to whom he published it: and that they (being seduced by his devilish doctrine and illusions) …".[136] Fletcher then went on to repeat the mediaeval claim that the "hellhound" Sergius helped Muhammad to write the Qur'an[137] and continued in the same strain. Henry Marsh condemned "the most blasphemous designs of this vile and lewd deceiver".[138] George Sandys claimed that Muhammad had "compiled his damnable doctrine with the help of one Sergius a Nestorian and Abdulla a Jew (containing a hodge-podge of sundry religions)",[139] that Muhammad had "taught a pigeon to feed at his ear, affirming it to be the Holy Ghost which informed him in divine precepts", and that the Qur'an was "farced with fables, visions, legends and relations ... many things being secretly put in and thrust out ...";[140] and William Lithgow "entirely follows the view of Islam as it had evolved in the polemical literature of early medieval Europe".[141] Even those like Paul Rycaut who had lived for many years in the Ottoman Empire and had a deep interest in and admiration for their host society were not immune from using the standard anti-Islamic invective. In Book Two of his *History of the Present State of the Ottoman Empire*, entitled *Of the Turkish Religion*, Rycaut was happy to recycle the legend of Sergius, and to call Islam a "superstition" and Muhammad "infamous".[142] In fact, apart from some short captivity narratives which had no interest in describing Turkish/Islamic/North African society (e.g. Rawlins, Phelps, Coxere), almost the only person relatively innocent of the accusation of being anti-Islamic is the rational traveller Henry Blount.[143] Gerald Maclean sums up the contemporary English attitude towards Islam thus:

> Refracted through competition with other European nations, especially those loyal to the Roman Catholic religion, Anglo-Protestant attitudes toward, and understanding of Islam and of the Muslim nations of the Maghreb remained just as unstable and contradictory throughout the early modern period as the sense of what it meant to be English or an Englishman or woman of the time.[144]

Given this *Zeitgeist*, it is no surprise that Joseph Pitts, when confronted with the monolithic enmity towards Islam in English publications of the 17th century, should often express himself negatively about Islam. Indeed, given his need to justify his conversion, and emphasize his Christian identity on his return to England, it would have been remarkable had he not done so, since for most people in 17th-century Europe identity equalled religion. As Peter Lambert Wilson says:

> The seventeenth century knew no such thing as a secular ideology. Neither states nor individuals justified their actions by philosophical appeals to science, sociology, economics, natural rights or dialectical materialism. Virtually all social contacts were predicated on religious values or at least expressed in religious values.[145]

So Pitts can be found using phrases such as *"false* Worship" and "vile and debauch'd *Impostor"*[146] to describe Islam and the Prophet Muhammad, calling the Qur'an *"that* Legend *of Falsities, and abominable Follies and Absurdities"*,[147] alluding to *"Dr.* Prideaux's *excellently written Life of* Mahomet", mentioning Sergius, and declaring Islam a "Miscellany *of* Popery, Judaism *and the* Gentilism *of the* Arabs".[148] It is also true that Pitts's negative attacks on Islam and Muhammad are equalled by his positive remarks on Christianity (of the Protestant variety) and the goodness of God. Indeed, he declares of his book:

> … my principal End in its *Publication*, is giving Glory to GOD, by whose gracious Providence I am releas'd from *Slavery*, and brought again into my own *native Country*, where there are no *Means of Salvation wanting*, and where the *Blessed Doctrine* of *Jesus* is established, and the *Holy Trinity* ador'd.[149]

However, Pitts stands out in differentiating between, on the one hand, Islam as a belief system, and, on the other, the practical worship of Muslims. He has no interest in Islamic history or the *sīrah* (biography) of Muhammad, or in cataloguing the varieties of Sufi orders, theological schools, legal precepts or philosophical questions. He mentions no famous Muslim religious scholar or philosopher.[150] He does, however, take considerable pains to describe, in a relatively objective way, the Islamic rituals as he witnessed them, indeed, as he himself practised them, often illustrated by personal comments and observations. He spends many pages on detailed and accurate descriptions of how and when Muslims prayed, and what the purity rituals entailed.[151] These descriptions explain the exact positions of the body during the different sequences of the ritual, how many *rak'āt* are performed at the different times of prayer, and how to avoid invalidating *wuḍū'* or ablution, etc., and correspond almost exactly to existing Ḥanafī practice.[152] Pitts was not unique in his descriptions, which can also be found in other authors of the period, for example Rycaut,[153] Fletcher[154] and Marsh,[155] but his are the most exhaustive and accurate. Pitts was deeply impressed by the Muslim devotion to prayer:

> But as for those who are Religious *in their way*, they'll not live in the Neglect of performing their *Salah* or *Nomas*, i.e. their *Worship* (*Salah* is the *Arabick*, and *Nomas* the *Turkish* Word for their *Worship*, or *Devotion*), might they gain ever so much. Nay, there are some among them *so* zealous, that after they are reformed from their former Extravagancies, they labour to *make up* what they have *run*

*back* in the time of Youth by their neglect of *Salah*, and in order to fetch up their *Arrears*, they will be out of their Beds an Hour or two before Day, and having *prepar'd* themselves, will be engag'd in their *Devotion* till they are quite *tired*.[156]

Indeed, he was able to back up his views from his own experience:

I very well remember my last *Patroon*, who was an ancient Man, would spend many Mornings in this Exercise [i.e., prayer]. Whilst I was a-bed he would be up, and having *wash'd* himself *as usual*, would be at his *Devotion*. I ask'd him the Reason of it. He told me, When he was young he lived in the Omission of his Duty; for as for *Nomas*, he paid no Regard to it; but now he would endeavour to make amends for all past Neglects.[157]

Pitts also deals with the other pillars of religion, such as the *shahādah*,[158] the declaration of belief in the Oneness of God, which must be recited publicly in order to become a Muslim. He goes on to refer to the popular belief that there are two levels of hell, one for unbelievers and one for Muslims,[159] which he likens to the "Romish Purgatory",[160] although he adds that "*the* Turks [do not] *make the use the* Papists *do of it*".[161] He also gives a detailed description of the ceremony which accompanies the conversion of a non-believer to Islam,[162] how he is ridden round the city for several hours, accompanied by drums and music, and that "after this *Show* and *Ceremony* is over, he is immediately entred into pay, and directed to the Place where he shall quarter, with some of his Fellow-Soldiers".[163] Regarding the other pillars of Islam, he barely touches on *zakāt*,[164] but describes at some length the fast in the month of *Ramaḍān*,[165] again embellishing his description with examples drawn from his own experiences:

When we were sailing on the *Red-Sea* towards *Mecca*, my Patroon (who was an ancient, and corpulent Man) being very faint with Thirst, broke his *Fast* voluntarily; but when we arrived at *Mecca*, he was not easy till he had *fasted* so many Days for it, and sacrified a Sheep *into the Bargain*.[166]

Pitts also tells the story of how, when he was on the pilgrimage, and while he was still fasting, he had drunk rainwater which had fallen from the *Bayt Allāh*, and because he believed he had broken his fast by drinking he began eating as well. A fellow pilgrim rebuked him, telling him he had been blessed by God to have drunk of the heavenly water which came off his own [i.e. God's] house, and that drinking it would not have "*marr'd* [his] Fast", but by then eating he had, through his ignorance, "*miss'd of so great an Advantage*".[167]

Regarding other aspects of the faith, Pitts mentions circumcision,[168] and talks briefly about the prohibition from eating pork and drinking wine.[169] In connection with the ban on images, he draws on his own experiences again:

> But they have nothing of any *fine Ornaments* in these their *Geameas* or *Mosques*, neither any *Pictures, Images*, or any thing of *that* Nature; but the Walls are *naked white*, for they utterly abhor *Images*, or any thing *like* them. They blame the *Papists* for having so many *Trumperies* in their *Churches*, and have a greater Respect for *Protestants*, because they have not the like. I once had a Draught [drawing] of an *English* ship, which I hung against the Wall; but my *Patroon* perceiving it had a *Cross* in its *Ancient* [flag], obliged me to blot it out, and then seemed well enough pleased with the Picture.[170]

Not surprisingly, Pitts was also interested in the Muslims' view of Christianity.[171] He was well aware that Muslims considered the Trinity to be a heretical concept, while still acknowledging Jesus as a great prophet, and asserted categorically that anyone who claimed "*THAT* MAHOMET *BELIEV'D ALL THE ARTICLES OF THE CHRISTIAN FAITH* must needs be in the wrong".[172] He also discounts the story that a convert "throws a Dart at the Picture of *Jesus Christ*, in token of his disowning him", saying "But there is no such Usage; ... I am sure I have reason (God pardon me!) to know everything in use among them of this Nature",[173] clearly referring to his own experience as a renegade.

Pitts shows some interest in the Qur'an,[174] not specifically in its contents about which he is silent, but in what he considers the admirable reverence paid to it by Muslims as the word of God (*Calam Allah*, as he called it[175]). He explains that Muslims take great care of their copies of the Qur'an and that even

> ... *Traders* and *Shopkeepers* ... set themselves a *daily* Task, to recite so much of the *Alcoran* without Book, as in *thirty* Days to take up the whole; and *this* many continue to do all their Life-time, believing that they *merit* much by it. ("I *wish* that Christians *were as diligent in studying the* Holy Scriptures, *the* Law *and the* Gospel ...)[176]

And he contradicts the common belief among Christians that reading the

Qur'an was discouraged among the poor:

> I was lately perusing an *English ALCORAN*, where I find, in the
> *Preface*, That the *Translator* saith, That the *Vulgar* are not permitted to
> read the *ALCORAN*, but (as the poor *Romanists*) to live and die in
> an implicit Faith of what they are taught by their Priests.[177] This I
> utterly deny; for it is not only permitted and allowed of, but it is (as
> I intimated before) looked on as very commendable in any Person
> to be diligent in the reading of it.[178]

However, he was not always impressed with all aspects of personal worship
and ritual in Islam, and regarded the worship of saints' tombs and the activities
of "*marabbots*" with great suspicion,[179] believing that the sacrificing of a sheep
when in danger at sea was "applying themselves to *Imaginary* Intercessors,
instead of the *Living, and True God*", something that, in contrast to Protestants,
only "blind *Infidels*" and "the *Papists*" did.[180]

By far the longest, most detailed, most personal and most interesting of Pitts's
description of Islam concerns the pilgrimage, and it is this section which has
intrigued scholars the most, since it is the first detailed and eye-witness
description in English of the *hajj* and of the Muslim Holy Places. The previous
information in English on the pilgrimage was restricted to very brief
descriptions in general accounts of Islam, for example by Paul Rycaut,[181] and
the translation by Richard Eden (*ca.* 1520–76) in 1577 of the travels of
Ludovico de Varthema (*ca.* 1470–1517) to Arabia in 1503.[182] Although Richard
Burton claimed that "… all things well considered, Lodovico Bartema, for
correctness of observation and readiness of wit, stands in the foremost rank of
the old Oriental travellers",[183] nevertheless he was still obliged to admit that
Varthema was "credulous" and that his descriptions "are disfigured with a little
romancing".[184] For example, although there is evidence that there was a
considerable Jewish population in one of the regions visited by Varthema, these
Jews must have been taller than the two feet high claimed by the traveller;[185]
moreover, Varthema talks about "two live unicorns" at the Temple in Mecca,[186]
he confuses Ishmael and Isaac (Ismā'īl and Isḥāq),[187] and repeats the old
Christian legend about a dove speaking to Muhammad.[188] While much of
Varthema's description of the temple and the rites of the *hajj* is reasonably
accurate, it is very brief and occasionally confused, particularly over the part
that Mount 'Arafat plays in the ritual.[189]

Pitts's description, on the other hand, is long, detailed and filled with personal
experiences. Burton's verdict was that:

His description of these places [Mecca, Medina, Alexandria and Cairo] is accurate in the main points, and though tainted with prejudice and bigotry, he is free from superstition and credulity. Conversant with Turkish and Arabic, he has acquired more knowledge of the tenets and practice of Al-Islam than his predecessor [Varthema], and the term of his residence at Algier, fifteen years, sufficed, despite the defects of his education, to give fullness and finish to his observations.[190]

Burton was aware of only two errors on Pitts's part, once when Pitts says that the *Ḥajar Aswad* was formerly white,[191] and the second time when he, like Varthema before him, confuses Isaac with Ishmael.[192] In addition to his accuracy, Pitts also refutes several myths about Mecca and Medina; in the preface to both authorized editions of his book, he states that he intends to be "very exact, as to *Truth*" and continues:

> How many *Stories* have been scattered about in the World, concerning *Mahomet's* Tomb? As of its hanging up by the Virtue of a *Loadstone*, &c.,[193] which are all as false as any thing can be.
>
> The Story of the *Pigeon*, which is said to have been taught by *Mahomet* to pick Corn out of his Ear, and which the *Vulgar* took to be the Whispers of the *Holy Ghost*, hath no better Foundation, that I could ever learn, than a *Castle* (or his Tomb) in the *Air*. And since I came home, I have seen many Books, some of which have treated of *Algier* in particular, and others of the *Mahometan* Religion in general; which are stuff'd with very great Mistakes.[194]

Clearly, after his return to England and before committing himself to print, Pitts read much of what had been published in English on the Muslim Holy Places. In the first edition of 1704, he quotes scholars of Islam such as Humphrey Prideaux, as well as more general works on the Middle East by travellers and encyclopaedists. That he continued to keep abreast of contemporary scholarship on Islam and Arabia can be inferred from the fact that, for the third edition, he consulted scholars to improve the transcription of the Arabic, and incorporated two engravings which had been published in the 1720s (although it is not possible to ascertain whether this was his own idea or at the insistence of his publishers – for more information on the engravings and their source see p. 88 below). In his book he corrects previous scholars who have repeated information from informants, making it clear to his readership that he has visited the places described and observed the various rituals. For example, he takes Jeremy Collier (1650–1726) and Pierre d'Avity (1573–1635) to task about the decoration of the Prophet's tomb, how many days' journey there are between Mecca and Medina, and the number of inhabitants in Mecca;[195] criticizes and corrects both Jeremy Collier and Jean de Thévenot (1633–67) about the number of mosques in Cairo;[196] and Thévenot alone about the taste of the water in Mecca,[197] and the ritual of stoning of the devil at Mina.[198]

Pitts enlivens many of his descriptions with personal anecdotes and stories about the pilgrims he encountered. He describes the dervishes or hermits "travelling up and down the Country like *Mendicants*",[199] and who "get Money here [Mecca], as well as at other Places, by burning of *Incense*, swinging their *Censers* as they go before the People that are sitting; and this they commonly do on *Fridays*, their *Sabbath*",[200] and he also embellishes his story with an episode out of his personal experience:

> Many *Turks*, when they reform, give themselves up to a *Dervise* sort of Life: And for an Instance, my second *Patroon* had a younger Brother, who had liv'd a very debauch'd Life; but on a sudden a great Change seem'd to be wrought upon him, insomuch that he let his *Beard* grow, never shaving it, and put on his great, green *Turbant*, which none presume to wear, but such are of the Blood and Race of *Mahomet*, and betook himself to the learning of his *Elif, Be, Te*, i.e. A. B. C. In a little time he attain'd to read very well, and spent a great part of his time in Reading. Some of his old jolly Companions would laugh at him for it; but he still kept on in this strict way of Living, notwithstanding all their *Banters*.[201]

Pitts was clearly impressed by the devotion of Muslim pilgrims, and often describes his own feelings during the rituals. However, he makes it clear that he distinguishes between the religious zeal and ardour of Muslims, which he admires, and the religion of Islam itself, which he is unable to accept, as can be seen from two of the most famous passages in his book:

> It was a Sight, indeed, able to pierce one's Heart, to behold so many Thousands in their Garments of *Humility* and *Mortification*, with their *naked Heads*, and *Cheeks watered with Tears*; and to hear their grievous *Sighs* and *Sobs*, begging earnestly for the *Remission of their Sins*, and promising *Newness of Life*, using a Form of *penitential Expressions*; and

thus continuing for the Space of four or five Hours, *viz.* until the
Time of *Acsham Nomas,* which is to be perform'd about half an Hour
after Sun-set. [It is a matter of sorrowful Reflection, to compare the
*Indifference* of many *Christians,* with this *Zeal* of those poor blind
*Mahometans,* who will, 'tis to be fear'd, *rise up* in Judgment *against
them, and condemn them.*][202]

And again:

> And I profess, I could not chuse but admire to see those poor
> Creatures, so extraordinary *devout,* and *affectionate* when they were
> about these *Superstitions,* and with what *Awe,* and *Trembling,* they
> were possess'd; insomuch, that I could scarce forbear shedding of
> *Tears,* to see their Zeal, tho' *blind* and *idolatrous.*[203]

Naturally Pitts was always at pains to remind his Christian readership that
he never fully accepted Islam and that his outward devotion disguised his
inward rejection of the religion. In one of the few passages where he makes
mock of Islam (probably because he associates the practice with Roman
Catholicism), he demonstrates this ambivalence very clearly: talking about
Mecca, he describes the Muslims' use of the rosary or *subḥah*:[204]

> Under the Room of the *Hanifees,* (which I mentioned before)
> People do usually gather together (between the Hours of *Devotion*)
> and sitting cross-legged, it may be, twenty or thirty of them, they
> have a very large pair of *Tesbeehs,* or *Beads,* each *Bead* near as big as
> a Man's Fist, which they keep passing round, Bead after Bead, one
> to the other, all the time, using some *devout* Expressions. I my self
> was once got in amongst them, and methought it was a pretty Play
> enough for *Children;* however, I was to appearance very *devout.*[205]

Indeed, there are occasions where his lack of genuine zeal became apparent
even to his fellow Muslims:

> … after I had sat a while [in Mecca], and for my more ease at last
> was lying on my Back, with my Feet towards the *Beat* [*Bayt Allāh*],
> but at a distance, as many others did; a *Turk* which sat by me, ask'd
> me what Countryman I was: *A* Moghrebee (said I), *i.e.* one of the
> *West. Pray,* quoth he, *how far* West *did you come?* I told him from

*Gazair*, i.e. *Algier. Ah!* replied he, *have you taken so much Pains, and been at so much Cost, and now be guilty of this* irreverent Posture *before the* Beat-Allah?[206]

However, for most of the chapter on the pilgrimage, Pitts is content to describe what he saw without reference to his own feelings, thus giving the West its first accurate and complete description of the pilgrimage.

It is clear from his preface (in both the first and third editions) that Pitts was aware that he was breaking new ground, particularly with respect to the pilgrimage and the Muslim Holy Places, but also, more broadly, *vis-à-vis* Islamic religious practices in general. He may well have written the sections of his book dealing with Islam both from a natural pride in the uniqueness of his experience, but also as a public expiation of his sin of apostasy. Pitts was clearly deeply affected by his conversion to Islam, which challenged his basic identity, and, as argued above, had he not received letters from his father, it is possible that he would have remained in Algiers to seek his fortune as so many other renegades did. However, the connection that he managed to maintain with England and Englishness sustained his belief in Christianity and gave him the courage to return to the land of his birth, despite the many dangers he knew he would have to face on the journey. On his return, having made the decision to write about his experiences in Algiers and Islam, Pitts was torn between his resolve to tell the truth, which obliged him to give an accurate description of Islamic ritual, and his desire to be seen by his fellow Christians in England as a man who repented bitterly of his apostasy, which led him to attack Islam as a false religion. This ambivalence[207] can be felt throughout the book. The result is that, on balance, despite some bigoted observations on Islam and its Prophet, Pitts's views of religious observances of Muslims are not wholly unsympathetic. Indeed, as can be seen from some of the passages quoted above, Pitts was impressed, despite himself, by Muslims' devotion to prayer and to the Qur'an, and by their often deep sense of repentance, and he reserved his condemnation of Islamic practices to those aspects which seemed to him most closely to approach Roman Catholicism, such as the belief in the intercession of saints or the use of the rosary. His nonconformist Protestant upbringing, which insisted on the believer having an individual relationship with God and with His book, clearly led him to admire both the directness of Islamic religious observances and the zeal of the worshippers.[208]

Pitts could have used his book to vilify Islam as Prideaux did, but the majority of his observations are neutral and factual, rather than mocking or censorious. Given his background, his experiences and his beliefs, Pitts's book is, on the whole, as balanced and accurate an account of the practice of Islam as any Englishman born in the 17th century was likely to produce. It may not be quite the "best Account of the *Mahometan* Religion we have extant in our Language", as the preface to the third edition claimed,[209] since Pitts as an authority on Islam displayed very much the same lack of curiosity about history, doctrine and why things were the way they were, as he did as a traveller. Just as he never inquired into the reasons why Muslims do not visit each other's houses, so he never questions why Muslims perform certain actions or the purpose behind particular rituals. He describes what he saw and experienced but in general reflects on matters in an emotional and personal rather than intellectual way. On the other hand, his book was almost the only description of Islam of its time which was written from the author's "own knowledge" and, as such, it had, and in some ways still has, a validity which cannot always be found in the more academic works on Islam produced by Pitts's contemporaries.

## Publishing history

THE FIRST EDITION of Pitts's book was published in Exeter by P. Bishop and E. Score in 1704 with the ponderous if accurate title of *A True and Faithful Account of the Religion and Manners of the Mohammetans, in Which is a Particular Relation of their Pilgrimage to Mecca, the Place of Mohammet's Birth, and a Description of Medina and His Tomb there; as Likewise of Algier and the Country Adjacent; and of Alexandria, Grand-Cairo &c; With an Account of the Author's Being Taken Captive, the Turks Cruelty to Him and of His Escape; in Which are Many Things Never Publish'd by any Historian Before* (pp. [13], 183). It was dedicated to William Ray (dates unknown),[210] the late Consul at Smyrna, and written at the insistence of his friends to provide "an account of the Mohammetan faith ... as exact as possible",[211] and to "make some manner (at least) of restitution and reparation for my past defection".[212] Clearly, the book was successful, since a second, unauthorized edition was published by M. Bishop and E. Score in Exeter in 1717 with a title page identical to the 1704 edition but different pagination (pp. [10], 204), while another unlicensed impression of the second edition appeared in London in 1719 published by W. Taylor (also pp. [10], 204). These illicit editions upset Pitts considerably, as he lamented in the Preface to the third edition:

> The *second* Edition was printed without my Consent; nay, I knew nothing of the Matter, till they had gone about half way. I have wish'd

since, I had then published an *Advertisement*, that I would in a little Time print a *second Edition with Additions*. This might, perhaps, have put a Stop to the Press; for I scarce ever saw a Book printed on worse Paper, and so incorrect: But this must not lie at my Door.[213]

Pitts did eventually decide to bring out a revised edition, which was published in London in 1731 by J. Osborn, T. Longman and R. Hett, with a slightly different title: *A Faithful Account of the Religion and Manners of the Mahometans, in Which is a Particular Relation of their Pilgrimage to Mecca, the Place of Mahomet's Birth; and a Description of Medina, and of his Tomb there: as likewise of Algier, and the Country Adjacent; and of Alexandria, Grand-Cairo &c. With an Account of the Author's Being Taken Captive; the Turks Cruelty to him; and of his Escape; in which are many Things never publish'd by any Historian Before. By Joseph Pitts, of Exon. The Third Edition, Corrected, with Additions. To this Edition is added a Map of Mecca, and a Cut of the Gestures of the Mahometans in their Worship* (pp. xxiv, 260). An almost identical fourth edition was published (presumably with the author's permission, since there are minor additions to the 1731 text) by T. Longman and R. Hett in 1738 (pp. xxiv, 259).[214] Both Radford and Foster[215] record that a version of the fourth edition with modernized spelling was published as an appendix to the 1810 London edition of the work of Henry Maundrell (1665?–1701) entitled *A Journey from Aleppo to Jerusalem at Easter, A.D. 1697*,[216] while an annotated version of the 1704 edition with modernized spelling and textual notes was produced by Daniel Vitkus in 2001.[217] This, as already noted, includes an excellent introduction to the whole genre of English captivity narratives by Nabil Matar.[218] Partial reprints of the section on Mecca and Medina have been published since the 1750s, but the two most important partial editions, both annotated, are those by Sir Richard Burton, first published in 1855–56,[219] and that produced for the Hakluyt Society in 1949 by Sir William Foster.[220]

Pitts published his revised version in 1731 because he had "been informed, that there hath been a great Demand for it (especially in *London*)".[221] He goes on to say the third edition has enabled him to improve the style, correct mistakes and reorganize the order of the material,[222] to improve the rendering of the Arabic words,[223] and to include material which he had now remembered,[224] particularly the text of Consul Baker's letter of which he had now procured a copy and which he considered to be "the Ground-work of my *Deliverance*".[225] The differences between the two authorized editions of 1704 and 1731 are perhaps more substantial than is generally realized. Besides improving and re-arranging the text, Pitts has added almost ten percent more material to the third edition of his book. It is true that many of the changes have been implemented for the sake of a smoother style, and to change the

A True and Faithful

# ACCOUNT

OF THE

Religion and Manners

OF THE

# 𝕸𝖔𝖍𝖆𝖒𝖒𝖊𝖙𝖆𝖓𝖘.

In which is a particular Relation of their

## *Pilgrimage to Mecca,*

The Place of *Mohammet*'s Birth;

And a Defcription of *Medina*, and of his
Tomb there. As likewife of *Algier*, and
the Country adjacent: And of *Alexandria, Grand-Cairo,* &c. With an Account
of the Author's being taken Captive, the
*Turks* Cruelty to him, and of his Efcape.
In which are many things never Publifh'd
by any Hiftorian before.

By *JOSEPH PITTS* of *Exon.*

*E X O N:* Printed by *S. Farley,* for *Philip Bifhop,*
and *Edward Score,* in the *High-Street.* 1704.

Title page of the first edition of Pitts's book: *A True and
Faithful Account of the Religion and Manners of the
Mohammetans*, 1704.

A True and Faithful

# ACCOUNT

OF THE

RELIGION & MANNERS

OF THE

# MAHOMETANS.

In which is a particular

# RELATION

OF THEIR

Pilgrimage to *Mecca*,

The Place of *Mahomet's* Birth;

And a Defcription of *Medina*, and of his
Tomb there · As likewife of *Algier* and
the Country adjacent; and of *Alexandria, Grand-Cairo*, &c. With an Account of the Author's being taken
Captive, the *Turks* Cruelty to him, and
of his Efcape. In which are many
Things never publifh'd by any Hifto
rian before.

*The* SECOND EDITION.

By JOSEPH PITTS of *EXON*

*L O N D O N* -

Printed for W. TAYLOR, at the *Ship* in
*Pater-Nofter Row*. M DCC XIX.

Title page of the reprint of the second edition (1717) of
Pitts's book: *A True and Faithful Account of the Religion &
Manners of the Mahometans*, 1719.

way Arabic words were rendered, though this has not always worked for the better: for example, "Mecha" on page 40 of the 1704 edition has been replaced on page 58 of the 1731 edition by the more common "Mecca", but on the same page of the 1704 edition "Kiblah" has been replaced by the less correct "Keblah". It is also difficult to know why the "Mohammetans" in the title of the first edition are transformed into the "Mahometans" of the third edition, since both were common currency in the 17th century and, if anything, the first form more closely corresponds to its putative Arabic original.[226] In addition, Pitts has sometimes re-arranged the text to give more coherence to the narrative,[227] and corrected errors. For example, in the 1704 edition he declares that "it hath been reported, That a *Mohametan* may have as many Wives as he pleaseth, and I believe it is so",[228] while in the 1731 edition this has been changed to: "It hath been reported, That a *Mahometan* may have as many Wives as he pleaseth, tho', if I mistake not, the Number may not exceed *four*."[229] There are even a few passages in the 1704 edition which have been omitted in the later editions.[230]

One of the most important differences between the two editions is that Pitts adds two engraved plates to the 1731 edition, the first between pages 56 and 57 showing "The various gestures of the Mahometans in their prayers to God", and the second between pages 124 and 125 showing "The most sacred and antient Temple of the Mahometans at Mecca". Both these plates were copied without acknowledgement from Muhammad Rabadan's *Mahometism Fully Explained*, which was a description of Islam purportedly written in Spanish and Arabic in 1603 for the benefit of the Moriscos, translated into English by Joseph Morgan and published in London between 1723 and 1725. They had also appeared in different form in Adrian Reeland's *La Religion des Mahometans*, published in The Hague in 1721.

Apart from the illustrations, the bulk of the differences between the two editions are either additions to the information Pitts gives us about life in Algiers, or personal anecdotes to illustrate a particular point. For example, in the 1731 edition there is new information, among other subjects, on food and cooking,[231] on Muslim burials,[232] on the connections between social relations and house design,[233] on baker's boys and water-carriers,[234] on *ḥammāms*,[235] on Muslim knowledge of the Old Testament,[236] on Pompey's Pillar in Alexandria,[237] on why Christians and Jews are forbidden to wear green headgear,[238] on Egyptian porters,[239] on the glass lamps in the *Bayt Allāh*,[240] on the organization of the camel caravan to Medina,[241] on Mount Sinai and 'Aqabah,[242] and on the manner of executing renegades.[243] As for personal anecdotes, Pitts adds stories about his third master's devoutness,[244] his second master's unfaithful wife,[245] on confusion regarding ships' colours,[246] on a game played by a Spanish renegade in the Church of a Thousand and One Pillars in Alexandria,[247] on rain in Egypt,[248] on his experiences as a *bombagee* in the siege of Oran,[249] on being sold a second time,[250] on secretly eating pork after he had become a Muslim,[251] on a failed attack by an Algerian galley on the French fleet,[252] on how he was entertained by the family of a Jewish bridegroom while in quarantine in Leghorn,[253] on Sir William Falkener's [Fawkener] letter to the Admiralty,[254] and, poignantly, how he met his father on his return to Exeter.[255]

There are, perhaps, four additions to the 1731 edition that are of greater importance than simply giving us more factual descriptions or illustrative anecdotes about Algerian society. These are, first, Pitts's correction of the impression he gave in the first edition that that Mr Eliot had been careless when writing to him at Scio [Chios];[256] second, the letter from ship's captain George Taylor to Pitts's father;[257] third, the letter that Consul Thomas Baker of Algiers wrote to the English Consul in Smyrna;[258] and, fourth, Pitts's description of how his skill at writing and reckoning gave him expectations of preferment.[259] The first addition corrects "the Blunder in *Page* 172 and 173 of the *first Edition* of my book, which seemed to cast a Reflection (tho I did not design it as such) upon that worthy Gentleman",[260] and so removes any slur that Pitts's book may have cast on Mr Eliot's name. The second and third additions are significant in that they help to give us a much more exact chronological framework for Pitts's life in Algiers than is available in the 1704 edition.[261] The fourth and final addition is perhaps the most interesting, since it illustrates that even thirty-five years after Pitts's escape from Algiers, his attitude to his time there remained ambivalent. In this additional passage Pitts admits, in a deeply personal way, that he was tempted to remain in Algiers, since his third master had offered to make any children Pitts might have his heirs. "Many more Kindnesses, of this my last *Patroon*, I could relate; for which I cannot but say, I had a great Love for him, even as a Father. But still this was not *England*, and I wanted to be at *home*."[262] It is difficult to see how Pitts could express more succinctly the mixed emotions that still seemed to affect him even as he approached old age in Exeter. It is often easy to forget that Pitts was taken into slavery when he was only about fifteen years old, and that he suffered deep loneliness, physical abuse and the shame of renouncing his faith during his first three or four years in Algiers. He spent at least ten years with his third master both as a slave before he was given his freedom at Mecca and later as a freeman, and Ömer's kindness clearly had a lasting effect on him, for which he remained deeply grateful. All this may explain why Pitts included this passage in the new edition, even though it reminded his critics yet again of his apostasy, and his abiding emotional attachment to a Muslim.

Pitts seems to have grown in confidence over the years with the success of his book. He makes no material changes to the information on Islam between the first and third edition (apart from correcting the number of wives permitted a Muslim and adding the engravings), but as can be seen from the list of the many additions to the third edition, he adds much circumstantial detail about Algerian society and to some extent about himself. He may well have felt that in 1704 he had done his duty in supplying a manual of Islamic practice as expiation for his apostasy, and that it was now, twenty-five years later, worth making the book more interesting both as a travel narrative and as an autobiographical account. Humberto Garcia has argued recently, in the first major article to be published on Pitts since Cecily Radford's in 1920, that there was a considerable amount of self-censoring in the 1731 edition and that the change in the title from *A True and Faithful Account of the Religion and Manners of the Mohammetans* (1704) to *A Faithful Account of the Religion and Manners of the Mahometans* (1731) "foregrounding the word 'faithful' and deleting 'true' from the original title – relocates the conditions of truth-production in other-worldly belief rather than in this-worldly virtue",[263] but this is a heavy philosophical burden for one word (or its omission) to bear, and it is possible that the change of title might just be an expression of Pitts's inherent modesty. Garcia continues:

> The belief–practice nexus was reconfigured between Pitts's first and third/fourth editions in response to the Exeter controversy, which rendered the performance of belief (in the Trinity) the prime legalistic criterion for debating toleration. Seeking to remedy the widespread decline of Anglican piety, Pitts exalts Muslims as role models for how to instil, for example, "pious education" among Christians starting at a young age. Between 1704 and 1731, the emphasis of "sincerely conform[ing] their practice to their belief" shifted from religion-as-practice to religion-as-performed belief, even as these two definitions of religion remained in flux in Pitts's dual Anglican-deist voice (present in both editions) and throughout the eighteenth century. This shift is a side effect of the editorial decision to downplay transcultural identifications with Muslims. In an effort to avoid theological strife, the third edition recasts Islam as, first and foremost, an abstract system of "sincere" beliefs belonging

to a foreign geographical locale and civilization and, secondly and less prominently, as a bodily habitus composed of virtuous practices, dispositions, and emotions that persist across generations, cultures, and nations.[264]

However, Garcia's argument that the third edition represents a major shift in Pitts's theological outlook, and thereby his views on Islam, places perhaps too much weight on minor changes in vocabulary and phrasing. If one examines all the changes to Pitts's two authorized editions together, then it is clear that ninety-nine percent of them are stylistic, personal and illustrative rather than didactic, and this, allied to the facts that Pitts makes no direct mention of the Arian/Deist controversy anywhere in either edition, and that he glorifies the Trinity in the preface to both the first and the third editions, and concludes both with praise to the Father, Son and Holy Spirit, offers powerful evidence that Pitts's views on Christian doctrine and Islam underwent no significant change between 1704 and 1731. However, Garcia's identification of a dual "Anglican-deist voice" does echo Pitts's equivocal emotions with regard to his time in Algiers, and his uneasy mixture of admiration for the directness of Muslim devotions with contempt for their adherence to some "Papist" practices, and is yet another way of explaining the fundamental ambivalence he demonstrates towards his experiences in the "foreign countries" he so much wanted to see.[265]

# CONCLUSION

PITTS'S BOOK RANKS among the most interesting of the captivity narratives, since it not only embodies the crisis of identity which was felt by so many slaves and which has been noted by so many critics, but also takes it one stage further by detailing the author's torments over his forced conversion to Islam. Pitts emphasizes his belief in the Protestant Christian God on regular occasions both negatively, by criticizing Islam and Roman Catholicism, and positively by declaring his attachment to Christianity. Pitts is also at pains to tell the reader that he never converted to Islam in his heart, and that he was often slipshod in his adherence to Islamic devotions. However, he also makes it clear that as a renegade he "was in a much fairer Way for *Honour* and *Preferment* in *Algier*, than I could expect ever to have been in *England*",[1] where, as a dissenter, many career paths would have remained closed to him.

Pitts had many doubts over publishing a book which identified him as an apostate[2] (an accusation which continued to dog him throughout his life after his return), but once he had made the decision to publish, he not only stresses his fundamental Protestant identity throughout the book, but also is candid about having spent several years as a free man in Algiers fighting for the Turks, and about his warm personal attachment to his third master. Linda Colley points out "that he did his best to extract an orthodox moral of a kind"[3] from his book by inserting in the preface "if they [Muslims] are so zealous in their *false* Worship, it must needs be a Reprimand to *Christians*, who are so remiss in the *True*",[4] and by suggesting that "many poor ignorant Souls, which have turn'd *Mahometans*, would never have done what they did, had they been *catechised* as they ought".[5] However, as Colley goes on to say, "he also struggled to find some sort of closure that might connect and not thrust apart the Islamic and Christian phases of his life",[6] and Pitts's captivity narrative remains perhaps the most ambivalent of all in its attitude to the alien society in which he found himself, and one of the most revealing about the psychological stresses which slavery placed on a captive, both before and after his escape.

As a travel narrative, Pitts's book is revealing about Algerian Muslim society, both in its observations on domestic life and in its descriptions of the role of slaves within this society. However, he has little to say about the history of Algiers (the Fleming Emanuel d'Aranda, the Frenchman Pierre Dan and the Spaniard Diego de Haëdo are better sources, as is the Englishman Joseph Morgan), and is by no means unique in describing life as a slave (Francis Knight and William Okeley are also informative about this, as are d'Aranda, Dan and Haëdo). What distinguishes Pitts is his intimate acquaintance with Algerian society from the inside and his personal knowledge of the details of Islamic worship, often illustrated with examples from his own experience. These anecdotes have the ring of truth to them, and describe his relations with his masters, fellow slaves, fellow renegades, Turks whom he met on his travels, and the many people who helped him escape, and they add considerable shape and depth to his narrative.

Pitts is certainly not free from lapses into generic animosity towards Muslims – for example, the cowardice of the Algerians Turks,[7] the laziness of the Moors,[8] the lewdness of the Egyptians,[9] the cheating nature of the Cairenes,[10] the generally unsavoury character of Meccans.[11] But, on the other hand, he is also unstinting in his praise of his third master, and impressed by the devoutness of Muslims, both on the *ḥajj* and in Algiers itself. Pitts is more of an observer than a professional traveller, and makes few references to other sources of information, never refers to classical authorities, and hardly ever resorts to hearsay evidence – indeed his preface is filled with assertions of the truth of his narrative which he assures readers is founded on his own first-hand experiences. As a travel narrative, Pitts's book is as ambivalent as it is as a captivity narrative, veering from insulting and contemptuous comments on the morality of Muslims to affecting descriptions of devotion, but on the whole it is a straightforward, unadorned, reasonably objective account of what he saw and experienced in Algiers and elsewhere, and there is little reason to doubt the veracity of the information he gives his readers.

As a study of Islam, Pitts's book departs from almost all other publications of the period. This is not to say that he does not display the same dislike, even contempt, of Islam as a religion as his more academic contemporaries do, and his book is peppered with references to false Gods and vile impostors. However, he does not seek to emulate the more scholarly publications by providing a history of Muhammad's life, the contents of the Qur'an, or the tenets of Muslim theology beyond those required to become a Muslim. Instead, his dedication to the "truth" obliges him to describe in considerable detail what he himself had experienced as a Muslim, specifically how individual Muslims worshipped

God through prayer, fasting and, above all, the pilgrimage, about the *hajj* ceremonies of which he gives the first detailed and accurate account in English. Pitts has been accused of being an Islamophobe, in the orientalist mode, by Aziz Al-Azmeh, who claims that his book

> ... rehearsed the usual repertoire of folkloric absurdities current for centuries, absurdities which arise from a fundamental structure of all orientalist discourse: namely, that observations, and judgments without reference to observations constitute two separate registers, with hardly any means of contact between the two.[12]

More subtly and perceptively, Pitts is seen by Nabil Matar as someone "who served to ground the demonization of the Moors not on fancy or fictions but on the authenticity of personal experience".[13] It is, indeed, true that Pitts attacks Islam throughout his book; since he was a renegade seeking re-admittance to the Christian community, he could hardly do otherwise. However, he does on the whole distinguish between Islam as a theology, which he dislikes, and the practice of Islam which, while never endorsed, is often regarded with a not unsympathetic eye (unless he feels that the ritual smacks of Roman Catholicism) and even a grudging admiration. Of all the books on Islam of the period, it is the only one to give any approximation of what it is actually like to be a Muslim, and even if it continually and fundamentally rejects Islam, it does give readers some inkling of why so many Muslims held the beliefs they did and why they worshipped in the way they did. The "personal experience" mentioned by Matar is indeed a double-edged sword: for the readers of the period, it may well have been a convincing refutation of a hostile faith, even while the preface to the third edition would indicate that not all Pitts's contemporaries were persuaded of the sincerity of his return to Christianity.[14] However, a modern audience can better detect the ambivalence of Pitts's attitude to Muslims. Had Pitts been less honest, he could have suppressed all his comments on Islam which were not overtly negative. That he did not do so testifies to his basic honesty and his inability ever fully to lay to rest his Muslim past, and his book remains one of the most accurate, empirical accounts of Muslim worship which has come down to us from the early modern period.

In their most recent publication, Gerald Maclean and Nabil Matar have also come to view Pitts in a much more favourable light *vis-à-vis* Islam. In *Britain and the Islamic World, 1558–1713* (Oxford, 2011), they judge that:

> With the hindsight of history, Pitts's account can be seen to be pivotal in the English understanding of Islam. It was written by a

non-scholar without access to the tomes of orientalist learning. But Pitts, a mere mariner, always cautiously, corrected the doyens. After living among Muslims for fourteen years, he realized that understanding Islam could not be achieved by mere reading and study. And although he read what he could find about Islam and Islamic lands upon his return to Exeter, the authoritativeness of his voice derived from having been part of the Muslim community – having eaten, travelled, served, prayed, and conversed with, and among, Muslims. His book shows, for the very first time in English, that learning about Muslims and Islamic required proficiency in languages,[15] adaptation to custom, integration into religious culture, and some humility … Had Pitts been a distinguished man of wealth or status, his text might have more forcibly encouraged a perspective that relied on approaching the different culture on its own terms, just as he, a captive, had been forced to do. Only by approaching religious difference without preconceptions, rather than through the a priori of Christian certitude and English triumphalism, can there be both understanding and criticism.[16]

Colley sees Pitts's book in the context of other captivity narratives, as an attempt to gain control over his own life by exorcising the trauma of captivity.[17] Matar sees it as "a journey to the 'alien' and a return to the familiar, a separation from England and a resumption of Englishness, a conversion to Islam on the 'outside', as he repeatedly affirmed, and an adherence to Christianity on the 'inside'".[18] Vitkus explains the book as "a confessional tract … it also represents the narrator's attempt to atone for his apostasy by offering something substantial – intelligence about the Muslims – that will be useful to his own society and therefore a valid form of compensation for his crime".[19] Seen through the prism of 21st-century criticism of the English captivity narrative, all these assessments are valid, and Pitts in his prefaces admits as much.

The book does of course throw valuable light on how English Protestants of the 17th century viewed their identity and on the attitudes of early modern England to the world of Islam, and it can rightly be seen as a classic example of the providentialist tale in which a Christian, after many adventures, finally escapes from mortal danger and finds salvation. However Pitts offers very much more than this insight into contemporary English attitudes (although as such, it is a valuable contribution to our knowledge), and his book is more than just an interesting example of a minor sub-genre of English literature. It is noteworthy that hardly any critics have impugned its factual veracity and, whether as travel narrative or commentary on Muslim practice, historians seem to have accepted the accuracy of most of the data it contains. Seen from this viewpoint, Pitts's account stands out as a mine of information on life in Muslim North Africa, and also as one of the most comprehensive manuals in English before the 19th century on Islamic ritual and practice. Over and above all of this, the book is the autobiography of a humane man, a literate but not highly educated individual who was very much a product of his time, class, religion and upbringing, but also someone who combined modesty with pride, resourcefulness with intelligence, and a capacity for self-reflection and observation with a gift for expression.

# Part II

## A Faithful Account of the Religion and Manners of the Mahometans

By Joseph Pitts, of Exeter

The 1731 third edition, corrected and expanded by the author from the 1704 first edition, including a plan of the Haram al-Sharif at Mecca, and an engraving of the postures of Muslims performing their prayer.

A FAITHFUL

# ACCOUNT

OF THE

## Religion and Manners

OF THE

# 𝕸𝖆𝖍𝖔𝖒𝖊𝖙𝖆𝖓𝖘.

In which is a particular

RELATION of their *Pilgrimage* to
*Mecca*, the Place of MAHOMET's
Birth; and a Description of *Medina*,
and of his Tomb there: As likewise
of *Algier*, and the Country adjacent;
and of *Alexandria*, *Grand Cairo*, &c.
With an Account of the Author's
being taken Captive; the *Turks* Cruelty to him; and of his Escape. In
which are many Things never publish'd by any Historian before.

By *JOSEPH PITTS*, of *Exon.*

The THIRD EDITION, *Corrected*, with *Additions*. To
*this Edition is added a Map of* Mecca, *and a Cut of*
*the Gestures of the* Mahometans *in their Worship*.

*L O N D O N ,*

*Printed for* J. Osborn *and* T. Longman, *at the* Ship *in*
Pater-noster-Row; *and* R. Hett, *at the* Bible *and*
Crown *in the* Poultry. M.DCC.XXXI

TO THE

Right HONOURABLE

# PETER,
# Lord KING,[1]

Baron of *Ockham*,
Lord High Chancellor of
*Great Britain*,

This Edition of the following
Account of the *Religion* and
*Manners* of the *Mahometans*, is,
with the profoundest Respect,
dedicated by

*Your Lordship's*
*most devoted,*
*most obedient, and*
*most humble Servant,*
JOSEPH PITTS.

---

[1] Peter King, Baron Ockham (1669–1734) was an Exeter man, who served as Lord High Chancellor of Britain from 1725 to 1733. King had been educated at Joseph Hallett's dissenting academy at Exeter, and would almost certainly have been known to Pitts's father, who was well acquainted with Joseph Hallett. Pitts may have dedicated this third edition to King both because the person to whom he dedicated the first edition, William Raye, the former British Consul at Smyrna, may have died by 1731, but also because King was the most prominent Exonian of his day and a man whose patronage Pitts was anxious to secure.

# The Preface.

IT may be thought *Presumption* in me, to put forth this little Book, Of the *Religion* and *Manners* of the *Mahometans*, &c. after what so many great and learned Men, and Travellers, capable of making the Observations with the greatest Exactness, have publish'd on the same Subject; and indeed, I thought
[p. vi] an Offer towards a Publication of my poor *Memoirs* to be so: But I was importun'd by many of my Friends; and upon a serious Consideration of the *Intent* of their Request, I was prevailed with to do it, hoping I might thereby be a Means of doing good to some one or other.

I may undergo the Censures of some, but I hope not of the best, and most candid Men. I do not pretend to give an exact and methodical *Account* of what I have observ'd; for I am sensible that I have not the Abilities which are required in a Person that writes such an *History:* Only, I beg leave to say plainly, I have the *most valuable Qualification* of an *Historian* on my side, *i.e. Truth.*

I never thought, till importun'd thereto, of exposing my *Observations* to *publick* view; I had many Objections in my self to the contrary, and great *Reluctancy*, which the *Reader* may guess at. But I have now launch'd out, and therefore intreat the *Reader*,
[p. vii] that he would pass by the inaccuracy of the Method, the Meanness of the Stile, and any Errors that happen to be seen; though I know of none material.

One Thing I will desire of the *learned Reader*, which is, that if the *Arabick* Words in any Place be not rightly written, he will please to take notice, that I aim'd at the vulgar Sound of the Words, and writ as near as I could to their way of speaking. And moreover, I can't pretend to a Perfection in the *Arabick* Language; which was the Occasion of that Mistake in *Page* 41 of the *first Edition*, where the *Arabick* was not truly *englished*; but I have since procured a *just Translation* of it.[2] If I happen in any place to be mistaken in point of Time, it is not wilfully done; and therefore I hope the *Reader* will overlook it.

I might have contriv'd it so, as to have made a much bigger Book of it, if I had thought fit; but I was willing it should be for every body's reading
[p. viii] and therefore would not make the Price too great.

I have hinted at some Mistakes in *Authors*, who are Persons of great *Learning* and *Worth*, and whose Names I acknowledge my self unworthy so much as to mention, were it not for the sake of *Truth*, which ought to be the dearest Thing in the World to every Man; and upon that account alone I have made bold to mention some Things, in which I am sure they have been misinform'd. What I speak I *know* to be true; nor have I recited Things meerly upon *Hearsay*.

I question whether there be a Man now in *England*, who has ever been at *Mecca*; and if I were assured of it, yet I would never take Encouragement from thence to tell the World any Thing but *Truth:* If I should, I am sensible it would be but a bad Testimony of my Repentance for my *Apostasy*, and I dread the Thoughts of so doing; so that the *Reader* may be
[p. ix] assured of my *Sincerity* in the following *Relation*.

But after all, 'tis not to be expected, but that I shall come under the Censures and Reproaches of some; yet this is my Comfort, Who is there

---

[2] *Arabick Language*: Pitts has corrected his translation of a phrase chanted during Muslim prayers from "All praise and blessing and thanksgiving be to God and to our Master Mohammet", found in the 1704 edition, to the much more correct: "O our God, be favourable to and let peace be upon our Lord (Master) and teacher Mahomet and upon the family of our Lord (Master) Mahomet."

that ever *publish'd* a Book of this Nature, and did not come under *Censure? You must give him leave* (say they, in a way of *Proverb*) Travellers *must be allowed to tell what* Stories *they please*; *'tis better to* believe *what he saith than to go and seek out the* Truth *of it.* I have borne much more than this e'er now; but *Censure* is no *Proof.* If I have committed any *Error*, it is an *involuntary* one, and I shall be glad to be inform'd of it, and will correct it; but for such Men as are *partial* in their *Censure*, or *Criticks* at random, and find fault for the sake of finding fault, I think they are more unreasonable than the *People* I came from, and therefore I desire no Familiarity with them.

In the Sixth *Chapter*, which contains an Account of the *Mahometan* Faith
[p. x] and Worship, it behov'd me to be as exact as I possibly could; and there is nothing material, as far as I can remember, that I have omitted.

The Seventh *Chapter*, which treats chiefly of the *Mahometans* Pilgrimage to *Mecca*, where *Mahomet* was born (tho' some deny that he was born there, yet it is universally believed among the *Turks*) and of their Visit to his Tomb at *Medina*, I think to be very exact, as to *Truth*; though the Method and wording may need an *Apology*.

How many *Stories* have been scattered about in the World, concerning *Mahomet's* Tomb? As of its hanging up by the Virtue of a *Loadstone*, &c. which are all as false as any thing can be.

The story of the *Pigeon*, which is said to have been taught by *Mahomet* to pick Corn out of his Ear, and which the *Vulgar* took to be the Whispers of the *Holy Ghost*, hath no better Foundation, that ever I could learn, than
[p. xi] a *Castle* (or his Tomb) in the *Air*. And since I came home, I have seen many Books, some of which have treated of *Algier* in particular, and others of the *Mahometan* Religion in general; which are stuff'd with very great Mistakes. I speak not this to raise a Value for what I have here written; for I protest, I am asham'd, and in pain about *publishing* it, notwithstanding the Encouragement my Friends have given me, because I am sensible I want Ability to do a Thing of this Nature as I ought. But whatever the Success of this *Book* may be, I declare my principal End in its *Publication*, is giving Glory to GOD, by whose gracious Providence I am releas'd from *Slavery*

and brought again into my own *native Country*, where there are no *Means of Salvation wanting*, and where the *Blessed Doctrine* of *Jesus* is established, and the *Holy Trinity* ador'd.

It is a Shame, indeed, to *Christians*, to take a View of the Zeal of those poor blind *Mahometans*; which in the
[p. xii] following *Account* will be found to be in many Things very strict. If they are so zealous in their *false* Worship, it must needs be a Reprimand to *Christians*, who are so remiss in the *True*. And, I pray GOD they may take the Hint, and learn thereby to bless the Goodness of GOD, that he hath continued his *Gospel* to them, while such a vast part of the *Globe* is devoted to a vile and debauch'd *Impostor*.

'Twas, as I have read, the many *Heresies*, and *blasphemous Errors*, broach'd in that, and the preceding Ages, which provok'd GOD to deliver the *Eastern* Churches over to cursed *Mahomet*, and to *remove the Candlestick out of its Place*.[3] GOD grant the same *Cause* may not have the same *direful* Influence on us; but that all professing *Christianity* may both entirely believe the *Doctrines* of our blessed *Saviour*, and sincerely conform their *Practice* to their Belief. And though the former, in some *Instances*, may seem difficult to *Reason*, and the latter to *corrupt* Nature; yet both duly and
[p. xiii] humbly considered, will be found to be our *reasonable Service*. And, according to the best of my Capacity, I see not much difference between a Man's refusing to believe the *mysterious* Doctrines of our *Religion*, because they exceed his Reach and Comprehension, so long as they are *clearly* reveal'd; and his denying to obey the *practical*, and *moral* Precepts of *Christianity*, because some of them are not suited to his *Humour* and *Complexion*, and adapted to his own *Scheme*. We must have a *new Religion* to please all; but the *old* must and will stand, in spight [*sic*] of the *Gates of Hell*; for our Lord hath assur'd us, that *They shall not prevail against it; and, that He will be with His* Church *to the End of the* World, wheresoever it may be transplanted for the Sins of Men.

---

[3] *Candlestick*: a reference to *Revelations*, chapter 2, verse 5, in which God threatened to destroy the Church in Ephesus in Asia Minor unless they mended their ways: "Remember therefore whence thou art fallen, and repent and do the first works; or else I come to thee, and will move thy candlestick out of its place, except thou repent."

I cannot but recommend to all Parents, an *early, religious Education* of their Children; and to take all imaginable Care, in their tender Years, to instruct them well in the *Principles* of *Christianity*: For I am apt to think [p. xiv] had I my self had as little Knowledge as some have, who are taken as *Slaves*, I had been for ever lost. And I am verily perswaded, [*sic*] that many poor ignorant Souls, which have turn'd *Mahometans*, would never have done what they did, had they been *catechised* as they ought. No Man knows how far the Benefit of a good *Education* may extend.

I think myself obliged to make an *Apology* for calling the *Turkish Imam*,[4] or *Emaum*, *Priest*, and their *Mosques Churches*; but I hope the *Reader* will pardon it, because I knew not well, otherwise, how to express my self so as to be understood.

The *second* Edition was printed without my Consent; nay, I knew nothing of the Matter, till they had gone about half way. I have wish'd since, I had then published an *Advertisement*, that I would in a little Time print a *second Edition with Additions*. This might, perhaps, have put a Stop to the Press; for I scarce ever saw a Book printed on [p. xv] worse Paper, and so incorrect: But this must not lie at my Door.

I was very unwilling to reprint my Book; but I have been informed, that there hath been a great Demand for it (especially in *London*) and, that it is the best Account of the *Mahometan* Religion we have extant in our Language: I will say, 'tis as *true* as any, for I wrote from *my own Knowledge*, which I never yet heard any *English-Man* did; nor indeed could he, unless he had been in the like *unhappy* Circumstances with my self.

Several have been very urgent with me, to have it printed at *London*, assuring me, it would meet with good Acceptance. Upon this I endeavoured to recollect some Things which had slipt me in the *first* Edition; and many soon occur'd. These have been placed under their respective Heads. Besides which, there is *Consul Baker's* Letter in this Edition,[5] which could not be in

---

[4] *Imam*: an Imām in Sunnī Islam is the leader of worship at a mosque, but since Islam has no clerical hierarchy, his position does not equate to that of the Christian priest.

[5] *Letter*: the text of the letter was printed on pp. 236–7 of the 1731 edition. More information on Consul Thomas Baker can be found in Pennell (1989).

that, because I had not then a Copy of it. This I cannot but look upon as *a* [p. xvi] *very material Addition*; for it was what I may call the Ground-work of my *Deliverance*. There are some small Alterations also made in the Stile [*sic*], many Mistakes corrected, several Things which were misplaced put into somewhat better Order, and two Cuts, *viz.* of the several Postures of the *Mahometans* in their publick Worship, and the *Temple* at *Mecca*; so that it may very properly be called, *The Third Edition, with Additions and Amendments.*

The late Mr. *Lowndes*,[6] who was so long *Secretary* to the *Treasury*, had a great desire to see and converse with me. Accordingly, when I was some years since in *London, Consul Baker* took me to him. Amongst other Discourse, he told me, *He was proud that he could say he had seen an* English-Man *who had been at* Mecca; and withal assured me, if I would accept of some *Place*, he would use his Interest to procure it for me. But I waved [*sic*][7] it in the best Manner I could, for some *private* Reasons.

[p. xvii] I have been often reflected upon for my *Apostasy*; which I desire to bear with Patience. I deserve abundantly more than this; however, I have this to comfort me, that they are, for the most part, ignorant or vile Persons, whose Censures are not much to be minded: Nay, I don't remember, that I have been once reproached for it by any of Learning or Piety. I do not pretend to excuse what I did; but whether it was *voluntarily*, or I was a true *Mussulman*, let any judge, when they have considered what Hazard I ran in making my Escape. I was in a much fairer way for *Honour* and *Preferment* in *Algier*, than I could expect ever to have been in *England*.

I have several *Letters* by me which I sent my *Father* while I was in *Turkey*, and found after my Return; but shall not trouble the *Reader* with them. Inclosed in one of them, is a *Letter* to him from Mr. *George Taylor* (who was Master of the Vessel wherein I was taken) dated the Twenty second Day of [p. xviii] *October*, 1682 from Algier; in which are these Words, speaking of me, "I have not seen him these thirteen or fourteen Months; but do hear,

---

[6] *William Lowndes* (1652–1724) was Secretary to the Treasury from 1695 until his death in 1724.

[7] *waved*: refused.

by all that come in Company of him, that he hath still a *Christian* Heart, which I hope will continue with him to the End of his Days."

I don't know of any Thing material I can farther add, as to the *Religion* and *Customs* of the *Mahometans*; and therefore my Book, though I am sensible 'tis very imperfect, is as complete now as I can make it.

J. P.

EXON
May 28th, 1731.

# THE CONTENTS.

# THE RELIGION *and* MANNERS OF THE
# Mahometans, &c.

## CHAP. I.

*Containing an Account of the Author's being taken. Of an Insurrection designed by
the Slaves, but disappointed. Of the Manner of selling Slaves in* Algier.

WHEN I was about fourteen or fifteen Years of Age, my *Genius* led me
to be a Sailor, and to see *foreign* Countries; (much contrary to my
Mother's Mind, though my Father seem'd to yield to my humour) and
having made two or three short
[p. 2] Voyages, my Fancy was to range further abroad; for which I sufficiently
suffer'd, as in the sequel of the *Story* will appear.

I shipped my self on *Easter Tuesday, Anno* 1678. with one Mr. *George
Taylor,* Master of the *Speedwell,* of *Lymson,*[8] near *Exeter* (Mr. Alderman *George
Tuthill,* of *Exon,*[9] Owner) bound to the *Western Islands,*[10] from thence to
*Newfoundland,* from thence to *Bilboa,*[11] from thence to the *Canaries,* and so
home, had God permitted. We got safe to *Newfoundland;* and our Business

---

[8] *Lymson:* now spelled Lympstone, this is a small village on the east bank of the Exe estuary,
south-south-east of Exeter and roughly midway between Topsham and Exmouth.
[9] *Exon:* Exeter. [10] *Western Islands:* Ireland.
[11] *Bilboa:* Bilbao, on the coast of northern Spain.

being ended there, with a fair Wind we set sail for *Bilboa*; and after we had been out about 40 Days from *Newfoundland*, coming near the Coast of *Spain* (which we knew was the Place where the *Algerines* us'd to haunt[12] for poor Ships that come from the *Westward*) we look'd out sharp for Ships, avoiding all we saw; but especially did we look out in the Morning, at Sun-rising, and in the Evening, at Sun-setting. The day in which we were taken, our *Mate*, Mr. *John Milton*, was early at Top-mast-head, and cried out, *A Sail!* The *Master* ask'd him, *Where? At Leeward*, replied the *Mate*, *about five or six Leagues*. And so, to be *brief* in my *Relation*, About Mid-day, being almost overtaken by them (the Enemy being but about a Mile distance from us) our *Master* said, it will be in vain for us to make our Flight any longer, seeing it will

[p. 3] be but an Hour or two e'er we shall be taken, and then, probably, fare the worse if we continue our flight. I may leave any Person to judge what an heartless Condition we were in; but yet still we could not forbear kenning[13] the Ship, that unwelcome Object, which, *Devil-like*, was eager in the Pursuit of us. All hope now failing, there being no place for Refuge, we haled up our Sails, and waited for them. As soon as the *Pirate* came up with us, the *Captain* being a *Dutch Renegado*, and able to speak *English*, bid us hoist out our Boat; which we could not do without much Trouble and Time, by reason that a few Days before, one of our Men in a great Storm was wash'd over-board, and I my self was so scalded with boiling Water, as to be disabled for working; so that we had but four Men that were able: And therefore, before we could make half ready to hoist out our boat, they came a-board us in their own. I being but *young*, the Enemy seem'd to me as monstrous ravenous Creatures; which made me cry out, *O, Master! I am afraid they will kill us and eat us. No, no, Child*, said my Master, *they will carry us to* Algier, *and sell us*.

The very first Words they spake, and the first Thing they did, was beating us with Ropes, saying, *Into Boat you* English *Dogs!* And without the least Opposition, with Fear, we tumbled into their Boat, we scarce knew

[p. 4] how; which, when they had loaded, they carried us aboard their Ship, and diligent Search was made about us for Money, but they found none. We were the first Prize they had taken for that Voyage, though they had been out at Sea about six Weeks. As for our Vessel, after they had taken out of her what they thought fit, and necessary for their use, they sunk her; for

---

[12] *haunt*: hunt.   [13] *kenning*: looking at.

being laden with *Fish*, they thought it not worth while to carry or send her home to *Algier*.

About four or five Days after our being thus taken, they met with another small *English* Ship, which also came from *Newfoundland*, with five or six Men aboard; which was served as ours was: And two or three Days after that, they espied another small *English* Vessel, with the like Number of Men aboard, laden with *Fish*, and coming from *New-England*. This Vessel was, at their first View of her, some Leagues at *Windward* of them, and as there was but little Wind, they were out of hopes of getting up to her; they therefore used this cunning Device, *viz.* haled up[14] their Sails, and hung out our *English* King's *Colours, and so appearing* Man of War *like, decoyed her down, and sunk her also.*

Two or three Days after this, they took a fourth little *English* Ship, with four or five Men aboard, laden with *Herrings*, of which they took out most part, and then sunk her.

**[p. 5]**

And last of all, they met with a small *Dutch* ship, with seven Men, laden partly with *Pipe Staves*;[15] which they also sunk. This Ship was, as one of the before-mentioned, at a great distance to *Windward* from them, when first espied, and they us'd the like Stratagem to decoy her down, *viz. put up* Dutch *Colours*; but when the *Dutchman* came so near as about half a League from him, and perceived him to be a *Turk*, he began to loof up[16] with all his Sail, but to no purpose; for e'er it was Night he was overtaken.

I would advise my *Country-men*, when at Sea, to avoid *all* Ships they see, unless they are in *great Distress*; because many have been in this manner taken, who might otherwise have escaped.

This being a Summer's Voyage, in which Season of the Year their Ships are usually but very badly mann'd (the Reason is, because their Camps are out at this time of the Year, of which hereafter) I think the *Algerines* had not above thirty or forty fighting Men aboard; so that there was a great Inclination amongst us to rise, and venture our Lives for our Liberty; and we had no small Encouragement, considering that we were near thirty *new-taken* Slaves, besides between twenty and thirty *old* Slaves brought with the *Pirate* out of *Algier. For such they usually bring to sail the Vessel, and to do all the Ship's*

---

[14] *haled up*: hauled up, hoisted.  [15] *Pipe Staves*: lengths of wood for making barrels.
[16] *loof up*: to luff, or steer nearer the wind.

**[p. 6]** *work for them, while the* new *Slaves are put into Irons in the Hold, and for a Month's time are not able to stand on their Legs, nor suffered to come upon Deck, being confin'd either to sit or lie down, without the least provision of Bedding to ease themselves.* In this sorrowful Case we were, insomuch that we were almost weary of our Lives; for you may imagine, that the Food we had to sustain Nature was answerable to the rest of their Kindness; and indeed, this generally was only a little Vinegar (about five or six Spoonfuls) half a spoonful of Oil, and a few Olives, with a small quantity of black Bisket, and a Pint of Water a Day.

Well, as I hinted, a Platform was laid for our mutinying, and the old *English* Slaves were as fully resolv'd as the new. The *Purtezara*[17] *(which is, as we may call him, the* Boatswain's Mate, *an English-Man, who had the Rigging, and other Iron Work, in his disposal)* was of the Confederacy, and had ingaged [*sic*] to supply all the rest with some Weapon or other. I think, the first Adviser of an Insurrection was one Mr. *James Goodridge,*[18] now of *Exon,* who was one of the *old* Slaves, and a Cabin-Servant; and in order to it, brought down two naked Swords, and a pair of Pincers to loose the Iron Bar on which we were shackled. All this while none of the *Spaniards,* or Slaves of other Nations, knew any thing of our Design; and we so ordered **[p. 7]** it, for fear we should be discovered by them, that only the *English* and *Dutch* were privy to it. The Night being come when we were resolved to rise, and in order thereto had loosened the Iron Bar on which we were shackled, the Heart of the *Dutch* Master flagg'd, and so a Stop was put to our Design; whereas, had we been all unanimous, the Thing might, and in all probability would have been accomplish'd with a great deal of *Honour* and *Profit; for it was the Time of* Ramadan, *(their Month of Fast) when they eat Meat only by Night; and therefore in the Morning, somewhat before Day came, they would in all likelihood, have been fast asleep. This was the time when we design'd to put our Plot in practice; but the* Divine Providence *had further Trials for us (especially for me) to undergo; as will appear in the Progress of this* History.

And now with a fresh westerly Wind we enter'd the *Straights*[19] by Day, which the *Algerines* seldom attempt to do during their Wars with us, fearing

---

[17] *Purtezara*: presumably a term used in *Lingua Franca,* but the word does not appear in Kahane (1958) or Corré (2005). For an explanation of *Lingua Franca,* see Part I, Chapter 1, note 257.
[18] Possibly the James Goodridge who was a well-known Quaker in Exeter; see Brockett (1962), 112.
[19] *Straights*: Straits of Gibraltar.

our *Men of War.* When we came almost within the sight of *Algier,* the *Boatswain* of the Ship was order'd *to loose the Slaves that were in Irons;* who coming down with a Candle, and finding that the Key which was put into the end of the Iron Bar was broken; *O ye* English *Dogs,* said he, *what, your Design was to rise!* And after we were loosed, and brought upon Deck

[p. 8] he presently told the *Captain* of it, who immediately fell into a very great Rage, and caused Mr. *John Milton of Lymson,*[20] our *Mate (who sat at the end of the Bar on which we were shackled, and so was suspected to open the Key, as indeed he did)* to be called forth to the *Bastinadoes.*[21] Accordingly he was forthwith laid down on the Deck, and had his Arms turned and held behind him, one Man sitting on his Legs, and another at his Head; and in this Posture the *Captain,* with a great Rope, gave him about an hundred Blows on his Buttocks; but he would not confess the Fact, *generously* choosing rather to suffer himself, than to bring us all under the *Bastinadoes* also.

Soon after our Arrival at our *undesired Haven,* viz. *Algier,* we were carried ashore to the *Captain's* House, and allowed nothing but a little *Bread* and *Water* that Night. The next Morning (as their Custom is) they drove us all to the *Dey's,*[22] or *King's,* House, who makes his Choice and takes the *Pengick,*[23] i.e. the eighth part of the Slaves for the publick Use, and the same part of the Cargo. After which we were all driven from thence to the *Battista,*[24] or *Market-place,* where *Christians* are wont to be sold: There we stand from eight of the Clock in the Morning, until two in the Afternoon (which is the limited time for the Sale of *Christians*) and have not the least bit

[p. 9] of Bread allowed us during our Stay there. Many Persons are curious to come and take a view of us, while we stand exposed to sale; and others, who intend to buy, to see whether we be *sound* and *healthy,* and *fit for Service.* The *taken Slaves* are sold by way of Auction, and the *Cryer* endeavours to make the most he can of them; and when the *Bidders* are at a stand, he makes use of his Rhetorick, *Behold what a* strong Man *this is! What Limbs he has!*

---

[20] *Lymson:* Lympstone.

[21] *Bastinadoes:* being beaten with a stick often (though not in this case) on the soles of the feet. A common punishment in the Mediterranean world.

[22] *Dey:* the ruler of Algiers. For more information on the political structure of Algiers, see the section of Part I, Chapter 1, entitled "Algiers: A Corsair State".

[23] *Pengick:* modern Turkish *pencik.* For more information, see Part I, Chapter 1, note 155.

[24] *Battistan:* modern Turkish *bedestan* or *bedesten.* The central building in an Ottoman covered market, where the most valuable goods were sold.

*He is fit for any* Work. *And, see what a* pretty Boy *this is! No doubt his Parents are* very rich*, and able to* redeem *him with a* great Ransom. And with many such like fair Speeches does he strive to raise the Price. After the *Bidders* have done bidding, the Slaves are all driven again to the *Dey's* House, where any that have a mind to advance above what was bidden at the *Battistan*, may; but then whatsoever exceeds the Bidding in that Place, belongs not to the *Pickaroons*, or *Pirates*, but goes to the *Dey*.

As to the City of *Algier*, it is situated on the side of a Hill, and its Walls are adjoining to the Sea. The tops of the Houses are all over White, being flat, and covered with Lime and Sand, as Floors. The upper part of the Town is not so broad as the lower, and therefore at Sea it looks just like the *Top-sail* of a Ship. It is a very strong Place, and well fortified with Castles and Guns.

[p. 10] There are *seven Castles* without the Walls, and two Tire[25] of Guns in most of them; but in the greatest Castle, which is on the *Mole* without the Gate, there are three Tire of Guns, many of them of an extraordinary length, carrying 40, 50, 60, 70, yea, 80 Pound Shot. Besides all these, there is at the higher end of the Town, within the Walls, another Castle with many Guns. And moreover, on many Places on the Walls, towards the Sea, are great Guns planted. It is well wall'd, and surrounded with a great Trench. It hath five Gates, and some of these have two, some three other Gates within them; and some of them plated all over with thick Iron; so that it is made strong and convenient for being what it is, a *Nest of Pirates*.

About two or three Leagues *West* of *Algier*, is a Town [*sic*; sc. Tower] of considerable Bigness. I never was so near it as to be able to give an exact Description of it; but I was informed, that it was *one entire Stone*, which I can hardly give credit to. They have a *Tradition*, that a *Christian* Woman was *enchanted* there, and therefore call it *Cub. el Romeea*, i.e. *The Cupola* of a Christian *Woman*.[26]

About ten Miles off *Algier*, to the *West-ward* also, is a pretty little Town called *Bleda*,[27] accommodated with *fine Gardens, full of all manner of Fruits, and plenty of Water*; insomuch, that there are upon the River *Grist*

---

[25] *Tire*: a battery of guns.

[26] *Cub. El Romeea*: Pitts has mistaken the Arabic word *Qubr* (tomb) for *Qubbah* (cupola). The *Qubr al-Rūmiyyah* (known now the Royal Mausoleum of Mauretania or more popularly as the Tomb of the Christian Woman) is a monument dating back to Numidian times and is located about forty miles west of Algiers.

[27] *Bleda*: modern-day Blida (Arabic, Bulaydah), a large town about thirty miles south-west of Algiers.

[p. 11] *Mills*, which is such a Rarity as I seldom, or never saw in any other part of that Country. In this Town I lived many Years with my second *Patroon*.[28] It lies in a spacious and pleasant Plain, call'd *Mateeja*,[29] adjoining to an high Mountain, on which live a rude sort of People, called *Cabyles*,[30] who speak a Language different from that of the *Turks* or *Moors*; of whom I shall have Occasion to make mention hereafter.

This Town lying so near to *Algier*, and being so exceeding pleasant and delightful, many *Turks* marry and reside there; so that there is no need of keeping *Garrison* there, as they do in most other Towns within the Territories of *Algier*. This *Mateeja*, or Plain, contains about *twenty Miles in length*, and *six or seven in breadth*. It is *very fruitful*, and abounds with many *handsom* [*sic*] *Farm-houses*. There are several *Markets* weekly kept on it. The *Turks* do frequently (for their Diversion) take their Muskets, and make a Progress, two or three in a Company, through this Plain, for ten or twenty Days space, living at *free Quarter*, at one Farmer's House or other, none daring to refuse them; and many Times they *abuse* their Wives too: These, and many more Injuries and Abuses the poor *Moors* suffer from the *Turks* of *Algier*, which makes them very uneasy under their Government; insomuch, that I have often heard them say,

[p. 12] *That they wished the* Christians *would come and take* Algier, *assuring themselves, that they should have* better Usage *from them.*

Further *West*, almost a Day's Journey, is another Town, called *Mylliana*,[31] a small but handsom [*sic*] Town. *West* of *Mylliana*, about fifteen Miles, is another Town called *Mazuna*,[32] where the *Turks* keep Garrison. Further *West*, about three or four Days Journey, is a Town called *Mustegollem*,[33] where the *Turks* keep Garrison also. And the *farthest* Town in the *Western* Territories of *Algier* is *Tillimsan*,[34] a Town of great Note in former Days, before *Mahomet* began his *Imposture*: And indeed, by its strong Walls and Gates, and the Ruins

---

[28] *Patroon: Lingua Franca*, Master (Patron is also found with this meaning).

[29] *Mateeja*: the Mitidja (Arabic, Mitījah or Matījah) is a large fertile plain in the hinterland of Algiers.   [30] *Cabyles*: Berbers.

[31] *Mylliana*: Miliana (Arabic, Milyāna) is a medium-sized town about 100 miles south-west of Algiers.

[32] *Mazuna*: Mazouna (Arabic, Mazūnah).

[33] *Mustegollem*: Mostaganem (Arabic, Mustaghanim), an important port founded in the 11th century.

[34] *Tillimsan*: Tlemcen (Arabic, Ṭilimsān) is the most important Algerian town west of Oran. Originally founded by the Romans, in the mediaeval period it was the capital of independent and semi-independent kingdoms, before its incorporation into the Ottoman province of Algiers in the 16th century.

thereof, which I saw, it seem'd so to have been. This is a Place abounding in all sorts of *curious and delicious Fruits*. And the Women and Boys *here* are reputed the fairest, and most beautiful in all the *Algerine Dominions*, even to a *Proverb*. Here the *Turks* keep Garrison also. When I went into their great *Mosque*, (*i.e.* their Place of *publick Worship*) I admired the great Door thereof, which was a Folding-Door, and all solid Brass, or Bell-metal, with curious Workmanship wrought on it. *This great Gate, they say, was found by the Sea-side, supposed to be some Wreck, and was brought from thence by a* Marabbot[35] (*or Saint*) *on his Shoulders to* Tillimsan, *which is about twenty Miles*. Which *Marabbot* [p. 13] lies intomb'd just before the said great Door.[36]

To the *Northward* of *Tillimsan*, joining to the Sea, is a strong fortified Town call'd *Oran*,[37] held by the *Spaniards*; of which I shall speak anon.

*Eastward* of *Algier*, there is scarce a Town worth taking Notice of, (for I have frequently travell'd it) 'till we come to *Constantine*,[38] which lies above two Hundred Miles from *Algier*. This is the greatest, and strongest Town they have in all the *Eastern* Parts of their Dominions. It is situated on the top of a great Rock, so that it needs no Walls for its Defence. It is difficult *for* Horses to get up to it, the Way being Steps hewen [*sic*] out in the Rock. Here the *Turks* likewise keep Garrison, and the *Bay*[39] or *General* hath his Dwelling-House. The usual way of Executing great Criminals here at *Constantine*, is pushing them off the Clift. About two Days Journey *East* of this Place, is another Town adjoining to the Sea, called *Beladernab* by the *Moors*, but in our Maps *Bona*;[40] a Sea-port Town for small Vessels, or Gallies. 'Tis walled, very fruitful, and hath a strong Castle built on the top of an Hill, in which also the *Turks* keep Garrison.

---

[35] *Marabbot*: a Marabout (Arabic, Murābiṭ) is a Muslim religious teacher, often a highly venerated Sufi, whose tomb could sometimes become a centre of pilgrimage.

[36] It is possible that Pitts is confusing the Great Mosque of Tlemcen (Arabic, al-Jāmiʿ al-Kabīr li-Ṭilimsān) with the Mosque of Sidi Boumediene (Arabic, Masjid Sīdī Abū [or Abī] Madyān), which lies about a mile from the centre of Tlemcen.

[37] *Oran*: Oran (Arabic, Wahrān) is now Algeria's second-largest city, but was held by the Spanish for around three hundred years, until its reconquest by the Algerians in 1792.

[38] *Constantine*: Constantine (Arabic, Qusanṭīnah) is Algeria's third-largest city and, as in Pitts's day, is still regarded as the capital of its Eastern Province.

[39] *Bay*: Bey or provincial governor.

[40] *Bona*: Bône (Arabic, ʿAnnābah) is the classical Hippo, and the most important port in Eastern Algeria.

A few Leagues *East* of *Bona*, is a little *Island*,[41] which is inhabited by the *Genoese*, whose chief Employment is dragging for
[p. 14] *Coral*. Both the *Algerines*, and *Tuniseens* claim a Right to this *Island*, and therefore the *Genoese* pay Tribute to each. I know not certainly how much they pay, but if I mistake not, it is an *Horse-load* of *Coral* every two Months to each. The *Turks* being unskilful in fishing for this *Coral*, for their Profit permit the *Genoese* to dwell here, and have the free Enjoyment of *their own Religion*.

*Westward* of *Bona* is a little Town call'd *Cool*.[42] And *West* of *Cool*, another call'd *Bugia*,[43] lying also by the Sea-side, where the *Turks* likewise keep Garrison. Here Sir *Edward Sprague*, in the Year 1670,[44] destroy'd several of their Ships that were got under the Castle for Protection, which plaid [*sic*] briskly on the *English* with their Cannon.

*South*, or rather *South-East* of *Algier*, about three or four Days Journey, are two Towns, the one called *Piscree*,[45] the other *Zammora*,[46] both Garrisons. They lie near to the *Sahra*, or *Desert*, which is all Sand, and therefore produces no sort of Fruit but *Dates*, which always prosper best in sandy Countries.

---

[41] The island was called the Ilot de France and lay just off the port of La Calle (Arabic, al-Qāllah). Coral is still harvested today in this area and also across the border in Tunisia near Tabarka.

[42] *Cool*: Collo (Arabic, al-Qull) is a small port in Skikda Province.

[43] *Bugia*: Bougie, now Bejaia (Arabic, Bijāyah), is still a significant port-city within the Kabylie region of Algeria.

[44] *Sir Edward Sprague*: Sir Edward Spragge (*ca.*1629–73) attacked the Algerian fleet in Bijāyah in May 1671, not 1670 as Pitts claims.

[45] *Piscree*: Biskra (Arabic, Biskirah) dates from Roman times and is still an important oasis town.

[46] *Zammora*: possibly Zemmoura (Arabic, Zammūrah), a small town in the province of Bordj Bou Arreridj (Arabic, Burj Bū Arrīrij), south-east of Algiers, although Zemmoura lies a long way from the Sahara.

[p. 15]

## CHAP. II.

*Containing an Account of the* Algerines *Behaviour when at Sea: And their superstitious Addressing the* Marabbots[47] *for Success.*

THE first Thing the *Algerines* do when any Ship comes home from Cruising, is with all Expedition to take every Thing out, Ballast and all; and then careen[48] again, and tallow all under Water to the very Keel. Having so done, they take in all again as fast as they can, and when they are ready, and fit to put to Sea, a *Signal* is given for any that will, to come on Board, and they refuse none that offer themselves, whether they be *able*, or *unable, old*, or *young*. The *Gunners* have *two Parts* or Shares of what is taken; and the *Soldiers* the same; the *Slaves* that labour, some *two*, some *three*, and some *four*, but it goes to their *Patroons*; and all the rest have *one Part*.

The Guns being fired, they all take their Leave of their Friends, saying, *Allah smorla dick*,[49] i.e. *I leave you with God*. Their Friends usually return, *Allah Deumlick weara;*[50] i.e. *God give you a good Prize*. And here it is to be noted, That if there be several Ships go out together, then the
[p. 16] *Captain* which was *first registred* is *Admiral* of the said Ships; and none can be registred a *Captain*, until he bring in *Eight Christian Slaves*, that so the *Governor* may have the *Pengick*; i.e. The *One Eighth*. And every such *Captain* has, when he dies, in Honour of him, an *Ancient Staff*[51] set up at the *Head of his Sepulchre*, and every *Sabbath-day*, which with them is *Friday*, his surviving Relations hang up their *Flag* on it; and this they do for many Years after his Decease.

At their return from Sea, if they have taken any Prize, all the *Slaves* and *Cargo* are sold by way of *Auction*; and all sorts of People, whether *Turks, Moors, Jews*, or *Christians*, have their liberty to advance in bidding; and after

---

[47] *Marabbot*: see note 35 for an explanation of this term.

[48] *Careen*: to take a ship out of the water, and turn it on its side for cleaning and repairs.

[49] *Allah smorla dick*: modern Turkish, *Allahaısmarladık*, to God we commend you, still a customary way of bidding farewell in Turkish.

[50] *Allah Deumlick weara*: it is difficult to determine the modern Turkish version of Pitts's phrase, but it may be something like *Allah devamlilik versin*, which literally means: May God give continuity, or *Allah dümenlik vere*, which approximates to: May God steer you well.

[51] *Ancient Staff*: flagstaff.

the Money is paid which is bid, every Person receiveth his Part, or Parts.

The *Algerines* are very *timorous* sort of People, willing to *sleep in a whole Skin*,[52] and therefore care not how little they fight; but shew themselves *wondrously* Valiant upon *poor small* Merchant-men. But many times they have made some Attempts on *great* Merchant-men, and have come off with Shame and broken Bones. And this is not much to be admired at, because they have *no Order* in their Engagements, neither is there *any Punishment* for such of the Inferiour Soldiers as fight not.

[p. 17]

They dread much our *English Men of War*, and when we have War with them, will seldom venture in or out the *Straights-mouth*[53] by Day, but chiefly in the Night-time, and *that* when they have a brisk Wind, keeping as near as they can with Safety to the *Barbary* Shore. And they were more especially afraid to do it, while *Tangier*[54] was ours. But if they have Peace with *Us*, tho' they have War with all *Christendom* besides, they will then not scruple to pass the *Straights-mouth* by Day, more than by Night.

I have often heard them say, That there are none like the *English* to give them Chace [*sic*]; "*For as for other ships*, say they, *when they have chased us a while, and see no great probability of soon overtaking us, they will give over their Pursuit; but as for the* English *Infidels, they will chase three Days after they have lost us.*"

When they are in the *Straights-mouth*, they make a gathering of small Wax Candles, which they usually carry with them, and bind them in a bundle; and then, together with a Pot of Oil, throw them overboard, as a Present to the *Marabbot*, or Saint, which lies intomb'd there on the *Barbary* Shore, near the Sea, and hath so done for many Scores of Years, as they are taught to believe; not in the least doubting, but the Present will come safe to the *Marabbot's* Hands. When this is done, they all together

[p. 18] hold up their Hands, begging the *Marabbot's* Blessing and a prosperous Voyage.⋆ [[⋆*Here's true* Sergius;[55] *this is exactly* ora pro nobis,[56] *and indeed their whole* Religion *is a* Miscellany *of* Popery, Judaism, *and the*

---

[52] *sleep in a whole Skin*: to escape being harmed or injured.

[53] *Straights-mouth*: Straits of Gibraltar.

[54] *Tangier*: Tangier was a British possession from 1661 to 1684.

[55] *Sergius*: Sergius was said to be a Nestorian monk who taught Muhammad. For more information, see Part I, Chapter 3, note 125.

[56] *Ora pro nobis*: "Pray for us", a phrase from the prayers for intercession used in Roman Catholic ritual.

Gentilism *of the* Arabs; *as may be seen in Dr.* Prideaux's *excellently written Life of* Mahomet.[57]]] And if they at any Time happen to be in a very great Strait, or Distress, as being Chased, or in a Storm, they will gather Money, and do likewise. Besides which, they usually light up abundance of Candles in remembrance of some dead *Marabbot* or other, calling upon him with heavy Sighs, and Groans. At such times also they collect Money, and wrap it in a piece of Linen-cloth, and make it fast to the Ancient Staff of the Ship, so dedicating it to some *Marabbot*; and there it abides till the arrival of the Ship, when they bestow it in Candles, or Oil, to give light, or in some Ornament to beautify the *Marabbots* Sepulchre. For these *Marabbots* have generally a little neat Room built over their Graves, resembling in figure their *Mosques*, or *Churches*, which is very nicely cleansed, and well look'd after. There are several of them about *Algier*, to which the Women on *Fridays* flock to pay their Visits, and perform their *Salah* or Prayer, begging of the *Marabbot* to hear and answer their Petitions. Many People there

[p. 19] are who will scarce pass by any of them without lifting up of their hands, and saying some short Prayer. And so great a Veneration have they for these *Marabbots*, that they will hardly believe one another, unless Oath be made by one or other of them.

But to *return* to their Custom at Sea. If they find no Succour from their before-mentioned Rites and Superstitions; but that the Danger rather encreases [*sic*], then they go to *sacrificing* of a Sheep (or *two or three* upon occasion, as they think needful) which is done after this manner: Having cut off the Head with a Knife, they immediately take out the Entrails, and throw them, and the Head overboard; and then with all the speed they can (without skinning) they cut the Body into two parts by the middle, and throw one part over the right side of the Ship, and the other over the left, into the Sea, as a kind of *Propitiation*. Thus those blind *Infidels* (as the *Papists* do, to whom they really seem to be a-kin in several things) apply themselves to *Imaginary* Intercessors, instead of the *Living, and True God*, who alone is able to command the swelling, and mounting Billows of the *Sea to be quiet and still.*

As I intimated before, they are *wondrously* Valiant against a weak Enemy, and vigorous in their Chace after *small* Vessels; and so careful are they that nothing may

---

[57] *Prideaux's Life of Mahomet*: Humphrey Prideaux published his attack on Muhammad and Islam in 1697. For more information see Part I, Chapter 3, note 148.

[p. 20] hinder their speed, that they will scarce suffer any Person in the Ship to stir, but all must sit stock-still, unless Necessity otherwise require. And all things that are capable of any motion, must be fasten'd, or unhang'd, (even the smallest weight) lest the Pursuit should be something retarded thereby.

But as they are eager upon a *small* Ship, so if it happen at any time that they chase a *great* One, they'll slack their pace as soon as they come near enough to apprehend what she is: Or if at any time they see a Ship preparing to *fight* them, their Courage is apt to be very soon daunted. Many Ships of twelve, ten, or but eight Guns, have escaped their Hands very manfully, whilst the *Turks* have come Home shatter'd, and with Shame. Many Instances of this nature might be related, but I will only mention one, which happen'd not long before I came away out of the Country.

There was an *Algerine* at Sea, and he met with a *Dutch* Vessel, which as I well remember had but ten Guns, and it may be about sixteen Men; whereas the *Algerine* had between twenty and thirty Guns and was very well-man'd. The *Dutch* Vessel by Courage got clear, and the cowardly *Algerine* made haste Home much shattered, and reported that he had fought with a great Flushing[58] *Privateer*, and it past all for *Truth*. But it happen'd, that a few Days after, the

[p. 21] same *Dutch* Merchant-man was met by another *Algerine* of about the same bigness with the former, and the poor *Dutch-man* having lost some of his Men, and others wounded, and being much disabled, was at last forced to yield, and was brought into *Algier*, to the great Shame of the other *Algerine*, who was sufficiently checkt for his Cowardise, and had much ado to escape the *Bastinadoes*. So that the *Algerines* are not in truth such *daring* Sparks as they are thought to be. And I verily believe that many Ships, much unequal to them in Strength, might escape being taken, if they would but *appear brave*, and look them *boldly* in the Face.

---

[58] *Flushing*: the English name for the Dutch town of Vlissingen, which in the 17th century was the main port used by the Dutch East India Company.

## CHAP. III.

*An Account of the* Turks *manner of Eating. They are much addicted to the cursed, and unnatural Sin of Sodomy.*

I T may not be altogether frivolous, or unacceptable, to give you a very brief *Account* of the *Turks* manner of *Eating*.

Their *low* Round-Table being placed, not above three or four Inches from the Floor, they all sit down cross-legg'd, as *Taylors* [*sic*] do when they are at work on their Shopboard;[59] having

[p. 22] a Napkin[60] that reaches all round to wipe with. The Victuals being put on the Table, every one says his *Grace*, (more 'tis to be fear'd, than thousands of such as call themselves Christians do) and that is, *Be, isme allah*;[61] i.e. *In the Name of* God. The same Expression they use in all things they set about, to the Shame of those who pretend to more, and *yet have not God in all their Thoughts*, as the *Psalmist*[62] speaks of some wicked Men. The Meat is always seasoned before it comes to the Table, so that they make use of no Salt there. Neither are Knives, or Forks of any use then, because the Flesh which they boil is always cut into pieces while raw, (and so is what they roast) and after that, they parboil it, then take it out with the Liquor, and then put in the Flesh again, with *Roots* or *Cabbage*, or what the Season doth afford, cut small, together with a little *Pepper*, *Herbs* and *Onions*; after which they pour in a small quantity of the Liquor again, and stew it so long, that it is no very hard matter to shake the Flesh off the Bones; this they call by the Name of *Terbeea*.[63] The *Sauce* for it is an *Egg* beaten with the Juice of a *Lemon*.

With the remainder of the before-mentioned Liquor they make a Dish which they call *Pillou*.[64] They take two Measures of this, and one of *Rice*, or

---

[59] *Shopboard*: a platform on which tailors sit when working.  [60] *Napkin*: tablecloth.

[61] *Be, isme allah*: Arabic, *bi-ism Allāh, bismillāh*, "In the name of God", a phrase found several times in Muslim daily prayers, and used before beginning many activities including eating.

[62] *Psalmist*: a reference to *Psalms*, chapter 10, verse 4: "The wicked, through the pride of his countenance, will not seek after God: God is not in all his thoughts."

[63] *Terbeea*: modern Turkish, *terbiye*, whose basic meaning is education or upbringing (from Arabic, *tarbiyah*), but the word was also used in Ottoman times to mean seasoning or sauce for food.

[64] *Pillou*: modern Turkish, *pilav* (from the Persian); rice cooked with spices and usually mixed with meat and/or vegetables.

*Burgoe,*[65] i.e. Wheat boil'd, dry'd, and ground not very small.

[p. 23] When the Liquor boils, the *Rice* being wash'd, or the *Burgoe* unwash'd, is put into the Pot; in a little time the Liquor is soked [*sic*] up, and the Pot taken off the Fire. They then melt some *Butter* to an *Oil*, and pour it into the Pot, and keep it close covered; after which they take out the *Rice* or *Burgoe* with a Spoon into a Dish, and form it in the Shape of a *Sugar-Loaf*, shaking *Pepper* over it. The *Butter* should be pretty much seen in the Dish around the *Rice*.

Another Dish they call *Dolmah*, of which there are divers Sorts, as *Sueoane Dolmah,*[66] i.e. *Onion Dolmah*; for *Dolmah* signifies to fill. They take large *Onions*, skin them, and cut both Ends; then cut them half way in by the side, and take out the several Skins or Parts, filling them with their Meat, which is minced very small, putting a little *Rice*, *Pepper*, and *Salt* mix'd together. The Bones they put in the Bottom of the Pot, next stew the *Onions* so filled, then a little Water not covering the *Onions*, and so let it stew. They also wrap such minced Flesh in *Vine Leaves*, and then 'tis called *Yoprock Dolmah;*[67] the Name of this Leaf is *Yoprock*. Sometimes it is done with *Cabbage Leaves*, which they call *Lauhna Dolmah.*[68] The *Sauce* for this is only *Lemon*.

As for *rost* [*sic*] Meat, they cut the Flesh into small Pieces, stick three, or four of them upon an Iron Skewer, and so set them
[p. 24] before the Fire; at the Cooks Shops, the Pieces are no bigger than the *Bowl* of a *Pipe*. This is called *Cobbob.*[69]

Sometimes, when they have minced the Meat as above without *Rice*, they make it into little Cakes, and *fry* them in a Pan with *Butter*, to which they give the Name of *Keufta.*[70] The *Sauce* is *Onions* sliced thin, and fry'd in *Vinegar*, and so poured upon it.

What they call *Mackaroon*[71] is some *Paste* made only with Flour, and Water, of which they take a Bit as big as a *Bean*, and put it on the middle of a Wire, rolling it between their Hands till it be two or three Inches long,

---

[65] *Burgoe*: modern Turkish, *bulgur*; English, bulghur.

[66] *Sueoane Dolmah*: modern Turkish, *soğan dolması*, or stuffed onion.

[67] *Yoprock Dolmah*: in modern Turkish, *yaprak* is a leaf; properly speaking a vine leaf is *asma yaprağı*.

[68] *Laubna Dolmah*: modern Turkish, *lahana dolması*.

[69] *Cobbob*: modern Turkish (and English), *kebab*.

[70] *Keufta*: modern Turkish, *köfte*.

[71] *Mackaroon*: macaroni.

and no bigger than the small End of a *Tobacco-Pipe*; then boil it in Water with three or four whole *Onions*, and when in the Dish, mix it with *grated Cheese*, and pour *Butter* upon it, as above.

I could enlarge here upon the several sorts of their Victuals, and their manner of *Cookery*, which I am well acquainted with; but this would eat up too great a part of my little Book. As they use no Knives or Forks at Table, so neither do they Trenchers, or Plates; for their Tables serve instead of them. They usually eat quick, and having done, every one returns Thanks, saying *el ham do lillali*;[72] i.e. *Thanks be to God*.

The Table being removed, (before they rise) a Slave, or Servant, who stands attending on them with a Cup of Water to give
[p. 25] them drink, steps into the middle with a Bason, or Copper-pot of Water, (somewhat like a Coffee-pot) and a little Soap, and lets the Water run upon their Hands one after another, in order as they sit; and they also wash their Mouths after Eating.

As for their *Drink*, 'tis well known that *Wine* is forbidden by the *Mahometan* Law, (and so is *Swines-Flesh*) and *Beer* and *Cyder* they are altogether Strangers to; so that their common Drink is Water; except at some certain Times they make a *Sherbet* with Water and Sugar. They are great Coffee-drinkers, but Coffee is not to quench Thirst. However, tho' *Wine* be forbidden, there is no Punishment for those who offend in this Respect; and yet none use to drink it but the *Rascality*.[73] For a Person of Figure and Reputation will by no means drink *Wine*, because it is contrary to his Principles, and so is a Scandal to his Reputation. And as for such as take to drink it, they generally do it so immoderately, that they hardly leave off till they are *drunk*, and then they are extreamly [*sic*] abusive, and quarrelsome, sometimes even to Murder: For they are no *good-natured* Drunkards, as some among us are said to be; though I am of Opinion they would be much *better natured* if they were not to be *drunk* at all.

When their Camps are setting forth, (of which in the next *Chapter*) then especially
[p. 26] are the *Soldiery* apt to drink, and are abominably rude, insomuch that it is very dangerous for *Women* to walk in any By-place, but more for *Boys*; for they are extremely given to *Sodomy*: and therefore Care is taken

---

[72] *el ham do lillali*: Arabic, *al-ḥamdu lillāh*, or "Praise be to God", a phrase used after ending many activities including eating.
[73] *Rascality*: rabble.

that it be cried about the Town, *That all People take care of their Wives, and Children.* And yet this horrible Sin of *Sodomy* is so far from being punish'd amongst them, that it is part of their ordinary Discourse to boast of their detestable Actions of that kind. 'Tis common for Men there to fall in Love with Boys, as 'tis here in *England* to be in Love with Women: And I have seen many, when they have been drunk, give themselves deep Gashes on their Arms with a Knife, saying, *'Tis for the* Love *they bear to such a* Boy. There are many so addicted to this prodigious Sin, that they *loath the Natural Use of the Woman;* (such as the Apostle inveighs against, *Rom.* i, 27).[74] And I *assure* you, That I have seen several who have had their Arms *full* of great Cuts, as so many Tokens of their Love (or rather worse than *bestial Lust*) to such their *Catamites.* But this being so *inhumane,* and *unnatural* a thing, I profess I am asham'd to enlarge further upon it, as I could: But what I could say on this Subject must needs be *disgustful* to every modest, and *christian* Reader; and therefore, I think, I am obliged to forbear: Only I crave leave to make this

[p. 27] *Reflection,* viz. "*That* Intemperance *in Drinking hurries Men on to the worst of Vices; and tho' the Inclination of these* hot *People, and the* Countenance *which is given to such Crimes, are two great Incentives; yet, avoiding* Intemperance, *they would be* less *liable to them.*"

As I have observ'd, when their *Camps* are setting out, it is a sort of *licentious* time, and a Rendezvous of all Wickedness imaginable; a true *Account* of the Order, and Management of these therefore I will now give you, in the following *Chapter.*

---

[74] *Epistle to the Romans,* chapter 1, verse 28: "And likewise also the men, leaving the natural use of the woman, burned in their lust one toward another; men with men working that which is unseemly, and receiving in themselves that recompence of their error which was meet."

## CHAP. IV.

*An Account of the* Algerine Camps, *with the Reason of them. Of the* Cabyles, *a rugged People, who dwell in the* Mountains.

THE *Algerines*, in the Month of *April*, have *three* several *Camps* go forth; one to the *East*, another to the *West*, and a third to the *South*; of which the *first* is the greatest, and consists of about an Hundred Tents, each Tent containing *twenty* men. The *Western* Camp consists of about *seventy* or *eighty* the like Tents; and the *Southern* Camp but of *fifteen*. Each of these Divisions [p. 28] hath a *Bay*, or General, who gives so many Thousand *Pieces of Eight* Monthly for his Place to the *Dey*, or *Governour* of *Algier*; besides which, he is to defray the whole Cost, and Charges of the *Camp*, to make due Provision of Bread, Butter, Oil, and Wheat to make *Burgu*, as also Flesh for them twice a Week, and Barley for the Horses. It is to be observed, that every Tent have their *Allowance*, which is far *more* than they can dispense with: And therefore, they have the liberty to take what they think will serve them, and the rest in Money, which they divide among themselves.

The *Bay's* Tent is pitch'd in the *middle* of the *Camp*, and all the others are pitch'd so *close* together that an Horse cannot pass; and this is so order'd, that there may be but *one* Entrance into the *Camp*, which is directly toward the Door of the *Bay's* Tent, (I suppose for the better Security, and also) to signify that *that* way they are to take, upon their next Removal, to which the Door of the *Bay's* Tent points. Each *Bay* may have, as I conjecture, about Four or Five Hundred Miles in his Circuit, excepting him that leads the *Southern* Camp, for the Country is not far Inhabited to the *Southward*. Every Tent hath sixteen *Soldiers*, one *Oscha*,[75] or *Cook*, one *Otha Bashe*,[76] or *Sergeant*, one *Beulick Bashe*,[77] who is *above* the
[p. 29] *Sergeant*, or Head of a *Company*, (what we call a *Captain*) and one *Vekil-harg*,[78] or *Steward*, (under the *Otha-Bashe*) who looks after the Provision; which amounts, as I said before, to the Complement of *twenty* Men to every Tent.

At the end of *seven* Years, an *Otha-Bashe* is preferr'd to be a *Beulick-Bashe*, and so by degrees to an higher Office, till he comes to be an *Aga*, or *Colonel*.

---

[75] *Oscha*: modern Turkish, *aşçı*.  [76] *Otha Bashe*: modern Turkish, *odabaşı*.
[77] *Beulick Bashe*: modern Turkish, *bölükbaşı*.  [78] *Vekil-harg*: modern Turkish, *vekilharc*.

And with a great deal of Splendor he remains in *that* Post for the space of two Months; after which, he is not obliged to do any *Service* at all, but receives his Pay, which is duly brought to him every two Months. So that Offices of this Nature are conferr'd, without *respect of Persons*, in a constant *Order*.

Each Tent hath, moreover, three or four Horses, and two or three Camels, to carry the Provision, and Baggage; and three or four Servants are allowed to drive and look after these Beasts. The *Vekil-harg*, or *Steward* of every Tent, hath an Horse to himself, which carries the Tent. These *Stewards* go before, with the Servants, and Baggage, and after them go the *Cooks*, with their Horses, *viz.* each *Cook* an Horse, carrying the *Utensils*, and other things belonging to his Profession; which are a very good Burden. The *Cooks* go in *order*, one close after another, but always on *foot*, being never permitted to ride on their Horses, because
[p. 30] they have a sufficient Burden without them.

When they come to the place where they intend to *pitch*, as soon as the *Bay's* Tent is mounted, every *Cook*, with his respective *Steward*, mount their Tents all at once. This being done, the *Cook* of every Tent rides with all convenient speed, to fetch Water in his *Goatskins* to dress Victuals for the *Soldiers*, and for them to drink.

The *Servants* belonging to each Tent make all the speed they can to get ready *Provender*, &c. for the Horses. And the *Steward* is no less busy to put all things in order, before the *Soldiers* arrive: So that when these come to their Tents, they find all things ready, and have nothing to do but to take off their *Accoutrements*, clean their Arms from the Dust, and dispose of them into their proper Places, and then, if it so please them, to spread their Bedding on the Mats, and so lie down to take their Repose, till the *Steward* awakes them to eat; insomuch that I am apt to believe, no *Soldiers* in the whole World take *less Pains*, and live *more at Ease*, than they do.

In their *March* they move but *two* in a Breast, each Rank keeping at a considerable distance; so that a *Thousand* Men make a great *Shew* [*sic*], and a very long *Train*. The *Cayah-Beulick*,[79] or *Lieutenant*, rides in the Van of the Army, with two *Hoages*,[80] or
[p. 31] *Clerks*, each of them bearing a *Flag*. The *Sergeants* follow on foot:

---

[79] *Cayah-Beulick*: modern Turkish, *kâhya bölük*; *kethüda* is often used instead of *kâhya*.
[80] *Hoages*: modern Turkish, *hoca*, from the Persian: *khvājah*.

133

And then comes the *Aga*; and him follows the *Bay* with Trumpets, Drums, Pipes, Kettle-Drums, and such-like Warlike Musick. They have a pretty odd way of *beating* their Drums, *viz.* The *Drummer* beats with a Drum-stick knobb'd at the end in his Right-hand, upon the *Head* of the Drum; and the *bottom* of it, he at the same time strikes with a small Wand, which he holds in his *Left-hand*.

The *Bay* is accompanied with his *Spahyes*,[81] or Troopers, who generally wear a Crimson-Cloak, woven all in one Piece; so that there is no need of a *Taylor* to cut, or shape it, only a little joining together under the Chin, and on the Breast; it hath a Cape to cover the Head in Case of Rain. But some of their Cloaks are white. On their Heads they have Turbants[82] of red Silk Sashes. Every *Trooper* hath a Pack-horse to carry his Bedding, Clothes, and all Necessaries, with his Servant riding thereon. And every *Soldier* is very *neat* in keeping his Arms, and will not suffer the least Spot to be upon them.

In their March they are attended with several *Sacces*,[83] or *Water-Carriers*, to supply them with Water, which every *Soldier* takes at his pleasure with a copper Dish, which he hath hanging at his side for that purpose: And as soon as the Water is spent, the *Carriers* ride hastily for more.

[p. 32]

They do not travel very *hard*, for they march, in a Day, not above *eight*, *ten*, or *twelve Miles*; unless it be at the season of their *returning* Home, and then they travel from *Morning* to *Night*.

The *Eastern* Camp makes its Return from a Town call'd *Constantine*, about Fourteen Days Journey from *Algier*, after having kept out about *six* Months. The *Western* Camp stays out about *four*, and the *Southern* about *three* Months. And as soon as ever the very Day of their Expedition is *expired*, the *Soldiers* will return home in spight [*sic*] of the *Bay*'s Commands, or Menaces, whether the Business and Design of it be *effected* or no. The Reason and Intent of the *Algerines* setting forth these *Camps*, is to *overawe* the *Moors*, and to cause them to hasten in their Tribute to the *Bay*; which whether they do or no, I say, the *Soldiers* will not stay in the *Camp* beyond their *stated* time.

And now, as I did in the *Second Chapter* acquaint my Country-men with the *Cowardice* of the *Algerines* at Sea, (*of which really Advantage may be made by*

---

[81] *Spahyes*: modern Turkish, *sipahi*.   [82] *Turbants*: turbans.
[83] *Sacces*: modern Turkish, *saka*, from Arabic, *saqqā'*.

*those who shall at any time happen to be attack'd by them,*) so I will here give you a little Account of their *Valour* by *Land*, which is much like that at *Sea*.

They know very well, that the *Moors*, their *Tributaries*, are but of *small* Courage, and are commonly for a *running* Fight: But if they happen to *stand*, the *Turks* are easily

[p. 33] daunted. But it seldom happens that the *Moors* keep their Ground, except it be some sort of them, *viz. Cabyls*,[84] who live in Mountains, and are a very rugged sort of People, and care not to pay the *Tribute* demanded of them by the *Bay*: At which he is enraged, and oftentimes gives Toleration to the *Soldiers* to do what Mischief they can to them, to take their *Cattle, Persons, Wives,* and *Children,* and gratify their base Lusts as they please; and also to destroy their Corn, burn their Houses, and ruine their Vineyards, if in their power so to do. These *Cabyls* dwell in small Houses, but little better than *Hogsties*; and the *Moors* who live in the Plains, dwell in Tents of Hair-Cloth.

I do not wonder to see the Cruelty, and Barbarity they often use towards poor *Christians*, whilst they are so inhumane to those of the *Mahometan* Religion with themselves, as to destroy them and theirs for a *small* matter. For frequently the Cause of falling out between the *Moors* and the *Bay* is very *trivial*; it may be, for not paying in full to *two* or *three* Shillings; or something as *inconsiderable*. But after all their Resistance, and Obstinacy, the *Moors* are (most commonly) so distressed by Numbers, that they are forced to come, and submit themselves to the *Bay*, paying the full Sum demanded, to petition for their Wives and Children, and pay dearly for their *Ruggedness*.

[p. 34]

Many of these *Moors* never knew what a *Christian* is. I have travell'd *Eastward* and *Westward*, to the utmost Bounds of their Territories; and I remember, when I was journeying with my *Patroon* from *Bona*, which is some Hundreds of Miles *Eastward* of *Algier*, we did every Night quarter in the *Moors* Tents; and they would, Men, Women, and Children, flock to see me; and I was much *admired* by them for having flaxen Hair, and being of a ruddy Complexion. I heard some of them say, *Behold, what a pretty* Maid *it is!* Others said *I never saw a* Nazarene (*i.e.* a Christian) *before. I thought they had been* (said some) *like unto* Hallewfs[85] (*or* Swine) *but I see now that they are* Benn Adam,[86] (*or* Children of Men).

The *Moors* are a People much given to *Sloth*, for after *Sowing time* they

---

[84] *Cabyls*: Berbers.   [85] *Hallewfs*: Arabic, ḥallūf.   [86] *Benn Adam*: Arabic, Banū Ādam.

have little to do, nor do they betake themselves to any thing, but only wait for the *Harvest*; at which Time their Corn being cut, and brought all together, they immediately tread it, and winnow it, and then put it into great Pits in the open Field. The Mouth of these *Mutmors*,[87] or Pits, is but small, but *within* the Cavity is much greater; being dug all round, and of some considerable depth: They put Straw into the bottom, and round by the sides of those Pits, and then they put in their Corn, and so cover it over with Earth laid on some sticks, and Straw

[p. 35] upon that, on the Mouths of them, which they cause to be even with the Surface of the Ground; so that by this means their Corn is preserv'd when they are put to flight by the *Bay*, but much damnified,[88] being kept in so damp a Place, instead of a Barn.

They never *dress* or *dung* their Ground, as we do, and yet they have great Plenty; for it is a common thing to see ten, sometimes fifteen, yea, twenty Stalks, shoot up together: nay, I have heard told of sixty, or more, which is *wonderful!* This Plenty is of *Wheat* and *Barley*, for *Rye* and *Oats* they have none; and truly they have *no need* of them, for as many of *our* Country People feed on *Rye*, so *they* feed on *Barley*, and most of their *Wheat* they sell in *Towns*, and Markets, to raise the Money exacted of them by the *Turks*. And, as *our* Horses are fed with *Oats*, so *theirs* with *Barley*.

These *Moors* are so very *lazy*, that they make their *Wives* saddle their Horses while they go to ease themselves, which they are asham'd to do in a *plain and open Place*, and therefore go a pretty way off, accounting it a great piece of Rudeness to do it in the sight of another. As for their *Wives*, they are, indeed, little better than *Slaves*; for they do not only what is properly Women's Work, but grind *all the Corn* us'd in the House, and fetch *all the Wood and Water* on their backs, and oftentimes at a considerable

[p. 36] distance. They also bake their Bread *daily*, on *earthen Pans*, and *milk their Kine*,[89] and do all other Things of the like Nature, that are to be done. And notwithstanding all this, if they have any *vacant* time in the Day, they imploy [*sic*] it in grinding of Corn; which they do with such *chearfulness* and *singing*, that I have often admired how they could go through so much Work without *complaining*, much more, how they could do it with so much Pleasure.

The Women are not permitted to eat at the Table with their Husbands, but must take what they are pleas'd to leave them. Their Fare is generally

---

[87] *Mutmors*: Arabic, *maṭmūrah*.    [88] *damnified*: damaged.    [89] *Kine*: cows.

*Bread* and *Milk*, and *Cuska seu*,[90] which is made of Meal and Water. They take a little Meal, and sprinkle Water on it in a broad wooden Platter, and then stir it about with the Palm of their Hand till it becomes as small Seeds or *Gunpowder*, when they have done this, they put it into a Cullender, which they set on the Mouth of the Pot that is boiling on the Fire with Victuals &c. In a little Time the Steam gets up thro' the *Cuska seu* (in the Cullender) and it becomes all together of a *lump*, then they turn it out into a Platter, and beat it abroad, and so mix it with *Butter*. After this they turn out of the Pot that is boiling, the Broth, &c. upon the *Cuska seu*, and almost cover it with the Liquor, which in a little time it soaks up, and then they
[p. 37] eat it with their Hands, making use of no Spoons, *i.e.* in the Country, amongst the *Boors*. Their Fare therefore being so *mean*, and yet the Women not being suffer'd to partake of it with their *Husbands*, one would think it should be but a small Encouragement to *Marriage*: I am perswaded *our Country Dames* would esteem it so. This leads me to give some Account of the *Algerines* way of *Marriage*, which I shall therefore do in the *next Chapter*.

---

[90] *Cuska seu*: couscous.

## CHAP. V.

*Of the* Algerines *way of* Marriage; *and the great* Lamentation *the* Women *make for their dead Husbands. Also their way of* teaching Children. *And of the ill Usage I received from* Mustapha *my first* Patroon, &c.

THERE is no such Privilege allowed among the *Turks* as *Wooing* or *Courting* their *Mistresses*; nay, a Man is not permitted to speak one Word to her whom he intends to make his *Spouse*, nor to have the least glimpse or sight of her, till just before such time as he is to go to the *Nuptial Bed* with her.

[p. 38]

The *Father* of the *Damsel* usually makes up the *Match*; tho' there are some Persons who make it their Business to be *Match-makers* (a dangerous Employment in *Europe* and too often a Curse-procurer:) When Matters are adjusted, and every Thing agreed upon, the Man to be married, together with some of his intended Wife's Relations, goes to the *Kadee*,[91] i.e. *Judge*, or *Magistrate*, and before him draws up some small Instrument in writing, wherein he promiseth to pay so much to his Wife, which shall be for her *Sadock*,[92] or *Jointure*; and there's an end of the *Matrimony*, without any further Ceremony or Formality, as of, *I* John *take thee* Joan, &c. The Father of the *Damsel* promiseth little or nothing, but, it may be, will set forth his Daughter with a few fine *Clothes* and *Bedding*, or the like, and that's all.

The time being come when they are to *bed* together, they usually make a little *Feast*, and invite their Friends, who are to depart (*i.e.* the Men) immediately after eating their Meat; but the Women tarry till they see the *Bride-folks* in *Bed*. After the Entertainment is over, the *Bridegroom* is put into the Chamber alone with a Candle, and after a little time the *Bride* is put in to him, and the Chamber-door made fast; the Women mean while waiting without the Door.

[p. 39]

Upon Notice given they enter the Room, and if the *Bride* proves as was expected, express a great deal of Joy, with loud Singing, that all the

---

[91] *Kadee*: modern Turkish, *kadi* or *cadi*, from Arabic, *qāḍī*.
[92] *Sadock*: Arabic, *ṣadāq* or *ṣidāq*, which means wedding gift.

Neighbourhood can hear it. If the Man and Wife agree together in love, the before mentioned *Sadock* is not at all required, because there is no occasion for it: but if Things happen ill, a *Divorce* commonly ensues, and then the Man is liable to pay the Woman what was the *original Agreement*, and maintain such Children as are begotten by him during the Time of their *Cohabitation.*

The Parties being thus *divorc'd*, they are both free to *marry* again, whom and when they please; and 'tis a Thing very common amongst them so to do; for I have known many Instances of it.

It hath been reported, That a *Mahometan* may have as many Wives as he pleaseth, tho', if I mistake not, the Number may not exceed *four*; but there is not one in a *Thousand* hath more than *one*, except it be in the Country, where some *here* and *there* may have *two*; yet I never knew but *one* which had so many as *three.*

The *Women* (in the *Country* especially) do for the most part, manifest a great deal of Sorrow for their deceased Relations; especially for their *Husbands. Some*, if they can, will get their Garments dy'd *black*, but at least they will be sure to take a little Oil or Grease,
[p. 40] and Soot, and therewith *smut*[93] their Faces almost all over, and make most *hideous* Cries and Lamentations. The neighbouring Women usually come and condole, it may be, twenty or thirty of them together; who all place themselves round the Woman that hath lost her Relation, making so prodigious a Noise, as may be heard sometimes near half a Mile off; all the while scratching their Faces with their Nails till they make the *Blood run down their Cheeks.*

Thus they continue to do half an Hour, and more, at a time, *every Day*, for a considerable space; and afterwards *once a Week*, or as the Fit shall take the *Widow*; and thus in and out, it may be, for a *whole Year.*

The Method of the *Mahometans* Burials is thus, They carry the Corpse upon a Bier, the Head foremost, going along a good Pace, and some singing before it; when they come to a *certain* Place without the *Gate*, they pitch (or rest) the Corpse, and some who accompany it perform two *Erkaets*,[94] or *Prayers.* After this they take up the Corpse again, and go on to the Grave, which is dug pretty broad at the Bottom, but narrow at the Top, just fit to

---

[93] *Smut*: blacken.
[94] *Erkaets*: modern Turkish, *rek'at*, from Arabic, *rak'ah* (plural: *raka'āt*), specifically the bodily positions adopted during the Muslim prayer ritual.

put in the Corpse, which they always lay with the Head towards the *Kebla*,[95] or *Mecca*. They cover the Body with broad Stones, and then throw in the Earth. Some poor People do usually attend at the Grave, reciting
**[p. 41]** something which they have got by heart. This they do, though they are not hired, for the sake of a piece of Bread-cake, and a handful of Figs, which it is common to distribute at such times.

As for the Burial of *Christian* Slaves, I was informed, that formerly they would not permit such to be interr'd, but threw their dead Bodies into the Sea. The King of *Spain* being moved at this, purchased a Piece of Ground for a Burial-place for *Christian* Slaves, where they are buried to this Day. 'Tis without *Bab el wait*,[96] or, the *western* Gate, adjoining to the *Jews* Burying-place, within a Stone's cast of their own, *viz*. the *Algerines*, a sandy Place close to the Sea.

All the Charges a *Patroon* is at in burying his Slave, is to hire four Slaves, for about six Pence a–piece, giving them also a Blanket, or some such–like old Thing, to wrap him up in, and then he leaves it wholly to them. In a Time of the *Plague*, when several die in a Day, it is common to carry two at once upon a Bier, and throw them into the same Pit.

The Slaves are buried very soon after Death hath done his Office; nay, sometimes 'tis to be feared, *before*. I have been told of one, who, when he was carrying along to be interr'd, rose up on the Bier, to the Astonishment of the Bearers, and was
**[p. 42]** brought back again to his *Patroon's* House, where he lived many Years after.

In the *Country*, not one among an Hundred wears any *Shoes*, but they generally go bare-foot and bare-leg'd. The Men wear neither *Shirts* nor *Drawers*, and but few of them any thing on their Heads; only a *Flannel* wrapt about their Bodies: Some of the better sort, indeed, have something like a *Cloak* about them.

And as for the *Women*, they wear a piece of *Flannel* before, down half way the Leg, and so behind, pinning the two ends on their Shoulders, with Skewers, or little Iron Pins; and they have a woollen Rope about their Middle.

---

[95] *Kebla*: modern Turkish, *kıble*, from Arabic, *qiblah*, which is the direction of Mecca towards which Muslims turn when praying.

[96] *Bab el wait*: now known as Bab El Oued, from the Arabic, Bāb al-Wādī, Gate of the Valley or Stream.

They have great Plenty of Camels and Sheep, as well as Corn; tho' (as I hinted) they bestow no Dressing at all.

As for their *Children*, when young, they take no Pains to bring them to go; but leave them to *crawl* about, till they can walk of themselves. They teach them to *swear* by their *Maker* as soon as they can speak. The *Female-sex* are seldom taught to read.

The compendious[97] Method which they (*i.e.* the *Moors*) take to teach their *Children* to *read* and *write*, is this, *viz.* every one hath a thin Board of *Oak*, scower'd white, to write on: their *Ink* is commonly a little burnt *Wool*, mix'd with *Water*, and their

[p. 43] *Pen* is made of a *Cane*; for they hold it to be unlawful to write with a *Quill*, as *Christians* do. The *Scholar* being thus furnish'd, after some few Directions, the *Master speaks* the *Boys* Lesson, which is some of the *Alcoran*,[98] and the *Boy* writes it; and having written it, is not only bound to *read* it, but to *learn* it without Book. And thus he is to do *every* Day, till he hath retain'd a *considerable Part* of the *Alcoran* in his Memory. The *Boy* having learn'd his *Day's Lesson*, rubs it out, and then whitens his Table again, to write down the *next* Day's Lesson on.

I have known it to be a common thing ("*Though I must speak it with shame, to consider how the* Holy Bible, *the* Heavenly Oracles, *the* Word *by which we must be judged at the* last Day, *is slighted and neglected among us*") for *Traders* and *Shop-keepers*, and such as have *more* leisure than many others have, to set themselves a *daily* Task, to recite so much of the *Alcoran* without Book, as in *thirty* Days to take up the whole: and *this* many continue to do all their Life-time, believing that they *merit* much by it. ("*I wish that* Christians *were as diligent in studying the* Holy Scriptures, *the* Law *and the* Gospel, *wherein we have eternal Life, as those* Infidels *are, in poring upon that* Legend of Falsities, *and abominable Follies and Absurdities.*") At the *end* of every time they read, in order to remember

[p. 44] *such* a part of the *Alcoran*, they hold up their two Hands at a little distance from their Face, say some short Prayer, begging a *Blessing* on what they have done, then smooth down their Face with their Hands, and so much for that time. This many do in their Youth, and retain what they read to their *dying Day*. They are (for the greater part) *illiterate*, and yet value Reading at an *high* Rate; insomuch, that many, to my knowledge, have

---

[97] *compendious*: concise, economical.
[98] *Alcoran*: al-Qur'ān.

begun their *Elif, Be, Te*,[99] i.e. as I may say, their *A. B. C.* when they have had grey Hairs; and I have heard several say, *Ocue mok billei dem!*[100] i.e. *Oh! that I could but read!* lamenting much the squandering of their Youth.

The Pronunciation of *Arabick* is very difficult, for every Letter must have its *proper* Sound. Some are *Gutturals*, and must be pronounced from the *Roof* of the Mouth, and sometimes the Mouth must be brought *awry* to pronounce the word aright: All these Things, likewise, the *Scholar* must give an Account of to his *Master*.

They have a very great *Veneration* for their *Books*, but most especially for the *Alcoran*, which they call *Calam allah*,[101] (*i.e.* to say) the *Word of God*; and on the Cover of it there is written (commonly in golden Letters) *la ta Messa ha billa Metah herat*,[102] i.e. *Touch not without being clean*, or *being wash'd*. [[Of their *cleansing* I shall speak hereafter.]]

[p. 45] They will never suffer the *Alcoran* to touch the *Ground*, if they can help it; and if it chance at any time to fall, they check themselves for it, and with *haste* and *concern* recover it again, *kiss* it, and put it to their *Forehead* in token of *profound* Respect. When they hold it in their Hands, they'll never let it be below their *middle*, accounting it too *worthy* to be touch'd by any of the *lower* parts.

If they are going a Journey, and carry it with them, as usually they do, they will be sure to secure it well in a *Searcloth*,[103] and in a *Cloth-bag*, hanging it under their Arm-pits. And if at any time they have Occasion to *go to Stool*, or *make Water*, they must take it off, and lay it at a distance from them, at least one fathom,[104] and then wash before they take it in hand again; or if they cannot come by any Water, then they must *wipe* as clean they can, till Water may conveniently be had (or else it suffices to take *Abdes*[105] upon a *Stone*, (which I call an *imaginary Abdes*) i.e. smooth their Hands over a Stone two or three times, and rub them one with the other, as if they were washing them with Water. (The like *Abdes* sufficeth when any are *sickly*, so that to use *Water* might endanger their Life.) And after they have so wip'd, it is *Gaise*,[106] i.e. *Lawful* to take the Book in hand again: But they are still uneasy,

---

[99] *Elif, Be, Te*: Arabic, Alif, Bā', Tā', the first three letters of the Arabic alphabet.

[100] *Ocue mok billei dem*: modern Turkish, Okumak bileydim.

[101] *Calam allah*: Arabic, *kalām Allāh*.

[102] *La ta Messa ha bila Metah herat*: Arabic, Lā tamasshā bilā muṭahharāt.

[103] *Searcloth*: waxed (i.e. waterproof) cloth.   [104] *fathom*: six feet.

[105] *Abdes*: modern Turkish, *aptes*, from the Persian, *ābdast*, meaning ritual ablution.

[106] *Gaise*: Arabic, *jā'iz*.

till they come to Water. They think

[p. 46] they cannot prize the *Alcoran* enough, and that there cannot be *too much* Care in preserving it. Nay, I have known many that could not read *one* tittle of it, to carry some part of it always about them, esteeming it as a *Charm* to preserve them from Hurt, and Danger. And if any Mishap do notwithstanding befal [sic] them, they will rather impute it to their *own* Demerit, than to any *Defect* of Virtue in the part of the *Alcoran*.

They have so *great* an Esteem for *this Book*, that they'll not suffer a *scrip* of clean Paper to lie on the Ground, but take it up, and *kiss* it, and then put it into some Hole or Cranny or other, because on such the Name of *God* is, or may be written. I have heard them oftentimes condemn the *Christians* for the little regard they have to their *Books*: For, say they, *you'll use the Paper of them to* burn, *or* light your Pipes, *or to put to the vilest Uses*.

They have a great Veneration for *Idiots*, accounting them no less than inspired; and the reason is, because *Mahomet*, when he devoted himself to a solitary Life in the Cave near *Mecca*, by much Fasting, and an austere Way of living, greatly impair'd his Health, so that he began to talk, and behave himself like a *Natural*.[107]

The *Correction* they give *Scholars*, or *Children* at Work, is *beating them* on the *bare Feet*; and the Punishment inflicted on *Soldiers*,

[p. 47] is *beating them* on the *Buttocks*, and this frequently with such Severity, tho' the Crime be not very great, as to make the *Blood* come out through their Drawers; and sometimes the Flesh *mortifies*[108] thereupon, so that they must have some Part cut off in order to a cure. If they are so *rigorous*, and *severe* among *themselves*, well may you think what Cruelty they exercise towards the poor *Captives!*

Within eight and forty Hours after I was sold, I *tasted* of their *Barbarity*; for I had my tender Feet tied up, and beaten twenty, or thirty Blows for a *beginning*: And thus was I beat for a *considerable* time, every two or three Days, besides Blows now and then, *forty, fifty, sixty*, at a time. My *Executioner* would fill his Pipe, and then give me *ten*, or *twenty* Blows, then stop, and smoak his Pipe for a while, and then he would at me again, and when weary stop again; and *thus cruelly* would he handle me till his Pipe was out. At other times he would hang me up *Neck and Heels*, and then beat me *miserably*. Sometimes he would hang me up by the *Arm-pits*, beating me all over my

---

[107] *Natural*: simpleton.   [108] *mortifies*: becomes gangrenous.

Body. And oftentimes *hot Brine* was order'd for me to put my Feet in, after they were sore with beating; which made them smart exceedingly, and put me to *intolerable* Pain. Sometimes I have been beaten on my Feet *so long*, and *cruelly*, that the *Blood* hath ran down to

[p. 48] the Ground. I have given an Account in another *Chapter*, of the *Cruelties* I suffered, and therefore I shall only tell you for the present, that I have oftentimes been beaten by my *Patroon* so *violently*, that I have not been able to *sit* for a considerable time.

I was Sold *three times*; my first *Patroon* was call'd *Mustapha*, the second *Ibrahim*, and the third *Eumer* [Omar]: But I must needs acknowledge, that with my *last Patroon* I lived very comfortably. But this was not *Satisfaction*; I long'd still to be gone out of this Country. And my chief Reason was, *That I might worship God as I ought.* As for the *Mahometan* Worship I was persuaded it could not be agreeable to his Will: And I suppose every one must agree with me herein, when they have read the *Account* I give of it in the next *Chapter*.

[p. 49]

## CHAP. VI.

*Of the* Mahometan *Faith. The Preparation they make before they go to their* Worship *in their* Mosques: *And the Manner of their* Worship *there. Of their* Hammams, *or Bathing-Houses.* The Ramadan *Fast,* &c.

Though a strict *Outward* Devotion be found amongst the *Mahometans*, yet almost all manner of *Wickedness*, and *Immorality* (except *Murder*, and *Theft*) are left unpunish'd. But as for those who are Religious *in their way*, they'll not live in the Neglect of performing their *Salah* or *Nomas*, i.e. their *Worship*★, might they gain ever so much.[109] [[★Salah *is the* Arabick, *and* Nomas *the* Turkish *Word for their* Worship, *or* Devotion.]] Nay there are some among them *so* zealous, that after they are reformed from their former Extravagancies, they labour to *make up* what they have *run back*[110] in the time of Youth by their neglect of *Salah*, and in order to fetch up their *Arrears*, they'll be out of their Beds an Hour or two before Day, and having *prepar'd* themselves, will be engag'd in their *Devotion* till they are quite *tired*.

[p. 50]

I very well remember my last *Patroon*, who was an ancient Man, would spend many Mornings in this Exercise. Whilst I was a-bed he would be up, and having *wash'd* himself *as usual*, would be at his *Devotion*. I ask'd him the Reason of it. He told me, When he was young he lived in the Omission of his Duty; for as for *Nomas*, he paid no Regard to it; but now he would endeavour to make amends for all past Neglects.

Their *Salah* is to be performed *five* times every Day, at *Mosque*, or *Church*, unless in case of extraordinary Business or Hinderance [*sic*]; and even then, though they may be prevented at the set *Times*, yet they are not wholly excused from the Performance of it, but are obliged to do it afterwards, either in the *Mosques*, or some other convenient Place.

The *stated* Times of *publick* Worship are, *First*, In the Morning when *the Day-light is broke*, before the Candles are out, be it Winter or Summer; this is called *Sobboh-Nomas*.[111] The *second* Performance of *Salah*, is near about

---

[109] *Salah*: Arabic, *ṣalāh. Nomas*: modern Turkish, *namaz*.    [110] *run back*: omitted.

[111] *Sobboh-Nomas*: modern Turkish, *subh namazı*; Arabic, *ṣalāt al-fajr*, the dawn prayer.

*two* of the *Clock* in the Afternoon; which is call'd *Eulea Nomas.*[112] The *third* is about *four* of the *Clock*, call'd *Ekinde Nomas.*[113] The *fourth* is just after *Candle-lighting*, call'd *Acsham Nomas.*[114] And the *last*, about *an Hour and half after Night*, called *Gega*, or *El-Asheea Nomas.*[115]

[p. 51]

In *all* these times of *Service* they differ as to the *Number* of their *Devotions* (which are all taken out of the *Alcoran*) and also the *Manner* of performing them; in *both* [of] *which* they are very exact, as I shall further acquaint you by and by. And I believe I may be bold to say, That hardly *any Man* hath ever given so *full*, and *punctual*[116] a Description of the *Manner* of their *Worship*, as the *Sequel* contains.

I shall speak, *First*, Of the *Care* and *Pains* they take to *prepare* themselves, e'er [*sic*; sc. ere] they can set about their *Devotion*. And, next, Of their *Behaviour in the performing of it.*

*First* then, concerning their Preparations. In the *Morning, as soon as they are* up, the first Thing they do is, going to the *Necessary House*, carrying with them a Pot of Water, somewhat like a *Coffee-Pot*, holding about a Quart. After they have *evacuated*, they take the Pot in their *Right-hand*, and let the Water run into the *Left-hand*, and therewith *wash* their *Posteriors*, &c. [[*Note*, That when Men make Water, they do it in the same Posture as Women do; the Reason of which is, lest the least Drop should fall upon their Clothes, or even their Shoes; for they hold, that *Urine* doth defile as much as *Ordure*;]] and thus they keep *washing* till the Pot of Water is all spent; which being done, they take *another* Pot of Water, and turning up their Sleeves above the Elbow,

[p. 52] therewith *wash* their *Hands*, first of all, *three* times; then they fill the *Right-hand* full of Water, and soop it into their *Mouth*, and with the *right* Thumb rub the *right* Jaws, and with the *right* Fore-finger rub the *left*: Which being done *three* times, they fill the Right-hand again with Water, and *snuff it up* into their *Nostrils* three times, as *often* blowing their Nose. After which they *wash* their *Face* three times, then *wash* their *Arms* up as far as the *Elbow*; then wet the *Right-hand*, and with the *Left* take off their Cap, bringing their

---

[112] *Eulea Nomas*: modern Turkish, *öğle namazı*; Arabic, *ṣalāt al-ẓuhr*, the noon prayer.

[113] *Ekinde Nomas*: modern Turkish, *ikindi namazı*; Arabic, *ṣalāt al-ʿaṣr*, the late afternoon prayer.

[114] *Acsham Nomas*: modern Turkish, *akşam namazı*; Arabic, *ṣalāt al-maghrib*, the sunset prayer.

[115] *Gega*, or *El-Asheea Nomas*: modern Turkish, *gece namazı*, or *işa namazı* (now more commonly *yatsı namazı*); Arabic, *ṣalāt al-ʿishāʾ*, the night prayer.

[116] *Punctual*: punctilious, exact.

*Right-hand* over their naked Head (for they shave their Heads weekly;) then they wet *both* Hands again, and thrust the two *Fore-fingers* into their *Ears*, rubbing the *Ears* behind with the two *Thumbs*; and then wet their Necks with the two *Little Fingers.* They also *wash* their *Feet* very well, as far as the *Ancles.* And, in the *last* place, they wet both Hands again, and then hold up the *Fore-finger* of the *Right-hand*, saying, *La allah ellallah*, Mohammed *Resul Allah*,[117] i.e. *There is but one* God, *and* Mahomet *the Prophet, or Messenger of* God; and the holding up the *Fore-finger* when they express these Words, is done to signify the *Unity.*[118]

Now when they have *wash'd*, or taken *Abdes* in the Morning, it may serve for the *whole Day* after, with this *Proviso*, viz. that they keep themselves *clean*, i.e. from *going* to *stool*, and *making Water*, and *breaking Wind* [p. 53] *backward*, and from the least sign of *Blood* on any Part of their Body; for if they discover the *smallest* Speck of *Blood*, it is thought to make them *unclean* as much as *any* of the *other* Escapes: And if it be no more than the *scratch* of a *Pin*, they must *wash* again after it, before they can go to their *Worship*. Or if after they have taken *Abdes*, they find the least drop of *Candle Wax* on their Hand, they must take a *fresh Abdes*, because the Place under the said Wax was not *wet*.

*Three* Times a Day, at least, they take *Abdes*; but they must do it *five* Times, if they are not satisfied of their being *clean*. They are so very Ceremonious in these Matters, that they commonly keep the *Nails* of their Fingers closely pared, because their Fingers are always in the Victuals when they eat, so that the Fat or Grease is apt to gather under their Nails, and so to hinder the Water from penetrating there, when they take *Abdes*; and therefore to have long Nails is not *Gaise*,[119] i.e. *Lawful*. But yet they say 'tis more lawful for those that live in the *Country*, because *their* Food is not so *gross* as theirs who live in *Towns* and *Cities* is. And besides, seeing their Labour is mostly about *Husbandry*, and consequently the *Earth* gathers under their Nails, which the water can easily soak through, the *Country People* are not so strict in paring of *their* Nails.

[p. 54]

If they chance to *sleep* between the Times of *Prayers*, then they must also take a *fresh Abdes*; and the Reason is, because they are nor sure whether they *brake Wind* in their Sleep or no.

---

[117] *La allah ellallah, Mohammed Resul Allah*: Arabic, *Lā ilāha illā-Llāh, Muḥammadun rasūlu-Llāh.*
[118] *Unity*: Arabic, *Tawḥīd*, or the unity of God.   [119] *Gaise*: Arabic, *jā'iz.*

Nay, I assure you, I have seen many go out of the *Mosque* in the midst of their *Devotion*, to take a *fresh Abdes*; because the former hath been spoil'd some or other of the forementioned ways.

The Performance of *Sallah* is incumbent upon the *Female Sex*, as well as the *Men*; though I think there are few of them but live in the neglect of it, for they are never permitted to enter into their *Mosques*; nay, it would be thought *rude* in them to be seen there. And besides, it is more difficult for the *Women* duly to perform *Sallah* upon another account, *viz.* because they must be very careful to watch their *Menstrua*; for while these are upon them, there is no performing of *Sallah*.

I have been very *particular* in relating these their *preparatory Ceremonies*, because they think themselves strictly obliged to be most *exact* and *critical* in the Observance of them.

After having thus done, they are fit, and in a readiness to go to the *Geamea*,[120] i.e. *the publick Place of Worship*, whither they immediately hasten (after the *Clerk* hath call'd from the Top of the Tower or Steeple.) In none of

[p. 55] their Places of publick Devotion have they any *Pews* or *Seats*, but the *Area* is a plain beaten Floor, like the Floor of a *Malt-House*, spread all over with thin Mats of Rushes, excepting near the *Emaum* [Imam] or *Priest*, where they lay Carpets. Their *Galleries* they have likewise spread with the *same*. But they have nothing of any *fine Ornaments* in these their *Geameas* or *Mosques*, neither any *Pictures*, *Images*, or any thing of *that* Nature; but the Walls are *naked white*, for they utterly abhor *Images*, or any thing *like* them. They blame the *Papists* for having so many *Trumperies* in their *Churches*, and have a greater Respect for *Protestants*, because they have not the like. I once had a Draught[121] of an *English* Ship, which I hung against the Wall; but my *Patroon* perceiving it had a *Cross* in its *Ancient*,[122] obliged me to blot it out, and then seemed well enough pleased with the Picture.

When they come to the Door of the *Geamea*, they slip off their *Shoes*, or rather Slippers; for the upper Leather, which is either red or yellow, scarce covers half the Instep, without any Quarters, except about half an Inch high above the Sole at the Heel: These they clap one Sole against the other, and so go in *bare-foot*, and lay them down before them, kneeling down, and bringing their Back-parts on their *Heels*, as for a Resting-place.

---

[120] *Geamea*: Arabic, *al-jāmi'*.  [121] *Draught*: drawing.  [122] *Ancient*: flag.

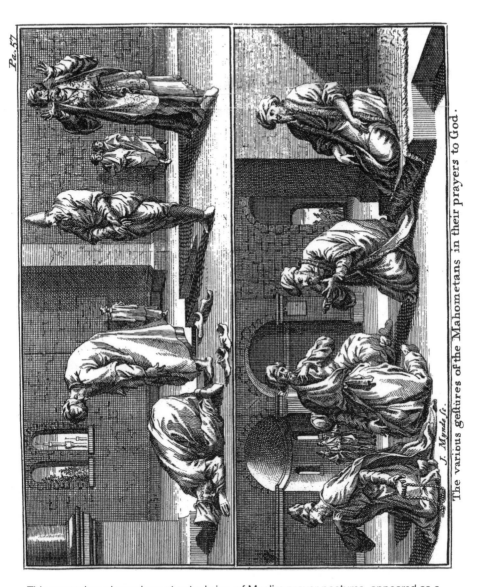

This engraving, shown here at actual size, of Muslim prayer postures, appeared as a foldout in the 1731 edition of Pitts's book between pages 56 and 57. For more information on the origin of this image, see Part I, p. 88.

[p. 56]

Now, being in all a Readiness, the *Emaem* (*Emaum*) or *Priest**, in the *Front*, upon equal Ground with the Congregation, and his Back towards them, the *Mezzins*[123] or *Clerks* are ready to observe his Motions, being plac'd in a little *Gallery* by themselves for that purpose. [[*There is no such Thing as Ordination of the* Emaum, *as I think, or ever heard; but the Dey appoints him.*]] But before the *Emaum* begins, they (*i.e.* the Clerks) stand up, and speak out so loudly, that all the Congregation may hear them, in a *curious* Tune, *Allah waik barik* (or *ekbar*) *Allah waik barik; Ashaed la Allahe ill Allah, ashaed la Allah ill Allah; Ashaed* Mohammed *rasul Allah, ashaed* Mohammed *rasul Allah: alla Sallah, hy alla Sallah: Hy alla Fellah; alla Fellah; Watacum alla Sallah, watacum allah Sallah: Allah waik barik* (or *ekbar*, &c.)[124] i.e. *God is great; God is great; I testify (or declare) that there is no God besides God; I testify that there is no God besides God; I testify, that* Mahomet *is the Messenger of God; I testify, that* Mahomet *is the Messenger of God. Haste to Prayers; Haste to Prayers; haste to a good Work, haste to a good Work. Now Prayers are beginning; now Prayers are beginning. God is great; there is no God besides God,* &c. (Much the same Words they use on the Top of the Steeple,[125] when they call 'em to *Service*, &c.). In the *Clerk's* saying the *last* Words, all the Congregation bring

[p. 57] their *two Thumbs* together, and kiss them *three* times, and at *every* Kiss they touch their *Forehead* with their *Thumbs*, and then rising up all on their Legs, they stand exactly *close* by one another in Rank, like a Company of Soldiers at *close* Order.

They all imitate the *Emaum* in the *Front*, who, as soon as he is upon his Legs, brings his *two Thumbs* to touch the lower part of his *Ears*; at which the *Clerk* above, having his Eyes always fix'd upon the *Priest*, cries out, *Allah waik barik*; at the hearing of which they all at once touch their *Ears*, as the *Priest* did, saying the *same* Words privately to themselves; and then they (*i.e.*

---

[123] *Mezzins*: modern Turkish, *müezzin*, from Arabic, *mu'adhdhin*.

[124] *Allah waik barik or ekbar* etc. are the words of the *iqāmah* which is pronounced immediately before the start of prayers; in Arabic the words are: *Allāhu akbar* (repeated), *Ashhadu an lā ilāha illā-Llāh* (repeated), *Ashhadu anna Muḥammadan rasūlu-Llāh* (repeated), *Ḥayya ʿala al-ṣalāh* (repeated), *Ḥayya ʿala al-falāḥ* (repeated), *qad qāmat al-ṣalāh* (repeated), *Allāhu akbar* (repeated). The *iqāmah* concludes with *Lā ilāha illā-Llāh*, which Pitts has omitted in his transcription of the Arabic but included in his translation ("there is no God besides God"). *Allah ekbar* is Pitts' transcription of *Allāhu akbar; Allah waik barik,* is a transcription of *Allāhu tabārak*.

[125] *Steeple*: minaret.

the *Hanifees*,[126] who are, as we may say, one of the four Sorts of *Mahometans)* put their Hands on their Belly, one on the other, and the *Emaum* says some short Lesson in the *Alcoran*; which being ended, he bows with his *hands* resting upon his *knees*; at which Motion of the *Priest*, the *Clerk* cries again, *Allah waik barik*; and when the *Priest* recovers himself upright, the same Expression is used again: It signifies, *Great*, or *Blessed God!*

Then the *Priest* placeth his Hands on his Thighs, and gently goes down his *Knees*; then *stretcheth* forth his Hands on the Ground, and with the same brings his *Forehead* to touch the *Ground*; at which *Ceremony* the *Clerk* repeats again, *Allah waik barik*: Then

[p. 58] the *Emaum* recovers himself on his *Knees*, with his Hands on his *Thighs*, and stretches his Hands on the Ground, *&c.* as before, and the *Clerk* repeats the *same* Expression, *Allah*, &c. All which Postures and Ceremonies the *Emaum* performs a *second* Time, and the *Clerk* useth the *same* words as at *first*; which being done, the *Emaum* sits still [[or rather sits and kneels at the same Time, as I hinted before]] about a *minute*, with his *Hands* on his *Thighs*, and fixing his Eyes upon the *Ground*, says a short *Prayer*; at the *end* of which, he looks about over his *right* Shoulder first, and then over his *left*, saying, *Salem Maelick*[127] at each; *i.e. Welcome* (viz.) *my Angels*; or *Peace be to you* (for the *Turks* hold, that every one hath *two Angels* to attend him, especially at the Time of their *Service* or *Worship*) this is call'd two *Erkaets*, or two *Messes*. You must observe, that *every* one in the Congregation doth use the very *same* Gestures with the *Priest*, and that *all at once*, in order; and the *Clerk's* speaking loudly in the Audience of them all, is a sufficient Token when to bow or rise; and *Note*, That they all stand with their Faces *one way*, i.e. towards the *Keblah*, or the Temple at *Mecca*, in the midst of which is a Place call'd *Beat-Allah*,[128] or the *House of God*.

At the *Conclusion* of their *Worship*, and after all the *Erkaets* are over, the *Emaum*

[p. 59] who officiates at the very upper end of the *Mosque*, being kneeling in an oval Place in the Wall,[129] and turning his Face towards the *Congregation*

---

[126] *Hanifees*: Ḥanafīs, one of the four main schools of law in Sunnī Islam. Pitts's description of the prayer ritual follows the Ḥanafī tradition.

[127] *Salem Maelick*: Arabic, *Salām 'alaykum*, "Peace be upon you", also the traditional Arabic greeting. Pitts may also be referring to the tradition of guardian angels (*malā'ikah*) being present during prayer.

[128] *Beat-Allāh*: Arabic, Bayt Allāh, the Ka'bah.

[129] The *miḥrāb*, the niche indicating the *qiblah*.

(and so consequently his Back is towards the *Keblah*) who are all upon their Knees, and imitate him, takes out his *Tesbea* (*Tesbih*)[130] or *Beads*, which are *Ninety Nine*[131] in number, and have a *Partition* between every *Thirty three*; these they turn over, and for every one of the *first* Thirty three they say, *Subhan Allah*; i.e. *Admire God*. For the *second* Thirty three they say, *El ham do l'Allah*; i.e. *Thanks be to God*. And for the *third* Thirty three, *Allah waik barik*. All which being ended, the *Emaum*, with the whole Assembly, hold up their Hands at a little distance from their Faces, putting up their silent *Orisons*; and to conclude all, *smooth down* their Faces with their Hands, take up their *Shoes*, which lie before them, and so go their way.

This is the *Manner* after which they behave themselves in their *publick Worship*, which lasts about a quarter of an Hour.

And here I shall give you an Account of the *Number* of *Erkaets* which they perform at *every* time of *Service*. And,

First of all, for the *Sobboh-Nomas*, or *Morning-Service*; as soon as they come in to the *Geamea*, they perform two *Erkaets* silently by themselves, and then wait till

[p. 60] the Time of *Service* (which is when it is Day-light, before the Candles are out in the *Mosque*) and then they perform two more with the *Emaum*. At this Time of *Service*, the *Emaum* speaks aloud, so that all the Congregation may hear him.

The *second* Time of their *Service* is (as I said) about *two* of the Clock in the Afternoon, which they call *Eulea Nomas*; at which time they hoist up a white Flag on a Pole, on the Top of the Steeple (*i.e.* about an Hour before *Service* begins) to give Notice to People that they be in a due *Preparation*. At this time, when they enter into the *Geamea*, they perform four *Erkaets* by themselves, *four* with the *Emaum*, and *four* afterwards apart by themselves. The *Emaum* now speaks so softly that he cannot be heard.

The *third* Time of *Service*, which they call *Ekinde Nomas,* is about *four of the Clock* in the Afternoon, and is performed exactly as the *second* was, excepting performing four *Erkaets*, after the *Emaum* has done, by themselves.

*Acsham Nomas*, being the *fourth* Time of *Service*, is a little after Sun-set, which they perform with Candle-light. About a quarter of an Hour before it begins, they have a short Form of Singing with the *Emaum*, who *reads a*

---

[130] *Tesbea* (*Tesbih*): modern Turkish, *tespih*, from Arabic, *tasbīh*, glorifying the name of God, by using the beads of the rosary (*subhah*) to repeat *Subhān Allāh*, or Praise God.
[131] *Ninety Nine*: traditionally God in Islam has ninety-nine names (*al-asmā' al-husnā*, or the most beautiful names).

Sentence, and then he and they *sing*. They always sing one Thing, and one [p. 61] Tune goes with it, *viz. Allahum solle, wasalem alla Seyedena, wa moulauna* Mohammed,[132] *i.e. O our God, be favourable to, and let Peace be upon our* Lord (*Master*) *and* Teacher, Mahomet, *and upon the Family of our* Lord (*Master*) Mahomet. This Singing is not *Farz*,[133] i.e. *a Matter strictly and universally enjoyn'd as a Duty by express command*, but only *Seunet*, [[or *Sunnah*]][134] i.e. *a voluntary Devotion*. At this *fourth Nomas*, the *Erkaets* which they perform, are *three* with the *Emaum*, who *now* also speaks with an audible Voice, and *two* afterwards by themselves,

The *fifth* and *last* Time of their *Service* is, *viz. Gega*, or *El-asheea Nomas*, about an Hour and half after the *fourth*, the *Lamps* continuing burning in the *Geamea* all *that* while; at their entring [*sic*] into which, they perform *four Erkaets* by themselves, *four* with the *Emaum*, who then speaks two with an *audible* Voice, and two *softly*, and five afterwards by themselves. *Note*, That those *Erkaets* or *Prayers*, which they perform *before*, and *after* the *Emaum*, are called *Seunet*, i.e. *voluntary Devotions*; and those performed with the *Emaum* are stiled *Farz*, i.e. *Commanded*. At the end of every *two Erkaets they* look over their *right* and *left* Shoulder, as I told you before the *Emaum* did, *viz.* to salute the *Angels*. But before they turn their Heads they say this Prayer, *viz. Atte* [p. 62] *hyjatu, lillahe wasale watu watte ubatu*.[135] Which is in the lesser *Chapters* or *Prayers*.

They seem to be *very* devout in the time of their *Worship*, fixing their Eyes on the Ground just before them, not in the *least gadding* or *wandring* with them.

Friday is their *Gemahgune*,[136] or *Sabbath*; but yet on *that* Day there is but little difference in their *Devotion* from that of *other* Days, excepting, that the *Hatteeb*,[137] i.e. a *Priest*, which is above the *Emaum*, *then* officiates, and that at One of the Clock, and for about the space of an Hour; after which

---

[132] *Allahum solle, wasalem alla Seyedena, wa moulauna* Mohammed: Arabic, *Allāhumma ṣallī wa-sallam ʿala sayyidinā wa-mawlānā Muḥammad wa-ʿala āl sayyidinā Muḥammad.*

[133] *Farz*: modern Turkish, *farz*, from Arabic, *fard*, an obligatory religious duty.

[134] *Sunnah*: modern Turkish *sünnet*, from Arabic, *sunnah*, an accepted action based on the Prophet's practice.

[135] *Attehyja-tu, lillahe wasale watu watte ubatu*: Arabic, *al-taḥiyyāt li-Llāh wa-al-ṣalawāt wa-al-tayyibāt*, which means literally, "All greetings, prayers and godly acts are for God".

[136] *Gemahgune*: modern Turkish, *Cuma günü*, from Arabic, *yawm al-jumʿah*.

[137] *Hatteeb*: modern Turkish, *hatip*, from Arabic, *khaṭīb*, the official who delivers the Friday sermon in the mosque.

he mounts a pair of Stairs (about six or seven) with a *Staff* in his hand, and there makes a sort of a short *Sermon*, about a quarter of an Hour, or a little more, and then performs *Sallah*, as the *Emaum* doth at other times.

At this time of their *Worship*, the *Gates* of the City (*Algier*) are shut, and many shut their *Shop-Windows* during *Service*; and some, that are more zealous, will not open their Windows all the Afternoon, but *walk*, and recreate themselves; but after the *fourth* time of Service (or *Acsham Nomas*) or rather a little before, not only the Gates of the *Town*, but all the Shop-Windows, are shut, and their Buying and Selling, and Work, are all over for that Day. And although the *Town* is very populous, yet very few People are to be seen in the Streets after Candle-

[p. 63] lighting, and the Shops are seldom open'd again till *Sun-rising*. After the *Gega Nomas* (or *last* time of *Service*) is over, the *Baulick Bashes*[138] (i.e. *Captains*) walk the Streets to see that no Disorders are committed.

On their *Sabbath* the Women flock out by *Thousands* in the Morning, to visit the *Sepulchers* of their deceased Relations, weeping over their Graves, and petitioning to them; and when they have done, they'll carefully weed, and cleanse them from Soil and Dirt.

Many People among them have their Burying-places wall'd in, with a Door to enter at, which places are very clean and whitened with Lime. The Women also pay their Visits to the *Marabbots* (of whom I gave you some Account before, *Chap.* II.) which have lain entomb'd, it may be, some hundreds of Years before; and to them they petition also: and, indeed, this is most of the *Liberty* the Women have; nay, many of them cannot attain unto this: Though, as I observ'd before, they are equally oblig'd to perform *Sallah* with the Men. And as for their Liberty in *Conversation*, it is as little; for tho' some may pay their Visits one to another upon occasion, yet they never *unvail* [sic] themselves till the Man of the House (if then present) depart.

[p. 64]

If there be two, three, or four *Families* in one House, as many times there happen to be, yet they may live there many Years, and never see one another's Wife. But perhaps you'll say, *That it is odds but that the Women may at some time or other be accidentally seen by the Men, coming in, or going out.* But in answer to that you must know, that the Men are seldom within-doors in the Day time (especially those of the poorer sort, who often thus live many Families under one Roof;) and when they chance to come home to their

---

138 *Baulick Bashe*: modern Turkish, *bölükbaşı*.

Houses, before they enter at the Door they usually speak aloud these Words, *viz. Ammiltreak,*[139] i.e. *Make way!* At the hearing of which every Woman *scuds* into her House from the Court, (for every House hath a Court in the middle Four-square, and on every Square there is a Room; and above there are Galleries, or Balconies all round, from whence you may look down into the Court.) The tops of their Houses are all flat, beaten Floors made with Lime, and Sand. 'Tis very seldom that any Men are to be seen on the Tops of their Houses; 'tis looked upon as very *rude* to be there: The Reason of which is, because, as their Houses are, generally speaking, of an equal Height; it would be easy to go from the Top of one to another, and so be able to look into the neighbouring Courts, and by this Means see other Mens Wives. Tho' some Men of

[p. 65] Note have low Walls on the Tops of their Houses, to prevent any Attempts of this Nature.

As for the Men, they never visit one another at their Houses; nay, it is not esteem'd civil, or decent for one *married Man* to enquire for another at his House. Nay, what is more, it is thought a rude thing to ask of any Person, *Sir, Where is your House?* Or, *Where do you live?* I my self once spake innocently to one when in *Egypt,* saying *Whereabouts is your House in* Algier? And he took me up somewhat roughly, and said, *Why do you ask that Question? My* Shop *is in such a place of the Town.*

The Doors of their Houses are always kept fast latch'd, for the Men have no Business at each others Houses; only the *Bakers Boys* go about the Street making a loud Noise, to take Peoples Bread, and carry it to the *Bake-House.* Upon this the Women within come and knock at the Inside of the Door, which the Boy hearing, makes towards the House. The Women open the Door a very little way, and hiding their Faces deliver the Cakes to him. Which when baked he brings to the Door again, and the Women receive them in the same Manner, as they gave them out. If there be a *Negro-Woman Slave* in the House, she goes to the Door; but if they are poor People, the Woman of the House must go her self.

[p. 66]

The *Water-Carriers* also (who are for the most part *Moors*) go about with a large Copper-Pot on their Shoulders full of Water, crying *Hab Elma:*[140] i.e. *will you have any Water?* Those who want, knock within the

---

[139] *Ammiltreak*: Arabic, *A'mal al-ṭarīq*.
[140] *Hab Elma*: Arabic, *ḥubb al-mā'*, literally, "desire for water".

Door *as above.* Way being made, the *Moor* goes in, empties his Pot, receives his Money, and away, without making any Stay. Many get their Living only by this; tho' 'tis commonly thought some of these *Water-Carriers* are frequently employed by the Women to procure *Gallants* for them, especially when their Husbands are *out of Town.*

The manner of the *Turks* complimenting, if Equals, is putting the Right Hand on the Left Breast with a little Bow, and kissing each others Cheek; though sometimes without kissing. If an Inferior comes to pay his Respects to a Superior, he takes his Superior's Hand and kisses it, afterwards putting it to his Forehead. But if the Superior be of a condescending Temper, he will snatch away his Hand as soon as the other hath touch'd it; then the Inferior puts his own Fingers to his Lips, and afterwards to his Forehead; and sometimes the Superior will also in Return put his Hands to his Lips. As for the *Moors*, if they are Equals, they'll hold fast each others Hand, striving to kiss it several times; and they'll ask how each other do; but in all their Compliments

[p. 67] they never ask one the other how their *Wives* and *Children* do. They take care of that for a reason well enough known. They never take off their *Turbants*, as we do our *Hats*, in Complaisance to one another; neither do they stand bare in the greatest Presence: Nay, they are never uncovered even in their *Mosques* when they are at their *Worship*, but wear their *Turbants* while they are at *Prayers.*

The Women (as I intimated before) wear *Veils,* so that a Man's own Wife may pass by him in the Street and he not have the least Knowledge of her. They will not stop to speak with Men, or even their own Husbands, in the Street. They always go bare-footed within-doors, except it be wet Weather, and then they wear their thin Slippers, which some have of Silver, but in their Chambers they always go barefoot. They keep their Houses very clean, and wash them so often and well, that they may go out of their Chambers into the Court bare-foot without dirting [sic] their Feet: Their *Shoes* they generally leave in the Entry or Passage.

The *Algerines* never take either Apprentices, or hired Servants, into their Houses, because they are a People given so much to *Jealousy* (and truly they have Reason enough for it on both sides) that there would be but little Love or Content under their Roof, if

[p. 68] they should. And therefore such as have occasion for Servants, do buy *Slaves,* and bring them up to their Houshold [sic] Work, as our *Servant-Maids* are here in *England;* who, as soon as they have done up all their Work in the House, are usually allow'd the liberty to go abroad, and visit their Country-men, commonly bearing each a Child with them; and if the Child be a *Boy* it rides on the *Slaves* shoulders.

*Slaves* in such places do always strive to get into the *Childrens* Affections; which if they can, they fare much the better for their Sakes. For oftentimes Faults are conniv'd at, and many Blows forborn upon the Child's account, lest it should grieve too much to see the dear Slave punish'd.

The *Turks* are but seldom *jealous* of their Slaves, tho' 'tis thought oftentimes they are made *Cuckolds* by them, and that by the *Solicitations* of the *Patroona's*, or *Mistresses* themselves; for it would be dangerous *Presumption* for the *Slave* to dare to make the least Item that way without Encouragement from his *Mistress*. My second *Patroon's* Wife was, I am persuaded, very unfaithful to him: I have Reason to think she was intimate with a Neighbour in the *Town*. Many a Temptation did she lay in my Way, tho' not by Word of Mouth, yet by *Signals*; but I made my self ignorant of her Meaning, and so (I bless God) escaped the Snare.

[p. 69]

I have heard of some who have suffer'd much like *Joseph*, for refusing to comply with the lascivious Desires of their *Mistresses*, who, like *Potiphar's*[141] Wife, have forg'd a quite contrary Story to their Husbands, which has occasioned the poor *Slave* to be severely beaten, and afterwards to be sold.

They have many *Hammams* or *Wash-houses* to bathe themselves in; which they go into almost naked, only with a thin white *Wrapper* on. There are several whose Business it is to give Attendance, and they are very ready to do it as soon as any Person comes. When any go in, they leave their Clothes in an Outer-Room, put on a pair of *Clogs*, or *Pattins*,[142] and so walk with their *Guides* into the *hot places*; where after they have been for a while, they grow into a great Sweat, and having continued in it for some Time, they have their Arm-pits shav'd by their *Guide*, and then retire into a private Room, where they have their *Pudenda* also shav'd, accounting it very beastly to have it otherwise: After which they lie down on the smooth Pavement, and one of the *Guides*, or *Tenders*, being ready with a Glove made of coarse Stuff or Camblet,[143] without Fingers, and stuft with something for that

---

[141] *Genesis*, chapter 39: while Potiphar was away, his wife attempted to seduce Joseph, but when he rejected her advances, she accused him of making advances to her and he was thrown into prison by Potiphar on his return.

[142] *Pattin*: another word for clog.   [143] *Camblet*: a light woollen fabric.

purpose, rubs their Body all over, and cleanses it from Filth: This they are very dexterous at, for as they are rubbing most Parts of the Body, they will bring the Rolls of Filth (like a

[p. 70] Worm, it may be two Inches in Length) under the Glove upon the Person's Arm, that he may see what need he stood in of *cleansing*. And I profess, I have often wondred [sic] to see so much Filth come off from a single Person, considering how frequently they use thus to *bathe*, or *wash*.

Having wash'd all over, and at last with Sope [sic], the *Tender* for a while leaves every Person to himself to throw Water on his Body; and this they may have from two Cocks,[144] one *hot*, the other *cold*, which run into an Earthen-pan, or else a great Bason [sic] of *Marble*; so that they may make the Water of what *temper of heat, or cold* they please: Having thus done, and taken *Abdes*, the *Tender* waits with *Wrappers*, one for the *upper*, and the other for the *lower* Parts of the Body; which having put on, the bath'd Person comes out into a *cooler* Room, and there lies down a while, till his Sweating is well over, and then puts on his Clothes again; and at his going out, the *Tender* sprinkles *Rose-water* on his Face. And all these refreshing Accommodations may be had for *three* or *four Pence*.

The Time of the *Mens* coming in, is till *One a clock* in the Afternoon; and *then* the *Women* take their turn of *Bathing*, till it be *Candle-lighting*.

I mention these *Hammams* in *this* Place, because they are not only design'd for *Recreation*,

[p. 71] and keeping the Body *clean*, but chiefly upon a *Religious* Account; because upon some Occasions they cannot perform *Sallah* without thus *washing* the *whole Body*. As for instance; if they have *lain with an Whore*, or be it with their *own Wives*, or if their Nature has gone from them in a Dream;[145] then the first thing they do is going to one of these *Hammams*, where they wash their Body all over; so then take *Abdes*, and are fit for *Sallah*.

And I really believe, that *few*, or *none* of them would venture to perform *Sallah*, being in any of the foremention'd Circumstances, without *washing* their *whole Body*, might they gain never so much. Wherever they are, be it at *Sea*, or in the Camp, yea, let the Weather be never so cold, they cannot be easy till they have *wash'd*. Nay, the most *negligent* among them, and such as scarce perform *Sallah* throughout the *whole Year*, will be sure, if

---

[144] *Cocks*: taps.
[145] *if their Nature has gone from them in a Dream*: if they have ejaculated while asleep.

in any *such* Circumstances, to *wash* themselves, take *Abdes*, and then perform a few *Erkaets*.

Now the *great* and *fundamental Article* of the *Mahometan* Faith, which chiefly makes them *Mussulmans*, or *Believers*, consists in these words, *La Allah Illallah* Mohammed *Resul Allah*,[146] i.e. *There is but one* God, *and* Mahomet *his Prophet, or the Messenger of* God: Or thus, *there is no* God (*i.e.* true God) *but* God, *and* Mahomet *is the Messenger of* God.

[p. 72]

For the saying of these Words, be it but *once* in a Man's whole Life, all his Debaucheries, and Sins (they say) shall be forgiven, and he shall assuredly get to Heaven, tho' for *some* time he may lie in Hell till his Sins are burnt away★: *i.e.* Supposing he be a *Mussulman*; for *Mahomet* will make Intercession for him, and obtain his Release. But for a *Christian* they have no Charity; for they say, that let him live never so well all his Days, yet all's in vain; for without believing in *Mahomet* there can be no *Salvation*. [[★*This is very much like the* Romish Purgatory, *which (among the* Papists) *is an Invention to get Money by.* 'Tis a plain Cheat, *to any observing* Man; *and, for ought [sic; sc.* aught] *I know a Doctrine of the most* damnable *Consequences of any in their whole Religion: And we may challenge the* Consistory of Cardinals[147] *to produce one Place of* Scripture, *which in the sense of any rational* Man *can be suppos'd to prove it. I don't find the* Turks *make the use the* Papists *do of it.*]]

I remember a Story that was told me, not foreign to the Matter in hand, and I believe it was true.

A *Turk* and a *Greek* were in Company together, and the *Greek* had with him his *Sister*, who was a very beautiful Woman. The *Turk*, among other talk, said, *That's a very pretty Woman; why dost thou not lie with her?* She is my Sister, replied the *Greek. What then*, quoth the *Turk, thou wilt never*

[p. 73] *go to* Hell *the sooner, for to* Hell *thou wilt go, whether thou liest with her or no.*

The *Mahometans* hold the Doctrine of the Blessed *Trinity* to be the greatest *Blasphemy* imaginable: For, *most prophanely say they, Was* God *ever married to beget a* Son? They will not hear of the *Son* of God with any Patience. 'Tis true, they own *Christ* to be a great *Prophet*, and born of the Virgin *Mary*; so they have it in their *Alcoran* very often hinted, *Eusa Ebn*

---

[146] *La Allah Illallah Mohammed Resul Allah*: Arabic, *Lā ilāha illā-Llāh, Muḥammadun rasūlu-Llāh.*
[147] *Consistory of Cardinals*: the formal meeting of the College of Cardinals of the Roman Catholic Church.

*Mariam,*[148] i.e. *Jesus the Son of* Mary; and they do also acknowledge him to be one of the *greatest Prophets* that has ever been on Earth: but they never own him to be the *Son* of God, (as some have related) or acknowledge his Doctrine as the *last Will* and *Word* of God, and his *Apostles* as the *Ministers* of it; for all these things they *utterly* deny, tho' some have asserted, That they believe the *Old* and the *New Testament,* the *Law* and the *Gospel*: But I say, How can it be? As for the *Law,* they do indeed pick some things out of it, but yet not in any due Order, or as it is *there* set down.

For *Circumcision* they observe not on the *Eighth Day,* as the *Jews,* but *when they please*; sometimes when the Child is *two, three, four* or *five* Years old. So do they vary from the *Old Law*[149] about Payment of *Tithes, Sacrifices,* &c. They do (or however should) pay the *fortieth* Part to the *Priests,* and when

[p. 74] they kill sheep in a Way of *Sacrifice,* they distribute them to the Poor.

And as for the *Gospel,* it is what I cannot but admire at, that any Writers, especially *Learned Men,* should affirm *they* believe it; since they do expressly *deny Christ* to be the *Saviour of the World*: and therefore, They who assert THAT MAHOMET *BELIEV'D ALL THE ARTICLES OF THE CHRISTIAN FAITH* must needs be in the wrong. They will hardly bear to hear of those *Miracles* which were done by *our Lord* and his *Apostles*. 'Tis true they have some Acquaintance with the *Historical* Parts of *Scripture,* especially the *Old Testament,* and give an Account of all the *Prophets* from *Adam* to *Christ*; but then they will have it that they were all of them *Mussulmans.* They will tell you that they (*viz.* their Fore-fathers) believed in all the *Prophets,* and obeyed the Messages which they brought, and they also believed in *Christ.* So should we (say they) to this Day, had he been *el we daw Pe gam ber,*[150] i.e. the *Last* of the *Prophets,* as they stile [sic] *Mahomet.* I have often heard them argue thus, while our *King* is living we yield our selves subjective to his Laws: But when after his Decease, another succeeds him, 'tis highly reasonable we should obey any *New* Laws made by him. So was the Practice of all *Mussulmans* in the Time of the *Prophets.*

[p. 75]

---

[148] *Eusa Ebn Mariam*: Arabic, ʿĪsā bin Maryam.

[149] *Old Law*: the law as found in the Old Testament.

[150] *el we daw Pe gam ber*: modern Turkish, *Elveda pegamber,* from the Arabo-Persian, *Vadāʾ-ı paygāmbar,* which means Farewell of the Prophet, or Farewell to the Prophet. The last of the prophets would be *hetemul-enbiya* in modern Turkish, the direct phonetic equivalant of the Arabic, *khātam al-anbiyāʾ,* literally, Seal of the Prophets.

Now, besides the *great* and *fundamental Article* of the *Mahometan* Faith, but now mentioned, there are Six Things, which they are *all* bound to believe; the disbelieving of *one* of which will exclude a Person from being a true *Mussulman*.

The First of these Six Things is, *viz.*

I.    *Aman to billahe*, i.e. To Believe in God.

II.   *Wa Malaikatehe*, i.e. And his Angels.

III.  *Wa Chetubehe*, i.e. And in his Written Word.

IV.   *Wa Reseulehe*, i.e. And in His Prophets.

[p. 76]

V.    *Wayom ilahere*, i.e. And the Last Day

VI.   *Wa bilcoder hirehe wa-sherrehe min allahe taallah*,[151] i.e. And that all Things that happen, whether Good or Evil, are disposed by the Providence of God; or in the Decrees of Good and Evil by the most high God.

These several Points the *Turks* do assent to, which is *more* than most Men (as I am apt to think) do imagine the *Mahometans* know, or give any Credit to.

But besides the *One* great Fundamental Article of their *Faith*, and these *six Credenda*,[152] there are several *Practical* Duties enjoined them, and which many of them do indifferently well observe. As,

I.    *Shahedet cala mace gettermeck*,[153] i.e. Often to repeat the following Words in which (as I told you) is contained the *prime*,

[p. 77] and *fundamental* Article of their Faith, *viz. La allah illallah ashaed Mohammed Resul allah.*[154]

II.   *Seunet etmeck*, i.e. To observe Circumcision.

III.  *Wa obtas [abdes] olmok*, i.e. To Wash before *Sallah*.

IV.   *Wa Nomas Culmok*, i.e. Duly to perform *Sallah*, or *Prayers*.

V.    *Wa zekaet wearmok*, i.e. And to give such a part (if I mistake not, the *fortieth*) of their Gettings[155] to the Poor: but this Command but few perform aright.

---

[151] *Aman to billahe, Wa Malaikatehe, Wa Chetubehe, Wa Reseulehe, Wayom ilahere, Wa bilcoder hirehe wa-sherrehe min allahe taallah*: Arabic, *amantū bi-Llāh wa-malā'ikātihi wa-kutubihi wa-rusūlihi wa-al-yawm al-ākhir wa-bi-al-qadar khayrihi wa-sharrihi min Allah ta'ālā.*

[152] *Credenda*: things which must be believed.

[153] *Shahedet cala mace gettermeck*: modern Turkish, Şehadet kelimesi getirmek.

[154] *La allah illallah ashaed Mohammed Resul allah*: Arabic, *Lā ilāha illā-Llāh, wa ashhadu anna Muḥammadan rasūlu-Llāh.*

[155] *Gettings*: income.

[p. 78]

VI. *Wa Caeba warmok*, i.e. And to go on Pilgrimage to *Mecca*, (*scil.*) if Health, and Ability permit.

VII.                    *Wa Orouch dootmok*,[156] i.e. And to keep the *Fast Ramadan*.

All which Injunctions some among them do *strictly*, and *conscientiously* observe; which, with their abstaining from certain things which they account *Sins*, viz. *Smoaking* [*sic*] *Tobacco, Eating Swines Flesh, Drinking of Wine*, &c. makes them to be look'd on *very much*: And yet (which is strange) there is no *Punishment* for those that do what is forbidden by the *Mahometan* Law, or neglect what is commanded. For (as I observ'd before) there is scarce any Sin punish'd among them, except *Murder*, and *Theft*. As for *drinking of Wine*, it is flatly *forbidden*, yet but few of them, in their Youth, refrain from it, nay the Excess of it. But, indeed, when they begin to *grow old*, they usually fall in love with *Money*, which bars other Extravagancies.

[p. 79]

However, though *Wine* be altogether *as* strictly forbidden as *Swines-flesh*, yet those who drink it, do seem to loath and abhor the thoughts of *Pork*. And yet, on the other hand, I have heard many say, *That it is* more *Lawful to eat* Pig, *than to drink* Wine; and they give this good Reason for it, *That the* former *doth satisfy* Hunger, *and nourish the Body*; *but the* latter *doth* intoxicate *so as to breed* Quarrelling, *and oftentimes the Consequence of that is* Murder.

But to *return* to the Points of *Practical* Duty, the two last of which only I shall insist on, and begin with the *Seventh*, (viz.) the *Fast of Ramadan*; because the other, *viz.* going on Pilgrimage to *Mecca*, I shall reserve to a distinct *Chapter*.

As *Christians* date by the *Month*, so the *Turks* date by the *Moon*; so that that this month of *Ramadan*, or month of *Fast*, doth every Year fall back *ten*, or *eleven* Days; and in the space of *thirty six* Years, or thereabouts, goes round the *whole* Year. And here the Reader may be pleased to *Note*, that they are altogether *ignorant* of *Astronomy*, and hold it to be a great Piece of *Arrogance*, and indeed *profane*, for any to *dive* into those things which belong to that *Science*. And they moreover say, *That no Man in the World knows when the*

---

[156] *Seunet etmeck Wa obtas* [*abdes*] *olmok Wa Nomas Culmok Wa zekaet wearmok Wa Caeba warmok Wa Orouch dootmok*: modern Turkish, *ve aptes almak, ve namaz kılmak, ve zekat vermek, ve Kâbeye varmak, ve oruç tutmak*. Pitts's list of seven practical duties of Islam comprises the classic Five Pillars – the *shahādah*, *ṣalāh*, the Ramaḍān fast, *zakāh* (*zakāt*) or alms-giving, and the *ḥajj* – plus circumcision, and ritual ablution before prayer.

New-moon *is, but* God alone *knows. That none but* Christians *will presume to enquire into such* hidden *and* abstruse

**[p. 80]** *matters.* Nay, they think it *Blasphemy* to say it will be *New-moon* at such an Hour or Minute. And therefore when by Reason of Hazy Weather, they are at a Loss whether there be a *New-moon,* or no, because it is not visible, all Hands will be looking out to spy it first, if possible. While they are thus employed, and are in Doubt about it, sometimes One, or more will come from the Hills near the *Town,* and testify that they have seen the *New-moon*; which is immediately taken for Truth, and the *Fast* thereupon begins. Many will not believe there is a *New-moon* till they *see* it. So that they begin their *Fast* the *next* Day after the Moon appears, and fast till they see the *next* Moon: Unless it so happens that the *Weather* hinder the sight of the Moon, and then they compleat *thirty Days Fast,* after they have seen the *Ramadan* Moon.

As soon as they see the *New-moon* in *Seaport Towns,* they fire a *Cannon* to give Notice when they are to begin the *Fast*; upon which *Signal* they'll immediately make Provision for the Night, and rise every Morning, about *two,* or *three* a Clock, (which I reckon the Night) to *eat,* and *drink,* and then continue without *meat* or *drink, smoaking,* or *chewing Tobacco,* or *taking snuff,* (which *three things* are much in use amongst them) till it be half an Hour after Sun-set. Nay, there are some so *scrupulous,* that they

**[p. 81]** question whether it be lawful for them to go into the Room where there is a *Grist-mill,* for fear any Flour should get into their *Throats,* and thro' their *Nostrils.* Others have been afraid to *wash* their Bodies, lest Water should *soke* [*sic*] into their *Belly* thro' the *Navel.* By all which you may see, how *extraordinarily strict* they are in their way.

During *Ramadan,* there is *no* difference at all in their *Devotion* from that at *other* times, excepting that in the *last* time of *Service,* at Night, there are a *multitude* of *Lamps* lighted up in their *Mosques,* and they perform *abundance* of *Erkaets,* the *Priest* saying a great many short Prayers with an *audible* voice, but as *fast* as he can speak, so that they are no sooner *down* upon their Knees, but they are *up* again. Altho' they carefully keep themselves from *Wine* this Month yet there is a *Toleration* for them to walk the Streets after Night, at which times much *Uncleanness* is *committed*: For though the *Whores* as well as *other* Women, at other times use to *veil* themselves in the Streets, yet in the Nights of *this* Month, they'll walk with Men in *Men's Apparel,* with their Hair down about them, in a most *shameful* manner. But tho' the *Turks* are so very strict, as I hinted, in the Observation of this their

*Fast*; yet if anyone be *Sick*, or in a *Journey*, and finds himself *faint* for want of inward Refreshment, he may *lawfully eat*, or

[p. 82] *drink*; but then he must be sure to *fast* for it afterwards: However, if he can deny himself altogether, it is more commendable.

I have seen many in the Country, to work *all day* very hard, in the most fervent *Harvest-time*, who tho' they have been ready to *fall down* for very parching Thirst, would by no means drink a little Water till the time came when they are used to *break-fast*. And the Reason they give is, because they are not sure of living so long as to make it up again in *Fasting*. Nay, they are yet more strict, if *Ramadan* happens to be during their *Pilgrimage* to *Mecca*; for if any do *then* break their *Fast* unseasonably, they must sacrifice a Sheep for such a Default.

When we were sailing on the *Red-Sea* towards *Mecca*, my *Patroon* (who was an ancient, and corpulent Man) being very faint with Thirst, broke his *Fast* voluntarily; but when we arrived at *Mecca*, he was not easy till he had *fasted* so many Days for it, and sacrificed a Sheep *into the Bargain*.

But if it happens so, that any do *eat* or *drink accidentally*, and *unwittingly*, not thinking of the *Fast*, it is accounted as nothing, neither is the *Fast* marr'd thereby, provided they forbear eating *as soon* as ever they think upon it. Nay, they account such a thing to be a great Favour of God, and *call it God's Treat*.

[p. 83]

I remember when I was at *Mecca*, in the month of *Ramadan*, it happened one Day to rain much, when my *Patroon's Water-Carrier*, who daily supplied us with the Holy Water of *Beer-el zem zem*,[157] brought some of the Rainy Water which fell from the *Beat-allah* to my *Patroon*, as a valuable Present, for which he was well rewarded. This Water being before me, I drank of it, not minding the *Fast* till it was down, when I reflected with my self that I had broken my *Fast*, and therefore fell to *eating* too. I told One, who dwelt in the same House with us, of this my Mistake (*viz.*) in drinking unadvisedly of the said Water. He then asked me, *Whether I had wittingly eaten since?* I told him, *Yes. Yozzik der!* replied he; i.e. *'Tis Pity! Ne deulet bashingah Coenmish;*[158] i.e. *What Dignity was put on your Head!* And withal, said he, God *was about to treat you in a more than ordinary way, even with*

---

[157] *Beer-el zem zem*: Arabic, Bi'r Zamzam, the holy well situated to the East of the Ka'bah in Mecca.

[158] *Yozzik der! Ne deulet bashingah Coenmish*: modern Turkish, *Yazık der! Ne devlet başına konmuş*.

Heavenly *Water, which came off from his own House, neither would it have marr'd your* Fast; *but now, through your Ignorance, you have miss'd of so great an Advantage:* Wishing, at the same time, *That* God *would so deal with* Him.

It was in this *Month of Ramadan,* they say, that the Angel *Gabriel* dictated to *Mahomet* the *Alcoran* (that is, that *Chapter* of it, which he *first* published) in the Cave which is by the Town of *Mecca,* on the top of a little Hill. While I was at *Mecca,* I went

[p. 84] thither; and tho' it was meerly to satisfy my Curiosity, yet it was thought very commendable in me: but I could find nothing remarkable in this *so famous* Cave. From the Hill, you have a good Prospect of the *Town,* and of the *Kabea,* [[*Caba*]]¹⁵⁹ or *Temple* of *Mecca;* of which, and their *Pilgrimage* thither, I shall give you a *faithful* Account in the following *Chapter.*

---

¹⁵⁹ *Kabea:* Arabic, Ka'bah: "The most famous sanctuary of Islam, called the temple or house of God (*Bayt Allāh*). It is situated almost in the centre of the great mosque in Mecca." (EI²).

## CHAP. VII.

*Containing an Account of the* Mahometans Pilgrimage *to* Mecca: *The Manner of their* Devotion *there. Of some of the most considerable Places between* Mecca *and* Algier; *as* Alexandria, Grand Cairo, *&c.*

GOING on *Pilgrimage* to *Mecca*, is (as I inform'd you before) a Duty incumbent on every *Mussulman*, if in a Capacity of *Health*, and *Purse*: But yet, a great many who are so, live in the final neglect of it.

There are *Four Caravans*, which come to *Mecca* every Year, with *great* numbers of *People* in each.

There is *First*, the *Moggarib*[160] *Caravan*, which comes from the *West*, from the Emperor of *Fez* and *Morocco's* Country, (from which parts they all go by Land,) and

[p. 85] toucheth at *Egypt*, where they take in what Provision will serve to *Mecca*, and back again to *Egypt*. The *Emmir Hagge*,[161] or *Chief-Leader* of the *Caravan*, makes a stop at *every* Town he passeth through, that so *all* such Persons as are desirous to go to *Mecca* that Year, may, if they please, go in company with him.

This *Emmir Hagge*, into whatsoever Town he comes, is received with a great deal of Joy, because he is going about so *Religious* a Work; and it is, who can have the Favour, and Honour of Kissing his Hand, or but his *Garment*! He goes attended in much Pomp, with *Flags, Kettle-Drums,* &c. and loud Acclamations do as it were rend the Skies; nay, the very *Women* get upon the Tops of the Houses to view the *Parade*, or *fine Show*, where they keep striking their four Fingers on *their* Lips softly, as fast as they can, making a joyful Noise all the while, which sounds somewhat like *Yow, Yow, Yow,* hundreds of Times.

The *Second Caravan* goes from *Misseer*,[162] or [[*Messe*]] i.e. *Grand Cairo* in *Egypt*; which is join'd by great *multitudes*, because it is better arm'd, and so they go with more *Safety* under its Protection. And it is also more *pleasant*, because they go every one in *Order*, and each knows his place; so that there arise no Quarrels or Disputes at all on the Road about Precedency.

---

[160] *Moggarib*: Arabic, Maghrib.   [161] *Emmir Hagge*: Arabic, *Amīr al-ḥajj.*
[162] *Misseer*: Arabic, Miṣr.

[p. 86]

With this Caravan is sent the Covering of the *Beat-Allah,* or *House of God;* of which I shall give a Description by and by.

The Third Caravan is call'd *Sham Carawan,*[163] which brings those that come from *Tartary,*[164] and Parts *thereabouts,* and also from all *Turkey, Natolia,*[165] and the Land of *Canaan,*[166] without touching at *Egypt.*

The *Fourth* is call'd *Hind*[167] *Carawan,* which comes from the *East-Indies,* and brings many rich and choice Goods, which are sold to all sorts of Persons who resort to *Mecca.*

These Four *Caravans jump* all into *Mecca* together, there being not above *three,* or *four* Days difference in their Arrival, which usually is about *six* or *seven* Days before the *Curbaen Byram,*[168] i.e. the Feast of Sacrifice.

But it may be ask'd, perhaps, by some who know, or at least have heard, or read of the Town of *Mecca, How such* great Numbers *of People can possibly have Lodging and Entertainment, for themselves, and Beasts, in such a* little ragged Town *as* Mecca is★. [[★*I had the Curiosity to look into the great and worthy Mr. Collier's Dictionary,*[169] *to see what wa*s there *said of* Mecca, *and* Medina; *and I find his Author very much out in both: And yet* Davity, *he saith, was a late*[170] *Writer: For* Davity *describes* Mecca *to be a very* large *Place; and that the constant Inhabitants make up about* six Thousand *Families; whereas it, indeed, is nothing near so populous, for I believe I may safely say there are not* One

[p. 87] Thousand *Families in it. And the Buildings are very* mean *and* ordinary. *I am sure, while I was in the* Town, *and when I took a View of it from a neighbouring Hill, I could see nothing of Beauty in it. I am not fond of contradicting* Authors, *especially such as are thought to be* Great Men; *but I speak from* Knowledge, *they only by* Hearsay. *And as for* Medina, Davity *saith 'tis but* four, *I say about* ten Days *journey from* Mecca. *He saith likewise, That the Pillars of the* Mosque *of* Medina, *are charg'd with*[171] 3000 Silver *Lamps, whereas in truth there are but* few *Lamps, and almost all of* Glass. *He saith, moreover, That*

---

[163] *Sham:* Arabic for Syria, understood in Pitts's time to include Lebanon and other areas of the Levant.

[164] *Tartary:* Central Asia.   [165] *Natolia:* Anatolia or Asia Minor.

[166] *Canaan:* modern-day Israel, Palestine and Jordan.   [167] *Hind:* Arabic for India.

[168] *Curbaen Byram:* Arabic/Turkish, Qurbān Bayram, in Arabic 'Īd al-adḥā, "the one great sacrificial ritual in Islam, occurring during the daylight hours of the tenth of the month of Dhū al-ḥijjah as a part of the major pilgrimage" to Mecca (EI²).

[169] *Mr. Collier's Dictionary:* for more information on Collier and d'Avity and their claims, see Part I, Chapter 3, note 195.

[170] *late:* recent.   [171] *charg'd with:* filled with.

Mahomet's *Tomb is* richly *adorn'd with Plates of Silver, and cover'd with Cloth of Gold; which is* not so, *but I suppose he mistakes* this *covering for that of the* Beat-Allah, *of which I have given an Account. There are no Lamps lighted about* Mahomet's *Tomb by Day. Nor are all* Turks absolutely *bound to visit the* Tomb *at* Medina. *For those who belong to the* Caravan *which comes from the* East Indies, &c. *go directly home from* Mecca; *because if they were to make a visit at* Medina, *it would necessarily hinder them twenty Days, or more.*]]

I answer, as for House-room, the Inhabitants do *streighten*[172] themselves very much, in order, at *this* time, to make their Market. And indeed, they make the *Hagges,*[173] or *Pilgrims,* pay for their House-room during their Stay there (which is generally only about 16 or 17 Days) *more* than the Rent of a whole Year amounts to. And as for such as come *last,* after the Town is fill'd, they pitch their Tents without the Town, and there abide till they remove towards Home. As for *Provision,* they all bring sufficient with them, except it be of *Flesh,* which

**[p. 88]** they may have at *Mecca;* but as for all other Provisions, as *Butter, Honey, Oil, Olives, Rice, Bisket,* &c. they bring with them as much as will last through the *Wilderness,* forward and backward, as well as the Time they stay at *Mecca;* and so for their *Camels,* they bring store of *Provender,* &c., with them; for they meet with very little, if any, Refreshment on the Road.

When a Ship is going for *Alexandria,* it is cried about the Town of *Algier,* where I liv'd, That she will sail *such* a Day; and then every one that designs for[174] *Mecca* that Year, joyfully embraces the Opportunity of going so far by *Sea,* because they thereby save both a great deal of *Trouble* and *Cost,* which they must be at if they were forc'd to go by Land.

You must observe, That no *Turks* who are in Pay, dare to undertake this *Pilgrimage* without leave from the *Dey;* and if they exceed a Year in it, how much soever it be, when they return to *Algier,* they must be contented with one Year's Pay and lose all the rest.

That Year I went from *Algier* to *Mecca,* we arrived at *Alexandria* in between *thirty* and *forty* Days; which is reckon'd to be a *very good* Passage.

In our Voyage, we espied a small Vessel one Morning, which we chased till almost Night. We hung out *French* Colours, and

---

[172] *streighten:* close ranks (as in an army).
[173] *Hagges:* Arabic, colloquially *ḥajjī,* more properly *ḥājj,* an honorific title given to all those who had performed the *ḥajj* or pilgrimage to Mecca.
[174] *designs for:* plans to go to.

[p. 89] the chased Vessel did the like; but still, shunn'd us, which made us continue our Chace. When we came up with her, we found the Men to be all *Turks* and *Moors* in a *French* vessel, who were brought from Malta, and were designed to be carried to *Leghorn*,[175] and sold there. They told us, That *that* very Morning they were at an Anchor at a certain Place, and most of the *French* Crew went ashore in their Boat, leaving only two Men and a Boy aboard; upon which the Slaves rose, and kill'd the two *French*-Men, and so became Masters of the Ship: That therefore upon our hanging out *French* Colours, they were in a great Consternation at the first, but when they knew we were *Turks*, they as much rejoiced as before they feared. Some of them, Men, Women, and Children, came on board of us, and would by no means be perswaded to return to the *French* vessel again. They steer'd directly for *Tunis*, where, we heard, they safely arrived.

At *Alexandria* we tarried about twenty Days. *Historians*, undoubtedly, have given a far more satisfactory Account of this Place than I can pretend to; however, I hope my Observations may be accepted.

No doubt this was a very *famous* City in *former* times, and celebrated for its Greatness and Neatness; for the very *Ruins* thereof leave an Image of *Magnificence* upon a

[p. 90] Man's Mind. In my Walks about it, I saw many curious Pieces of *Arch-work* under Ground. It is accommodated with a small Branch or Cut of *Nilus*,[176] which fills their Wells: and to these Wells *New Alexandria*, which is about a Quarter of a Mile distant from the *old*, and all the Ships that resort thither, are beholden for *fresh Water*. The Mouths of these Wells are intire [*sic*] Stones of Marble.

I think all the Walls of this City are yet standing, with firm Iron Gates; unless some part of the Upper-work be fallen.

There are two Churches in *Old Alexandria*, one of which is call'd by the Name of *Bingbeer Drake*,[177] i.e. a Thousand and one Pillars; for so many, they say, it hath. When I went into it, there was with me a *Spanish Renegado*, who belong'd to another *Patroon*, and a *Turk* of our Company. This last show'd us a Pillar of Stone, unpolish'd, which looked not much unlike the Stump of a dead Tree, with Knots on it. This, he told us, was the *Fig-tree* which

---

[175] *Leghorn*: now known as Livorno, a major port on the West coast of Italy.
[176] *Nilus*: the River Nile.
[177] *Bingbeer Drake*: modern Turkish, *bin bir direk*. This is possibly a reference to the mosque which stood on the site of the original St Mark's Coptic Cathedral.

*Christ* cursed when he found it fruitless, saying, *Let no Fruit grow on thee henceforward for ever*. Here, *added he*, you will be tried whether you are right *Mussulmans*, or no. You must stand about eight or ten Paces from this Tree, and being *hood-wink'd*[178] must go towards it; if you go directly to it, you are *right*; but if you miss, you are not true *Mussulmans*.

[p. 91] He ty'd his own Handkerchief about our Eyes; the *Spaniard* went first, and miss'd; I then try'd what I could do with my Arms spread, and happening to touch the *Pillar*, was pronounced the better *Mussulman* of the two.

There are several Pillars in the Ruins of *Old Alexandria*, of a vast bigness and height; one, especially, I did much admire, for it is as big about as *three* or *four* Men can fathom, and higher than I could throw a Stone; it shines like Glass, and the Colour of it is much like *Porphyrian* Marble; it looks as if it were one *intire* [sic] Piece, with some curious Stone-work on the Top of it; but I am perswaded it is artificially made, and consists of several Parts, though so well done, that the Joinings are not discernible; for I can't see how it would otherwise be possible to mount it, and place it in its present Position. The Country being very low, it serves for a *Sea-Mark*; for, as it is erected on a little rising Ground, it is visible, as well as some *Palm-Trees*, a considerable Time before the *Land*. 'Tis called *Pompey's Pillar*.[179]

This City of *Alexandria* is situated about two Bow-shots from the Sea-side; and the *New Alexandria* joins to the Sea.

Here is not such a Plenty at all Times to be had, as further up in the Country; and the Reason is, because abundance of Ships, [p. 92] of all Nations, do continually resort hither, and take off such Supplies as they want.

Having tarried at *Alexandria* about twenty Days, we embark'd for a Place call'd *Roseet* [[or *Rosetta*]][180] which is about two Leagues, as I guess, up the River Nilus, which River they also call *Bahor el Nile*,[181] i.e. The Sea of Nilus.

I think we sail'd from *Alexandria* about five or six Leagues *Eastward* of it, before we came to the open *Mouth* of the famous River *Nile*, where it emptieth it self into the *Mediterranean Sea*, with its muddy Colour

---

[178] *hood-wink'd*: blindfolded.

[179] Pompey's Pillar, as Pitts rightly says fashioned from "porphyrian" (correctly, porphyry), a purplish-red igneous rock quarried in Egypt, is a Roman triumphal column erected in AD 297. It is in fact a monolith, despite Pitts's incredulity on this score. It stands 26.46 m high with a diameter of 2.71 m at its base.

[180] *Roseet* or *Rosetta*: Arabic, Rashīd.   [181] *Bahor el Nile*: Arabic, Baḥr al-Nīl.

threat'ning as if it would change the whole Sea into its own Colour and Sweetness. I drank of its Water a considerable Way off at Sea, and found that it was no way salt, to my great Satisfaction, and according to what I had heard of it.

I have been credibly informed, that the *Leghornese* and *Venetians* oftentimes take in fresh Water off the Mouth of the *Nile*; and they may do it, indeed, without the least Danger, the *Turks* having no Ships to defend this Coast.

This River is not only famous, among other Things, for *Depth*, but also for *Breadth*. I cannot give an exact Account of the *Breadth* of it, but I well remember, that being on one side, I could scarce distinguish a *Man's* from a *Woman's* Habit on the other. As for its *Depth*, you may guess

[p. 93] 'tis very considerable, because there are many of the *Turks* Merchant-Men, navigated by *Greeks*, which are called by the Name of *Shykes*,[182] somewhat like our *English Ketches*, of two or three Hundred Ton, which come up to *Roseet*; and from thence it is Navigable up to *Boelock* [[or *Boulack*]][183] by great Boats or Barges deeply laden, and how much further up I know not.

*Roseet* is the Place where all the Boats unload which come from *Cairo* and *Alexandria*; for the Boats which come from Cairo, are not fit to sail down for *Alexandria*; neither are the *Alexandrian* big Boats fit to sail up to *Cairo*, for want of sufficient Depth of Water.

The Mouth of *Nilus* is oftentimes very dangerous, and Vessels are cast away[184] there, by reason of its being chok'd up with Sands; and many times Vessels are forc'd to wait *ten* or *twelve* Days for a clear Mouth. Whether this *Bar* may not be owing to an *out hard Wind*,[185] which checks the River, and stops the Sand which it brings down with it at its Mouth, and when the Wind is off the Shore the Freshet[186] drives it away again, I shall leave to Persons of better Judgment to determine.

I very well remember, we were forced to wait several Days for a *clear* Mouth; in the mean Time, an ancient Man of our Company fell sick, and died, and the next Day, if

[p. 94] I mistake not, we had a *free* Passage. The *Turks* made this Observation

---

[182] *Shykes*: modern Turkish, ṣayka (pl. ṣaykalar).
[183] *Boelock* or *Boulack*: Arabic, Būlāq, the port on the Nile which served Cairo in pre-modern times.
[184] *cast away*: wrecked.    [185] *out hard Wind*: a strong onshore breeze.
[186] *Freshet*: flood of water towards the sea.

upon it, *viz*. That it was the Place where God had *determined* he should be buried, for which reason we were obliged to wait so many Days.

This River is well known, and famous in most Parts of the World.

It hath *another* great Mouth, where it empties it self also, some Leagues *Eastward* of the former, which is call'd by the Natives *Dimyot*.[187] Some have written of several *more* Mouths, but if there be any such, they must be *small Streams*, which I never [[observ'd or]] heard of from the *Natives*: I am sure of this, *viz*. that *these two* I have mentioned are the *great* ones, and *navigable*.

I was not in *Egypt*, but at *Mecca*, at the Time of the *Nile's overflowing*; but they say, it comes *gradually* and *gently*, not at all damnifying[188] the Inhabitants, who receive it with a great deal of Joy; it remains about *forty* Days on the Land, and when it is gone off, they make very great Feasting and Rejoicing; and good Reason for't, for they have a great Dependance on the *Overflowing* of this River; nay, were it not for it, *Egypt* would be a very barren Country, even as the *Wilderness*, which is not above half a Day's Journey from *Grand Cairo*, because they have little or no *Rain*. After *Nilus* hath left the Land, then is their Time of *Tilling* and *Sowing*. When their Seed is in the

[p. 95] Ground, they are not much solicitous whether it *rain* or not, hardly reckoning themselves obliged to the *Showers of Heaven*.

Many will not believe that it ever *rains* in *Egypt*, because most *Historians* say the contrary; but I will be bold to affirm what I saw my self: While I was at *Cairo* it rained to that Degree, that having no Kennels[189] in the Streets to carry off the Water, it was Ancle-deep, and in some Places half way the Leg. My *Patroon* had, at that Time, two Bales of Linen-cloth on board a Bark at *Boelock*, which were so damaged by the *Rain*, that we were forced to open them, and dry the Cloth piece by piece.

They have a particular *Mark* when the Flood is at its height; and *they say*, That if it rise a *Finger's breadth above it*, it is a sign of *Plenty*; but if it come *so much* short of it, 'tis a sign of *Scarcity*.[190]

This River affords Plenty of *Fish* and *Fowl*, as *Wild-Ducks*, *Geese*, &c.

I was credibly inform'd of a pretty Way they have there to take *Wild-Ducks*, viz. Some one that can swim, and dive very well, takes the Head of

---

[187] *Dimyot*: Damietta; Arabic, Dimyāṭ.
[188] *damnifying*: damaging. The annual Nile inundation occurred between June and September.
[189] *Kennels*: surface drains.
[190] Pitts is probably referring to the best-known Nilometer, on Rhoda island (Arabic, Jazīrat al-Rawḍah) in Cairo, built AD 861.

a dead Duck, and swims with it in his Hand, and when he comes pretty near the Ducks, he dives, holding the Duck's Head just above the Surface of the Water, till he comes to the Ducks, and then takes hold of them by the Legs, and so catches them.

**[p. 96]**

I have seen and handled a Bird taken on this River, about the bigness of a *Heron*, which hath under his Throat a Bag of Skin, with the Mouth of it towards the Beak.

This Bird they call *Sacca Cush*,[191] i.e. *Bird-Water-Carrier*, and (like *Dotterels*)[192] they say, that when *Abraham*[193] built the Temple at *Mecca*, these Birds supplied him with *Water*.

I remember, that when we were sailing up the River *Nilus* towards *Cairo*, one of our Company shot one of these *Water-Carriers*, thinking it to be a *Wild-Goose*; but when it was known what it was, it was much lamented, even with Tears, that such a Creature should be so kill'd.

As for *Crocodiles* here, I saw none.

The River of *Nile* is not clear of *Robbers*, who rob in Boats. They are most bold at that Time of the Year in which the *Hagges* are a going from *Rosetta* to *Grand Cairo*, knowing they must carry Sums of Money with them. We were afraid, once, they were coming to attack us; but having Arms we fired upon them, and they soon made off.

There are Towns all along its Banks, in-so-much that you are no sooner out of the sight of one, but you are in sight of *two* or *three more*.

They say it is above 250 Miles up from *Rosset* to the Country where the famous

**[p. 97]** City of *Cairo* stands; and in *all* this way scarce an Hill as big as an House to be seen.

About *four* or *five* Miles on this side Cairo this River parts, and betakes it self into two Streams; the one runs to *Rosset*, the other to *Dimyott*.

The Inhabitants of Egypt are a mixture of *Moors, Turks, Jewes, Greeks* and *Copties*;[194] which last I understand to be the Race of the ancient *Egyptians*.

---

[191] *Sacca Cush*: pelican, from the Arabic, *saqqā'*, water-carrier or pelican, and Turkish, *kuş*, a bird. In modern Turkish, however, *saka kuş* means a goldfinch.

[192] *Dotterel*: a species of plover (*Eudromias morinellus*).

[193] *Abraham*: Arabic, Ibrāhīm. In the Qur'ān, Ibrāhīm and his son Ismā'īl are described as having laid the foundations of the Ka'bah, the cuboid structure at the centre of the Great Mosque in Mecca.

[194] *Copties*: Copts, the native Christians of Egypt.

The chief Commodities in the Country are, *Rice*, *Flax*, most sorts of *Grain*, *Sugar*, *Linen*, and *Hides* in abundance, especially of *Buffleas*;[195] *Balsams*, &c.

As for their *Fruits*, they have but little, if any, *Tree-Fruits*, as *Apples*, *Pears*, *Cherries*, &c. but abundance of other Sorts, such as *Melons*, *Water-Melons*, *Cucumbers*, &c

Here is also great Plenty of *East India* Commodities, as *Silks*, *Muslins*, *Callicoes*, *Spices*, *Coffee*, &c.

And also, of *Milk*, *Butter*, *Cheese*, *Oil*, *Olives*, &c.

The Habits of the *Moors* and *Egyptians*, or *Copties* [[*Copticks*]] differ only in their *Turbants;* the *Moors* Turbants being all *white*, and the *Copties* white *striped* with blue.

They speak all *one* Language, and generally wear a long, black, loose Frock, sown together all down before.[196]

**[p. 98]**

The *Jews* wear a Frock of the same Fashion, but of *Broad-cloth*; but their Caps are of an odd Figure, being somewhat like the *Poll* of a Man's Hat-case[197] covered with *Broad-cloth*.

And as for the *Jewish Women*, they wear a long sort of Head-dress, which is like one of our Womens *high crown'd Hats*, but not quite so *taper* at the top, yet of a greater length, jutting out behind at the Poll; in which they look very *awkard* [sic] indeed.

The *Greeks* differ but little from the *Turks* in their Habit, except it be in their *Turbants* and *Caps*; but they dare not wear any Thing of a *green* Colour, tho' it be ever so small; if they did, they would be in danger of having their Clothes torn off their Backs, at least, that part which is *green*; and 'tis well if they escape the *Bastinadoes*. And though all *Mussulmans*, whether *Turks* or *Moors*, have liberty to wear *Green*; yet none will presume to wear a *Turbant* of *that* Colour, unless they belong to the Race of *Mahomet*, who are always most respected.

There is in no Part of the World, I am apt to think, greater Encouragement given to *Whoredom*, than in *Egypt*. It is *impossible* for me to give you a full Account of their *Licentiousness* of this kind, and which is

---

[195] *Buffleas*: water buffaloes.
[196] *all down before*: all down the front.
[197] *Poll of a Man's Hat-case*: crown of a man's hat-box.

*tolerated* too; but yet I cannot forbear speaking *something* of it, hoping it may be a

[p. 99] Motive to cause my Country-men to make a *good use of it*, and to bless God, that we have such Punishment, by the *Laws*, to be inflicted, in order to the Suppression of this *Soul-destroying* Sin.

In *Egypt* then, they have distinct Streets and Places, which are *all* full of *lewd Houses*; into any of which none of *Repute* will enter, but upon absolutely *necessary* Occasions.

The *Whores* use to sit at the Door, or walk in the Streets *unveil'd*.

They are commonly very *rich* in their Clothes, some having their Shifts and Drawers[198] of *Silk*, with silk *Coats* like Mens (as for Petticoats, they never wear any in this Country) and a silk *Sash* about their Middle (as indeed all others in these Parts have, Men, Women, and Children) with a Knife tuck'd in at their Girdle, the Sheath of which is commonly Silver.

These *Courtezans*, or *Ladies of Pleasure*, as well as other Women, have broad *Velvet Caps* on their Heads, beautified with abundance of *Pearls*, and other *costly* and *gaudy* Ornaments; and they wear their Hair in *Tresses* behind, reaching down to their very *Heels*, with little Bells, or some such Things, at the end, which *swing* against their Heels, and make a *tinkling* Sound as they go.

[p. 100]

They also wear Nose-Jewels; and therefore 'tis not altogether improbable that these, or some like them, were the Vanities of bewitching *Apparel*, which the *Prophet* exclaims against, *Isa.* iii.16.[199]

These *Madams* go along the Streets smoaking their Pipes of *four* or *five* Foot long; and when they sit at their Doors, a Man can scarce pass by but they will endeavour to decoy him in.

I have often wonder'd, how these Creatures can maintain themselves at the Rate they do, seeing, *I am told*, that for three or four *Parrahs*,[200] i.e. Pence, any Man may gratify his Lust upon them.

---

[198] *Shifts and Drawers*: underclothing.

[199] *Isaiah,* chapter 3, verse 16: "Moreover the LORD saith, Because the daughters of Zion are haughty, and walk with stretched forth necks and wanton eyes, walking and mincing as they go, and making a tinkling with their feet."

[200] *Parrahs*: modern Turkish, *para*, a small coin (now obsolete) which was worth one-fortieth of a piastre.

But they are so cunning, that they will not encourage any to stay longer with them than in the Fact, and Payment for it; because they will be ready for a *fresh* Gallant.

And now to speak something more of *Grand Cairo*, a Place eminent in History.

In this Place they have *Wells* in most of their *Mosques*, into which Water is by an *Aqueduct* convey'd, at the time of the Overflowing of *Nilus*; and there are Men appointed, who stand at the Windows of several of their *Churches*, to give Cups of Water to all such as pass by.

[p. 101]

If I mistake not, it is reported, that in this City, *there are five* or *six Thousand publick* and *private Mosques★*. [[ *★Not six Thousand publick* Mosques, *and twenty Thousand particular ones, as I find in the worthy Mr.* Collier's[201] *great Dictionary from his Author: I am* positive *it cannot be near the number, nor three and twenty thousand, as Mons.* De Thevenot *hath it, Part I. pag. 129. though I honour that Author, for he is as exact in the* Turkish *History as any that ever I yet saw: I speak of what I* know, *and have seen.*]]

Among which, some are very large and stately, with curiously wrought Fronts and Gates, as likewise high round *Minarets* or *Steeples*; and some of the said *Minarets* have several *Balconies* round them, some *two*, some *three*; which *Balconies*, and also the Streets, during the Time of *Ramadan*, are illuminated with abundance of *Lamps*, glorious to behold.

Many Miles before we come to *Cairo*, the two *Pyramids*, which are six or seven Miles beyond it, discover themselves;[202] they are of a prodigious Height, and in the form of a *Sugar-loaf*.

There is a Town joining to the River *Nile*, about a Mile and half before we come to *Cairo*, call'd *Bolock*, where resort many hundreds of *Barks* laden with *Corn*, &c.

Here we hired *Asses* or *Camels* to carry our Things to *Cairo*; where, notwithstanding the resort of Strangers and Merchants,

---

[201] *Collier:* for more information on Collier and his dictionary, see Part I, Chapter 3, note 195. For more information on Thévenot, see Part I, Chapter 3, note 196. Thévenot's remarks on the number of mosques in Cairo can be found on p. 129 of part one of the 1687 edition.

[202] *discover themselves:* can be seen.

[p. 102] and all the Fame that this City hath in *History*, all the Entertainment for Strangers, is a naked Room or Chamber, without the least Furniture; and yet, though the Accommodations are so mean, every Stranger, whether *Pilgrim* or *Merchant,* when he takes a Room, is obliged to pay fifty *Parrahs* for *Entrance*, and one *Parrah* a week afterwards, stay as long as he will.

In this City are said to be spoken no less than *seventy two* Languages.

As for the *Buildings* here, they are but very ordinary, and for the most part low, except some *Hawns*,[203] i.e. *Publick-Houses* of Entertainment, which are three or four Stories high. These are built after the same Figure with their other Houses, *viz.* Four-square, with a Court in the middle; and some of them are so large, that they have three or four score Rooms in them.

There are several *Hundreds* of these *Hawns* in this City, which have in the midst of their several Courts little *Mosques* built, for those who live or lodge there to perform *Acsham*, and *Gega Nomas*, or *Evening* and *Night* Prayers in, because it is dangerous walking in the Streets after Candle-lighting: when this is done the Gate of the *Hawn* is shut. Now, considering these, and the great Houses with large Courts, that every Man of Note hath, you must needs think it to be a very fair and magnificent City,

[p. 103] to take a distant Prospect of; but yet the Streets are very narrow, which (it being exceedingly populous) is an inconvenience; for People frequently are very much throng'd as they pass the Streets, and sometimes lose their Slippers off their Feet.

The People here usually ride on Asses, if they go but a Mile or two in the City [[and call for an Ass, as they do for a Coach in *London*;]] and the Women ride astride as the Men do. These Asses pace as fast as any Horse; and for one *Parrah* or *Penny*, you may ride a Mile: The Owner of the Ass drives it; and the Drivers, as they go, are bound to call out to Persons on the way, lest any hurt be done by sudden meeting or turning; so that all Day long is heard a great Noise caus'd by the Ass-drivers, who are continually crying, either *Wuggick*, or *Thorick*, or *Shemalick*, or *Yeamejenick*,[204] i.e. *Have a care of your Face*, or *Back*, or *Left-side*, or *Right-side*.

Twice a day they generally water their Streets, because of the excessive

---

[203] *Khawn*: modern Turkish, *han*, from the Persian *khān*, "an establishment where commercial travellers could lodge for a period of time and where facilities were provided for the sale of their wares" (EI²).

[204] *Wuggick*, or *Thorick*, or *Shemalick*, or *Yeamejenick*: Arabic (Egyptian pronunciation): *waghak* [*wajhak*], *ẓahrak*, *shimālak*, *yamīnak*.

Heat. And there are many that get a Livelihood by carrying of Water in Goat-skins, with two or three brass Cups, in which they offer Water to drink to those that pass by; for which some give them to the Value of *half a Farthing*.

**[p. 104]**

As for the Plenty which abounds here, 'tis wonderful; you may have twenty, nay, five and twenty Eggs for one *Parrah*.

And you may also have fourteen or sixteen little Cakes of Bread (each of which is very near as big as a *Half-penny* Loaf with us) for one *Parrah*; and all other Things are proportionately cheap.

The *Water* which they have in this City is very *Brackish*, and therefore most of what they make use of is brought on Camels from the River *Nile*; and many Hundreds get their Living by bringing it. This Water hath such a Quality in it, that it usually *purges* Strangers at first.

Here is great scarcity of Wood; so that they heat their Ovens commonly with Horse or Cow-dung, or Dirt of the Streets. What Wood they have is brought from *Parts* adjoining to the *Black-Sea*; and is sold by weight, as Seal-Coal[205] [*sic*] is with us by Measure.

There are daily brought into this City large Herds of Goats; and if any are minded to buy of their Milk, they milk it for them before their Faces, that they may be satisfied it is good and new. Indeed, most of common Necessaries are brought about to their Doors to be sold, except it be *Flesh*.

They have a very Pretty way of *hatching Chickens* hereabouts. (It's possible some may think what I am going to tell a *Fable*,

**[p. 105]** but I declare I have seen it, and aver it to be true,) *viz.* They have a Place under ground (not unlike an Oven) the Bottom of which is spread all over with Straw, on which they lay some Thousands of Eggs, close one by the other; which, without the Warmth of the Hens, or any other prolific Heat, but that of the Sun, Dung, and such ignite Particles as the Earth may afford, are brought to Life. When the Chickens are *thus* hatch'd, they sell them to poor People by the Measure; and when they are full grown up, and fat, the Value of them is no more than two or three *Parrahs* a-piece. When I was sailing up the *Nile*, I had the Curiosity sometimes to go ashore, and walk when the Wind was contrary; for at such Times they haled the Vessel along with a Rope: When I was once walking on the Bank, I was shown a Place where Chickens were thus hatched.

---

[205] *Seal-Coal*: coal that has been mined.

In this City there is a particular Place where a Market is held twice a Week for the selling of *Christian Slaves*, which are brought by Merchants from *Turkey*, and were taken mostly by the *Tartars*; they are for the most part only Women and Children, for the *Men-Slaves* are generally kept in Turkey for the Service of the Gallies.

These Slaves brought here to be sold are most of them *Muscovites* and *Russians*, and from those Parts; and some of the *Emperor*
[p. 106] of *Germany*'s Country.[206] They are curiously deck'd,[207] and set out with fine Clothes, when they are expos'd to Sale, that they may carry the better Price. The Boys, whose Heads are shaved, when they stand in the Market, have a Lock of Hair, one part under their Caps, the other hanging down their Cheeks, to signify they are *newly* taken, and are yet *Christians*.

And altho' the Women and Maidens are veil'd, yet the Chapmen[208] have liberty to view their Faces, and to put their Fingers into their Mouths to feel their Teeth; and also, to feel their Breasts; nay, further, as I have been inform'd, they are sometimes permitted by the Sellers (in a modest way) to be search'd, whether they are Virgins or no.

It hath been affirm'd by some, that the Slaves which are sold in this Country are never compell'd to turn to the *Mahometan Religion*.

In *Algier*, I confess, it is not common [[though I my self suffer'd enough from them, God knows]] but in *Egypt* and *Turkey*, I affirm, it is otherwise.

The younger Sort which are sold for Slaves, are immediately put to School to learn to read, for they are very poor ignorant Creatures; and indeed, after they have *turn'd* they fare very well in those Parts, almost as well as their *Patroons* Children, if they are any way ingenious.
[p. 107]
They say, that these *Renegadoes* have a greater Blessing than the *natural Turks*, for they commonly become great Men and bear sway; and it is observ'd by them, that the *Children* of those *Turks* which marry here in *Egypt*, seldom live to Mens Estate, but that the *Off-spring* of these *Renegadoes* live as long as the *Natives* do, and that they have a blessing on the account of *Joseph*'s being sold into *Egypt*.[209]

---

[206] *Emperor of Germany's Country*: the Hapsburg Empire.

[207] *deck'd*: clothed.

[208] *Chapmen*: merchants.

[209] *Genesis,* chapter 39, verses 1–2, tell how Joseph was sold into slavery but "the LORD was with Joseph, and he was a prosperous man; and he was in the house of his master the Egyptian".

Here are no *Turks*, you must know, but what come from *Turkey*, and they are all *Yeane-Sherres*,[210] or, *Janizaries*, i.e. *Soldiers*.

The People of this Country (and particularly of *Cairo*) are very rugged, and much given to Passion; they'll *scold* like *Whores*, but seldom care to *fight*, and when they do, they strike with the *Palm* of their Hand, and not with the *Fist*.

They are extreamly addicted to *Cozening* and *Cheating*, especially of Strangers, who are not well acquainted with their Coin, and their manner of Buying and Selling. When the Buyer gives a *Parrah* into the Seller's Hand, the latter, if it be possible, puts it into his Mouth, and makes it quiver between his Lips with his Breath, and then cunningly takes another, not so good, which he had in his Mouth *for the Purpose*, and gives it to the Buyer, telling him 'tis *Mokseus*,[211] i.e., *Clipt*. After I was acquainted with [p. 108] this Cheat, I would suffer none to *mouth* my *Parrahs*.

They are also very *abusive* to Strangers, insomuch, that it is dangerous for such to be in the Streets after *Candle-lighting*; nay, I have known them to fall on a Stranger at *Mid-day*, and rob him, and beat him to that degree, that it hath cost him his Life. An ancient Man, a Neighbour of ours at *Algier*, who put up at the same *Hawn* with us, was so abused by villains, as he was walking in some bye Lane, that he was never well after, but died in a few Weeks.

But though they love Cheating of *Strangers* so well, yet they are strict in punishing a *false Balance*; and therefore the Bakers Bread is examined into, and if it prove less than the *just* and *legal* Weight, they take it away and give it to the Poor, and punish the offending Baker with many hard Blows on the bare Feet; which I saw several Times: For fear of this, many Times, such as know their Bread to be less than the *Standard-weight*, run away, and leave it to be seiz'd on, thereby to avoid *corporal* Punishment.

There are abundance of *Buffleas* in this Country, which are somewhat bigger than our *Oxen*, all black, but not quite so hairy; they hold their Noses much forward, with their Horns pointing backward. The People use them for the same Purposes as *Oxen* are used with us.
[p. 109]

I need not tell you of the abundance of *Rice* here, for this is known to be the *chief* Country for that Commodity in the whole World. But notwithstanding the great *Plenty* which this Country abounds with, in all

---

[210] *Yeane-Sherres*: modern Turkish, *yeniçeri*.  [211] *Mokseus*: Arabic, *maqṣūṣ*.

my Life I never saw the like multitude of *Beggars* as *here*; for 'tis a common thing to see *Ten, Twelve,* or *more* of them, in a Company together; and especially *Thursday* Evening, which is the Evening before their *Sabbath*; at which time, if there be any *Charity* going, it is shewn.

People, in this Country, are much afflicted with *Sore Eyes*, and *Swoll'n Legs*; and such as are Porters, have some other Parts also commonly very much swoll'n, by bearing of extraordinary heavy Burdens. They are generally very strong Men, and will carry *three Hundred* Weight,[212] or more, on their backs at once; nay, if I mistake not, none are admitted into their Company, unless they can carry *five Hundred* Weight such a length.

They have a saying, *That* God *hath such a Love for* this City, *that he casts his eyes upon it* seven *Times a Day, to behold it with* Complacency.

Most of the *Gentry* of this Country keep *Eunuchs* or gelt[213] *Negroes*, in their Houses, with whom they intrust their Wives; and wheresoever they go, be it to the *Bathing-houses*, or *else-where*, these *Eunuchs* go with [p. 110] them, and make way for them with a long Staff in their Hands. Their Masters, indeed, intrust them with all, in a manner, and have a great Esteem for them, insomuch that they call them *Masters*. The Reason, no doubt, is, because they would engage them to be faithful in the Trust of their Wives.

These *Eunuchs* cost a considerable Price, because they are young when they are castrated, and several die to one that lives. They usually grow to a great *Stature*, have an *effeminate* Voice, and never have any Hair grow on their Faces.

There is a Well in this City of *Cairo* of a very considerable depth, and about 20 Foot square; there is a way to go down half way, dug round about it, to which Light is given from the top of the well, through great Holes dug in the sides of it.

If I mistake not, there are about three Hundred broad Steps down to the half-way, where there is a Stable, in which Oxen are kept to draw the Water from the bottom; and there is a great Cistern, into which the Water is emptied, from whence it is drawn by other Oxen, after the same manner, to the top.

The Way of drawing it up is thus, *viz*. They have a Wheel somewhat like a Mill-wheel, on which are two Ropes; and between these are fastened little earthen Pots to both of the Ropes, about four Foot distance one from

---

[212] *three Hundred Weight*: about 150 kilos.  [213] *gelt*: castrated.

the other. As the Ox goes round, so

[p. 111] the Wheel goes round, and brings the Pots up full, which empty themselves into the Cistern, and so go down empty with their mouths downward, to take in more Water.

This contrivance is for their *Baths*, and watering of *Gardens*, &c. But it is not so much for the sake of this *Machine* that I mention this Well, as for another reason, *viz.* Because this is affirm'd by them to be the Well, in which *Joseph* was kept a Prisoner by *Potiphar*.[214]

But I am afraid I have held the Reader too long in suspense before we come to *Mecca*; I shall beg his Patience but a little longer.

From *Cairo* we proceeded on our Journey towards *Mecca*, and at the bottom, or utmost bounds of the *Red-Sea*, we came to a Town call'd *Sues*, [[or *Suez*]] which is about a Day's Journey from *Cairo*, and hath a Port, where do anchor the Ships that use the *Mecca* Voyage. They are an odd sort of Vessels, having no Decks, and are deeply laden, altogether with Provisions for *Mecca*; for when we had Intelligence at *Cairo* that they were ready, we all furnish'd our selves with three, or four Months Provisions, enough to serve us back again to *Egypt*, and then hired Camels for *Sues*.

In this Town we paid a Groat or Six-pence a Gallon for *fresh Water*. Here I saw a great Number of large very good

[p. 112] brass Guns under Covert,[215] near the Sea, laid one upon another; but forgot to enquire how they were brought there, and what they were designed for.

'Tis but a few Miles after we come out of *Egypt* before we enter into the *Wilderness*.

After we had sail'd about two or three Days from *Sues*, we anchored at *Toor*, or *Tor*, or *Eltor*,[216] a very small Town, and Port, where we refresh'd our selves with Water; for every Passenger carries his own Water. We had also here plenty of *Apricocks* and other Fruit, which were brought from *Mount-Sinai*, which is call'd by them *Toor-dog*,[217] i.e. *Law-Mountain*, because the

---

[214] *Genesis,* chapter 39: Joseph is put in prison by Potiphar after Potiphar's wife accused Joseph of trying to seduce her; the reference to being kept in a well (or pit) comes from *Genesis,* chapter 37, verses 23–24: "So it came to pass, when Joseph had come to his brothers, that they stripped Joseph of his tunic, the tunic of many colours that was on him. [24]Then they took him and cast him into a pit. And the pit was empty; there was no water in it." The well in Cairo Pitts is referring to is probably the one found in the mediaeval Citadel (built between AD 1166 and 1207).

[215] *under Covert*: under shelter.   [216] *Eltor*: Arabic, al-Ṭūr, a small port on the Sinai Peninsula.

[217] *Toor-dog*: modern Turkish, Tur Dağı.

*Moral Law*[218] was there given. This *Mountain*, I take it, is about five, or six Miles from the *Sea-side*. The *Papists*, I was told, have a *Monastery*[219] on it, for which they pay dear to the *Turks*. Many *Papists* make visits there.

After we had sail'd a little further, we were shew'd the place where (they say) the *Children of* Israel *pass'd through the* Red-Sea; which they term by the name of *Kilt el Pharown;*[220] i.e. The *Well or Pit of* Pharaoh, meaning where he and all his Host were drowned in their Pursuit after the *Israelites.*[221]

They report, That in this place is much Danger without a fresh Gale of Wind, because it is a kind of *Vortex*, the Water running whirling round, and is apt to swallow down a Ship.

[p. 113]

I guess, that the Breadth of the *Red-Sea* in this place where the *Israelites* are said to have passed through, is about six or seven Leagues.[222]

There is no safe sailing in this Sea by Night, unless it be in one place of about two Nights sail; because of the multitude of Rocks, (tho' I don't observe that the *Maps* describe them) which are so thick, that we were always in sight of some or other of them, sometimes in the midst of a great many of them, and frequently so near, as to be able to throw a Stone to them.

Some of these Rocks are much bigger than others; some look like little *Islands*, others just appear above Water, and some are to be seen a little under Water; so that every Evening we came to an anchor to the *Leeward* of one Rock or other.

Their Sailors are Prisoners of their own, and, I think, are used as bad as (if not worse than) any *Galley-Slaves* in the World.

At the hithermost Bounds of the *Red-Sea, i.e.* at *Sues* where we took shipping, it's but of a little breadth. For the space of four or five Days sail from *Tor*, we keep near the side of the Wilderness, on the Left-hand; and after that, we lose sight of the Shore on the Right-hand.

The Water of the *Red-Sea* is generally thought to be much *salter* [sic] hereabout than in other Parts, insomuch, that when they took

---

[218] *Moral Law*: the story of Moses ascending Mt Sinai and receiving the Ten Commandments can be found in *Exodus,* chapters 19–20.
[219] *Monastery*: the Orthodox Monastery of St Catherine.
[220] *Kilt el Pharown*: Arabic, Qalt al-Fira'ūn.
[221] *Israelites*: the story of the Israelites fleeing Egypt and crossing the Red Sea can be found in *Exodus*, chapters 13–14.
[222] *six or seven Leagues*: approximately 18 to 21 miles.

[p. 114] *Abdes* with it, (for none did otherwise, because of the scarcity of *fresh* Water) it made their *Posteriors* exceedingly to smart.

We were on this Sea about a Month. After we had sail'd from *Sues* about twenty Days, we came to a place where was buried ashore a *Marabbot*, *i.e.* (as you have heard) a Saint, or one reputed eminently Devout, and Religious; and perhaps some hundreds of Years are pass'd since he was there inter'd.[223] When we came here, one of the Ship's Crew (with the consent of the rest) made a little Ship, about two Foot in length, and went to every one of the *Hagges* or *Pilgrims*, (for you must observe that if any die on the Journey before they come to *Mecca*, they are notwithstanding ever after termed by the Honourable Name of *Hagge*) desiring them to bestow their *Charity* in Honour of the said *Marabbot*; and at such a time they liberally bestow some piece of Money to the said end. They then took some small Wax-Candles, with a little Bottle of Oil, and put them into the Ship, together with the Money they had received of well-inclin'd People, *as they said* (but I am apt to think they put in but a very small part of it, if any at all, but kept it to themselves.) This being done they all held up their Hands begging the *Marabbot's* Blessing, and praying that they might have a good Voyage. And then they put the Ship over-

[p. 115]

board into the Sea, not in the least doubting of its safe Arrival to the *Marabbot*, for the benefit of his Sepulchre, tho' it be a *desolate* Place and not at all inhabited, where he is said to lie inter'd. Poor Ignorant Creatures!

This *Marabbot*, they have a Tradition, died in his Voyage towards *Mecca*; and therefore his Memory is most highly esteemed, and venerated by them.

The Veneration they have for these *Marabbots* is so great, that if any Person who hath committed Murder, flies to one of the little Houses (which, as I inform'd you, are built upon their Sepulchres) for Sanctuary, he's as safe as if he were in a *Convent*: For none durst touch him, in order to fetch him thence.

A few Days after this, we came to a place called *Rabbock*,[224] about *four* days Sail on this side *Mecca*, where all the *Hagges* (excepting those of the Female Sex) do enter into *Hirrawem*, or *Ihram*,[225] *i.e.* They take off all their

---

[223] Probably the tomb on Al-Ḥasānī island, a well-known landmark for Arab sailors, just north of Umm Lajj on the Hijaz coast. Royal Navy, *Red Sea Pilot* (1980) p. 158; Wellsted (1836) p. 65.

[224] *Rabbock*: Arabic, Al-Rābigh, a small port in Saudi Arabia about 100 miles north of Jiddah.

[225] *Ihram*: Arabic, *iḥrām*, the state of consecration required of Muslims engaged on the pilgrimage.

Clothes, covering themselves with two *Hirrawems*,[226] or large white *Cotton Wrappers*; one they put about their *middle*, which reaches down to their Ancles; the other they cover the *upper part* of the Body with, except the *Head*; and they wear no other thing on their Bodies but these *Wrappers*, only a pair of *Gimgameea*,[227] *i.e.* Thin-sol'd Shoes, like *Sandals*, the Over-leather of which covers only the Toes, their Insteps being all
[p. 116] naked. In this manner like humble *Penitents* they go from *Rabbock* till they come to *Mecca*, to approach the *Temple*; many times enduring the *scorching* heat of the Sun, till their very Skin is *burnt* off their Backs, and Arms, and their Heads *swoll'n* to a very great Degree. Yet when any Man's Health is by such *Austerities* in *danger*, and like to be impair'd, they may lawfully put on their Clothes, on condition still, that when they come to *Mecca*, they sacrifice a Sheep, and give it to the Poor. During the time of their wearing this *mortifying* Habit, which is about the space of *seven* Days, it is held unlawful for them so much as to cut their *Nails*, or to kill a *Louse*, or a *Flea*, tho' they see them sucking their Blood: But yet if they are so troublesome that they cannot well endure it longer, 'tis lawful for them to *remove* them from one place of the Body to another.

During this time they are very watchful over their *Tempers*, keep a jealous Eye upon their *Passions*, and observe a strict Government of their *Tongues*, making continual use of a *Form* of devout Expressions. And they will also be careful to be *reconcil'd*, and at Peace, with all such as they had any Difference with, accounting it a very sinful, and shameful thing to bear the least Malice against any. They do not shave themselves during this time.
[p. 117]
Next we come to *Gidda*,[228] the nearest Seaport Town to *Mecca*, not quite one day's Journey from it, where the Ships are unloaded. Here we are met by *Dilleels*,[229] *i.e.* certain Persons who come from *Mecca* on purpose to instruct the *Hagges*, or *Pilgrims*, in the *Ceremonies* (most of them being ignorant of them) which are to be used in their Worship at the Temple there; in the middle of which is a Place which they call *Beat Allah*, i.e. the House of God. They say that *Abraham* built it; *to which I give no Credit.*

---

[226] *Hirrawems:* Arabic, *harā'im*, plural form of *hirām*, which is the name for the actual garment worn while in a state of *ihrām*.
[227] *Gimgameea:* Arabic, *jamjamiyyah*.
[228] *Gidda:* Jiddah (often pronounced Jeddah; sometimes Juddah). Actually about 48 miles from Mecca, so a day's journey only in the sense of a 24-hour journey.
[229] *Dileels:* Arabic, *dalīl*.

As soon as we come to the Town of *Mecca*, the *Dilleel,* or *Guide,* carries us into the Great Street, which is in the midst of the Town, and to which the *Temple* joins★: [[Note, *that before they'll provide for themselves, they serve God in their way.*]] After the Camels are laid down, he first directs us to the *Fountains*, there to take *Abdes*; which being done, he brings us to the *Temple,* into which (having left our Shoes with one who constantly attends to receive them) we enter at the Door called *Bab el-Salem,*[230] *i.e.* the *Welcome Gate,* or *Gate of Peace.* After a few Paces entrance, the *Dilleel* makes a stand, and holds up his Hands towards the *Beat-Allah* (it being in the middle of the *Mosque*) the *Hagges* imitating him, and saying after him the same

[p. 118] Words which he speaks. At the very first sight of the *Beat-Allah,* the *Hagges* melt into Tears: then we are led *up to it,* still speaking after the *Dilleel*; then we are led *round* it seven times, and then make two *Erkaets.* This being done, we are led out into the Street again, where we are sometimes to run, and sometimes to walk very quick with the *Dilleel,* from one place of the Street to the other, about a Bow-shot.[231] And I profess, I could not chuse [*sic*] but admire to see those poor Creatures so extraordinary *devout,* and *affectionate* when they were about these *Superstitions,* and with what *Awe,* and *Trembling,* they were possess'd; insomuch, that I could scarce forbear shedding of *Tears,* to see their Zeal, tho' *blind* and *idolatrous.* After all this is done, we return'd to the place in the Street where we left our Camels, with our Provision, and Necessaries, and then look out for *Lodgings*; where, when we come, we *disrobe* and take off our *Hirrawems,* and put on our ordinary Clothes again.

All the *Pilgrims* hold it to be their great Duty well to improve their Time whilst they are at *Mecca,* not only to do their accustomed *Duty,* and *Devotion* in the *Temple,* but to spend all their leisure time there, and as far Strength will permit, to continue at *Towoaf,*[232] *i.e.* to walk round the *Beat-Allah,* which is about four and twenty Paces square. At one corner of the *Beat* there is

[p. 119] a black Stone fastned [*sic*], and fram'd in with silver Plate, and every time they come to that Corner they *kiss* the Stone; and having gone round *seven* times, they perform two *Erkaets-nomas,* or *Prayers.* This Stone, *they say,*

---

[230] *Bab el-Salem*: Arabic, Bāb al-Salām.

[231] Pitts is here referring to the *sa'y*, the "running" or walking quickly between the two small hills of Ṣafā and Marwah in Mecca, one of the rites of the Ḥajj performed immediately after the circumambulation of the Ka'bah and the prayer at the Station of Abraham.

[232] *Towoaf*: Arabic, ṭawāf, circumambulation.

was formerly *white*, and then it was called *Haggar Essaed*,[233] i.e. *the white Stone*. But by Reason of the Sins of the Multitudes of People who kiss it, it is become *black*, and is now called *Haggar Esswaed*,[234] or *the Black Stone*.

This place is so much frequented by People going round it, that the place of *Towoaf*, *i.e.* the Circuit which they take in going round it, is seldom void of People at any time of the Day, or Night. Many have waited several Weeks, nay Months, for the opportunity of finding it so. For they say, that if any Person is blessed with such an opportunity, that for his or her Zeal in keeping up the Honour of *Towoaf*, let them petition what they will at the *Beat-Allah*, they shall be answered. Many will walk round till they are quite weary, then rest, and at it again; carefully remembring [*sic*] at the end of every *seventh* time to perform two *Erkaets*. This *Beat* is in effect the Object of their Devotion, the *Idol* which they adore: For let them be never so far distant from it, *East*, *West*, *North*, or *South* of it, they'll be sure to bow down towards it; but when they are at the *Beat*, they may go on which side they [p. 120] please and pay their *Sallah* towards it. Sometimes there are several Hundreds at *Towoaf* at once, especially after *Acsham-nomas*, or fourth time of *Service*, which is after Candle-lighting (as you heard before) and these both Men, and Women; but the Women walk on the outside of the Men, and the Men nearest to the *Beat*. In so great a Resort as this, it is not to be suppos'd that every individual Person can come to *kiss* the *Stone* aforementioned; therefore in such a case, the lifting up the Hands towards it, smoothing down their Faces, and using a short Expression of Devotion, as *Allah-waick barick*, i.e. *Blessed God*, or *Allah Cabor*,[235] i.e. *Great God*, or somesuch like; and so passing by it till opportunity of *kissing* it offers, is thought sufficient. But when there are but few Men at *Towoaf*, then the Women get opportunity to *kiss* the said *Stone*; and when they have gotten it, they close in with it as they come round, and walk round as quick as they can to come to it again, and so keep possession of it for a considerable time. The Men, when they see that the Women have got the place, will be so civil as to pass by and give them leave to take their *fill*, as I may say, in their *Towoaf*, or walking round, during which they are using some formal

---

[233] *Haggar Essaed*: Arabic, Ḥajar Asʿad.

[234] *Haggar Esswaed*: Arabic, Ḥajar Aswad. Burton (1913),Vol. 2, 363 states: "This is an error. The stone is called *Hajar Aswad*, the Black Stone, or *Hajar Asʿad*, the Blessed Stone. Moreover it did not change its colour on account of the sins of the people who kissed it."

[235] *Allah Cabor*: a variant transcription by Pitts of *Allāhu akbar*, which is usually translated as "God is Most Great".

Expressions. When the Women are at the *Stone*, then it's esteem'd a very rude and abominable thing to go near them, respecting the Time and Place.
[p. 121]

I shall now give you a more particular *Description* of *Mecca* and the *Temple* there.

First, as to *Mecca*. It is a Town situated in a barren place (about one day's Journey from the *Red-Sea*) in a Valley, or rather in the midst of many little Hills. 'Tis a Place of no Force, wanting both Walls, and Gates. Its Building[s] are (as I said before) very ordinary, insomuch that it would be a place of no tolerable Entertainment, were it not for the *Anniversary*[236] Resort of so many thousand *Hagges*, or *Pilgrims*, on whose coming the whole dependence of the Town (in a manner) is; for many Shops are scarcely open all the Year besides.

The People here, I observ'd, are a poor sort of People, very thin, lean, and swarthy. The Town is surrounded for several Miles with many thousands of little Hills, which are very near one to the other. I have been on the top of some of them near *Mecca*, where I could see some Miles about, but yet was not able to see the farthest of the Hills. They are all Stony-Rock, and blackish, and pretty near of a bigness, appearing at a distance like Cocks of Hay, but all pointing towards *Mecca*. Some of them are half a Mile in Circumference, *&c.* but all near of one Height. The People here have an odd, and foolish sort of *Tradition* concerning them, *viz.* That when
[p. 122] *Abraham* went about building the *Beat-Allah*, God by his wonderful Providence did so order it, that every *Mountain* in the World should contribute something to the building thereof; and accordingly every one did send its *Proportion*. Though there is a *Mountain* near *Algier*, which is called *Corra Dog*,[237] i.e. *Black Mountain*. And the Reason of its Blackness, *they say*, is because it did not send any Part of itself towards building the *Temple* at *Mecca*. Between these Hills is good, and plain Travelling, tho' they stand near to one another.

There is upon the top of one of them a *Cave*, which they term *Hira*,[238] i.e. *Blessing*: Into which (they say) *Mahomet* did usually retire for his solitary Devotion, Meditations and Fastings; and here they believe he had a great

---

[236] *Anniversary*: annual.

[237] *Corra Dog*: modern Turkish, Kara Dağ.

[238] *Hira*: Arabic, Ḥirāʾ, the cave or grotto at the summit of Mt Ḥirāʾ, now usually called Jabal al-Nūr, the Mountain of Light.

part of the *Alcoran* brought him by the Angel *Gabriel*. I have been in this *Cave*, and observ'd that it is not at all beautified; at which I admir'd.

About half a Mile out of *Mecca* is a very steep Hill,[239] and there are Stairs made to go to the top of it, where is a *Cupola*, under which is a cloven Rock; into this, they say, *Mahomet*, when very young, *viz.* about four Years of Age, was carried by the Angel *Gabriel*, who open'd his Breast, and took out his Heart, from which he pick'd some black Blood Specks, which was his *original Corruption*; then put it into its

[p. 123] Place again, and afterward clos'd up the Part; and that during this Operation *Mahomet* felt no Pain.

Into this very place I my self went, because the rest of my Company did so, and performed some *Erkaets*, as they did.

The Town hath plenty of Water, and yet but few Herbs, unless in some particular places. Here are several sorts of good Fruits to be had, *viz. Grapes, Melons, Water-Melons, Cucumbers, Pumkins*, and the like; but these are brought two or three days Journey off, where there is a place of very great Plenty, call'd, if I mistake not, *Habbash*.[240] Likewise, Sheep are brought hither and sold. So that as to *Mecca* it self, it affords little or nothing of comfortable Provisions. It lieth in a very hot Country, insomuch that People run from one side of the Streets to the other to get into the Shadow, as the motion of the Sun causes it. The Inhabitants, especially Men, do usually sleep on the tops of the Houses for the Air, or in the Streets before their Doors. Some lay the small Bedding they have on a thin Mat on the Ground; others have a slight Frame, made much like *Drink-Stalls* on which we place Barrels, standing on four Legs, corded with *Palm Cordage*; on which they put their Bedding. Before they bring out their Bedding, they sweep the Streets and water them. As for my

[p. 124] own part, I usually lay open without any Bed covering, on the Top of the House; only I took a Linen Cloth, dipt in Water, and after I had wrung it, cover'd my self with it in the Night; and when I awoke I should find it dry; then I would wet it again: and thus I did two or three times in a Night.

---

[239] Pitts is possibly referring to Jabal al-Qubays.

[240] *Habbash*: Arabic, Ḥabash, or Ethiopia. Clearly Al-Ṭā'if, the traditional source of fruit and vegetables for Mecca, is meant. Burton (1913) discusses fruit in the Holy Places in Vol. 1, pp. 402–4, and mentions Taif (Al-Ṭā'if) and Medina but never Ethiopia.

*Secondly*, I shall next give you some account of the *Temple* of *Mecca*.

It hath about forty two Doors to enter into it, not so much, I think, for Necessity, as Figure; for in some places they are close by one another. The Form of it is much resembling that of the *Royal Exchange* in *London*, but I believe it's near ten times bigger. 'Tis all open, and gravell'd in the midst, except some Paths that come from certain Doors which lead to the *Beat-Allah*, and are pav'd with broad Stones. The Walks, or Cloisters, all round are arch'd over head, and pav'd beneath with fine broad Stone; and all round are little Rooms, or *Cells*, where such dwell as give themselves up to Reading, Studying, and a devout Life, who are much a-kin to their *Dervises*,[241] or *Hermits*.

The *Dervises* are most commonly such as live an *Eremitick*[242] Life, travelling up and down the Country like *Mendicants*, living on the Charity of others, wearing a white

[p. 125] Woollen Garment, and a long white Woollen Cap (much like some of the Orders of *Friers* in the *Romish Church*) with a *Sheep* or *Goats-Skin* on their Back to lie on, and a long Staff in their Hand. When they read, they commonly sit down, putting their Legs across, and keeping their Knees above the Ground. They usually carry their *Beads* about their Arms, or Necks; whereas others carry them in their Pockets. Many *Turks*, when they reform, give themselves up to a *Dervise* sort of Life: And for an Instance, my second *Patroon* had a younger Brother, who had liv'd a very debauch'd Life; but on a sudden a great Change seem'd to be wrought upon him, insomuch that he let his *Beard* grow, never shaving it, and put on his great *green Turbant*, which none presume to wear, but such as are of the Blood and Race of *Mahomet*, and betook himself to the learning his *Elif be te*, i.e. *A. B. C.* In a little time he attain'd to read very well, and spent a great part of his time in Reading. Some of his old jolly Companions would laugh at him for it; but he still kept on in this strict way of Living, notwithstanding all their *Banters*.

The *Beat-Allah*, which stands in the middle of the *Temple*, is Four-square, about twenty four Paces each Square, and near twenty four Foot in Height. 'Tis built with great Stone, all smooth, and plain,

[p. 126] without the least bit of carv'd Work on it. 'Tis covered all over from top to bottom, with a thick sort of Silk. Above the middle part of the

---

[241] *Dervises*: modern Turkish, *derviş*, from the Arabic, *darwīsh*, a poor, holy man, who depends on the charity of Muslims for food and lodging.
[242] *Eremitick*: hermit-like.

Covering[243] are imbroidered all round Letters of Gold, the meaning of which I cannot well call to mind; but I think, they were some *devout* Expressions. Each Letter is near two Foot in length, and two Inches broad. Near the lower end of this *Beat*, are large Brass Rings fastned [*sic*] into it, through which passeth a great Cotton Rope; and to this the lower end of the Covering is tack'd. The Threshold of the Door that belongs to the *Beat*, is as high as a Man can reach; and therefore when any Person enters into it, a sort of Ladder-stairs are brought for that purpose. The Door is plated all over with Silver,[244] and there's a Covering hangs over it, and reaches to the Ground, which is kept turn'd up all the Week, except *Thursday* Night, and *Friday*, which is their *Sabbath*. The said Covering of the Door is very thick imbroider'd with Gold, insomuch that it weighs several score Pounds. The top of the *Beat* is flat, beaten with Lime and Sand; and there is a long Gutter, or Spout, to carry off the Water when it rains; at which time the People will run, throng, and struggle, to get under the said Gutter, that so the Water that comes off the *Beat* may fall upon them, accounting it as the *Dew of Heaven,* and

[p. 127] looking on it as a great Happiness to have it drop upon them: But if they can recover some of this Water to drink, they esteem it to be yet a much greater Happiness. Many poor People make it their Endeavour to get some of it, and present it to the *Hagges;* for which they are well-rewarded.

In *Mecca* there are thousands of blue Pigeons, which none will affright, or abuse, much less kill them; and they are therefore so very tame, that they'll pick Meat out of one's hand. I my self have often fed them in the House where I resided while there. They come in great Flocks to the *Temple*, where they are usually fed by the *Hagges:* For the poor People of *Mecca* come to them with a little sort of a Dish made with Rushes, with some Corn in it, begging them to bestow something on *Hammamet Metta Nabee,*[245] *i.e.* the Pigeons of the Prophet. I have heard some say, that in their Flight they'll never fly over the *Beat-Allah*, as if they knew it to be the *House of God:* But it is a very great mistake, for I have seen them oftentimes fly over it.

This *Beat-Allah* is opened but two Days in the space of six Weeks, *viz.* one Day for the Men, and the next Day for the Women. As I was at *Mecca*

---

[243] *Covering*: Pitts is here describing the *kiswah*, or black cloth embroidered with passages from the Qur'ān and decoration in gold thread, which covers the Ka'bah.
[244] *Silver*: Pitts adds a note in the 1738 edition that the door "is of wood, only plated over with silver".
[245] *Hammamet Metta Nabee*: colloquial Arabic, *ḥamāmāt matā' al-Nabī.*

about four Months, I had the opportunity of entring [*sic*] into it twice; a *reputed* Advantage, which many Thousands of the *Hagges* have not met with. [p. 128] For those that come by *Land* make no longer stay at *Mecca* than sixteen, or seventeen Days.

When any enter into the Beat, all that they have to do is to perform two *Erkaets* on each side, with the holding up the two Hands, and petitioning at the Conclusion of each two *Erkaets*. And they are so very *reverent*, and *devout*, in doing this, that they will not suffer their Eyes to *wander*, and *gaze* about; for they account it very sinful so to do. Nay, *they say*, that one was smitten blind for gazing about when in the *Beat*, as the Reward of his vain, and unlawful *Curiosity*. I could not, for my part, give any *Credit* to this Story, but look'd on it as a *Legendary* Relation, and therefore was resolved, if I could, to take my View of it; I mean, not to continue gazing about it, but now and then to cast an observing Eye. And, I profess, I found nothing worth seeing in it, only two Wooden Pillars in the midst to keep up the Roof, and a Bar of Iron fastened to them, on which hang'd three or four Silver Lamps, (which are, I suppose, but seldom, if ever lighted.) The Floor of the *Beat* is Marble, and so is the inside of the Walls, on which there is written something in *Arabick*, which I had not time to read. The Walls, tho' of Marble on the Inside, are hung all over with Silk, which is pull'd off before the

[p. 129] *Hagges* enter. Those that go into the *Beat* tarry there but a very *little* while, (*viz.* scarce so much as half a quarter of an Hour) because *others* wait for the same Privilege; and while some go in, others are going out. After *all* is over, and all that will, have done this, the *Sultan* of *Mecca*, who is a *Shirreef*,[246] *i.e.* one of the race of *Mahomet*, accounts himself not too good to cleanse the *Beat*; and therefore with some of his Favorites doth wash, and cleanse it. And first of all, they wash it with the holy Water, *Zem Zem*, and after that with sweet Water. The Stairs which were brought to enter in at the Door of the *Beat*, being remov'd, the People crowd under the Door, to receive on them the Sweeping of the said Water. And the Besoms,[247] wherewith the *Beat* is cleansed, are broken in pieces, and thrown out amongst the Mob; and he that gets a small Stick, or Twig of it, keeps it as a *Sacred Relique*.

---

[246] *Shirreef*: Arabic, Sharīf, or descendant of the Prophet Muḥammad. The office of Sharīf of Mecca, or guardian of the Holy Places, was founded in the mid-10th century AD.
[247] *Besoms*: brooms.

Every Year the Covering of this *Beat-Allah* is renewed in *Grand Cairo*, by the order of the *Grand Seignior;*[248] and when the *Caravan* goes with the *Hagges* to *Mecca*, then is the new Covering carried upon two *Camels,* which do no other Work all the Year long. It is sent out of Egypt with a great deal of Rejoycing [*sic*], and received into *Mecca* with wonderful Joy, many People even weeping for Joy, and some *kissing* the very *Camels*

[p. 130] that carry it, bidding them *welcome* again and again, reaching their Hands up to the Covering, and then smoothing down their Faces. This and a great deal more they do, to show what a *Veneration* they have for this new Covering, tho' not yet put on about the *Beat.* Well may you think then what Esteem they have for the *Beat-Allah* it self.

When the Old Covering, or *Hirrawem*, [[or *Irham*]] (for so the name of it is) is taken down, the New one is put up by the *Sultan Shirreef* of *Mecca*,[249] with some to assist him. The Old Covering the *Sultan* takes into his own Custody, for it properly belongs to him, and cuts it in pieces, and sells them to the *Hagges*, who care not, almost, how much they give for a piece of it. They being so *eager* after these Shreds, a piece of the bigness of a *Sheet of Paper* will cost a *Sultane*,[250] *i.e.* nine, or ten Shillings. Yea, the very Cotton Rope (to which the lower part of the Covering was fastened) is also cut into Pieces, untwisted, and sold. Many buy a piece of the Covering of the *Beat* on purpose to have it laid on their Breast when they are *Dead*, and be buried with them; this they carry always with them, esteeming it as an excellent *Amulet* to preserve them from all manner of Danger. I am apt to believe that the *Sultan Shirreef* makes as much Money of the Old Covering as the New may cost, although, they say, that the Work that is in

[p. 131] it is alone the Employment of many People for a whole Year's space.

But to speak something further of the *Temple of Mecca*; (for I am willing to be very particular in matters about it, tho' in so being, I should, it may

---

[248] *Grand Seignior:* the Ottoman Sultan. The practice of the Ottomans' donating the *kiswah* or covering of the Ka'bah each year was discontinued in 1924, the year that the Caliphate was abolished and Mecca was taken by 'Abd al-'Azīz Ibn Sa'ūd. A year later the whole of the Hijaz including Jiddah and Medina was annexed by Riyadh, and 'Abd al-'Azīz Ibn Sa'ūd proclaimed himself King of the Hijaz on 8 January 1926. Since that time the Muslim Holy Places have been under Saudi control and protection. In 1927 the joint Kingdom of the Hijaz and Najd received international recognition, as a prelude to the formal proclamation of the Kingdom of Saudi Arabia in 1932.

[249] The Sharīf of Mecca during Pitts's pilgrimage in the mid-1680s would have been Aḥmad ibn Zaid (r. 1669–71 and 1684–87). De Gaury (1951), 291.

[250] *Sultane:* Arabic, *sulṭānī*, a gold coin used in the Ottoman Empire at the time.

be, speak of things which by some People may be thought trivial.) The compass of Ground round the *Beat* (where the People exercise themselves in the Duty of *Towoaf*) is paved with *Marble* about fifty Foot in breadth; and round this *Marble* Pavement stand Pillars of Brass about *fifteen* Foot high, and twenty Foot distant from each other; above the middle part of which Iron Bars are fastened, reaching from one to the other, and several Lamps made of Glass, are hang'd to each of the said Bars, with Brass Wires in the Form of a *Triangle*, to give Light in the Night-season; for they pay their Devotions at the *Beat-Allah* as much by Night, as by Day, during the *Hagges* stay at Mecca. These glasses are half filled with Water, and a third Part with Oil, on which a round Wire of Brass is buoy'd up with three little Corks; in the Midst of this Wire is made a Place to put in the Wick, or Cotton, which burns till the Oil is spent. Every Day they are washed clean, and replenished with fresh Water, Oil, and Cotton.

On each of the four Squares of the *Beat* is a little Room built, and over every one of

[p. 132] them is a little Chamber with Windows all round it, in which Chambers the *Emaums* (together with the *Mezzins*) perform *Sallah*, in the Audience of all the People which are below. These four Chambers are built, one at each Square of the *Beat*, by reason that there are four Sorts of *Mahometans*. The *First* are call'd *Hanifee*; most of them are Turks. The *Second Schafee*; whose Manners and Ways the *Arabians* follow. The *Third Hanbelee*; of which there are but few. The *Fourth Malekee*;[251] of which are those that live Westward of *Egypt*, even to the *Emperor of Morocco*'s Country. These all agree in *Fundamentals*, only there is some small difference between them in the *Ceremonial Part*.

As for Instance, The *Hanifees*, when they stand at their *Devotion*, having touch'd the lower part of the Ears with their two Thumbs, place their Hands on their Bellies, the Right-hand on the left, intimating, that they stand bound in the Presence of God, to live well. The *Malekees* and *Schafees* lift up their Hands in a sort of careless manner, and then let them fall down and hang by their sides; which intimates (as they say) a *Reverence of the Divine Majesty*.

As for the *Hanbelees*, they differ but little from the *Hanifees*; but of all these four Sorts, the *Hanifees* seem to be the most *serious*, *devout*, and *deliberate*, in their *Worship*, as well as in their *Preparatories*. Every

---

[251] *Hanifee*; *Schafee*; *Hanbelee*; *Malekee*: Arabic, Ḥanafī, Shāfiʿī, Ḥanbalī, Mālikī; the four *madhāhib*, or Sunnī schools of law.

**[p. 133]** *Mussulman* is bound to believe in all *Mahomet's* Apostles (as they call them) especially these four, *viz. Abu-Beker, Omar, Othman,* and *Ali,*[252] who were the great and principal Sticklers[253] for the Religion of *Mahomet* after his Death. But the *Hanbelees* do not own *Ali* to be one of *Mahomet's* Apostles; upon which Account they are look'd on by the rest as *Heretical.*

About twelve Paces from the *Beat* is (as they say) the Sepulchre of *Abraham,* who by God's immediate Command, *they tell you,* built this *Beat-Allah;* which Sepulchre is enclos'd within Iron Grates: 'Tis made somewhat like the Tomb-stones which People of Fashion have among us, but with a very handsome imbroider'd Covering. Into this Persons are very apt to gaze. A small Distance from it, on the Left-hand, is a Well, which they call *Beer el zem zem,* the Water whereof they call *Holy Water,* and as superstitiously esteem it as the *Papists* do theirs. In the Month of *Ramadan* they'll be sure to break their *Fast* with it. They report that it is as sweet as Milk; but for my part, I could perceive no other taste in it than in common Water, except that it was somewhat *brackish.* The *Hagges,* when they come first to *Mecca,* drink of it unreasonably; by which means they are not only much *purged,* but their Flesh breaks out all in *Pimples;* and this they call the *Purging of*

**[p. 134]** *their spiritual Corruptions.* There are hundreds of *Pitchers* belonging to the *Temple,* which in the Month of *Ramadan* are fill'd with the said Water, and plac'd all along before the People (with Cups to drink) as they are kneeling and waiting for *Acsham Nomas,* or *Evening Service;* and as soon as the *Mezzins* or *Clerks,* on the tops of the *Minarets,* begin their *Bawling* to call them to *Nomas,* they fall a drinking thereof, before they begin their Devotions. This *Beer,*[254] or Well, of *Zem Zem,* is in the midst of one of the little Rooms before-mentioned at each Square of the *Beat,* distant about twelve or fourteen Paces from it, out of which four Men are employ'd to draw Water, without any Pay or Reward, for any that shall desire it. Each of these Men have two Leather Buckets ty'd to a Rope on a small Wheel, one of which comes up full, while the other goes down empty. They do not only drink this Water, but oftentimes bathe themselves with it; at which time they take off their Clothes, only covering their lower Parts with a thin Wrapper, and one of the Drawers pours on each Person's Head five or six Buckets of

---

[252] *Abu-Beker, Omar, Othman,* and *Ali*: Arabic, Abū Bakr, 'Umar, 'Uthmān, and 'Alī, the first four Caliphs of Islam, usually known as al-Khulafā' al-rāshidūn, or the Rightly-guided Caliphs.

[253] *Sticklers*: supporters.

[254] *Beer*: Arabic, Bi'r.

Water\*. [[\* *The worthy Mons* Thevenot *saith, That the Waters of* Mecca *are* bitter; *but I never found them* so, *but as* sweet *and as* good *as any others, for ought* [*sic*; sc. aught] *as I could perceive.*]][255] The Person bathing may lawfully wash **[p. 135]** himself therewith above the middle, but not his lower Parts, because they account them not worthy, only letting the Water take its way downwards. In short, they make use of this Water only to drink, take *Abdes*, and for bathing; neither may they take *Abdes* with it, unless they first cleanse their secret Parts with other common Water. Yea, such an high Esteem they have for it, that many *Hagges* carry it home to their respective Countries in little latten[256] or tin Pots, and present it to their Friends, half a Spoonful, it may be, to each, who receive it in the hollow of their Hand with great Care and abundance of Thanks, sipping a little of it, and bestowing the rest on their Faces and naked Heads; at the same Time holding up their Hands, and desiring of God, that they also may be so happy and prosperous as to go on *Pilgrimage* to *Mecca*. The Reason of their putting such an high Value upon the Water of *this Well*, is because (as they say) it is the Place where *Ishmael* was laid by his Mother *Hagar*. I have heard them tell the Story exactly, as it is recorded in the 21st Chapter of *Genesis*;[257] and they say, that in the very Place where the *Child* padled [*sic*] with his Feet, the Water flowed out.

I shall now inform you how, when, and where, they receive the honourable Title of *Hagges*; for which they are at all this Pains and Expence. **[p. 136]**

The *Curbaen Byram*, or the *Feast of Sacrifice*, follows two Months and ten Days after the *Ramadan Fast*. The eighth Day after the said two Months they all enter into *Hirrawem*, i.e. put on their *mortifying* Habit again, and in that manner go to a certain Hill called *Gibbel el Orphat*,[258] [[or *el Arafat*]] i.e.

---

[255] *Thevenot*: For more information on Thévenot, see Part I, Chapter 3, notes 108 and 196. Thévenot's remarks on the waters of Mecca in general and ZamZam in particular can be found on p. 152 of Part Two of the 1687 edition.

[256] *latten*: a yellow metal resembling brass.

[257] *Genesis*, chapter 21, verses 16–19: "And she [Hagar] went, and sat her down over against him a good way off, as it were a bow shot: for she said, Let me not see the death of the child. And she sat over against him, and lift up her voice, and wept. [17]And God heard the voice of the lad; and the angel of God called to Hagar out of heaven, and said unto her, What aileth thee, Hagar? fear not; for God hath heard the voice of the lad where he is. [18]Arise, lift up the lad, and hold him in thine hand; for I will make him a great nation. [19]And God opened her eyes, and she saw a well of water; and she went, and filled the bottle with water, and gave the lad drink."

[258] *Gibbel el Orphat*: Arabic, Jabal 'Arafāt. Strictly, 'Arafāt is the plain 12 miles south-west of Mecca where the climax of the Ḥajj, the Standing at 'Arafāt, takes place on the 9th day of the pilgrimage month, Dhū-l-Ḥijjah. The Jabal, or Mountain, that overlooks the plain and on which pilgrims gather at the Standing is called Jabal al-Raḥmah, the Mount of Mercy.

the Mountain of *Knowledge*; for there, they say, *Adam* first found and knew his Wife *Eve*.[259] And they likewise say, that she was buried at *Gidda* near the *Red Sea*; at whose Sepulchre all the *Hagges*, who come to *Mecca* by way of the *Red Sea*, perform two *Erkaets Nomas*, and, I think, no more. I could not but smile to hear this their *ridiculous* Tradition (for so I must pronounce it) when observing the Marks which were set, the one at the Head, and the other at the Foot of the Grave, I guess'd them to be about a Bow-shot distant from each other. On the middle of her *supposed* Grave is a little *Mosque* built, where the *Hagges* pay their *Religious Respect*.

This *Gibbel* or *Hill* is not so big as to contain the vast *Multitudes* which resort thither; for 'tis said by them, that there meet no less than *Seventy Thousand Souls* every Year, on the *ninth* Day after the two Months after *Ramadan*; and if it happen that in any Year there be wanting some of that Number, God, *they say*, will supply the Deficiency by so many *Angels*.

[p. 137]

I do confess, the Number of *Hagges* I saw at this Mountain was very great; nevertheless, I cannot think they could amount to so many as *Seventy Thousand*. There are certain Bound-Stones[260] placed round the *Gibbel*, in the Plain, to shew how far the *sacred Ground* (as they esteem it) extends; and many are so zealous, as to come and pitch their Tents within these Bounds, some Time before the Hour of paying their *Devotion* here comes, waiting for it. But why they so solemnly approach *this Mountain*, beyond any other Place, and receive from hence the Title of *Hagges*, I confess, I do not more fully understand than what I have already said, giving but *little heed* to these *Delusions*. I observ'd nothing worth seeing on this *Hill*, for there was only a small *Cupola* on the top of it; neither are there any *Inhabitants* nearer to it than *Mecca*. About one or two of the Clock, which is the Time of *Eulea Nomas,* having *wash'd*, and made themselves ready for it, they perform *that,* and at the same Time perform *Ekinde Nomas*, which they never do at one time but upon *this Occasion*; because, at the Time when *Ekinde Nomas* should be perform'd in the *accustomed* Order (*viz.*) about *Four of the Clock in the Afternoon*, they are imploring Pardon for their Sins, and receiving the *Emaums* Benediction.

[p. 138]

It was a Sight, indeed, able to pierce one's Heart, to behold so many

---

[259] *Adam and Eve*: see Burton (1913), pp. 188–9 for a discussion of this story.
[260] *Bound-Stones*: boundary stones.

Thousands in their Garments of *Humility* and *Mortification*, with their *naked Heads* and *Cheeks watered with Tears*; and to hear their grievous *Sighs* and *Sobs*, begging earnestly for the *Remission of their Sins*, and promising *Newness of Life*, using a Form of *penitential Expressions*; and thus continuing for the Space of four or five Hours, *viz.* until the Time of *Acsham Nomas*, which is to be perform'd about half an Hour after Sun-set. [[It is matter of sorrowful Reflection, to compare the *Indifference* of many *Christians*, with this *Zeal* of those poor blind *Mahometans*, who will, 'tis to be feared, *rise up in* Judgment *against them, and condemn them.*]] After their solemn Performance of their *Devotions* thus at the *Gibbel*, they all at once receive that honourable Title of *Hagge* from the *Emaum* or *Imam*, and are so stiled [*sic*] to their dying Day. Immediately, upon their receiving *this Name*, the Trumpet is sounded, and they all leave the *Hill* and return for *Mecca*, and being gone two or three Miles on their Way, they there rest for that Night;[261] but after *Nomas*, before they go to rest, each Person gathers nine and forty small Stones, about the bigness of an *Hazle* [*sic*] *Nut*; the meaning of which I shall acquaint you with presently.

[p. 139]

 The next Morning they move to a Place call'd *Mina* or *Muna*;[262] the Place, *as they say*, where *Abraham* went to offer up his Son *Isaac*, and therefore in this place they sacrifice their Sheep: It is about two or three Miles from *Mecca*. I was here shown a Stone, or little Rock, which was parted in the middle. *They told me*, that when *Abraham* was going to sacrifice his *Son*, instead of striking him, Providence directed his Hand to this Stone, which he clave in two. *It must be a good Stroke indeed!*

 Here they all pitch their Tents (it being in a spacious Plain) and spend the Time of *Curbaen Byram*, viz. three Days. As soon as their Tents are pitch'd, and all Things orderly dispos'd, every individual *Hagge*, the first Day, goes and throws Seven of the small Stones, which they had gathered, against a small Pillar, or little square Stone Building★. [[★*Monsieur* de Thevenot[263] *saith, That they throw these Stones at the* Gibbel *or* Mount; *but, indeed, it is*

---

[261] i.e. at Muzdalifah, where pilgrims went to spend the night after the Standing at 'Arafāt, though Pitts does not name it.

[262] *Mina or Muna*: "Minā, later often pronounced Munā, a place in the hills east of Mecca on the road from it to 'Arafah." EI[2].

[263] *Thevenot*: For more information on Thévenot, see Part I, Chapter 3, notes 108 and 196. Thévenot's remarks on stone throwing can be found on p. 153 of Part Two of the 1687 edition.

*otherwise*: *Though I must needs say, he is very exact in almost every Thing of* Turkish *Matters; and I pay much* deference *to that great* Author.]] Which Action of theirs is intended to testify their Defiance of the *Devil* and his Deeds; for they at the same Time pronounce the following Words, *viz. Erzum le Shetane wazbehe*,[264] i.e., *Stone the* Devil, *and them that please him.* And there are two other of the like Pillars, which are situated

[p. 140] near one another; at each of which (I mean all three) the Second Day, they throw seven Stones; and the same they do the third Day. As I was going to perform this Ceremony of throwing the Stones, a facetious *Hagge* met me; saith he, *You may save your Labour at present, if you please, for I have hit out the* Devil's Eyes *already.*

You must observe, that after they have thrown the seven Stones on the first Day, (the Country People having brought great Flocks of Sheep to be sold) every one buys a Sheep and sacrifices it; some of which they give to their Friends, some to the Poor which come out of *Mecca*, and the Country adjacent, very ragged Poor, and the rest they eat themselves; after which they shave their Heads, throw off *Hirrawem*, and put on other Clothes, and then *salute* one another with a *Kiss*, saying, *Byram Mabarick Ela*,[265] i.e. *The Feast be a Blessing to you.*

These three Days of *Byram* they spend *Festivally*, rejoicing with abundance of *Illuminations* all Night, shooting of Guns, and Fire works flying in the Air; for they reckon that all their Sins are now done away, and they shall when they die go *directly* to Heaven, if they don't *apostatize*; and that for the future, if they keep their Vow and do well, God will set down for every good Action *ten*; but if they do ill, God will likewise reckon every evil Action *ten*: And any

[p. 141] Person, who, after having received the Title of *Hagge*, shall fall back to a vicious Course of Life, is esteem'd to be very vile and infamous by them.

Some have written, That many of the *Hagges*, after they have return'd home, have been so austere to themselves, as to pore a long time over red-hot Bricks, or Ingots of Iron, and by that means willingly lose their Sight, desiring to see nothing evil or prophane after so *Sacred* a sight as the *Temple* at *Mecca*; but I never knew any such thing done.

During their three Days stay at *Mina*, scarce any *Hagge* (unless impotent)

---

[264] *Erzum le Shetane wazbehe*: Arabic, *Urjum al-Shayṭān wa-ḥizbahu.*
[265] *Byram Mabarick Ela*: modern Turkish, *Bayram mübarek ola.*

but thinks it his Duty to pay his Visit, once at least, to the *Temple* at *Mecca*: They scarce cease running all the way thitherward, shewing their vehement Desire to have a fresh sight of the *Beat-Allah*; which as soon as ever they come in sight of, they burst into Tears for Joy; and after having perform'd *Towoaf* for a while, and a few *Erkaets*, they return again to *Mina*. And when the three Days of *Byram* are expired, they all with their Tents, &c. come back again to *Mecca*.

They say, That after the *Hagges* are gone from *Mina* to *Mecca*, God doth usually send a good shower of Rain to wash away the Filth, and Dung of the *Sacrifices* there slain: And also that those vast Numbers of little [p. 142] Stones, which I told you the *Hagges* throw in Defiance of the *Devil*, are all carried away by the *Angels* before the Year comes about again. But I am sure, I saw vast Numbers of them that were thrown the Year before, lie upon the Ground. After they are return'd to *Mecca*, they can tarry there no longer than the *stated time*, which is about ten or twelve Days; during which time there is a great Fair held, where are sold all manner of *East India* Goods, and abundance of fine Stones for Rings, and Bracelets, &c. brought from *Yeamane*;[266] also of *China-Ware* and *Musk*, and variety of other Curiosities. Now is the time in which the *Hagges* are busily employ'd in buying, for they do not think it lawful to buy any thing until they have received the Title of *Hagge*. Every one almost now buys a *Caffin*,[267] or Shroud, of fine Linen to be buried in (for they never use *Coffins* for that Purpose) which might have been procured at *Algier*, or their other respective Homes, at a much cheaper Rate; but they choose to buy it *here*, because they have the Advantage of dipping it in the Holy Water *Zem Zem*. They are very careful to carry the said *Caffin* with them, wherever they travel, whether by Sea, or Land, that they may be sure to buried therein.

The Evening before they leave *Mecca*, every one must go to take their solemn Leave [p. 143] of the *Beat*, entring in at the Gate call'd *Babe el Salem*, i.e. *Welcome Gate*; and having continued at *Towoaf* as long as they please, which many do till they are quite tired; and it being the *last* time of their paying their *Devotions* to it, they do it with Floods of *Tears*, as being extremely unwilling to part, and bid farewel [*sic*]; and having drank their *fill* of the Water *Zem Zem*, they go to one side of the *Beat*, their Backs being towards the Door call'd by the name of *Babe el Weedoh*,[268] i.e. the *Farewel Door*, which is

---

[266] *Yeamane*: Yemen.   [267] *Caffin*: Arabic, *kafan*.   [268] *Babe el Weedoh*: Arabic, Bāb al-Wadāʿ.

opposite to the *Welcome Door*; where having perform'd two or three *Erkaets*, they get upon their Legs and hold up their Hands towards the *Beat*, making earnest Petitions; and then keep going backward till they come to the above-said *Farewel Gate*, being guided by some or other; for they account it a very *irreverent* thing to turn their Backs towards the *Beat* when they take leave of it. All the way as they retreat, they continue petitioning, holding up their Hands, with their Eyes fix'd upon the *Beat*, till they are out of sight of it; and so go to their Lodgings weeping.

E'er [*sic*; sc. ere] I leave *Mecca*, I shall acquaint you with a Passage of a *Turk* to me in the *Temple Cloyster*, in the night-time, between *Acsham Nomas*, and *Gega Nomas*, *i.e.* between the Evening and the Night *Services*. The *Hagges* do usually spend that time, or

[p. 144] good part of it (which is about an Hour and a half) at *Towoaf*, and then sit down on the Mats, and rest themselves. This I did, and after I had sat a while, and for my more ease at last was lying on my Back, with my Feet towards the *Beat*, but at a distance, as many others did; a *Turk* which sat by me ask'd what Countryman I was: *A Mogrebee* (said I) *i.e.* one of the *West. Pray*, quoth he, *how far* West *did you come?* I told him from *Gazair*,[269] *i.e. Algier. Ah!* replied he, *have you taken so much Pains, and been at so much Cost, and now be guilty of this* irreverent Posture *before the* Beat-Allah?

Here are many *Moors*, who get a beggarly Livelihood by selling Models of the *Temple* unto Strangers, and in being serviceable to the *Pilgrims*. Here are also several *Effendies*,[270] or Masters of Learning, who daily expound out of the *Alcoran*, sitting in high Chairs, and some of the learned *Pilgrims*, whilst they are here, do undertake the same.

Under the Room of the *Hanifees*, (which I mentioned before) People do usually gather together (between the Hours of *Devotion*) and sitting round cross-legged, it may be, twenty or thirty of them, they have a very large pair of *Tesbeehs*,[271] or *Beads*, each *Bead* near as big as a Man's Fist, which they keep passing round, Bead after Bead, one to the other, all the time, using some *devout* Expressions. I myself was once got in

[p. 145] amongst them, and methought it was a pretty Play enough for *Children*; however, I was to appearance very *devout*.

There are likewise some *Dervises* that get Money here, as well as at other

---

[269] *Gazair*: Arabic, Al-Jazā'ir.
[270] *Effendies*: modern Turkish, Effendi, a title of respect for learned people.
[271] *Tesbeehs*: see note 130.

Places, by burning of *Incense*, swinging their *Censers* as they go along before the People that are sitting; and this they do commonly on *Fridays*, their Sabbath. In all other *Gamiler*[272] or *Mosques*, when the *Hattib* is preaching, and the People all sitting still at their *Devotion*, they are all in Ranks; so that the *Dervise*, without the least Disturbance to any, walks between every Rank, with his *Censer* in one hand, and with the other takes his powder'd *Incense* out of a little Pouch that hangs by his side.

But though this Place, *Mecca*, is esteem'd so very holy, yet it comes short of *none* for Lewdness and Debauchery: As for Uncleanness, it is equal to *Grand Cairo*; and they'll steal even in the Temple it self.

I shall now entertain you with a Story or two, which may be of use.

The First, of a certain Beggar at *Mecca*, who would use no other Expression to excite the People to *Charity* towards him, than this, *Her ne yapparsen gendinga*,[273] i.e. *Whatsoever thou dost, thou dost it to thy self*; implying the Reward that will hereafter be conferr'd on the *charitable* Man. There past by one of his Neighbours (none of the best

[p. 146] Men to be sure; but why he did attempt such a desperate Thing against the Poor Beggar, I can't give an Account) who thought with himself, he'd try whether this Saying of the Beggar were true or not; and so goes and makes a Cake of Bread, and mixes Poison with it, and then gave it as an Alms to the Beggar, who put it thankfully up into his Bag; the other, the mean while, thinking in a little time to hear of his Death. But the Beggar's Saying prov'd true at length, and that unhappily for the Man who gave him the *poison'd Cake*; for it happened that a Child of his being at play, and seeing the Beggar eating, ask'd him for a piece of Bread, and he very innocently gave the Child the very same he had received from his Father; who eat it, and died. I have reason to believe this Story; and if so, it is a wonderful Argument to encourage CHARITY TO THE POOR.

Another Beggar would always use this Expression in begging, *viz. Her ne wearersen elingla, O Gidder senne la*,[274] i.e. *Whatsoever thou givest with thy*

---

[272] *Gamiler*: modern Turkish, *camiler*.

[273] *Her ne yapparsen gendinga*: modern Turkish, *Her ne yaparsan, kendine*. There is a modern Turkish proverb: *Ne Yaparsan Yap Kendine Yaparsın … Nereye Gidersen Git Kendinden Kaçamazsın*, which means: Whatever you do, you do it to yourself, wherever you go, you cannot run away from yourself.

[274] *Her ne wearersen elingla, O Gidder senne la*: modern Turkish, *Her ne verirsen elinle o gider seninle*. In this case there is also an almost identical modern Turkish proverb: *Ne verirsen elinle o gelir seninle*.

*Hand, that will go with thee;* implying after Death. Which shews also, that these blind *Mahometans* do believe a Reward reserv'd hereafter for the noble Vertue [*sic*] of CHARITY.

Now, to what I have related concerning the *Mahometans* great Veneration for the *ALCORAN,* and Way of WORSHIP **[p. 147]** in their *Mosques,* together with their *Pilgrimage to Mecca,* and Manner of DEVOTION there; I shall only add, That I was lately perusing an English *ALCORAN★,* [[ ★ *The* ALCORAN *amongst the* Turks *is strictly forbidden to be translated into any other Language*]] where I find, in the *Preface,* That the *Translator* saith, That the *Vulgar* are not permitted to read the *ALCORAN,*[275] but (as the poor *Romanists*) to live and die in an implicit Faith of what they are taught by their Priests. This I utterly deny; for it is not only permitted and allowed of, but it is (as I intimated before) looked on as very commendable in any Person to be diligent in the reading of it. And the same Difference there is amongst us, between learned and illiterate Persons, there is with them, between such as can and cannot read. They give eight or ten *Dollars* for a Copy of the *Alcoran.* Their Dollar is about two Shillings and three Pence.

---

[275] *The Vulgar are not permitted to read the Alcoran:* Pitts is quoting directly from p. 2 of the Preface to André du Ryer's 1688 translation of the Qur'ān, entitled *The Alcoran of Mahomet* (London: Randal Taylor).

[p. 148]

## CHAP. VIII

*Of the* Pilgrims *Return from* Mecca. *Their Visit made at* Medina *to* Mahomet's
*Tomb there. The mighty welcome the* Hagges *receive at their Return Home; and
the great Rejoicing made on that Occasion. Of a dreadful* Plague *at* Grand
Cairo, *&c.*

Having thus given you an Account of the *Turks* Pilgrimage to *Mecca*,
and of their *Worship* there (the Manner and Circumstances of which
I have faithfully and punctually related, and may challenge the World to
convict me of a known Falshood,) I now come to take leave of the *Temple*
and *Town* of *Mecca*.

Having hired Camels of the Carriers, we set out; but we give as much
for the Hire of one from *Mecca* to *Egypt*, which is about forty Days Journey,
as the real Worth of it is (*viz.*) about five or six Pounds *Sterling*: If it happen
that the Camel dies by the way, the Carrier is to supply us with another;
and therefore those Carriers who come from *Egypt* to *Mecca* with the
*Caravan*, bring with them several spare Camels; for there is hardly a Night
passeth but many die upon the Road: For, if a Camel should chance
[p. 149] to fall, 'tis seldom known that it is able to rise again, and if it should,
they despair of its being capable of performing the Journey, or ever being
useful more. 'Tis a common Thing therefore, when a Camel once falls, to
take off its Burden, and put it on another, and then kill it, which the poorer
Sort of the Company eat: I my self have eaten of *Camels Flesh*, and 'tis very
sweet and nourishing. If a Camel tires, they e'en leave him upon the Place.

The first Day we set out from *Mecca* it was without any Order at all, all
*hurly burly*; but the next Day every one labour'd to get forward; and in order
to it, there was many times much Quarrelling and Fighting: But after
everyone had taken his Place in the *Caravan*, they orderly and peaceably
kept the same Place till they came to *Grand Cairo*. They travel four Camels
in a Breast, which are all tied one after the other, like as in *Teams*. The whole
Body is called a *Caravan*, which is divided into several *Cottors*,[276] or
*Companies*, each of which hath its Name, and consists, it may be, of several
Thousand Camels; and they move one *Cottor* after another, like distinct

---

[276] *Cottors*: Arabic, *qiṭār*.

*Troops.* In the Head of each *Cottor* is some great *Gentleman* or *Officer*, who is carried in a Thing like an *Horse-litter*, born by two Camels, one before, and the other behind, which is covered all over with Sear-cloth,

[p. 150] and over that again with green Broad-cloth, and set forth very *handsomly* [*sic*]. If the said *great Person* have a Wife with him, she is carried in another of the same. In the Head of every *Cottor* there goes likewise a *Sumpter*[277] Camel, which carries his Treasure, *&c.* This Camel hath two Bells, about the Bigness of our *Market-Bells*, hanging one on each side, the Sound of which may be heard a great way off. Some other of the Camels have round Bells about their Necks, some about their Legs, like those which our *Carriers* put about their *Fore-horses*[278] Necks; which, together with the Servants (who belong to the Camels, and travel on Foot) singing all Night, make a pleasant Noise, and the Journey passes away delightfully. They say *this Musick* makes the Camels brisk and lively. Thus they travel, in good Order, every Day, till they come to *Grand Cairo*; and were it not for this Order, you may guess what Confusion would be amongst such a vast Multitude.

They have Lights by Night (which is the chief Time of Travelling, because of the exceeding Heat of the Sun by Day) which are carried on the Tops of high Poles, to direct the *Hagges* in their March. They are somewhat like Iron *Stoves*, into which they put short dry Wood, which some of the Camels are loaded with; 'tis carried in great Sacks, which have an Hole near the Bottom,

[p. 151] where the Servants take it out, as they see the Fires need a Recruit. Every *Cottor* hath one of these Poles belonging to it, some of which have ten, some twelve, of these Lights on their Tops, or more or less; and they are likewise of different Figures as well as Numbers; one, perhaps, *Oval way*, like a Gate; another *Triangular*, or like an *N* or *M*, &c. so that every one knows by them his respective *Cottor*. They are carried in the *Front*, and set up in the Place where the *Caravan* is to pitch, before *that* comes up, at some distance from one another. They are also carried by Day, not lighted; but yet by the Figure and Number of them the *Hagges* are directed to what *Cottor* they belong, as Soldiers are, by their Colours, where to rendezvous: And without such Directions it would be impossible to avoid Confusion in such a vast number of People.

---

[277] *Sumpter*: pack camel, i.e. a camel for carrying heavy loads.
[278] *Fore-horses*: leading horses in a team.

Every Day, *viz.* in the *Morning*, they pitch their Tents, and rest several Hours. When the Camels are unloaded, the Owners drive them to Water, and give them their Provender. *&c.* so that we had nothing to do with them, besides helping to load them.

As soon as our Tents were pitch'd, my Business was to make a little Fire, and get a Pot of Coffee. When we had eat some small Matter, and drank the Coffee, we lay

[p. 152] down to sleep. Between eleven and twelve we boiled something for Dinner, and having dined, lay down again till about four in the Afternoon; when the *Trumpet* was sounded, which gave Notice to every one to take down their Tents, pack up their Things, and load their Camels in order to proceed in their Journey. It takes up about two Hours Time e'er they are all in their Places again. At the Time of *Acsham Nomas*, also *Gega Nomas*, they make a Halt, and perform their *Sallah* (so punctual are they in their Worship) and then they travel until next Morning. If Water be scarce, what I call an *imaginary Abdes*[279] will do. As for ancient Men, it being very troublesome for such to alight off the Camels, and get up again, 'tis lawful for them to defer these two Times of *Nomas* till the next Day; but they will be sure to perform it *then*.

As for Provisions, we bring enough out of *Egypt* to suffice us till we return thither again. At *Mecca* we compute how much will serve us for one Day, and consequently, for the *forty* Days Journey to *Egypt*; and, if we find we have more than we may well guess will suffice us for so long a Time, we sell the *Overplus*[280] at *Mecca*. There is a Charity maintained by the *Grand Seignior*, for Water to refresh the Poor who travel on foot all the way; for there are many such undertake this *Journey* (or *Pilgrimage*) without

[p. 153] any money, relying on the *Charity* of the *Hagges* for subsistence, knowing that they largely extend it at such a Time.

Every *Hagge* carries his Provisions, Water, Bedding, *&c.* with him, and usually *three* or *four* diet[281] together, and sometimes discharge a poor Man's Expences the whole Journey for his Attendance on them. There was an *Irish Renegado*, who was taken very young, insomuch that he had not only lost his *Christian Religion*, but his *Native Language* also. This Man had endured thirty Years Slavery in *Spain*, and in the *French Gallies*; but was afterwards

---

[279] *imaginary Abdes*: Arabic, *tayammum*, performing the ritual ablution with sand instead of water.
[280] *Overplus*: surplus.  [281] *diet*: eat and board.

redeemed, and came home to *Algier*. He was look'd upon as a very pious Man, and a great *Zealot*, by the *Turks*, for his not turning from the *Mahometan Faith*, notwithstanding the great *Temptations* he had so to do. Some of my Neighbours who intended for *Mecca*, the same Year I went with my *Patroon* thither, offered this *Renegado*, that if he would serve them on this Journey they would defray his Charges throughout. He gladly embraced the Offer; and I remember, when we arrived at *Mecca*, he passionately told me, that God had delivered him out of an *Hell* upon *Earth* (meaning his former Slavery in *France* and *Spain*) and had brought him into an *Heaven* upon *Earth*, viz. *Mecca*. I admired much his Zeal, but pitied his Condition.

**[p. 154]**

Their Water they carry in Goat-skins, which they fasten to one side of their Camels. It sometimes happens, that no Water is to be met with for *two*, *three*, or more Days; but yet, it is well known that a Camel is a Creature that can live long without drinking, [[God in his wise Providence so ordering it; for otherwise it would be very difficult, if not impossible, to travel thro' the parch'd Deserts of *Arabia*.]] Every Tent's Company have their convenient Place for easing Nature (*viz.*) four long Poles fixed square, about three or four Foot distance from each other, which is hung round with Canvas, because (as I said before) the *Mahometans* esteem it very odious to be seen while they are Exonerating.[282] And besides, otherwise, if they should go too far, they would hardly be able to find the Way to their Tent again.

In this Journey many times the skulking, thievish *Arabs*,[283] do much Mischief to some of the *Hagges*; for, in the Night-time they'll steal upon them (especially such as are on the out-side of the *Caravan*) and being taken to be some of the *Servants* that belong to the Carriers, or Owners of the Camels, they are not suspected: When they see an *Hagge* fast asleep (for it is usual for them to sleep on the Road) they loose a Camel *before* and *behind*, and one of the Thieves leads it away with the *Hagge* upon its back asleep.

**[p. 155]** Another of them, in the mean while, pulls on the next Camel, to tie it to the Camel from whence the Halter of the other was cut; for if *that* Camel be not fasten'd again to the *leading* Camel, it will stop, and all that are behind will then stop of course, which might be a Means of discovering

---

[282] *Exonerating*: relieving themselves.

[283] *Arabs*: in this case, Pitts means the nomadic Bedouin tribesmen, who were a notorious scourge of the pilgrim caravans.

the *Robbers*. When they have gotten the stolen Camel, with his Rider, at a convenient distance from the Caravan, and think themselves out of Danger, they awake the *Hagge*, and sometimes destroy him immediately; but at other Times, being a little more inclin'd to Mercy, they strip him naked, and let him return to the *Caravan*.

About the tenth easy Day's Journey after we come out of *Mecca*, we enter into *Medina*, the Place where *Mahomet* lies intomb'd [*sic*]. Although it be (as I take it) 2 or 3 Days Journey out of the direct way from *Mecca* to Egypt; yet the *Hagges* pay their Visit there, for the space of two Days, and come away the third.

Those *Mahometans* which live to the *Southward* of *Mecca*, at the *East Indies*, and thereaway, are not *bound* to make a Visit to *Medina*, but to *Mecca* only, because it would be *so much* out of their way. But such as come from *Turkey*, *Tartary*, *Egypt*, and *Africa*, think themselves obliged so to do.

*Medina* is but a little Town, and *poor*, yet it is wall'd round, and hath in it a great

[p. 156] *Mosque*, but nothing near so big as the *Temple* at *Mecca*. In one *Corner* of the *Mosque* is a Place built about fourteen or fifteen Paces square. About this Place are great Windows fenced with brass Grates. In the Inside it is deck'd with some Lamps, and Ornaments. It is arch'd all over head. [[I find some relate, That there are no less than three Thousand Lamps about *Mahomet*'s Tomb; but it is a Mistake, for there are not, as I verily believe, an Hundred: And I speak what I *know*, and have been an *Eye-Witness* of.]] In the middle of this Place is the Tomb of *Mahomet*, where the Corpse of that bloody *Impostor* is laid, which hath silk Curtains all around it like a Bed; which Curtains are not *costly* nor beautiful. There is nothing of his Tomb to be seen by *any*, by reason of the Curtains round it; nor are any of the *Hagges* permitted to enter there: None go in but the *Eunuchs*, who keep watch over it, and they only to light the Lamps which burn there by Night, and to sweep and cleanse the Place. All the Privilege the *Hagges* have, is only to thrust in their Hands at the Windows between the brass Grates, and to petition the dead *Jugler*,[284] which they do, with a wonderful deal of *Reverence, Affection,* and *Zeal.* My *Patroon* had his silk Handkerchief stole out of his Bosom, while he stood at his *Devotion* here.

---

[284] *Jugler.* Juggler or Magician, an insulting epithet commonly applied to Muḥammad from the Middle Ages until the 18th century.

**[p. 157]**

It is storied by some, that the Coffin of *Mahomet* hangs up by the attractive Virtue of a *Loadstone*[285] to the *Roof* of the *Mosque*; but believe me, 'tis a false Story. When I looked through the brass Grate I saw as much as any of the *Hagges*; and the top of the Curtains, which cover'd the Tomb, were not half so high as the *Roof* or *Arch*; so that 'tis impossible his Coffin should be hanging there. I never heard the *Mahometans* say any Thing like it. On the *outside* of this Place, where *Mahomet's* Tomb is, are some Sepulchres of their reputed *Saints*; among which is one prepared for *Christ Jesus*, when He shall come again *personally* into the World; for they hold that *Christ* will come again in the Flesh, forty Years before the End of the World, to *confirm* the *Mahometan* Faith, and say, likewise, that our *Saviour* was not crucified in *Person*, but in *Effigy*, or one like him.

*Medina* is much supplied by the opposite *Abyssine* Country, which is on the other side of the *Red Sea*; from thence they have Corn and Necessaries brought in Ships; an odd sort of Vessels as ever I saw, their Sails being made of *Matting*, such as they use in their Houses and *Mosques* to tread upon.

When we had taken our leave of *Medina*, the third Day, and travell'd about *ten* Days more, we were met by a great many *Arabians*, who brought abundance of *Fruit* to

**[p. 158]** us, particularly *Raisins*; but from whence I cannot tell. When we came within *fifteen* Days Journey of *Grand Cairo* we were met by many People who came from thence, with their Camels laden with *Presents* for the *Hagges*, sent from their *Friends* and *Relations*, as *Sweet-Meats*, &c. But some of them came rather for Profit, to sell fresh Provisions to the *Hagges*, and trade with them.

About ten Days before we got to *Cairo*, we came to a very long steep Hill, called *Ackaba*,[286] which the *Hagges* are usually much afraid how they shall be able to get up. Those who can will walk it. The poor Camels, having no Hoofs, find it very hard Work, and many drop here. They were all untied, and we dealt gently with them, moving very slowly, and often halting. Before we came to this Hill I observed no Descent, and when we were at the Top there was none, but all plain as before.

---

[285] *attractive Virtue of a Loadstone*: the attracting power of a lodestone or magnet.

[286] *Ackaba*: Arabic, *'aqabah*, a mountain road or pass, or the steepest part of a hill. From his description in this paragraph, it is unlikely that Pitts is referring to the district of 'Aqabah, the port of what is today the Hashemite Kingdom of Jordan.

We past [*sic*] by Mount *Sinai* by Night, and, perhaps, when I was asleep; so that I had no Prospect of it.

When we came within *seven* Days Journey of *Cairo*, we were met by *abundance* of People more, some Hundreds, who came to welcome their Friends and Relations; but it being Night, it was difficult to find those they wanted, and therefore as the *Caravans* past along they kept calling them [p. 159] aloud by their Names, and by this Means found them out. And when we were within *three* Days Journey of it, we had many *Camel-loads* of the Water of the Nile brought us to drink. But the *Day* and the *Night* before we came to *Cairo*, *Thousands* came out to meet us, with extraordinary Rejoicing. 'Tis *thirty seven* Days Journey from *Mecca* to *Cairo*, and three Days we tarry by the way, which together make up (as I said) *forty* Days Journey; and in all this way there is scarce any *green* Thing to be met with, nor *Beast* or *Fowl* to be seen or heard, nothing but *Sand* and *Stones*, excepting one place which we pass'd by Night; I suppose it was a *Village*, where there were some *Trees*, and, as we thought, *Gardens*.

We travell'd through a certain Valley, which is called by the Name of *Attash el wait*,[287] i.e. the *River* of *Fire*, the Vale being so excessively hot, that the very Water in their Goat-skins hath sometimes been dried up with the gloomy, scorching Heat. But we had the Happiness to pass thorough [*sic*] it when it rain'd, so that the fervent Heat was much allayed thereby; which the *Hagges* look'd on as a great *Blessing*, and did not a little praise God for it. When we came to *Cairo*, the *Plague* was very hot there, insomuch that it was reported, there died *sixty Thousand* within a *Fortnight's Time*; wherefore we hastned [*sic*] away to *Roseet*, and [p. 160] from thence to *Alexandria*; where in a little time, there was a Ship of *Algier* ready to transport us thither.

After we came to *Alexandria*, I was walking with the *Irish Renegado* I spake of but now (who was maintain'd in his Pilgrimage to *Mecca*, for his Service, and Attendance, *&c,*) on the Key[288] where was an *English* Boat with a Man in it. The *Renegado* was very earnest for me to speak to the Man; and I would have done it without a Request, had I thought it safe, or convenient. But the more importunate he was, the more shy I seem'd, for I fear'd some ill Consequence might attend it. However, watching an opportunity, I spake to him, and ask'd of him, From whence his Ship? He

---

[287] *Attash el wait*: modern Turkish, Ateş vadisi.
[288] *Key*: quay.

look'd intently in my Face, and said from *Topsham*.[289] At which Words my Heart smote me. I ask'd him further who was the *Master*? He replyed, Mr. *Bear* of *Topsham*.[290] He then ask'd me where I learn'd my *English*? I told him in *England. Are you an* English-Man *then*? quoth he. I told him, yes. *Of what part of* England? continued he. Of *Exeter*, said I. I told him also, with *whom* I was taken, and other Circumstances; but did not think fit to hold any long Discourse with him, and so pass'd from him. It happened, that there was at this time, on Board Mr. Bear, one *John Cleak* of *Lymson*, whom I very well knew,

[p. 161] when we were Boys together. He hearing of what had pass'd, came ashore the next Day, with the said Man, who spying me walking, told *Cleak*, I was the Man; whereupon he came running to me, and hugg'd me in his Arms, saying *Jo, I'm glad to see thee with all my Heart!* I did not know him at first, till he told me who he was; I call'd him to mind, but was afraid to hold any Discourse with him, tho' very desirous to have further talk with him. He desir'd to drink a Glass of *Wine* with me; but I refused, alledging, that I was newly come from *Mecca*, and therefore it would be much taken notice of. He then invited me to the Coffee-House with him; but I told him it would not be convenient for me to go with him thither neither, because the House was full of *Turks*. So we did not go. But I enquir'd of my Father's, and Friends Healths; and he told me he saw my Father but a little before he came away. I desired him to carry a Letter for me; he told me he would. The Letter you have inserted hereafter; and I sent by him a *Turkish* Pipe to my Father, and a green Silk Purse to my Mother, and at the same Time gave him a Sash for himself; withal telling him, that I hoped God would find out some Way for my *Escape*. But truly I was troubled that I could not conveniently have had some Conversation with my old Acquaintance. This was no

[p. 162] small renewal of my Affliction; and when I thought upon the Circumstances I was then in, my Heart did Bleed.

The *Plague* was hot in *Alexandria*, at this time; and some Persons infected with it being taken on board our Ship, which was bound for *Algier*, the *Plague* reigned amongst us: Insomuch that besides those that recovered, we

---

[289] *Topsham*: Topsham is situated four miles south-east of Exeter on the Exe estuary and in the 17th century was the main port for Exeter.

[290] *Mr. Bear of Topsham*: Pitts's book is the only evidence we have that ships from Topsham or Exeter travelled as far east in the Mediterranean as Alexandria in the 17th century; see Stephens (1958), pp. xxvi and 116.

threw twenty Persons overboard, who died of it. And truly I was not a little afraid of the *Distemper*,[291] and wish'd I were safe at *Algier*, hoping that if I were got there I should escape it. But soon after we got ashore there, I was seized with it, but thro' the *Divine Goodness*, escap'd Death. It rose under my Arm, and the Boil which usually accompanies the *Plague* rose on my Leg. After it was much swollen, I was desirous to have it lanced; but my *Patroon* told me it was not soft enough. There was a Neighbour, a *Spaniard* Slave, who advised me to rost [*sic*] an *Onion*, and apply a piece of it dipt [*sic*] in Oil, to the Swelling, to mollify it; which accordingly I did. The next day it became soft; and then my *Patroon* had it lanced, and thro' the Blessing of my good God, I recovered. Such a signal Mercy I hope I shall never forget; a Mercy so circumstantiated, considering every thing, that my Soul shall thankfully call it to mind, as long as I have any Being. For I was just return'd from *Mecca* when this Mercy was

[p. 163] dispens'd to me; I do observe the *Divine Providence* plainly in it, and hope ever to make the best use of it.[292]

Being now got back again to *Algier* from our long *Pilgrimage*, I shall acquaint you with some Things which have been hitherto omitted, and may as properly come in here as any where else.

The Women of *Algier* look on it as very ornamental to wear great Rings, almost like Gives [Gyves] or Fetters, about their Legs, and also their Arm-Wrists. Some wear them of Gold, others of Silver, others of Brass, and some of Horn, (*i.e.* in the Country.) And if the Country-women can get a few ordinary Stones, and Cloves to string up and make a Bracelet with, they think themselves very fine indeed. The Women here commonly paint their Hands and Feet with a certain Plant call'd *Kennah*[293] dried and beaten to Powder, which they moisten with Water, and so use it; and in a Month's time, or thereabout, it makes the Part of a deep *Saffron* Colour. The like is often done to their Horses, if white, *i.e.* they die [*sic*] their Feet, Tail, and Mane, and under the Saddle, of the said Colour.

There are some *Jews* here, who wear their shirts without their Drawers, or Breeches; for what Reason I never inquired, but it was undoubtedly

---

[291] *Distemper*: illness.

[292] Pitts has been interpreted here as attributing the intervention of Divine Providence to the fact that he had performed the Muslim pilgrimage (Netton (1996), p. 18). But a more accurate reading would be that Pitts finds evidence for the workings of Divine Providence in another sense: that his having been to Mecca *had not disqualified him* from its protection.

[293] *Kennah*: modern Turkish, *kına*; Arabic, *ḥinnā'*; in English, henna.

designed as a Mark of Distinction.

[p. 164]

A few Years before I came from *Algier*, there happened a terrible Fire among their Ships in the *Mole*, a little before Candle-lighting: Several of their fine Ships were burnt, among which was one that was reputed the biggest that was ever built in *Algier*. This noble Ship was just finished, and fit for a Voyage, able to carry sixty Guns, when this Fire broke out. Besides, several Prizes were burnt, in all about sixteen Sail: they had much ado to save their three *Galleys*; and had the Wind been harder the Fire must have burnt their Ships on the Stocks, and all the *Timber* that lay by. Their *Castle* on the *Mole* was likewise in danger, for they were not a little afraid that the Powder Magazines would take Fire. It was a most dreadful Fire, and yet, methought, I could not be much concerned for the Sufferers, because these very Ships would in all Probability have otherwise been a Means of bringing many poor *Christians* into Slavery.

While I was at *Algier*, there was a *Prize* brought in by a *Frigatto*, as they call it, (*i.e.* a long sort of Vessel, with eleven or twelve Oars on each side, and with sails *Gally*-like, fit only for the Summers Expeditions. These are generally mann'd with *Moors*, well arm'd with small Arms, having five or Six Pattareroes.[294] They get over to the *Spanish* Shore, but mostly about *Majorca*

[p. 165] and *Minorca*, and there sculk [*sic*] about the Creeks, waiting to snap[295] small Coasters: And where they know is an House, they'll land and carry off the whole Family.) When this *Frigatto* came to *Algier*, it was reported by the *Frigatogees*,[296] that the *Christians*, who were in the taken Ship, ran a-shore, and that the said *Prize* was found, without a Soul therein, on the Seas; which to some seem'd very strange, because the *Boat* was all this while in the *Prize*, and to be sure they could not *fly* to the Shore. It was the general Suspicion therefore, that they had barbarously thrown the poor Men of the Ship over-board. And a little time after, I my self was credibly inform'd, that one of the *Frigattogees* was heard, on a time, to say, that nothing griev'd him so much as to see such a pretty Boy thrown over-board. And it was in all likelihood an *English* Ship, of about thirty, or forty Tun [*sic*], richly

---

[294] *Pattareroes:* from the Spanish *pedrero*, small naval guns designed to fire stones.

[295] *snap:* capture.

[296] *Frigatogees:* modern Turkish, *firkataci*, the sailors on board the frigatto, or frigate which was, in Pitts's day, a small sailing ship designed for speed.

laden; which, probably, was the occasion of this *Barbarity*; for it was in a time when the *English* had Peace with the *Turks*. And I must tell you, 'tis not the first time, by a great many, that, when we have had Peace with them, they have turn'd *Isbandote*,[297] i.e. *Buccaniers*, *Robbers*, perfidious *Villains*, or what you'll call them, and have taken our Ships, and sold Ship, Men, Cargo, and all, to those who have, at the same time, been at War with us. I must confess, this Treachery

[p. 166] is not allow'd of in *Algier;* but yet, after some time, a Sum of *Money* to the *Dey* makes up all, and 'tis conniv'd at, and in a little time quite forgotten.

In *Algier*, as well as in other Places, on *Friday*, their *Sabbath*, in the Afternoon they generally take their Recreation. And amongst their several Sports and Diversions, they have a comical sort of *Wrestling*, which is perform'd about a quarter of a Mile without the Gate, call'd *Bab el Wait*, which is the *Western* Gate. There's a Plain just by the Sea-side, where, when the People are gathered together, they make a Ring, all sitting on the Ground, expecting the *Combatants*. Anon, there comes one *boldly* in, and strips all to his Drawers. Having done this, he turns his Back to the Ring, and his Face is towards his Clothes on the Ground. He then pitcheth on his Right Knee, and then throws abroad his Arms three times, clapping his Hands together as often, just above the Ground; which having done, he puts the backside of his Hand to the Ground and then kisseth his Fingers, and puts them to his Forehead; then makes two or three good Springs into the middle of the Ring, and there he stands with his Left-hand to his Left-ear, and his Right-hand to his Left-elbow: In this Posture the *Challenger* stands, not looking about, till some one comes into the Ring to take him up;

[p. 167] and he that comes to take him up does the very same Postures, and then stands by the side of him, in the manner aforesaid. Then the *Tryer* of the Play[298] comes behind the *Pilewans*,[299] (for so the *Wrestlers* are termed by them) and covers their naked Backs, and Heads, and makes a short Harangue to the *Spectators*. After which the *Pilewans* face each other, and then both at once slap their Hands on their *Thighs*, then clap them *together*, and then lift them up as high as their Shoulders, and cause the Palms of

---

[297] *Isbandote*: presumably a term used in *Lingua Franca*; the word *sbendut* meaning robber occurs in Corré (2005).
[298] *Tryer of the Play*: judge or referee.
[299] *Pilewans*: modern Turkish, *pehlivan*, from the Persian *pahlavān*, athlete or hero.

their Hands to meet, and with the same, dash their Heads one against another three times, so hard, that many times the *Blood* runs down. This being done, they walk off from one another, and traverse their Ground, eying each other like two *Game-Cocks.* If either of them find his Hands moist, he rubs them on the Ground, for the better hold-fast:[300] And they will make an offer of Closing twice or thrice before they do. They'll come as often within five or six yards one of the other, and clap their hands to each other, and then put forward the Left-leg, bowing their Body, and leaning with the Left-elbow on the Left-knee, for a little while, looking one at the other (as I said) just like two *Fighting-Cocks.* Then they walk a Turn again: Then *at it* they go; and as they are naked to the Middle, and so there is but little *holdfast,* there's

[p. 168] much ado before one hath a fair Cast[301] on his Back; they having none of our *Devonshire,* or *Cornish* Skill. He that throws the other goes round the Ring, taking Money of many that give it him, which is but a small matter, it may be, a *Farthing,* an *Halfpenny,* or a *Penny* of a Person, which is much. Having gone the Round, he goes to the *Tryer* and delivers him the Money so collected, who in a short time returns it again to the *Conqueror,* and makes a short Speech of Thanks. And, it may be, while this is doing, other two shall come into the Ring to *wrestle.*

But at their *Byrams,* or *Feasts,* those which are the most famous *Pilewans,* come in to show their Parts, before the *Dey,* eight or ten together. These anoint themselves all over with Oil, having on their Bodies but a pair of leathern Drawers, which are well oil'd too: They stand in the Street near *Bab el wait* (the abovesaid Gate,) without which are all their Sports held, spreading out their Arms, as if they would oil Peoples fine Clothes, unless they give them some Money; which many do to carry on the Humour. They are, as I said, the choice of all the stout *Wrestlers,* and *wrestle* before the *Dey,* who sits on a Carpet spread on the Ground, looking on: And when the Sport is over, he gives, it may be, two or three Dollars to each. After which

[p. 169] the *Dey* with the *Bashaw*[302] mount their Horses, and several *Spahys* ride one after another, throwing Sticks made like Lances, at each other; and the *Dey* rides after one or other of them, who is his Favourite, and throws his wooden Lance at him; and if he happens to hit him, the *Spahy* comes off his Horse to the *Dey,* who gives him Money. After all which Diversions,

---

[300] *hold-fast*: grip.   [301] *Cast*: a throw in wrestling.   [302] *Bashaw*: Pasha.

they ride to the place where the *Dey* hath a Tent pitch'd, and there they spend the Afternoon in eating and drinking of Coffee, and pleasant Talk, but no *Wine*. The *Dey* usually appears in no great Splendor at *Algier*. For I have seen him oftentimes ride into the Town from his Garden in a Morning on a Mule, attended only by a Slave on another [mule].

Being thus, as I have told you, return'd to *Algier* from *Mecca,* and my *Patroon* having given me my *Letter of Freedom*, I became a *Soldier*, and enter'd into Pay, which is about twenty Pound *Sterling per Annum*. There are about twelve Thousand *Janizaries* in *Algier*, including the *Invalids* who have *half Pay*.

The first Camp I made after I was thus for my self[303] (as I may say) was, as I remember, against *Oran,* a *Spanish Garrison* on the *Barbary* Shore, within the Territories of *Algier,* which is a great Eye-sore to the *Algerines*, and proves oftentimes no small Damage to the Country about them.

[p. 170]

When these *Spaniards* of *Oran* have War with the neighbouring *Moors*, they often make Incursions, and do great Spoil among them, and bring them Slaves into *Oran*, and from thence send them to *Spain*. But *as it commonly happens, that* private, *and* intestine[304] *Quarrels and Dissentions do more Mischief to a People than the Force of a Foreign Enemy*, so many times the *Moors* fall out among themselves, and the consequence is, that some one or other of them, to be revenged, steals away by Night, and gets to *Oran*, and there agrees, for a Sum of Money, with the *Marquess*, or *Governour*, to discover,[305] and lead him to such or such a Village, that he may pillage it. The *Spaniard* glad of the Bargain, goes forth by Night, falls upon the said *Village* by Surprize, and takes and carries away *Men, Women, Children, Cattel,* and all. This hath been often done. But then let the *Traitor* look to it, for there's no more coming back into his own Country without certain Death. But he must stay all his life time with the *Spaniards*, and if occasion be, *fight for* them; but he's allow'd to retain the *Mahometan* Religion.

The Advantage the *Spanish* King hath by keeping this *Garrison*, one would think, should be *inconsiderable*. But I know it to be of some, *viz.* that when the *Moors*, adjacent, have Peace with *Oran*, as they mostly

[p. 171] have, they bring a great many *Necessaries* into their Market to sell, and the Country affords great Plenty of *Wheat, Barley, Butter, Honey, Sheep,*

---

[303] *after I was thus for my self:* after I had become a free man.
[304] *intestine:* internal, domestic.   [305] *discover:* inform him.

*Wax*, &c. which the *Spaniards* buy and carry in Ships into *Spain*. It hath also been of great Service to Vessels when chased by *Algerines*; for they have oftentimes got into *Oran*, and so saved themselves.

As I was speaking, the first Camp I made was against this *Oran*. The *Dey* was there in Person, with about 3 or 4000 Men, which with them is reckon'd a great Force; with Bombs also, and several piece of Cannon. We lay'd Siege against it about *three Months*, plying sometimes our Cannon, and sometimes our Bombs; but all that we did, signified not much, for the *Turks* in *Algier* are nothing expert in Firing Bombs. The *Spaniards*, on the other side, had orders not to *sally* out, but to be upon the *Defensive*. And the *Algerines* had not Courage enough to come very near the Town. I was a *Bombagee*,[306] *i.e.* one who assists in Firing the Bombs. After we had raised a Battery to secure our selves from their Cannon, we placed our Cannon and Mortars behind it, and then began to ply them against a *Castle*, which was without the *Town*. We fired on them before they did on us. And no sooner was our first Cannon discharg'd, but the *Turks* sculked behind the Battery, as if the Enemies

[p. 172] Cannon could reach us the very Moment we fired. I mention this as an Instance of their *Bravery*. In this *great* Expedition we lost *three* Men, and I think the *Spaniards* not so many.

Whilst we were besieging *Oran*, the *French* came a third time to bombard *Algier*, *Anno* 1688.[307] (When that *Tragedy* happened, which you'll hear of hereafter) And there happened some Bombs to fall on the *Haznah*,[308] *i.e.* the *Treasury* or place where the Money was kept, which was to pay off the Soldiers. Immediately upon which, there was an Express dispatch'd to the *Dey*, as he lay before *Oran*, signifying the *absolute* necessity of his Presence at *Algier*. He forthwith rode Post thither, and having pacified matters, as 'twas thought, and secured the *Haznah*, in a little time, return'd to the *Camp*. But soon after this, there was a *Plot* hatching to take away this *Dey's* Life. His Name was *Ibrahim* [[i.e. *Abraham*]] *Hogea*, [[i.e. *Scribe*,]] because he was, before he came to be *Dey*, but an ordinary Man, tho' indifferently well skill'd in Letters.

The Nature of the Plot was this. *Ibrahim Hogea* was *Cayah*,[309] or *Deputy*

---

[306] *Bombagee*: modern Turkish, *bombacı*.

[307] *French ... 1688*: a French naval squadron under Admiral d'Estrées attacked Algiers in 1688.

[308] *Haznah*: modern Turkish, *hazine*, from the Arabic, *khazīnah*.

[309] *Cayah*: modern Turkish, *kâhya*; *kethüda* is often used instead of *kâhya*.

to *Hagge Heusin*, or *Medio-morto*;[310] (who, as you will find, succeeded him in the *Dey-ship*, tho' he was *Dey* before him too.) This *Medio-morto*, being a politick Man, and well knowing what a ticklish, tho' splendid, Place he was [p. 173] in, when first *Dey*, made what interest he could privately, to be advanced to be a *Bashaw*; for then he knew he should be safe from all evil Designs, which otherwise might be laid against him. For the *Bashaw* of *Algier* is no way concerned in the Government, but only represents the State of the Grand *Seignior*, and hath allowance sufficient to maintain it.

Now *Medio-morto's* design was not only to be made a *Bashaw*, but so to work Matters, as to be call'd home to *Turkey* by the *Grand-Seignior*, and so to be quite out of fear of danger. For 'tis customary, upon Reasons of State, to remand one *Bashaw*, and send another in his Room. This Scheme *Medio-Morto* soon accomplish'd; and then *Ibrahim*[311] became *Dey* in his Room:[312] And all things seem'd to be very quiet, and serene. According to *Medio-Morto's* design, a Ship came from *Constantinople* to *Algier* with a new *Bashaw*, and to carry the old one, *viz.* himself to *Turkey*. At this very time (as I was speaking) we were besieging *Oran*, whither came an Express to acquaint the *Dey* of the Arrival of the Ship to fetch *Medio-Morto*. The *Dey* immediately sent back an Express to tell him, that if he went from *Algier*, he should go as he came, *viz.* with just nothing. For he had intrusted *Medio-Morto* in his absence with the *Haznah*, or *Treasury*, and so was afraid left he should [p. 174] have gone off with a good part of the Riches. *Medio-Morto* being thus disappointed, excus'd himself from going to *Constantinople*, and remain'd still in *Algier*, where he made it his Business to gain a Party to himself, in order, if an occasion did offer, to set himself up for *Dey* again, to be revenged on *Ibrahim* for the ill treatment he had met with from him. Accordingly he carried on his Plot so successfully that the Conspiracy grew to such a Head, that an Express came to our Camp before *Oran* to arrest the *Dey*, *viz. Ibrahim*. The Express came to the *Aga*, or *Colonel* of our Camp; for the Letter was directed to him, and the *Dey* happening to be in the *Aga's*

---

[310] *Hagge Heusin*, or *Medio-morto*: modern Turkish, Hacı Hüseyin, also known as Medio-Morto or Mezzo-Morto, was an important figure in the government of Algiers in the later 17th century, becoming Dey between July 1683 and 1686, and later taking effective power from Ibrahim in 1688. He was forced to flee to Tunis in 1689 and then to Istanbul, where he was appointed Chief Admiral in the Ottoman Navy. He died in 1700.

[311] *Ibrahim*: Dey of Algiers from 1686 to 1688.

[312] *Room*: place.

Tent at the very same time the Express came, took the Letter first into his own Hand, and running it over to himself, went immediately to his own Tent, took what light Treasure he could, and with two, or three Friends made his Escape. Presently the Rumour went thro' the Camp, and it was all in a Confusion. So that had the *Spaniards* nick'd[313] that Opportunity, and made a Sally upon us, they might have done great Execution. But they did not; and the next Day we drew off our Forces, and march'd back to *Algier* again, where the said *Dey* never appear'd more after this. So that *Hagge Heusin* succeeded him in the *Deyship*, (tho' he had been *Dey* before) who was nicknam'd by the *Christians, Medio-morto,*

[p. 175] *i.e.* half dead; because he was a very weak, and sickly Man.

This *Dey* was also, a little time after he came to his new Honour, forc'd to fly for it, or else he had lost his Life; for becoming *Dey* again, he ceas'd to be a *Bashaw*. He got up to *Turkey*, where he became *Capatan-Bashaw,*[314] *i.e.* the Head of the Captains of the *Grand-Turks* Men of War, or *Admiral*. And indeed it's a rare thing for a *Dey* of Algier to die a *Natural* Death. It was but a few Years before I was taken, that *Hagge Allee,*[315] who was *Dey*, was murdered. And some Years after I had been there, *Baba Hassen,*[316] *i.e. Father Hassen*, was also slain.

The Year after this, the *Moors* belonging to the Emperor of *Morocco*[317] broke their Bounds, and damag'd the *Moors* within the Territories of *Algier, Westward* of *Tillimsan.* The *Algerine Turks* which kept Garrison in *Tillimsan* sallied out to assist the Moors of their side, but lost most of their Men in the Action. The *Dey* of *Algier* being enrag'd at this, immediately caus'd a great Camp to march forth of *Algier*, with Cannon, and Bombs, in order to be reveng'd on the Emperor of *Morocco.* We were in all about Three thousand Foot, and Two thousand Horse of *Turks*, and about Three thousand Horse of *Moors.* We marched into the Emperor of *Morocco*'s Country, and all the Inhabitants as we went declar'd for the *Dey.* At length

[p. 176] we came within half a day's Journey of the Enemies Camp, which consisted, as 'twas suppos'd, of Thirty thousand Men; notwithstanding, we thought they would not have fac'd us. When we came within five or six Miles of the Enemy, we call'd *a Council of War;* at which time Notice is

---

[313] *nick'd:* taken advantage of.
[314] *Capatan-Bashaw:* modern Turkish, Kapudan Paşa.
[315] *Hagge Allee:* modern Turkish, Hacı Ali, Dey of Algiers from 1665 to 1671.
[316] *Baba Hassen:* modern Turkish, Baba Hasan, Dey of Algiers from January 1682 to July 1683.
[317] *Emperor of Morocco:* Mulay Ismā'īl, who ruled Morocco from 1672 to 1727.

always given to the Soldiers to draw near to the *Dey's* Tent, where the Council of War is held. In the conclusion it was resolv'd to attack the Enemy, and in doing this 'twas ordered, That half the *Infantry* and half the *Cavalry* should march before with the Baggage, and the rest were to come behind. It was my place to be in the Rear, but being desirous to see the Beginning of it, I offered to exchange places with one of the Tent wherein I was, who gladly accepted it. Coming forth from between two Mountains, at the bottom of the Hill, we saw the Enemy before us, their Tents being all pitch'd on the further side of the River *Melweea*,[318] which may be seen in the Maps of that Country. Here we were at a stand; for positive Orders were given, that no Man should fire a Piece till our Camp was pitch'd. However, we had not Patience very long, but ran down the Hill to the River-side, and at it we went, without any Order, three or four behind one Bush, five or six behind another, *&c.* After we had been engag'd about half an Hour, the

[p. 177] Enemy seeing we were but few in number, in comparison of them, made an Attempt to pass the River, but we hindered them. This Attempt of theirs was a discovery to us where the River was passable, which we knew not before, being altogether Strangers; and in most places it was very deep. When we had been engag'd about an Hour, or somewhat more, our Party which was in the Rear came up with us, and then the Enemies Hearts began to flag. We then ply'd them with our Artillery, and Bombs; so that in a very short time they fled, and left to us their Tents and Baggage. We soon passed the River, every *Trooper* taking one of the Foot behind him, and our *Spahys*, which were about Three thousand, pursued their Horse; their Foot taking to the Mountains. But at length the Enemies Horse perceiving themselves to exceed ours in number, wheel'd about towards us, which made our Horse wheel towards our Foot, at which time was the greatest of our Loss. But the Enemy were afraid to come near our Foot, and so wheel'd about again, and march'd off. After we had buried our Dead, and tarried two or three Days by the River, we march'd forward three or four Days March, intending to storm *Fez*, and we advanced so far, as within one Day's Journey of it, where the whole body of the Enemy lay. The *Emperor* of *Morocco* hearing that his Son (the

[p. 178] *General* in the late Engagement) was defeated, came against us in Person, with what Forces he could make. We pitch'd within two or three Miles of him, in a vast Plain, in sight of each other. After we had look'd on

---

[318] *River Melweea*: Arabic, Malwiyyah or Mulūyah, known colloquially as the Wadi Moulouya.

one another for about an Hour or two, the *Emperor* sent an Ambassador to our *Dey*, to treat of Peace; who after he had tarried with the *Dey* about an Hour, return'd with an Ambassador of ours to his Master.

Upon his having Audience of the *Emperor*, it was concluded, that the next Day the *Emperor* and the *Dey* should meet on Horse-Back, in the middle way between the two Camps, each with fifty Horse to attend him. When they came near one another, the rest of the Horse halted, and the *Emperor*, and the *Dey*, with a Servant each, went to meet, and salute one another; and after high Compliments on both sides, a Carpet was spread on the Ground, and down they sat. In two or three Hours time all Matters were adjusted. The *Emperor* promised to give Satisfaction for the Charges the *Dey* had been at, urging this as an Argument of Accommodation, (*viz.*) "*Our Principles are to fight against the* Christians, *and weaken their* Interest, *and not to worry one another*". Upon this easy Agreement, the *Emperor* presented our *Dey* with his Saddle, which was all of Beaten

[p. 179] Gold; and the next Day we march'd back again for *Algier*, and thus ended the *Campaign*. All Matters being thus accommodated between the two Potentates, at the time appointed in the Treaty, the *Emperor* of *Morocco* sent his Son to *Algier*, with Treasure sufficient to pay for the Damage done the *Algerines*, and many rich Presents.

In a few Days after the Prince of *Morocco* came to *Algier*, it happened to be *Byram*; and it being a time of more leisure than ordinary, thousands of Country *Moors* flock'd thither to see him, and to behold the Sports and Entertainments which were prepared for him, without the Gate *Bab el wait*. At the time of these Sports, there happened a Quarrel betwixt a *Turk*, and some *Moors*; whereupon the *Turks* all began to cry out, that the *Moors* had a design to rise and *rebel*; which took the more easily with the *Turks* Mob, because the Prince of *Morocco* happened to be there at that very juncture. And therefore they all ran into the City of *Algier*, and betook themselves to Arms, and would suffer no *Moor* to enter the Gate without Examination. In this Fray there were, in the several quarters of the Town, about three or four Score innocent *Moors* kill'd; for the Outcry of the *Turks* was altogether groundless, and a false Alarm. However, this *Tragedy* dashed all their *Sports* and *Recreations*, and the *Prince* himself was

[p. 180] put into a great Concern, and much fear'd what the Event of it would prove.

## CHAP. IX

*An Account of the* Author's *turning* Mahometan, *through the barbarous Cruelties and Tortures which he suffered. Of the* Concern *and* Remorse *he had thereupon. A* Letter *from his* Father. *A* Letter *from him to his* Father. *A* Conspiracy *contrived by his second* Patroon *to be* Dey *of* Algier.

THE Reader, I suppose, will expect an Account, how I became qualified to write such an *History* as this (though it may be guessed at by what has gone before) and how I was let into the *Secrets* of the *Mahometan Religion*, so as to be able to give such an exact Description of it, and particularly of their *Pilgrimage* to *Mecca*, and their *Devotions* there; when 'tis as much as a *Christian's* Life is worth to go into the *Temple*. And truly, I will not dissemble, but (undervaluing all the Censures of the World) freely and particularly declare the whole Matter; and herein I will deliver nothing but Naked Truth, as I protest I have hitherto done (*i.e.* what I speak as of [p. 181] my own Knowledge) in this whole Relation.

I spake something before of the Cruelties exercised upon me by the *Turks*; but now shall give a more particular Account of them; which were so many, and so great, that I being then but *young*, could no longer endure them, and therefore turn'd *Turk* to avoid them.

*GOD BE MERCIFUL TO ME A SINNER!*

It is usually reported among us here in *England*, that when any *Christians* are taken by the *Algerines*, they are put to the *extremest Tortures*, that so they may be thereby brought over to the *Mahometan Faith*; and I doubt not, many who have been Slaves in the *Turks* Country and come home again, have asserted so much out of *Vanity*, to be thought to relate something very affecting to such as are Strangers to that Country. But I do assure the Reader it is a very *false Report*; for they *very seldom* use such Severities on that account, though it was my hard Lot to be so *unmercifully* dealt with: They do not use to *force* any *Christian* to renounce his *Religion*.

Indeed, in the *Grand Turk's Country*,[319] in *Egypt*, and the Parts thereabout, where those *Sorts* of Christians are which are taken

---

[319] *Grand Turk's Country*: Anatolia.

[p. 182] by the *Tartars,* coming out of the Country of the *Russians, Georgians, Circassians,* &c. these being a very *ignorant Sort of Christians,* and especially the *Younger of them,* are no sooner taken Slaves, and sold, but they are immediately clothed with the *Turkish Habit,* put to School, and brought up in the *Mahometan* way. But in *Algier,* I aver, 'tis otherwise; for I have known some *Turks* there, who when they have perceived their Slaves inclinable to *turn,* have forthwith sold them; though by some of them this is look'd on as very odd, and to favour too much of a *want of Religion.* But the Truth is, they are more in love with their Money than they are with the Welfare of their Slaves; for you must know, that when a *Christian Slave* turns *Mahometan,* there can be no *Ransom* for him; and it is look'd on as an *infamous Thing* for any *Patroon,* in some few Years Time after they have *turned,* to deny them their Liberty, and to refuse to set them out handsomly [*sic*] into the World.

'Tis an Error among some too (I find) that as soon as ever a *Christian* turns *Turk,* he is *emancipated,* or becomes *free* (and so some think of *Turks* who become *Christians,* that they also are *Freemen;*) but as for those *Christians* who turn *Turks,* it is not so; for it lies wholly in the *Patroon's* Breast to dispose of them as he pleaseth.

[p. 183]

I have known those who have continued Slaves many Years after they have turn'd *Turks;* nay, some even to their *Dying-day.* And many, I am sure, have been as little respected by their *Patroons* after the *changing* of their *Religion,* as (or less than) before. For my part, I remain'd several Years a Slave after my *Defection,* suffered a great deal of cruel Usage, and then was sold again.

My first *Patroon* would (when exercising his barbarous Cruelty upon me) press me to turn *Mussulman;* but all this while I did not believe that he was really willing I should so do, but only he might think, that he discharg'd his Duty in importuning me thereunto. And my Reason why I thought so, is, because I knew at that Time he could badly sustain such a Loss; for it was not very long before that he bought a little Boy of *Dover,* which soon renounc'd his *Holy Religion,* and died in some Years after. This cruel Man I lived with about two or three Months, and then he sent me to Sea in one of the Ships to attend upon the *Toepgee Bashe,*[320] or the head Gunner. We

---

[320] *Toepgee Bashe:* modern Turkish, *topçubaşı; topcıbaşı* is also found.

made (as they said) but a very indifferent Voyage, for we took but one Ship, and that a *Portuguese*, with eighteen Slaves. We were out about two Months, to my great Ease and Content; but when we were returning to *Algier*, and I out of hopes of being *retaken*

[p. 184] for that Time, my Heart began to be heavy with the Thoughts of entring again into my former Misery: But there was no Remedy but Patience; into the Hands of the *Tyrant* I must fall again. But (*blessed be God*) within a few Days he sold me, and so I was out of the Possession of that *inhuman Wretch.*

When I was Selling, in the Shop where I was at work, I understood nothing of the Matter; but the Bargain being concluded, my new *Patroon*, and two Friends who were with him, went up Stairs, and I followed them. My Clothes were taken and pack'd up, and away I must go. I thought now I should have three *Patroons*, which I was afraid would be worse than one; but a *Moor* who lived on the other side of the Way, knowing what an hard *Patroon* I had, because he had often seen me beaten in the Shop, bid his Slave, who was an *English*-Man, tell me my new *Patroon* was better than the old. This comforted me a little. My new *Patroon* not living in *Algier* took me to a Friend's House of his, who kept a *Mistress* in the House, and with her was I left. In the Evening the Man of the House came, with my *Patroon*, who brought a *Madam* with him. A *Taverner*, at the same Time, brought Wine and Victuals, on which they were very merry. The next Morning they went out, and left me again with the

[p. 185] Woman. When the *Taverner*, who was a *Spaniard*, came for his Bottles, I desired him to ask her, What my *Patroon* design'd to do with me? She told him, I was bought to be made a Present of to his Brother at *Tunis*. And there, says the *Spaniard*, you may, perhaps, in Time, be *redeemed* by the *Consul*; which made me much easier than I was before.

My second *Patroon* lived in the Country, and was called by the Name of *dilberre Ibrahim*,[321] i.e. *handsome Abraham* (for *Note*, that the *Turks* are mostly *Nick*-named, especially those that are Soldiers. If a Man be blind in one Eye, they call him *blind Hugh*, or what his name is. If tall, *long such an one*. If short, *short such an one*. If in his younger Days given to much drinking, *sorhowsh*,[322] or *drunken such an one*. If Black-brow'd, then *Black-brow'd such an one*; which is esteem'd the greatest Beauty among them, *&c*. Besides this way of *Nick*-

---

[321] *dilberre Ibrahim*: modern Turkish, Dilber İbrahim.
[322] *sorhowsh*: modern Turkish, *sarhoş,* from the Persian, *sarkhūsh*.

*naming,* they often use another Manner of distinction, calling Men by the Name of their Country: As, *Exeter John, Welsh Tom,* or the like. But all this by the by.) He had several Slaves, both *Christians* and *Negroes;* and I happen'd to lose a Shirt, which, indeed, was scarce worth looking after; and it seems one of the *Negroes* had stolen it. I had it again, and said but little about the matter. But some Time after this, I lost my Jacquet; where-

[p. 186] upon I made my Complaint to our *Patroon;* he told me, he would beat all the Slaves round[323] but he would find out the Thief. Upon which one of the *Negro-slaves* stood up and said, "*Sir,* There is no Reason that *all* should suffer for *one;* and therefore, if I may presume so far, there is at *Bleda* (a Place about three Miles from our Country House) a *black* Woman, who can, as they say, *tell Fortunes,* and inform People where their lost Goods are." Upon which, my *Patroon* appointed two *Negroes* to go with me to the said *cunning* Woman. When we came to her House, I told her, *That we came to be inform'd of some thing by her.* Upon which she took a Thing like a Dish, and put Meal into it, and after she had smooth'd over the Meal, and made it plain, she bid me *put my Hand on it,* and withal, *to think within my self what I would be informed of.* Accordingly I did and my Thought was to know where my *Jacquet* was. In two or three Minutes time she told me, *That I had some Time before lost a* white Thing. I told her I had so; which I understood to be my Shirt. She then assured me, *That the* same Person *who stole my* Shirt *had stolen my* Jacquet; which prov'd to be the *Negro* aforesaid, by his own Confession. I was much surpriz'd [*sic*] at this Discovery, but repent of my Folly in going to such a Person on any such account.

[p. 187]

This my second *Patroon* had two Brothers in *Algier,* and a third in *Tunis.* The middle Brother had design'd to make a Voyage to *Tunis,* to see his Brother there; and, it seems, I was bought in order to be given as a Present to him. I was then cloth'd very fine, that I might be the better accepted. The Ship being ready, we put to Sea, and in about fourteen or fifteen Days Time we arriv'd at *Tunis,* and went forthwith to my *Patroon's* Brother's House, who had two Wives, which liv'd each in a House distant from one another. The next Day, my *Patroon's* Brother's Son, taking a Pride to have a *Christian* to wait upon him, made me walk after him. I was ready and glad to do it, because I was desirous to see the city. As I was attending upon my new Master through the Streets, I met with a Gentleman habited like a

---

[323] *round:* severely, without restraint.

*Christian*, not knowing him to be an *English*-Man, as he was. He look'd earnestly upon me, and ask'd me, Whether I were not an *English*-man? I answered him, *Yea. How came you hither?* Said he. I told him I came with my *Patroon. What, are you a Slave?* Said he. I replied, *Yes. To what place do you belong?* Continues he. To *Algier*, quoth I. But he was not willing to enter into any further Discourse with me in the publick Street, and therefore desired the young Man on whom I waited, that he would please, at

[p. 188] such an Hour of the Day, to bring me to his House, with a Promise of an hearty Welcome. The young Man assured him he would; for being a *Drinker* of *Wine*, and knowing the Plenty of it in the said Gentleman's House, he was the rather willing to go.

After the Gentleman was gone from us, my young new Master told me, that he whom we talk'd with was the *English Consul*; which I was glad to hear. We went, as appointed, to the *Consul's* House, where, when we came, I was directed up to his Chamber, the young Spark in the mean Time being eating and drinking in another Room. The *Consul* ask'd me many Questions about my Country, Parentage, &c. And withal, whether I could write, and understood *Arithmetick*. I told him I could do both tolerably. He called for Pen, Ink, and Paper, and bid me write a Line. The Words which came into my Mind, I very well remember, were these, *The Lord be my Guide, in him I will trust*. Which he seemed very well pleased with. Then he ask'd me what I thought was the Inducement for my *Patroon* to buy me. I told him, he design'd me for a Present to his Brother here, at Tunis. Upon the whole, the *Consul* kindly told me, if I were left in *Tunis*, he would order Matters to my Satisfaction; but if my *Patroon* design'd to carry me back again to

[p. 189] *Algier*, I should acquaint him with it in season; and in the mean time, he bid me, if I had so much liberty, to come every Day to his House, where I should be welcome.

After I had been in *Tunis* about thirty Days, I understood that my *Patroon's* Brother cared not to accept of me, and that therefore I was to return to *Algier*. This very much troubled me; upon which I went to the *Consul* and acquainted him with it. The *Consul* told me, that he and other two Merchants (there being no more *English* Merchants in the Town) would the next Day come and talk with my *Patroon* about me; and that if his Demands were not too high, they would purchase my Redemption. *And if so*, says he, *you must tarry* two, *or* three *Years* (Seven, said I) *with me, and then you shall go home when I do*. They came accordingly with their *Interpreter*, and ask'd him whether he was willing to sell me. He told them he was, upon Terms. They ask'd him what Price he put upon me. He told them Five hundred *Dollars*, which was, I suppose, Three hundred more than he bought me for. They offered Two hundred. He made a slight of that, and laugh'd at them. They advanc'd to Two hundred and fifty *Dollars*. He still made a Pish of it.[324] They at length came up to Three hundred *Dollars*, which is near sixty Pounds *Sterling*; but my

[p. 190] *Patroon* plainly told them, he would not abate one *Asper* (*i.e.* about *five Farthings*) of his Demands. At which the *Consul* told me that I must have Patience, for *an Hundred* Pounds was a considerable Sum to be contributed by three only, and Providence might work some other way. Upon hearing this, I burst into Tears, notwithstanding, returning them a thousand Thanks for their generous Good-will. The *Consul* laid his Hand on my Head, and bid me serve GOD and be chearful; and promised me, that as soon as he return'd to *England* he would prefer a Petition to the *King* for me, and so parted from me.

This worthy Gentleman's name was *Baker* (I think *Charles*)[325] Brother to *Thomas Baker, Consul* at *Algier.* And here I must observe that what *One Brother* could not bring to bear, the *Other* several Years after undertook, though he ran the greatest Hazard in so doing; and was (though Divine Goodness) an Instrument of effecting it.

My Hopes were thus all *dash'd*, which was no small Trouble to me; but *Patience overcomes all Disappointments and Afflictions.*

My *Patroon* now carried me on board in order to go back again for *Algier.* The Vessel in which we went was bound no further than *Bona*, which is near about half

[p. 191] way to *Algier* ★; so that when we came thither my *Patroon* hired two Mules, on which we came by Land to *Algier*, which is about Two hundred and fifty Miles. [[ ★*Some years after this, when I had my* Freedom, *and went to* Camp, *I somewhere about this part of the Country passed through a River, the Water of which was so hot, I could scarce suffer it. And I was credibly* inform'd, *that a little farther up in the River the Water was* hot *enough to* boil an Egg.]][326]

---

[324] *still made a Pish of it*: still expressed contempt at the offer.

[325] *Charles Baker*: in fact, Thomas Baker's brother in Tunis was called Francis. For more information on the Baker brothers, see Pennell (1989).

[326] *boil an Egg*: Pitts is here referring to the Meskhoutine Spring (Arabic, Ḥammām al-Miskhūṭīn), which is one of the hottest in the world and lies halfway between Bône and Constantine, just off the N20 highway.

About two Months after this, my chief *Patroon*, being *Captain* of a Troop of Horse, was sent to *Tunis* by Land, with about twenty *Spahys*, and carried me with him also; so that I was not wanting from *Tunis* above four Months before my second coming thither. The next Day after we came now to *Tunis*, I was sent out on an Errand, and accidentally met with the worthy *Consul* again. When he saw me, *What, my Boy*, said he, *art thou come* again? Yes Sir, *said I*, I came now with my chief *Patroon*. *While you were absent*, said he, *I bought a Young Man for my purpose, for* considerably less *than I offered for you; but however, you may tell* this *your* Patroon, *that if he be disposed to sell you, I will still* stand *to my* Proposal. I gave him many Thanks, and went immediately , and told my *Patroon* of it; who surlily answered me, *Seu le mang keu pek,*[327] i.e. *Hold your Peace you* Dog! I saw that there was no good to be done with him, and therefore desisted.

[p. 192]

We return'd back to *Algier* in some small time; and a little after that, he carried me into Camp with him; and it so happen'd, that his two Brothers, being *Spahys*, or Troopers, were with him in one and the same Tent. His *younger* Brother would be frequently (behind his Back, and sometimes before his Face) perswading me to turn *Mahometan*, and to gain me, made me large Offers; but I little regarded them. And I can truly appeal to Almighty God, that it was not out of Choice, or Inclination, or Perswasion, or any Temporal Advantage, that I became a *Mahometan*; for I abhorred the Thoughts of such an *Apostasy*.

The eldest Brother, who was my chief *Patroon*, I found, was not very fond of my *turning*; for he would often threaten me, that if I did turn *Turk*, and did not learn my Book well, he would beat me soundly. But when his *younger* Brother, who had been so often tampering with me, saw that no Arguments nor Offers would prevail, he began to lie very close to[328] his Brother to force me to *turn*; and as an Argument, would often tell him, "That he had been a *profligate* and *debauch'd* Man in his time, and a *Murderer*; and that the *Proselyting* me would be some sort of an *Atonement* for his past Impieties; and *flatly told him* that otherwise he would never go to

[p. 193] *Heaven*". Whereupon (as guilty Men are willing to lay hold on every *pretence* to Happiness, though never so slight, and groundless) the eldest Brother endeavoured to perswade me; and finding that would not

---

[327] *Seu le mang keu pek*: modern Turkish, *söylemen köpek*.
[328] *lie very close to*: press, try to persuade.

do, he threatned [*sic*] to send me hundreds of Miles off into the Country, where I should never see the Face of any *Christian*. But finding all these Methods to be ineffectual to the End they drove at, the two Brothers consulted together, and resolv'd upon *Cruelty,* and *Violence,* to see what that would do. Accordingly, on a certain Day, when my *Patroon*'s Barber came to trim him, I being there to give Attendance, my *Patroon* bid me kneel down before him; which I did: He then ordered the Barber to cut off my Hair with his Scissers [*sic*]; but I mistrusting somewhat of their Design, struggled with them; but by stronger Force my Hair was cut off, and then the Barber went about to shave my Head, my *Patroon* all the while holding my Hands. I kept shaking my head, and he kept striking me in the Face. After my Head, with much ado, was shaved, my *Patroon* would have me take off my Clothes, and put on the *Turkish* Habit. I told him plainly I would not: Whereupon I was forthwith hal'd away[329] to another Tent, in which we kept our Provision; where were two Men, *viz.* the *Cook* and the *Steward*; one of which held me, while the other stript

[p. 194] me, and put on me the *Turkish* Garb. I all this while kept crying, and told my *Patroon*, that although he had chang'd my *Habit*,[330] yet he could never change my *Heart*. The Night following, before he lay down to sleep, he call'd me, and bid me kneel down by his Bed-side, and then used Entreaties that I would gratify him in renouncing my *Religion*. I told him it was against my *Conscience*, and withal, desired him to sell me, and buy another Boy, who perhaps might more easily be won; but as for my part, I was afraid I should be everlastingly *damn'd*, if I complied with his Request. He told me, he would pawn his Soul for mine, and many other *importunate*[331] Expressions did he use. At length I desired him to let me go to bed, and I would pray to God, and if I found any better reasons suggested to my mind than what I then had, to *turn*, by the next Morning, I did not know what I might do; but if I continued in the same mind I was, I desired him to say no more to me on *that* Subject. This he agreed to, and so I went to Bed. But (whatever ail'd him) having not Patience to stay till the Morning for my Answer, he awoke me in the Night, and ask'd me what my Sentiments now were. I told him they were the same as before. Then he took me by the Right-hand, and endeavoured to make me hold up the Fore-finger, as they usually do

[p. 195] when they speak those Words [[viz. *La Allah ellallah, Mohammed*

---

[329] *hal'd away*: taken away.  [330] *Habit*: clothes.  [331] *importunate*: persistent.

*Resul Allah*]] which initiates them *Turks* (as I have related before) but I did with all my might bend it down, so that he saw nothing was to be done with me without *Violence*; upon which he presently call'd two of his Servants, and commanded them to tie up my Feet with a Rope to the Post of the Tent; and when they had so done, he with a great Cudgel fell a beating of me upon my bare feet: And being a very strong Man, and full of Passion, his Blows fell heavy indeed; and the more he beat me, the more chafed and enraged he was; and declared, that, in short, if I would not *turn*, he would beat me to Death. I roar'd out to feel the Pain of his cruel Strokes, but the more I cry'd, the more furiously he laid on; and to stop the Noise of my Crying, would stamp with his Feet on my Mouth; at which I beg'd him to dispatch me out of the way; but he continued beating me. After I had endured this merciless Usage so long, till I was ready to faint and die under it, and saw him as mad and implacable as ever, I beg'd him to forbear, and I would *turn*. And breathing a while, but still hanging by the Feet, he urg'd me again to speak the Words. Very unwilling I was, and held him in suspence a while; and at length told him, that I could not speak them. At which he was

[p. 196] more enrag'd than before, and fell at me again in a most *barbarous* manner. After I had received a great many Blows a *second* time, I beseech'd him again to hold his Hand, and gave him fresh hopes of my turning *Mahometan*; and after I had taken a little more Breath, I told him as before, I could not do what he desired. And thus I held him in suspence three, or four times; but at last, seeing his Cruelty towards me insatiable, unless I turn'd, through *Terrour* [*sic*] I did it, and spake the Words as usual, holding up the Fore-finger of my Right-hand: And presently I was had away to a Fire, and care was taken to heal my Feet, (for they were so beaten, that I was not able to go upon them for several Days) and so I was put to Bed.

All the Ceremony that any Person who turns *Mahometan*, by *Compulsion*, useth, is only holding up the Fore-finger of the Right-hand, and pronouncing the Words before-mentioned. But when any Person *voluntarily* turns from his *Religion* to the *Mahometan*, there is a great deal of *Formality* used. Many there are who so *turn*, out of Choice, without any Terrour or Severity shewn them. Sometimes in a mad, or drunken Humour; sometimes to avoid the Punishment due to some great Crime committed by them, as Murder, or the like: I speak of Persons belonging to *English*, or other

[p. 197] Ships at Anchor at *Algier*, such will get ashore if possible, and often become *Mahometans*, being afraid to return to their own country.

Now when any Person so turns *Mahometan,* he goes to the Court, where the *Dey,* and *Divan,*[332] (*i.e.* his Council) sits, and there declares his willingness to be a *Mahometan;* upon which he is immediately accepted, without demanding of him any *Reason* for his so doing. After which, the *Apostate* is to get on Horse-back, on a stately Steed, with a rich Saddle, and fine Trappings: He is also richly habited, and hath a *Turbant* on his Head, (but to be sure, not of a *green* colour; for none durst wear their *Turbants* of *that* Colour, but such as are of *Mahomet's Blood*) but nothing of this is to be call'd his own; only there is given him about two or three yards of Broad-Cloth, which is laid before him on the Saddle. The Horse, with him on his Back, is led all round the City; and he carries an Arrow in his Right-hand, holding it straight up, and thereby supporting the Fore-finger of his Right-hand, which he holds up against it. This he doth all the while he is riding round the City; which he is several Hours in doing. But if he happens to be *tired* with long holding up his Fore-finger against the Arrow, he may now and then take it off for a *Moment,* and then up with it again in the said Posture. [p. 198]

The *Apostate* is attended with Drums, and other Musick, and twenty or thirty *Vekil-Harges,* or *Stewards,* who (as I told you) are under the *Otho-Bashes,* or *Sergeants.* These march in Order on each side of the Horse, with naked Swords in their Hands, intimating thereby (as I was informed) that if he should *repent,* and shew the least Inclination of *Retracting* what he had declared before the *Dey* and *Divan,* he deserv'd to be cut in Pieces; and the *Vekil-Harges* would accordingly do it. There are likewise two Persons who stand one on each side of the Street, as he marcheth thorow [*sic*], to gather what People are pleas'd to give, by way of Encouragement, to the New *Convert,* (as they call him) and it may be, one here and there drops a *Farthing* or *Halfpenny;* 'tis much if any be so *Zealous* as to give a *Penny.* After this *Show* and *Ceremony* is over, he is immediately entred [*sic*] into Pay, and directed to the Place where he shall quarter, with some of his Fellow-Soldiers. And within a few Days the *Seunet Gee*[333] of the Town, *i.e.* the *Circumciser,* comes and performs the Ceremony of *Circumcision.* And then he is a *Turk* to all Intents and Purposes. It is reported by some, that when any thus *voluntarily* turns *Mahometan,* he throws a Dart at the Picture of *Jesus Christ,* in token of his disowning him as the *Saviour* of the World, and

---

[332] *Divan:* modern Turkish, *divan,* from the Arabo-Persian, *dīwān.*
[333] *Seunet Gee:* modern Turkish, *sünnetçi,* from the Arabic, *sunnah.*

preferring *Mahomet* to him: But there
[p. 199] is no such Usage; and they who relate such things, deceive the World. I am sure I have reason (God pardon me!) to know everything in use among them of this Nature; and I assure the *Reader* there is never any such thing done.

The *Cryer* goes before, with a loud Voice giving Thanks to God, for the *Proselyte* that is made; and at some particular Places of the City, especially in the *Casharees*,[334] or the Places where many of the Soldiers dwell together, the Multitude hold up their Hands, giving Thanks to God.

I was very much concern'd for one of our *Country-men*, who had endur'd many Years of Slavery, and after he was *ransomed*, went home to his own Country; but came again to *Algier*, and *voluntarily*, without the least Force used towards him, became a *Mahometan*.

Another *English-man* I knew, bred to the Trade of a *Gun-Smith*, who after he was *ransomed*, and only waited for his Passage, *renegado'd*, and chose rather to be a *Mahometan*, than to return to *England*.

About two or three Months, as near as I can guess, after I was taken a Slave, I writ a Letter to my Father, giving him an Account of what had happen'd; to which I received a kind and affectionate Answer. A copy of the Letter I have not by me, but I well remember that therein he gave me [p. 200] very good Counsel, *viz.* "To have a care and keep close to *God*, and to be sure never, by any Methods of Cruelty that could be used towards me, be prevailed with to *deny* my *blessed Saviour.* And that he had rather hear of my *Death*, than of my being a *Mahometan*". But this first Letter from my Father came not to my Hands till some days after I had, through my *Patroon's* Barbarity to me, *turn'd* from my *Religion*. Which after (through *extreme* Torture, and out of Love to a *Temporal* Life) I had done, I became very sad, and melancholy, considering the Danger my poor Soul was in. The said Letter was taken up in *Algier* by my Master *George Taylor*[335] of *Lymson*, who sent it to the Camp, directing it to an *English* Lad, one of the *Bey's*, or *General's* Slaves; who being afraid to deliver me the Letter openly, slid it into my Hand as he past by me. As soon as I cast my Eye upon the Superscription, I knew it to be my Father's Hand, and in a great deal of

---

[334] *Casharees:* possibly *inkashāriyyah*, from the colloquial Arabic word for janissary, *inkishārī*, which itself derives from the Turkish, *yeniçeri*.

[335] *George Taylor:* the same George Taylor with whom Pitts sailed on his fateful voyage in the *Speedwell* in 1678. Presumably, Taylor had been ransomed and had returned to England.

Sorrow, made what haste I could out of the Camp (pretending to go to ease my self) to read the Letter; but when I had open'd it, could scarce read a Word for weeping. And I am apt to think, that if the Letter had come into my Hands before I had turn'd *Turk,* my *Patroon* would rather have accepted of the promis'd *Ransom* for me, than that I should become a *Mahometan.*

[p. 201]

After I had read some part of the Letter (for I could not read it through at once, for fear my *Patroon* should find me wanting) I was ready to sink. I put it up therefore, intending to read the whole another time, and return'd to our Tent, with a more dejected Heart and Countenance than before; insomuch that my *Patroon* perceiving it, ask'd me whether I had been weeping? I reply'd, *Sir, you don't see me weep.* Many other angry Words he had with me; and at length truly my Heart was so big, that I could not contain any longer, but fell into Tears, and at the same time produc'd him the Letter which I received from my Father, and told him that my Father would *ransom* me; and withal added, *I am no* Turk, *but a* Christian. My *Patroon* answered me with, *Hold your Tongue, you* Dog, *for if you speak such a Word again, I'll have a great* Fire *made, and therein* burn *thee immediately.* At which I was forc'd to be silent.

In two or three Days after this, I writ my Father a second Letter, (which I was forc'd to do by piece-meals, in a great deal of Danger, and Fear) in which I gave him a perfect Account of the whole matter, and told him the naked Truth, lest he should have thought that what I did, had been *voluntarily,* and without any *Coercion.* And in order thereunto, I privately desired the aforesaid *English* Lad, a Servant to the *Bey,* to lend

[p. 202] me Pen, Ink, and Paper; and took an occasion to go on the outside of the Camp, and there in Fear writ two or three Lines at a time, as I could, without discovery, till I had finish'd my *Epistle.*

The substance of my Letter was, "that tho' I was forc'd by the *Cruelty* which was exercis'd upon me, to turn *Turk,* yet I was really a *Christian* in my Heart; (some may term me *Hypocrite* for so doing, but I'll not reply any more, than this, That I speak it not to extenuate my Sin, but to set the Matter in a true Light, how I *turn'd,* and the *Reasons* of my so doing.) And withal, I assured my Father and Mother, that I would, as soon as ever I could find an opportunity, endeavour to make my Escape: And therefore intreated them to be as contented as they could under their great Affliction, and expect what time would produce."

Some time after my Father receiv'd this my second Letter, he sent me another, which was directed (as the former) to my Master *Taylor* in *Algier*; and he sent it forward, directing it to an *Englishman* at *Bleda*, where I then lived, of whom I receiv'd it; and I look upon it as a signal Providence, for there was but that one *Englishman* then living in the Town. The Substance of the Letter was as followeth, *viz.*

[p. 203]

*YET I cannot chuse but call thee* dear *and* loving Son, *although thou hast denied thy* Redeemer *that bought thee; especially, considering the* Tenderness *of thy Age, the* Cruelty *of thy Usage, and the* Strength *of thy Temptations. I confess, when I first heard of it, I thought it would have overwhelm'd my* Spirits; *and had it not been for* divine Supports, *it had been a* Burden *too too unsupportable for my weak Shoulders to have* crippled *under; especially considering the Loss of thy* Soul.

But withal, my Father in his Letter comforted me, with telling me, That he had been with several *Ministers*, who unanimously concurred in their Opinion, I had not sinned the *unpardonable Sin.* Their names were, Mr. *Hopping*, Mr. *Collings*, and Mr. *Hallett*,[336] who were *Ministers* in *Exeter.* The last advised my Father to write to me. Said my Father, *I shall write very smart*[337] *if I do.* The good Man replied, *by no Means, but write as* tenderly *as possible, otherwise you'll* spoil *all; and give him all the* Encouragement *you can.* My Father followed his Advice, and therefore went on as follows,

*Truly,* Child, *I do believe, that what thou hast done with thy* Mouth, *was not with thy* Heart; *and that it was contrary to thy* Conscience.

[p. 204] *Take heed of being* hardened *in thine Iniquity; give not way to* Despondency, *nor to* Desperation. *Remember, that* Peter[338] *had not so many Temptations to deny his* Lord *and* Master, *as thou hast had, and yet he* obtain'd Mercy; *and so may'st thou. Yet the Door of* Grace *and* Mercy *is open for thee. I can hardly write to thee for weeping, and my* Time *is but short; and what shall I say to thee more, my* poor Child? *I will* pawn *the* Loss *of my* Soul, *upon the* Salvation *of thine, that if thou dost but duly and daily* repent *of this thy horrid*

---

[336] *Mr. Hopping, Mr. Collings, and Mr. Hallett*: John Hopping and Joseph Hallett were both well-known Presbyterian ministers in Exeter. For more information, see Part I, Chapter 2, note 25.

[337] *smart*: sharply.

[338] *Peter*: St Peter denied Christ three times in the account found in the *Gospel according to St Matthew*, chapter 26, verses 69–75.

*Iniquity, the* Blood *of that* Jesus *whom thou hast* denied, *will cleanse thee from it, and there is sufficient* Satisfaction *in him* to save thee to the utmost, *or otherwise let me* perish. *I will promise thee as* welcome *to me upon thy* Return *and* Repentance, *as though thou hadst never done it. And if there be such* Bowels *of* Pity *in an* earthly Parent, *which are but as* Drops *to the* Ocean, *what dost thou think of the* boundless Mercies *of* GOD, *whose Compassions are like to himself,* Infinite? *I confess, it's something difficult for thee to make thy* Escape, *but yet I am* confident, *that if thou dost keep close to* GOD, *notwithstanding this thy* Miscarriage, *infinite* Wisdom *and* Power *will be set at work to find out Ways, in such* untrodden *Paths, as I cannot imagine, for thy* Relief. *Which is the* daily Prayers *of thy*

Affectionate Father,

JOHN PITTS.

**[p. 205]**

It pleased GOD that this my Father's second Letter, though cause of many sorrowful Reflections in me, did yet administer great Support and Comfort to me; and I would often go into some By-corner,[339] or under some Hedge of a Garden, to read it.

The Reader may easily think, that one under *my Circumstances*, could have but very few Opportunities of writing home to his Parents and Friends; which was the reason why I writ no oftner.

In my return from *Mecca* to *Algier,* at *Alexandria* I accidentally met with *John Cleak* of *Lymson,* who belong'd to Captain *Bear's* Ship of *Topsham* (as I related to you before) in whom, being my old Acquaintance, I could put Confidence; and so desired him to carry a Letter for me, which he readily granted. But since I came home to *Exon,* the said *Cleak* told me, that he was under great Fear and Concern, lest the *Turks* Officers on Board (who are much like our *Tidesmen*[340]) should, when searching their Chests, *&c.* find the Letter in his Custody; to prevent which, he hung it in the inside the Cieling [*sic*] of the Ship. The Reader will excuse my not dating the Letter, when I tell him, that truly I had then forgot the Month and the Year, because the *Turks* reckon after a different manner from us; and I did not only omit the Date of the Letter,

**[p. 206]** but sent it also unsealed; as the manner of sending letters is there: For indeed, they are very *illiterate,* not one in an Hundred being able to read; and therefore they run no great Risque in sending their Letters unsealed.

---

[339] *By-corner:* an out-of-the-way place.   [340] *Tidesmen:* customs officials.

Honoured, and dear Father and Mother,

*It is not the want of* Duty, *or* Love, *which makes me negligent of* writing *to you, but 'tis chiefly the Consideration of the little* Comfort *you can take in hearing from me, having been a great* Grief, *and* Heart-breaking *to you.*

Dear Father and Mother, *How often have I wished that I had departed the World when I hung upon your* Breasts, *that I might not have been* the bringer of your gray Hairs with Sorrow to the Ground. *Therefore, if you would be an Ease to my* Grief, *I desire you to wait* GOD's *Leisure.*

Your *Grief, through great, is but little, in comparison of* mine. *Put it to the worst, you have lost* but *a* Son; *but I, for my part, have lost both a dear* Father *and* Mother, Brothers, Relations, Friends, Acquaintance, *and all! But my greatest* Sorrow *is, that* GOD *hath deprived me of his* Holy Scriptures, *of any* good Counsel *or* Discourse; *for* I see nothing but Wickedness before mine Eyes.

*The* Lord *of* Heaven *reward you for your Endeavours to bring me up in the* Ways *of* Jesus Christ; *for the bad Improvement of which*

[p. 207] *Privilege, I now here find and suffer the want of it.*[341] I am in great Fears, *and great* Hazards *do I run, in writing these few Lines. About fourteen Months I have been wanting from* Algier, *for I have been with my* Patroon *to* Mecca, *where is* (they say) *the* House *of* GOD; *and after they have been to pay their* Devotions *thither, they do account that all their* Sins *are* forgiven.

Mecca *is about forty Days travel beyond* Grand Cairo; *being now therefore in my way back again to* Algier (*as far as* Alexandria) *I embrace this Opportunity of sending to you from hence. With my kind* Love *to all my* Brothers, Relations, Friends *and* Neighbours, *desiring yours, and the* Prayers *of all good People to* GOD *for me, I rest*

Your Dutiful Son, till Death,

JOSEPH PITTS.


I liv'd still a miserable Life with this my second *Patroon*, and was oftentimes so beaten by him, that my Blood ran down upon the Ground. *After* I had thus turn'd *Turk*, he had rather *less* Kindness for me than *before*; and one Reason was, because he thought that I was no true *Mussulman* in my Heart; for he observ'd me to be far from being *zealous* in the *Mahometan* way. (And I must declare, that oftentimes I would go to *Mosque* without

---

[341] *for the bad Improvement* ... : I have been unable to improve myself as a Christian since there is no Christianity here.

ever taking any *Abdes* at all; which none of the thorough pac'd[342]
*Mahometans*
**[p. 208]** would do, might they gain ever so much.) For which I fared (many
ways) much worse than my fellow Slaves, which had not *turned*; and did lie
with them in a Stable, and also eat with them. And indeed, our Victuals were
very *coarse* and *ordinary* (viz.) mostly *Barley-Bread* with *sour Milk* — — But
if a *Sheep* did chance to *die*, the Flesh would come for our share, and many
joyful and hearty good Meals should we make of it.

I remember there was a tame young Hog in the Village where we lived,
once happen'd to fall foul of a Milk-pan full of Milk; for which it soon lost
its Life. My fellow Slaves hearing it was dead, presently took and carried it
into the Field, where they made a Fire, burnt off its Hair, and then boiled
it. When they had eat their Allowance for Supper, down came the *second
Coarse*, viz. the boil'd Hog, on which they fared *sumptuously*, desiring me to
take part with them. I envied them their Dainties, but durst not taste, lest it
should have been discover'd, and cost me my Life. After they had enjoyed
themselves on this *noble* Dish, what remained was set by for another Time.
The next Day, when they were all gone to their Work in the Vineyards, I
had an Opportunity to see how I liked it, and fed on it very *heartily*. In the
Evening they had their *second Coarse* again, but finding that a good part of
it was gone, they fell
**[p. 209]** a-taxing each other, for it was no small Disappointment to them
all: But none of them did in the least suspect me.

This my *Patroon* was a married Man, and being wanting about *fourteen
months* from his Wife, upon a *stretch*, in that Interval she was deliver'd of
*bastard* Twins; so he turn'd her away, and in a little Time married another,
who was a great *Fortune* to him. Having now got great *Riches*, and being a
Man full of *Ambition*, he had a great Tooth[343] for the *Dey-ship* of *Algier*, and
to compass his design, had (by large Promises of *promoting* them) corrupted
many among the *Soldiers*, who declar'd they were resolv'd to stand by him.
The *Dey*, whose Name was *Hassan* (whom they also call'd *Baba Hassan*,[344]
i.e. *Father Hassan*) having had some private Information of this my *Patroon's*
Design, *banish'd* him. Now the way of *Banishment* is thus, (viz.) The *Cryer*
cries it about the Town, and proclaims the Person to be *banish'd*, promising
a great Reward to any who shall discover him from that Time.

---

[342] *thorough pac'd*: scrupulous.  [343] *Tooth*: desire.  [344] *Baba Hassan*: see note 316.

My *Patroon*, notwithstanding, left not his Country, nor his Country-house, but kept himself very private all Day, and lay in the Fields by Night, with me, and others of his Slaves. At length Search was made for him, and his two Brothers, and the *Troopers* would come sometimes and beset his Country-house, to take him. Finding himself
[p. 210] no longer safe in those Parts, be betook himself to the *Mountains* of the *Cabyles*, a rugged sort of People. I, with two or three more of his Slaves, and his two Brothers, were with him in the Mountains, where, by his plausible[345] Tongue, he at length got into the Favour and Esteem of the *Cabyles*; so that they resolved to stand by him.

Now it happen'd, that at this very juncture, the *French* came and bombarded *Algier*, because their Demands of the *French* Slaves there were not answer'd. Upon which, all being in great Confusion by the Bombs, the *Dey's* Wife set her self to persuade her Husband to release the Slaves; he was *accordingly* prevail'd upon, and yielded them up to the *French*, then before the Town. At which the Soldiers began to express their Dissatisfaction, that he had not consulted with them about it, and were somewhat turbulent, saying one among another, *We are brought to a* brave Pass *now, to become* tributary *to the* French! And in a little Time the Jealousies against him grew so high, that they slew him in the Night-time without the *Mole-gate*.[346]

[[A third time the *French* came, with a Squadron under the Command of *Mareschal d'Estree*,[347] who fired 10000 *Bombs* into the Town, as also abundance of *Carkashes*,[348] which are fired as a *Bomb* is, but a *Bomb* is
[p. 211] fill'd only with Powder, whereas these are fill'd with several Combustibles, and have Holes all round, and in every Hole something like the Barrel of a Pistol, laden with several Shot. These break not all at once, as the *Bombs*; and were design'd for the Ships that were in the *Mole*, but they did no great Execution upon them; for, to the best of my remembrance, they lost not one *Privateer*, only some Prizes which lay then in the Harbour; the *Algerines* having themselves sunk their *Privateers* before the *French* began to fire their *Bombs*.

---

[345] *plausible Tongue*: convincing speech.
[346] *Mole-gate*: Pitts is referring to the attack on Algiers by the French in 1683 after which *Baba Hassan* (Baba Hasan) was put to death.
[347] *Mareschal d'Estree*: Maréchal Jean, comte d'Estrées (1624–1707), bombarded Algiers in 1688.
[348] *Carkashes*: shells filled with inflammable material.

'Tis true, the City was so much beaten down, that you could not distinguish one Street or Lane from another, and 'twas several Years before the Damage was quite repair'd. The *French* Fleet anchor'd out of Gun-shot of the Town, but the *Bomb-Vessels* were within shot, at which the *Turks* plied their Cannon very briskly. But they saw no good was to be done, for the Shot could not pierce the Sides of the *French* Ships, but fell into the Sea. The *French* therefore were in no fear of their Cannon; and the *Turks*, at length, thought it their wisest way to save their Ammunition.

However, to show their Valour, they resolved to fit out a *Galley* to attack the *Bomb-Vessels*; and for Encouragement, promised to advance the Pay to such as would be *Voluntiers*; so that she was soon very well

[p. 212] mann'd. The *Galley-Slaves* being on board and chained to their Oars, away they tow'd by Night. Now, though there was a considerable Distance between the *French* Fleet and their *Bomb-Vessels*, yet they had Hausers which reached from one to the other, being fasten'd to each; but this was more than the *Algerines* knew. When the *Galley* attack'd one of the *Bomb-Vessels*, the *French* gave them a warm Reception with their *Hand-Granadoes* which falling into the *Galley*, did great Execution; for there were about two Hundred Slaves chained, and near as many *Turks* on board. The poor Slaves begg'd the *French* to take Pity on them, which made them fire the less. While they were thus hotly engag'ed, the *Galley* having grappled the *Bomb-Vessel*, the *French* Fleet being apprehensive of what was doing, fell a pulling the Hauser, which insensibly drew both of them towards them. But when the *Turks* perceived how near they were to the *French* Fleet, they at once cut their Fasts,[349] and scower'd[350] back for the *Town* as fast as they could. I thought it a very melancholy Sight, in the Morning, to see so many Slaves and *Turks* kill'd and wounded.

There were (as I remember) nine *Bomb-Vessels*, each having two *Mortars*, which kept firing Day and Night, insomuch that there would be five or six *Bombs* flying in the Air at once, which was a terrible sight.

[p. 213] At this the *Algerines* were horribly enraged, and to be revenged, fired away from the Mouth of their Cannon about *forty French* Slaves; and finding *that* would not do, but d'*Estree* was rather the more exasperated, they sent for the *French Consul*, intending to serve him the same Sauce. He pleaded his *Character*, and that he hoped they would not use a Person of his

---

[349] *Fasts*: ropes.   [350] *scower'd*: rushed.

*Post* and *Figure*[351] so barbarously: That 'twas against the *Law of Nations*, &c. They answer'd, they were *resolv'd*, and all these *Compliments* would not serve his turn. At which he desir'd a Day or two's Respite, till he could dispatch a Letter to the *Admiral*; which was granted him, and a Boat was sent out with a *white* Flag. But after the *Admiral* had perused, and considered the *Consul's* Letter, he bid the Messenger return this Answer (*viz.*) "That his *Commission* was to throw 10000 *Bombs* into the Town, and he would do it to the very last; and that, as for the *Consul*, if he died, he could not die better than for his *Prince.*" This was bad News, you may imagine, to the *Consul*, and highly provoked the *Algerines*, who immediately, upon this Message, caus'd the *Consul* to be brought down, and placed him before the Mouth of a Cannon, and fired him off also. This was very dreadful to behold.

The *French*, to make some Returns for the *Algerines* firing off their *Consul*, Slaves,

[p. 214] and an ancient *Priest*, took this Method, *viz.* They made a Stage of three or four deal Boards, when the Wind blew towards the Shore, and fasten'd some *Turks* or *Moors* on it, firing at them until they were dead. In a little Time the Wind would drive the Stage ashore with the dead *Turks*, which was a *dismal* Spectacle, indeed!

The *French* bombarded *Algier* three times[352] while I was there; The first Time, as I remember, was because the *Turks* would not yield up the *French* Slaves which they had. They then threw but few *Bombs* into the *Town*, and that by Night; nevertheless, the Inhabitants were so surprized, and terrified at it, being unacquainted with *Bombs*, that they threw open the Gates of the City and Men, Women, and Children, left the Town; whereupon the *French* had their Country-men, who were Slaves, for nothing. A little after they came again to *Algier* upon other Demands, when (as I have related) by the Perswasion of his Wife, the *Dey* surrender'd up all the *French* Slaves; which prov'd his Ruin. And then, (as I have also told) they came a third Time, and fired many thousands of *Bombs* into the *Town*; notwithstanding the *Dey* stood his Ground and would not yield up one Slave without an *Equivalent*; so that the French brought ashore thirty or forty *Turks*, or *Moors*, in their Boat, and had as many of their own

[p. 215] Country-men, that were Slaves, in exchange for them.]] But to return to the Story of my *Patroon*.

---

[351] *Post and Figure*: position and importance.
[352] *three times*: in 1682, 1683 and 1688.

Immediately upon the Death of *Baba Hassan*, some of my *Patroon's* Friends took Horse, and came Post-haste to acquaint him of this seemingly favourable Event. He instantly equips for *Algier*, which being a Day's Journey, there was a new *Dey* elected before he could get thither; whereas, if he could have come sooner than he did, 'twas the general Notion that he would have been *Dey*. However, though he came too late to be *Dey*, all former Matters were accommodated, and he, in all Appearance, in favour with the present *Dey*. But in a few Days this *Dey* became incens'd against him; whereupon he was a second Time *banish'd*.

My *Patroon*, at this, being very much puzzled what to do, or where to go, at length went to a *Marabbot*, to crave his Advice, what he was best to do in this Exigence. The *Marabbot* told him, "That he should distribute fifty *Dollars* to the *Poor*, kill four *Sheep*, and give to them; and after he had so done, go back to *Algier*, not doubting Success in his Enterprizes there." He took his leave of the *Marabbot*, having received of him his old patch'd Cloak, which he look'd on as a mighty Preservative from all manner of Danger; and, according to the *Marabbot's*

[p. 216] Advice, he, with his two Brothers, and two other *Turks* of their Acquaintance, being well-arm'd with small Arms under their Cloaks, mounted their Horses, and posted[353] to *Algier*; and were at the Gate as soon, almost, as it was open. They left their Horses at the Gate, and went directly to the House where the *Dey* sat with the *Divan*, or *Council*. At the Gate of the *Dey's* House the *Aga*, with other Officers, sits, and there usually Complaints are made. To him, therefore, my *Patroon* makes his Complaint, telling him, that he was not conscious of any Harm that he had done against the *Government*, that therefore he was unjustly *banish'd*; and that if there could any Thing be proved against him that deserved it, he was come, presently ready to suffer Death. The *Aga* having received his Complaint, sends for one of the seven *Chiauxes*, or *Chiaous*,[354] who are equal to our *Serjeants*, and bid him go in and acquaint the *Dey* with it. When the *Dey* heard they were without, he immediately ordered the *Chiauxes* to apprehend them, for fear what the Consequence of any Delays might prove. The *Chiauxes* therefore running upon them to seize them, my *Patroon* and his Company drew their Swords, and defied them; at which the *Chiauxes* were afraid, and fell back, and my *Patroon* and his Accomplices made to a

---

[353] *posted*: travelled with relays of horses.
[354] *Chiauxes, or Chiaous*: modern Turkish, *çavuş*.

*Casherea*, i.e. a sort of a *Guard-House*, where
[p. 217] were many Soldiers, and with large Promises engaged them to stand by him; and so they shut the Gate of the *Casherea*, making it a sort of Garrison. But in a little Time the *Town* was up in Arms, and the Soldiers beset the Place, and demanded the Gate to be opened; which was done, and my *Patroon* with his *Forlorn*[355] were seized, and they had all their Heads cut off.

Thus my *Patroon* miscarried in a seemingly rash Attempt; though it was certainly the general Opinion, that if, instead of complaining to the *Aga*, he had gone directly to the Room where the *Dey* was (as he might) and had killed him, he would infallibly have obtain'd his End. But it was best for me as it was, for if my *Patroon* had succeeded, because he always found me honest, he designed to make me his *Secretary* or *Treasurer*, which might have proved a *Snare* to me, and made me have less Inclination to return home.

The next Day after this *Tragedy*, the Soldiers were sent out to his Country-House, and all he had was seiz'd on, and brought to *Algier*; and I was called before the *Dey* to witness what I could; but he only ask'd me, whether my *Patroon* had any Children? I told him yes, whereupon all his seiz'd Goods were restor'd again for the Good of his Family, who were now making most dismal Lamentations, those of the Male Sex not
[p. 218] shaving their Heads for near the Space of two Months; which with them is a token of *extraordinary* Mourning.

I was in hopes that my *Patroona*, or Mistress, would now have given me my *Freedom*; but she would not, and intended to sell me there in the Country; and if so, I had, in all probability, been a Slave as long as I lived; for I don't see how I could possibly have made my *Escape*. I therefore earnestly desired that I might be sold in *Algier*, which at length she granted; and according to Custom, I was carried three Days (by the *Crier*) about the Streets, and was bought the *third* Time by an old *Batchelor* [sic]. My Work with him was to look after his House, dress his Meat, wash the Clothes; and, in short, to do all those Things that are look'd on as a Servant-Maid's Work in *England*.

I must own, I wanted nothing with him; Meat, Drink, Clothes, and Money, I had enough. After I had lived with him about a Year he made his *Pilgrimage* to *Mecca*, and carried me with him; but before we came to

---

[355] *Forlorn*: troops who risked their lives.

*Alexandria* he was taken sick, and thinking verily he should die, having a woven Girdle about his middle, under his Sash (which they usually wear) in which was much Gold, and also my *Letter of Freedom*, (which he intended to give me when at *Mecca*) he took it off, and bid me put it on about [p. 219] me, and took my Girdle and put it on himself; and withal told me, that if he died on the way, I should be sure to perform the *Alhage*, or *el Hagge*, i.e. the *Pilgrimage* to *Mecca*, in order to obtain the *honourable* Title of *Hagge*; not doubting, but that there would be sufficient care *besides* taken to bear my Charges. He meant, that the *Algerine Hagges* who were going with us to *Mecca* would have paid my Expences thither, and back again to *Algier*, out of his Cash. (For you must observe, that when any *Algerine Turks* die *without Children*, whether at home or abroad, their Effects are carefully secured, and returned into the *Bank* for the *publick Use*.) This was argument enough how much he lov'd me. But it pleased God that he recovered; and one Thing I observ'd in him was, that though he was before a great Smoaker of *Tobacco*, after that Sickness he never smoak'd at all; which was look'd on as a Token of his Repentance: For though abundance of *Tobacco* be smoak'd among the *Turks*, yet it is accounted a Sin.

A little before I went to *Mecca*, being newly come to this my last *Patroon*, we lived in a Court, or *Funduck*,[356] as they term it, where lived none but *Batchelors*, and every one had his Slave to do the like Service with him, as I did with my *Patroon*: Among these Slaves there was one *James* [p. 220] *Grey*, an *English-Man* of *Weymouth*, with whom I became very intimate, insomuch that I communicated my greatest *Secrets* to him, and particularly, how I came to turn *Mahometan*, and how uneasy I was upon it; and withal, that I had Thoughts of going to the *Dey*, and telling him, that I was forced to *turn*; and, that I hop'd he would let me be at my Choice, for I would be no *Mahometan*; and desired this *Grey's* Opinion, whether I were best so to do. He answer'd, I should by no means do it, for it would make the worse for me, and endanger my Life. He told me also, that 'twould not be long before my *Patroon* would go to *Mecca*, and there, in all likelihood, give me my *Liberty*; and after that, I might find some way or other to *escape*. Well, I hearken'd to his Advice, but afterwards had cause to repent of making him so much my *Confident*; for when I return'd from *Mecca* to *Algier*, I found this *James Grey* himself very much inclin'd to turn *Mahometan*. I was with my Heart willing to discourage him from it, and to lay the horrid Evil of it

---

356 *Funduck*: modern Turkish, *fünduk*, from the Arabic, *funduq*.

before him, but I was afraid lest he should betray me. One Day particularly, he came and ask'd my Advice, whether he was best to *turn* or not. I thought him perfidious, and therefore told him, he should use his own mind, I would use no Arguments with him *pro* or *con*; for, *said I*, if I should perswade you to

[p. 221] *turn*, and your *Patroon* should not be so kind to you as you expect, *viz.* to give you your *Liberty*, then you'd lay the Blame on me. But in a little Time this *Grey* did turn *Turk*, and that without the least Temptation, his *Patroon* no way desiring him so to do. I guessed him to be about thirty Years of Age when he turn'd.

About a Year afterwards his *Patroon* gave him his *Liberty*, and he enter'd into Pay. He became very diligent in learning to read the *Alcoran*, and very forward to perform *Sallah*, so that he was look'd on as a *Zealot*. He would often correct me for my backwardness to go to *Mosque*, and for my Intimacy with the neighbouring Slaves; and I was afraid to oppose or contradict him in any thing.

But it pleased God, that in a little Time this *Grey* died, and that in a very dismal manner; for he pined away after a strange rate,[357] and before his Death became a very miserable Object indeed. And I cannot say that I was very sorry for his Death.

I suppose this *Grey* had some Expectations of great Matters, which made him *turn*; but he found himself disappointed. I am sure 'twas not from any such Inducements that I became a *Mahometan*, but through my *Patroon's* cruel and merciless Usage; and yet I fared rather worse with him than before; though sometimes they

[p. 222] shew themselves partial enough to those of the *Mahometan* Religion with themselves; an Instance of which I shall not easily forget, *viz.*

While I was in Algier there were two *Negro* Slaves belonging to a *Tagaren*,[358] or *Andalousian*, one of which was a *Mahometan*, and the other a *Portuguese*, and a *Christian*. It seems that these two Slaves, while they were at their Work in their *Patroon's* Garden, having some old Grudge, conspired to take away his Life, and rob him of his Money. Accordingly, on a certain Day, understanding that their *Patroon* was to go to *Algier* with a considerable

---

[357] *after a strange rate*: at an unusual speed.

[358] *Tagaren*: Moriscos from Aragon, Valencia and Catalonia, that is Spanish Arabs and Berbers who had converted to Christianity and who remained in Spain after the reconquest, but were expelled between 1609 and 1614; from the Arabic, *thaghr*.

Sum of Money with him, and most of it in Gold, they way-lay'd him, and murder'd him.

This barbarous Fact was not presently discovered; but at length these *Negroes*, forsooth, must go and enjoy themselves, and in order thereunto went to the *Money-Changers*, to change some Pieces of Gold; by which means they were suspected and apprehended, and upon a strict Examination into the Matter were found guilty, and both executed. He that was a *Mussulman* had a great deal more favour shewn him than the other, for he was fairly hanged; the manner of which, in *Algier*, is thus, *viz.* They have an Hole made in a Wall, just up to the top, through which one end of the Rope is put, and fastened on the other side of the Wall, and the

[p. 223] other about the Criminal's Neck, he sitting upon the Wall; and after he hath spoken what he will, he is push'd off the top of the Wall, and so is hang'd.

But the poor *Portuguese* was stripp'd naked to the middle, and had his Hands ty'd behind him, and a Hole made in the Heel of each Hand, into which were put Wax Candles burning; the same was done in both his Shoulders; and in this manner was he led along the Streets with the *Crier* of the Town before him, publishing his Crime. I thought they intended to have burn'd him alive, and therefore went without the Gate to see him executed; but they cut off his Head first, and then burn'd his Body to Ashes.

There was a *Spaniard* killed a *Moor*, and was therefore condemn'd to be burn'd; but to escape the Fire, if not save his Life, he turn'd *Mahometan*. But this would not save his Life; however, it gain'd him the Favour, instead of being burn'd, to be push'd off the Wall at the Gate *Bab el zoon*,[359] which is the *common Place of Execution*.

The *Turks* and *Renegadoes* of Algier have the Privilege above the *Cull Ougles*[360] (that is, the Sons of the *Yenesherres, Janizaries*, or Soldiers) of being *Aga*, or Colonel, which none of the said *Cull Ougles* can be; for when any of them becomes a *Kaya*, which is under the *Aga*, and, as we may call it, a

[p. 224] *Lieutenant*, he is forthwith made *Mazel-Aga*,[361] i.e. one who hath gone through all his Offices, and has his Pay brought to his Hand, not being in the least oblig'd to perform any Duty, and so can advance no further. And the Reason of this Difference made between the *Turks, Renegadoes*, and the *Cull Ougles*, is this, *viz.*

---

[359] *Bab el zoon*: now known as Bab Azoun, from the Arabic, Bāb al-Ḥuzn, or Gate of Grief.
[360] *Cull Ougles*: modern Turkish, *kuloğlu*.   [361] *Mazel-Aga*: modern Turkish, *mazul ağa*.

Some scores of Years past, the abovesaid *Cull Ougles* had conspired together to murder the *Algerine Turks* in general; which was a dreadful Design, but it took no Effect, and many of the *Cull Ougles* lost their Lives; great heaps of whole Heads are at this Day to be seen on the Walls of *Algier*, over the Gate *Bab el zoon*, or *Eastern Gate*. Notwithstanding the *Cull Ougles* will, upon the least Provocation, twit the *Renegadoes*, with Words like these, *Eir youle bullersen catchersen*,[362] i.e. *Thou wouldst run away if thou knewest how*. And at other Times they will jeer them with, *Domus eate, the hoe dishing dader*,[363] i.e. *There is yet* Swine's-flesh *in thy Teeth*, (meaning they still have a Tang of *Christianity*) and especially, when any *Renegado* runs away, the rest shall be thus jeered by them.

And now I am speaking of *Renegadoes* running away, I can't well omit this Story, which is not foreign to the Matter in hand.

*Ibrahim Hogea*, the *Dey* of *Algier*, had several *Christian* Slaves, and also several

[p. 225] Renegadoes, and he would distinguish the *Renegadoes*, and prefer them when any Thing offered; and particularly, I remember there was a *Spanish Renegado*, whom I knew, which the *Dey* had preferr'd to be a *Captain* of a *Privateer*. This *Renegado*, after he had made two or three Voyages, had got together on Board him a parcel of *Renegadoes*, who were intirely devoted to his will, and would comply with any thing he propos'd to them. It happen'd that coming near *Tittewan*,[364] a *Moors Town*, near the *Straights-Mouth*, they sent, as usual, their Boat a-shore to take in Wood for their Cruising Voyage. The *Turks* were all willing to go a-shore, and did so; whereupon the *Renegadoes* being all agreed, as soon as the Boat was gone a-shore, hoisted up their Sails, and stood over for the *Spanish* Shore, where, in a few Hours, they safely arrived, and there they sold Ships and Slaves, and re-embraced their former *Religion*. This did not a little nettle the *Turks*, and therefore they would cast it in the Teeth of almost every *Renegado* they met; but my *Patroon* would not open his Mouth against me, unless when in a Passion; but would speak, upon Occasion, in my behalf, saying, *Ben ebn, Ouglanem eumra catch mes*,[365] i.e. *My* Son *will never run away*. He seldom called me any thing but *Son*, and bought a *Dutch* Boy to do the Work of the

---

[362] *Eir youle bullersen catchersen*: modern Turkish, *Bir yolu bularken, kaçarken*.

[363] *Domus eate, the hoe dishing dader*: modern Turkish, *Domuz eti daha dişin'da dır*.

[364] *Tittewan*: Tétouan; Arabic, Tiṭwān.

[365] *Ben ebn, Ouglanem eumra catch mes*: modern Turkish, *Ben ibn oğlanım ömründe kaçmaz*.

House, who attended upon

[p. 226] me, and obeyed my Orders as much as his. Many Times, after Dinner, when the Boy ask'd him what he should dress for Supper, he would bid him ask me. He desired me to mind my Reading, in which I made considerable Proficiency; and would have me also learn to write; and understanding something of writing, I could strike the *Turkish* Character beyond their Expectation; and all in the School admir'd me for it. But I began to consider with my self, that I should soon be *Master* of writing, as well as a pretty good *Accountant*, and my *Patroon* being related to the then *Dey*, could easily get me promoted, as such usually are; and for this very Reason I laid aside my Writing, fearing what the Consequence might be. I often saw several Bags of his Money, a great part of which, he said, he would leave me. He would say to me, *Though I was never married my self, yet you shall in a little Time, and then your Children shall be mine.* An Offer was made me of *that* Nature, but, *I bless God,* it was no Temptation to me. Had I been prevailed with to alter my Condition there, I tremble to think what the Issue might have been. Many more Kindnesses, of this my last Patroon, I could relate; for which I cannot but say, I had a great Love for him, even as a Father. But still this was not *England,* and I wanted to be at *home.* The Manner of my *Escape,* I suppose, will

[p. 227] be entertaining to the *Reader,* and therefore I shall give an Account of it in the next *Chapter.*

## CHAP. X

*An Account of the* Author's *Escape at* Smyrna. *Of his being* robb'd: *And many other Occurrences on his Journey home to* Exeter.

BEing now at liberty from my *Patroon* (who gave me my *Letter of Freedom* at *Mecca*) and enter'd into Pay, but living still with him (because he had a great Kindness for me, not doubting that I was a true *Mussulman*) I was of the mind to use the *Seas*, and did two or three Voyages, hoping to be *retaken*, or some Way or other to make my *Escape*; but *Providence* did not order it that way. It happened, at length, that there came a Messenger from the *Grand Turk*[366] to *Algier*, to bespeak[367] some of the *Algerines* Ships to assist[368] him; which was granted. I was in good hopes it would fall to my lot to go in one of the Ships, intending, if I could, to make my Escape at *Smyrna*;[369] but it fell to my Turn to go to the *Camp* that Year. However, I made an Exchange with one, who agreed to go in my room[370] to

[p. 228] the *Camp*, and I was to go to his room in the *Ship*, which I was earnestly desirous of, because I was acquainted with one Mr. *Butler*, who was a Merchant in *Algier*, and liv'd with the *Consul*, who (as it will hereafter appear) was my great Friend in facilitating my *Escape*. In order to give you an Account of which, it will be convenient to inform you how I came acquainted with that honest and worthy Gentleman, Mr. *Butler*.

Some few Months before I came away from *Algier*, I was afflicted with a very sore Eye, insomuch that I was in danger of losing my Sight; and understanding that there was an *English* Doctor (a Slave, for whom, I knew, Mr. *Butler* had a Kindness, and paid his *Patroon* so much a Month) whom he had taken into his House, I went to Mr. *Butler's* to advise with the said Doctor for a Cure of my Eye. He undertook it, and so I usually went twice or thrice a Day to his House; where sometimes I would take a *Bible* in to my Hand and read, for I thought my self out of danger of any *Turks* seeing me. It happened, that once Mr. Butler came in while I was reading in the

---

[366] *Grand Turk*: the Ottoman Sultan.

[367] *bespeak*: ask for.

[368] *assist*: The Ottomans faced naval attacks by the Venetians and Maltese in the Aegean during the summer of 1694.

[369] *Smyrna*: now İzmir, a major port in Western Anatolia and Turkey's third largest city.

[370] *room*: place.

*Bible*; he seem'd to wonder at it, and ask'd me, why I did so? (for he knew that it was very dangerous for Persons under my Circumstances to do it) I answer'd him, I had no hatred to the *Bible*; which was the most I durst say for that Time; but by frequent

[p. 229] coming to his House, to be dressed by the Doctor, in a little Time I grew better acquainted with him, insomuch that he invited me, one Day, to dine with him. I did, and then he told me, that if I would dine with him the next Day, he would entertain me with a curious Dish (a great Rarity indeed in that Country) which was, as I remember, a piece of *Bacon*, with other Things. He did this, I suppose, to try me, whether I would eat *Swines Flesh*, or not (for the *Mahometans* strictly abstain from it; nay, they have such an Aversion to it, that if any chance to kill a wild *Pig* (for tame they have very few) they look on the Merit of it to be almost equivalent to the killing a *Christian* in fight) that he might be confirmed in his Opinion of me; for he truly suspected that I was no real *Turk*. Nevertheless, I refus'd to eat of it, fearing what the Event of Eating might prove.

But at length, once being made merry by him, he told me, *That he wondered why I would tarry here, in* this Country; and said, *He wish'd that I were in* England. I smiled, but withal, desired him to forbear such Discourse. But still, every now and then, he would drop a Word or two about the same Matter, and at length went so far, as to assure me, that if I were resolved to make my *Escape*, he would assist me all that lay in his power. To which I replied, *Sir*, shall

[p. 230] I be plain with you? *Prithee be*, said he, *and I will be your bosom Friend.* This engaged me to open my Sentiments to him, and I freely told him, that I once little thought of being in this Condition; and while I was in it, was never in the least inclin'd to *Mahometanism*, but that it was through the cruel Usage I suffered at their Hands, that I was forc'd to do what I did (a particular Account of which I gave him) which made him sympathize with me; and not only did he do that, but projected a Way for my *Escape* also; which was this, *viz.* that when our *English* Men of War came to *Algier* to renew the Peace[371] (which they usually did once in two or three Years) he did not doubt but to get me safe on Board one of them. But I did not approve of that way, acknowledging, notwithstanding, all Obligations to the *Gentleman* for his kind Proposal. I told him I had thought of another Way, which I imagined might be more feasible, *viz.* That I was going with the

---

[371] *Peace*: Britain had signed a peace treaty with Algiers in 1682.

Ships of *Algier* up to the *Levant*, and that then I design'd, if possible, to make my *Escape*; and that, if he could do me any good that way, I should be very thankful to him. He answered me, that he would acquaint Mr. *Baker*, the *Consul* in *Algier*, with it, and confer with him about it.

When the time came, that within a few days we were to sail, I went and ask'd of

[p. 231] him, whether he had been pleased to acquaint the *Consul* with my Business? He told me he had, and desired me to walk out to the *Consul's* Garden, about a Mile from *Algier*, where he kept his Summer Seat. There happen'd to be one *John Thomas* of *Bristol* there, whom I had a long Time before let into my *Secrets*. He was just then redeem'd, only waited for his Passage; and having some Business with the *Consul*, we went together. I had never the Honour before of being known to the *Consul*. When I came before him, I ask'd him, whether Mr. *Butler* had told him any thing concerning me? He said he had, and made me very welcome. After I had been there some time, he discoursed me at large about my intended *Escape*, and upon the whole, finding me to be real in the matter, (for if I had been otherwise, so as to discover any thing of what passed between us, it would infallibly have cost him his Life, and therefore he sifted me narrowly,[372]) he told me, that he would give me a Letter of *Recommendation* to Mr. *Raye*, who was then the *English Consul* in *Smyrna*: He drew up one accordingly, in which he requested him to assist me in my Design; for he read it to me before he sealed it; and charg'd me to keep it very safe; and if at any time before my getting to *Smyrna*, I should be sick, or any way in danger of Death, or Discovery, I

[p. 232] should convey it over-board, for his safety. Upon which I thankfully took my leave of him; this being the only time of my having any Discourse with him.

Having sailed about thirty Days on our Voyage towards *Smyrna*, where I design'd to make my *Escape*, and being a little off of one part of the *Morea*,[373] we espied seven or eight *Venetian* Gallies at Anchor under the Shore. The *Turks* had a great Tooth for these Gallies, but knew not how to come at them, not being able to adventure so far as they safely may. At length they consulted, being fifteen Ships in number, to hoist up *French* Colours,

---

[372] *sifted me narrowly*: questioned me closely.

[373] *Morea*: the Peloponnese, the peninsula which makes up the whole of the southern Greek mainland.

if peradventure any of them might be decoyed out; having done this, we hal'd up our Sails and brought to, pretending as if we were desirous of some News from the *Levant*. They at this thinking we were *French* Men of War, sent out two of their Gallies; upon which the *Turks* were ordered to lie close, and not to stir, for fear of shewing their *Turbants*; and those Officers, or others, who were oblig'd to be moving, took off their *Turbants* to avoid Discovery, and put on a Hat, or Cap, instead of them; but the Slaves were all ordered to be upon Deck to colour the matter,[374] and make us look more like *Christians*. At length one of the Gallies being within Musquet-shot, we fired upon him, and soon made him *strike*.[375] The other seeing that, [p. 233] who was also under Gun-shot, turns and rows with all his Might and Main to get ashore; the *Algerines* all the while making what sail they could after him, but 'twas in vain, for the *Venetian* got clear, the Wind being off the Shore just in our Mouth.[376] In that Galley which we took, there were near Four hundred *Christians*, and some few *Turks* who were Slaves.

The *Turks*, to shew what an Exploit they had done in taking this Vessel, took the trouble to row the Prize up to *Turkey*, where they were received with an universal *Housh-galding*,[377] *i.e.* Welcome.

When we came to *Scio*[378] we were met and join'd with ten Sail of the *Grand Turk's* Ships, carrying seventy or eighty Brass Cannon Guns each: And being now twenty five in number, we had the Courage to *Cruize* about the Islands of the *Archipelago*; which looks in them a pretty *bold* Attempt, tho' it be in their *own* Country. For 'twas but a Year or two before this, that thirteen Sail of the *Venetians*, with one Fire-ship, put thirty of their Ships to Flight, some being of *Tripoli*, some of *Tunis*, and some of the *Grand Turks* Ships, together with thirty *Turkish* Gallies; which run some into one Harbour, some into another, as they could.

Being now, as I said, five and twenty Sail, as we were *Cruising*, we espied a Ship [p. 234] at an Anchor, at the Leeward of an *Island*, who suspecting what we were, slipt his *Cable*[379] and made all the Sail he could to fly from us. But

---

[374] *to colour the matter*: to misrepresent our true purpose.

[375] *strike*: take down his flag and surrender.

[376] *in our Mouth*: in our faces, i.e. blowing towards us.

[377] *Housh-galding*: modern Turkish, *hoş geldiniz*.

[378] *Scio*: Chios, a large island, now part of Greece, lying about five miles off the coast of Western Turkey.

[379] *slipt his Cable*: raised his anchor.

being to the Windward of us, and coming clear of the Island, the Wind was very hard, insomuch that his *Main Mast* was carried by the Board,[380] whereupon he was forc'd to bear away before the Wind, and so must unavoidably fall in amongst us. Notwithstanding, he was resolved to *Fight* his way through, and held it stoutly a considerable time; but unhappily for him, his *Fore-top-mast*, by a Shot, was carried by the Board also; and so being disabled, he was forc'd to yield; but politickly[381] yielded by the side of the *Algerine Admiral,* chusing rather to be carried to *Algier* than to *Constantinople*; for he well knew that at the *latter* Place no Money would prevail for his *Ransom*, as it would at the *former*. But after a long Contest between the two *Admirals*, who should have the *Captain* of this *Prize*, the *Admiral* of the *Grand Turks* had him, (rendring [*sic*] the *Algerine Admiral* many of the taken *Slaves* in lieu of him,) and carried him to *Constantinople*, whence he was never to be redeemed. This *Captain* was a *Leghornese*, and stil'd *Captain Paul*, whose Name *rung* among them; for he had been in his time a great Plague to them, both by *Sea*, and *Land*. His Ship carried about forty Guns, and an hundred Men. But tho' he had been such a *Scourge*

[p. 235] to them, for many Years, yet the *Slaves* which were at any time taken by him were kindly treated; insomuch, that when he came to an Anchor at some Places; the Inhabitants would bring him *Fruits*, and *Wine*, &c. on Board, as *Presents*: especially in the *Island* called *Eustanchue*,[382] or *Long-Island*, near *Scio*.

In this *Island*, and in the principal Town thereof (by the way) is a *Tree*[383] of a prodigious bigness, so large, that I question whether there be another like it for bigness in the *whole World*. Under which are several *Coffee-Houses*, *Barbers-Shops*, and other *Shops*; and several *Fountains* of *Water*, wherewith to take *Abdes*; and if I mistake not, there are five and thirty, or seven and thirty *Pillars*, some of which are *Marble*, and some of *Timber*, to support the Branches thereof. This *Tree* is famous, to a *Proverb*, all over Turkey.

Some time after we arrived at *Scio*, an *Island* (since taken by the *Venetians*,)[384] inhabited by the *Greeks*, but governed by the *Turks*, about

---

[380] *by the Board*: overboard.  [381] *politickly*: wisely.

[382] *Eustanchue*: the island of Kos, now belonging to Greece, which lies just off the coast of Turkey opposite Bodrum and is known in Turkish as İstanköy.

[383] *Tree*: Pitts must be referring to the plane tree of Hippocrates in whose shade the philosopher is said to have taught and which still stands today in the centre of the town of Kos.

[384] *Venetians*: the Venetians captured Chios in September 1694.

fifteen Leagues on this side *Smyrna*; the *Turks* had Liberty, for one Month's time, to go home to visit the respective Places of their Nativity.

I went to *Smyrna* and hired a Chamber there. And after I knew where the *Consul's* House was, went thither, and enquir'd of the *Janizaries*, i.e. *Turkish Soldiers*, which

[p. 236] kept Guard at his Door, whether the *Consul* was at home: They directed me to one of his three Interpreters, who brought me to him. The *Consul* not knowing who I was, complimented me much, because I was handsomely apparel'd; and I returned the Compliment to him after the *Turkish* manner, and then deliver'd him my Letter of *Recommendation*. Which was as follows★. [[★*A copy of this Letter* Consul Baker *gave me a few Years since, when I waited upon him at his House near St.* James's *Park,* Westminster. *On the back of it he had writ thus,* —— *Copy of my Letter to* Consul Raye *at* Smyrna, *to favour the* Escape *of* Joseph Pitts, *an* English Renegado, *from a Squadron of* Algier Men of War. —— *Had my Kindness to him been discover'd to the Government of* Algier, *my Legs and Arms had first been broken, and my Carcase burnt.* —— *A Danger hitherto not courted by any.*]]

*Algier, June* 14, 1694.

SIR,

*It must raise a melancholy Consideration in every merciful Heart, to observe a Well-disposed Body and Mind in Danger of inevitable Ruin, by a fatal Destiny of consuming its most improveable Years of Strength and Vigour in a detested Course.*

*It would therefore, by a generous Attempt to reinstate such an Object into the Discharge of its most immediate natural Duty, to be a distinguishing Mark of a true Votary to the Welfare*

[p. 237] *of his Country; whereto I am fully assured you will exert your Steadiness, and Conduct.*

I am, Sir,

Your most faithful,

Humble Servant,

THOMAS BAKER.

To *William Raye*, Esq;

*Consul* of the *English* Nation at *Smyrna*.

The *Consul* having perused the Letter, bid the *Interpreter* to withdraw, because he should not understand any thing of the matter. After he was gone, the *Consul* ask'd me whether I was the Man mention'd in the Letter.

I told him I was. He said the Design was very dangerous, and that if it should be known to the *Turks* that he was in any way concern'd in it, it was as much as his *Life*, and his *All* was worth. But after he had discours'd me further, and found that I was *fully resolv'd* in the matter, he told me that, "Truly were it not upon Mr. *Baker's* Request he would not meddle in such a dangerous Attempt; but for the Friendship and *Respect* he bore to him, he would do me all the Kindness he could;" *which put Life into me*.

We had no *English* nor *Dutch* Ships at *Smyrna* then, but daily expected some; he told me, I must wait till they came, and withal caution'd me not to frequent his House, unless upon some *more than ordinary*
[p. 238] *Business*. A day or two after this, I was sitting in a *Barber's* Shop, who was an *Armenian*, where both *Christians* and *Turks* did shave; and there was then an *English* Man shaving, whose Name was *George Grunsell*, of *Deptford*. He knew me not otherwise than a *Turk*, but when I heard him speak *English*, I ask'd him in *English*, *Whether he knew of any of the* West-parts *of* England *to be in* Smyrna? He told me of one, who he thought was an *Exeter-man*, which when I heard, I was glad at Heart. I desired him to shew me his House, which he very kindly did; but when I came to speak with Mr. *Eliot*, for so was his Name, I found him to be one of *Cornwal*, who had serv'd some part of his Apprenticeship in *Exon*, with Mr. *Henry Cudmore* a Merchant; he was very glad to see me for Country's sake: After some Discourse, I communicated to him my *Design*, and how I had been with the *Consul*. He was very glad to hear of it, and promised to assist me, and told me, that I need not run the hazard of going to the *Consul's* House, but if I had any thing of *Moment* to impart to him, he would do it for me. I thought it good to follow his *friendly* Advice.

In a Month's time it was cry'd about the City of *Smyrna*, that all *Algerines* should repair to their Ships, which lay then at *Rhodes* (another Island inhabited by *Greeks*, as *Scio*, and govern'd by the *Turks*.)
[p. 239] You must observe, that no *Algerine* is forced to return to *Algier* again, but they may discharge themselves when they please.

All this while no *English* or *Dutch* Ships came to *Smyrna*; the *Consul* and Mr. *Eliot* therefore consulted which was my best way to take; to stay at *Smyrna* after all the *Algerines* were gone, would look suspiciously; and therefore they advised me not to tarry there, but either to go to *Scio* with the *Algerines*, which is part of our way back to *Rhodes*, or else to go up to *Constantinople*; and when there, to write to the said Mr. *Eliot*, and acquaint him where I was; and stay there till I had Directions from them to return to *Smyrna,* or what else to do.

I pursued their Advice, and went with some of the *Algerines* to *Scio,* and there made a stop till all the *Algerines* were gone from thence, and then writ Mr. *Eliot* where I was. A short time after, he writ me, that he was very glad that I was where I was, but withal, gave a damp to my Spirits, with the bad News, that our *Smyrna* Fleet were said to be intercepted by the *French,* with the cold reserve of Comfort, that it *wanted Confirmation,* and that they *hop'd* it was not true.

Now the *Devil* was very busy with me, tempting me to lay aside all thoughts of *escaping,* but to return to *Algier,* and continue a *Mussulman.* What with the Temptation, and what with the Disappointment, I was [p. 240] very melancholy. But here the *Goodness* of God was manifested to me in such a measure, that I at last surmounted all the Temptations and Fears that so furiously beset me, which were indeed very great: For it was suggested to me, first, That it was a very difficult, if not *desperate* Attempt, to endeavour to make my *Escape;* and that if I were discovered in it, I should be put to death after the most cruel, and exemplary manner: And also, in the next place, the Loss that I should sustain thereby, in several respects, *viz.* The Loss of the profitable Returns which I might make of what Money I had, to *Algier,* and of receiving eight Months Pay due to me there, and the frustrating my Hopes and Expectations which I had from my *Patroon,* who made me large Promises of leaving me considerable Substance at his Death; and I believe he meant as he promised; for I must acknowledge he was like a *Father* to me.

After I had my Liberty to go from him, or live with him, I chose the latter; and he was so willing of it, that he gave me my Meat, Coffee, Washing, Lodging, and Clothes, freely; and in short, lov'd me as if I had been his own Child; which made me sincerely to love him, I do acknowledge. This was also a great Temptation to me to return to *Algier.*
[p. 241]

In the midst of all, I would pray to *God* for his Assistance, and found it. For *I bless God,* that after all my Acquaintance were gone from *Scio,* to *Rhodes,* I grew daily better and better satisfied, though my Fears were still very great, you must imagine; and I was indeed afraid every-body I met did suspect my *Design.* And I can truly say, that I would not go through such a *Labyrinth* of Sorrows and Troubles again, might I gain a *Kingdom.* Nay at this very Hour, when I reflect upon my Danger, my Concern revives, and my very Flesh trembles; for if my *Design* had by any Means been discover'd,

I should undoubtedly have been put to Death, perhaps there at *Scio*, or else secured in the *Algerine* Ships, and my *dreadful* Punishment would have been reserved till I was brought back to Algier, there to be made a *publick Example* for all *Renegadoes* to take Warning by for the future. For 'tis certain Death for all in the like Circumstances with me, who endeavour to make their *Escape*, if it be known.

The Manner of executing *Renegadoes* when they are found attempting to make, or are retaken after they have made their *Escape*, is *as follows*. As soon as such an one is brought before the *Dey*, Sentence is at once past upon him. Upon which the *Mizwear*,[385] *i.e.* Executioner ties his Feet with one end of a Rope, and fastens the other

[p. 242] at the Tail of a Mule which is got ready for the purpose, at about ten, or twelve Foot Distance, and then drags the *Apostate* (as they stile him) about the Streets on the Stones some Hours. The *Mahometans* are so far from shewing the *poor Wretch* the least Pity, that they do nothing but *revile* him. The *Executioner* going before the Mule loudly proclaims his Crime. After they have exposed him in this *terrible* Manner till he is almost dead, they draw him without the Gate *Bab el Wait*, to a Place where the *Jews* bury their Dead, where they get a Fire, and burn him to Ashes. This I have seen done with my own Eyes; and had I been discover'd, or taken, must have been serv'd in the same Manner my self. But the good *Providence* of God order'd it better for me.

While I was at *Scio*, I wrote, as I said, a Letter to our *English Consul* Mr. *Raye*, and to Mr. *Eliot*, acquainting them with what strong Temptations I was assaulted. They answered me with very kind, and comfortable Lines, which gave great Life to my drooping Spirits.

The first Letter that Mr. *Eliot* sent me while I was at *Scio*, he directed to a *Greek* there, who did Business for the *Consul* of *Smyrna*, to be delivered to me, naming me by my *Turkish* Name. I was altogether unknown to the *Greek*, so that he was forced to enquire among the *Algerines* for one of

[p. 243] that Name; and indeed there were one or two more of the same Name with my self, but they were gone from *Scio* to *Rhodes*. When the Letter came into my Hands, and I saw the Superscription, I *trembled exceedingly*, imagining there had been Danger of its falling into either of the

---

[385] *Mizwear.* Arabic, *mizwār*, a local North African term meaning principally the head of the candar, or guards, and by extension, an executioner; from the Berber word for first, *iezzaren* (transcribed by Dozy (1881), Vol. 1, 613 as *imzawār*).

other *Algerines* Hands; for I did not then know that Mr. *Eliot* had been so good and careful as to send the *Greek* a particular Description of me, as my Age, Stature, Complexion, that I was an *English*-man, a Native of *Exeter*, &c. on purpose to prevent any Mistake in the Delivery of the Letter. This he hath since informed me of, and my Ignorance of it was the Cause of that Blunder in *Page* 172 and 173 of the *first Edition*[386] of my Book, which seemed to cast a Reflection (tho' I did not design it as such) upon that worthy Gentleman, to whom I am more obliged than to all the other Friends I have in the World. For this I have beg'd his Pardon, and take this Opportunity of doing it in the most publick Manner.

When I first came to *Scio* from *Smyrna*, according to the Advice of these my true Friends, the *Consul* and Mr. *Eliot*, I happened to take up my *Lodging* at a *Hawn*, or *Inn*, adjoining to the *Harbour*, where were two *Algerines*, who were *Spanish Renegadoes*; I had no acquaintance with them at all, for they belonged not to the same Ship that I

[p. 244] did, nor do I remember that I had ever seen them before; but being all *Algerines*, we soon became familiarly acquainted; insomuch that they would fain have me lodge in the *same* Room with them; accordingly I did, but the next Day I better consider'd on't, and thought it not convenient to be so near the *Harbour*, because the *Algerines* would be often asking of me when I would return to *Algier*; and laying matters together,[387] I thought likewise, that I were better break off Society with these two Fellows; which I did, and removed to one end of the *Town*, to a *Greek's* House, where I hired a Room. The two said *Renegadoes* found me out, and were still very desirous to be with me; to which I at length consented. And when I better knew them, their Company pleas'd me, because I could not observe any thing of the *Mahometan* Religion in them; neither would they at any time talk of going to *Rhodes*, where our Ships lay; which made me at last suspect that they were of my mind, designing to make their *Escape*. And what somewhat confirm'd me in this suspicion, was this, The younger of them would sometimes speak slightly of *Mahomet*, calling him *Sabbatero*,[388] i.e.

---

[386] *first Edition*: in the first edition, on p. 173, Pitts wrote, "Upon this, I wrote to Mr. *Elliot* [*sic*] earnestly desiring him to direct to me after an other manner", since he was unaware that Mr Eliot had ensured that the Greek messenger had a description of him.

[387] *laying matters together*: drawing conclusions.

[388] *Sabbatero*: modern Spanish, *zapatero*. There does not seem to be a mediaeval tradition of insulting Muḥammad by calling him a shoemaker or cobbler, and the term is not mentioned in Daniel (1993).

*Shoe-maker*, and the other would seem *faintly* to *reprove* him for it; and I also would shew my Dislike of it, tho' I was truly pleas'd to hear it. But it seems this was all to *try* me. And indeed

[p. 245] I would sometimes *try* them too, and therefore would take an *Arabick Alcoran* in my Hand to read, of which they were both wholly ignorant, and they would laugh at me, and at last came to pop the *Alcoran* out of my Hand, and blow out the *Candle*, telling me, I should read no more. At length we came to know one anothers Mind, and I found that they applied themselves to some *French Priests* in *Smyrna*, to make their *Escape*, as I did to the *Consul* and Mr. *Eliot*.

About this time I receiv'd another Letter from Mr. *Eliot*, in which he inform'd me, that the reported bad News concerning our Ships being intercepted by the *French* was true, but that he and the *Consul* had consulted that Day what was best to be done for my Safety; and upon due Consideration, were of opinion that it would be in vain for me to wait for any *English* Ships, for it might be a long time before any came, and it would be Charge and Loss of Time for me to stay for them. And therefore they advised me to go off in a *French* Ship, tho' somewhat more expensive, and in order thereunto, to hasten back again to *Smyrna* in the first Boat that came.

Accordingly I came to *Smyrna* again, and went immediately to Mr. *Grunsell*'s House, who received me gladly; for he, with some other of my Friends, was afraid that I had gone back to *Algier*.

[p. 246]

I lodg'd at Mr. *Grunsell*'s House, and kept my self very *private* for the space of twenty Days, till the *French* Ship was ready to sail; Where I was visited daily by Mr. *Eliot*, who (I thank him) did always administer *Comfort* to me, under my Fears, which were not small; particularly because I had heard how an *English* Man was serv'd who turn'd *Turk* in *Algier*, and made his *Escape*, but afterward, using the Seas, made a Voyage to *Smyrna*: The *Algerines* happened to be there at that time, and as he was in a *Barber's Shop*, some of them passing by, seem'd to remember him; he suspecting it, went away immediately: The *Turks* followed him, and he perceiving it, made the more haste, at which the *Turks* pursued him the more closely, and he, to avoid them, ran into an *English-Factor's* House: But the *Turks* were so close upon him, that he had not Power to make fast the Door after him; so that they *cut him in pieces*. This was but a few Years before I came away; which (together with my being acquainted too well with their Cruelty, which they glory in, when it is, as they think it, for the cause of *Religion*) fill'd me with great *Fears*, and dreadful *Apprehensions*.

Now the *French* Ship, in which I was to make my *Escape*, was intended to sail the next Day; and therefore in the *Evening* I went on Board, apparel'd as an *English*-Man, with my Beard shaven, a *Campaign-Periwig*,[389] [p. 247] and a *Cane* in my Hand, accompanied with three or four of my Friends. The Boat which carried us aboard, was brought just to the House where I lodged; and as we were going into it there were some *Turks* of *Smyrna* walking by, but they smelt nothing of the matter. My good Friend Mr. *Eliot* had agreed with the *Captain* of the Ship to pay *four Pounds* for my Passage to *Leghorn*; but neither he nor any of the *French*-Men knew who I was. Mr. *Eliot* only told him that my Parents were desirous of my Return home to *England*. My Friends, after they had brought me safe a-board, took their leave of me, and told me that if the Ship did not sail the *next Morning*, they would visit me again, which accordingly they did, (the Ship not sailing,) and brought *Wine* and *Victuals* a-board; upon which they were very *merry*, but, for my part, I was exceedingly *uneasy* till the Ship had made Sail. I pretended my self ignorant of all *Foreign* Languages, because I would not be known to the *French*, who (if we had met with any *Algerines*) I was afraid would be so far from shewing me any Favour so as to *conceal* me, that they would readily *discover* who I was, had they been let into the *Secret*, and give me up into their Hands.

In our Voyage we were chased by a *Privateer*, which made me very melancholy, fearing it might be one of the *Algerines* who [p. 248] sailed from *Rhodes* but a few Days before us. I leave the *Reader* to judge of the Distress I was then in; but it was not able to come up with us. We thought, afterwards, that it was a *Spanish* Privateer, with whom the *French* had then War.

We had a *Month's* Passage from *Smyrna* to *Leghorn*, and I was never at rest in my Mind till we arrived; where, as soon as ever I came a-shore, I *prostrated* my self, and *kissed the Earth*, blessing *Almighty God* for his undeserved Mercy and Goodness to me, that I once more set footing on the *European, Christian* part of the World. The Custom of *Leghorn* (as well as of some other Parts) is, when any Ships come from *Turkey* or *Barbary*, not to suffer the Men (*straightway*) to come a-shore, fearing lest their Country should be infected with the *Plague*, because the *Turks* and *Moors* Country is

---

[389] *Campaign-Periwig*: a plain and close-fitting wig for travelling.

seldom *intirely* [*sic*] free from it: Therefore, I say, they will not permit any to come a-shore directly, but they and their Cargo are put on an *Island*, and there they are to perform their *Quarantaine*, i.e. to stay forty Days; after which, every Man of them is search'd by the *Physician*, and if they find no *Infection* upon any of them, they are admitted a-shore; but if any one of them should chance to die within forty Days, then they must begin the *Quarantaine* again. When we came out of *Smyrna* it was pretty free from [p. 249] the *Plague*; which they having intelligence of, ordered us to remain on the said *Island* only five and twenty days; during which Time, every Day, Necessaries are brought to be sold, but the Sellers keep themselves at a distance from us, laying down their *Provisions*, and telling aloud the Price; then we that buy put the Price of them into a *Vessel of Water*, placed there on purpose, and afterwards they come and take out the Money.

There were several *Jews* and *Greeks* came Passengers with me from *Smyrna*; one of the former a Merchant, who was to be married at *Leghorn*. When we got thither, the *Jews* would have me perform *Quarantaine* with them; and the *Greeks* (two of whom were *Jesuits*) desired I would let *them* have my Company. I thought there could be no great Difference which ever of them I took up with, as I expected to pay my *Scot*[390] with either. However, I went with the *Jews*, and scarce spent any thing; for the Man's new Relations which were to be, daily brought us *fresh* Provisions, *Wine* and *Fruit*.

It happened a few Days after I had been upon the *Lazaret*,[391] i.e. the said *Island*, that there came a *French* Vessel from *Algier*, in which there were some redeem'd Slaves, amongst whom were some *Dutchmen*, and one of them was a nigh Neighbour of mine in [p. 250] *Algier*, who was mightily surpriz'd but very glad to see me; and said, that he, with the rest of his Country-men, would be glad of my Company homeward, for that they had rather travel home by Land than by Sea. I was no less glad of their Company than they of mine; and therefore, after being permitted to go a-shore, and tarrying in *Leghorn* one Night, the next Day we set out on our Journey. It was about *Christmas* time, when there was very frosty Weather, and great Snows fell, so that we travelled twenty Days in the Snow. The first Day we set out from *Leghorn* we came

---

[390] *pay my Scot*: pay my share.
[391] *Lazaret*: a lazaretto, a place set apart from other habitations to accommodate travellers performing their quarantine, or forty-day isolation, to prevent the spread of disease.

to *Pisa*; from thence to *Florence*; from thence to *Bolognia*;[392] and so onward. We had a note of all Cities and Towns we were to pass through, as far as to *Ausburgh*.[393] After I had travelled with my Company about two Hundred Miles in *Italy*, and was just entering into *Germany*, my left Leg fail'd me, so that I was not able to hold on with them;[394] whereupon they went away and left me, fearing their Money would fall short if they should stay for me.

Being thus left behind I was much troubled; but it pleased God to mitigate my Pains, and the next Day I followed them, but never could overtake them, they being always a Day's Journey before me.

When I had gone these two Hundred Miles with them, I was forced to travel five
[p. 251] Hundred more (as they told me it was) on foot in *Germany*, till I came to *Francfort*.[395] I fell into some Troubles in travelling through *Germany*; and among them this was one, *viz.* One Day I had travelled through a great Wood, and as I came out of it, I met with four or five *German* Soldiers, who bid me stand; I did; they examined me, and I gave them an Account of my self; they made me go back with them, saying, I was a *French-Man*, come as a *Spy* into their Country. I earnestly beg'd of them to let me go; they would not, but carried me back into the Wood again, and brought me to a *by-place*,[396] which made me very much afraid they would take away my Life; and I have been since told by one of that Country, that I had a very narrow Escape, because the *Germans* seldom *rob* without committing *Murder*. There they *robb'd* me of my Money, as much as they could find, then beat me, and bid me be gone: But as *Divine Providence* order'd it, they did not strip me; for if they had, they would have found more Money about me.

When I came to *Ausburgh*, which was the last Place on our Note of Directions (of which I took a Copy, when my Company left me) I thought the River *Rhine* had come up so far, but was mistaken; for I was informed, that I must travel still further on foot, *viz.* to *Francfort*, upon the
[p. 252] *Maine*, which was about an hundred and fifty Miles more. It could not be help'd, and therefore put to it I must. I got Directions for as far as that Place, and found it many a weary Step; but the Thoughts of getting *home* at last put new Life and Strength into me. When I got to *Francfort* it was about Sun set, and the Gates of the City were just ready to be shut; for

---

[392] *Bolognia*: Bologna.  [393] *Ausburgh*: Augsburg in southern Germany.
[394] *hold on with them*: keep up with them.
[395] *Francfort*: Frankfurt-am-Main.  [396] *by-place*: out-of-the-way spot.

they had then War with *France*. When I offered to go in, the *Centinels* [*sic*] who were upon Duty at the Gate demanded of me, Who I was? I told them, an *English-Man*. They asked me, Whence I came? I replied, from *Leghorn*; but they would not believe me. They bid me produce my *Passport*, but I had none, because the above-mentioned Company took it with them, when I was left behind; and the want of it was the Occasion of many Troubles to me in my Travels. Upon this they would not allow me Entrance, but told me to go such a particular Way, and about a Mile and half off I should find a *Village*, where I might lodge; for there was not so much as one House without the Walls. I desired them to have some Compassion upon me; and told them, that I knew not the Way; that it was almost dark; and withal, that I was weary and faint, having travelled a great Way that Day. But all the Arguments I could make use of were to no purpose, and so the Gate was shut.

[p. 253] (I suppose they had *express* Orders not to admit any *Strangers*, for fear they should be *Spies*.) Upon meeting with such an unexpected Repulse, I sat down on the Ground and wept, bewailing the melancholy Circumstances I was then in; for I had not a bit of Bread to eat, nor any Fire to warm my self, in the extreamly cold Season which then was, though I had a little Money, which soon supplied all my Wants; for looking about me, I, at last, spied an *Hut*, or little House of Boards, not far from the Gate, where some Soldiers kept Guard; I made towards it, and the *Corporal* seeing the Condition I was in, took pity on me, and called me in, where they had a good Fire. After I had warmed my self, he gave me some of his *Victuals*, for which seasonable Kindness I gave him Money to fetch us some good *Liquor*. One of the Soldiers very gladly went to the *Village* whither I had been directed for a Lodging, and brought some *Wine* in a Bucket; so that with their *Victuals*, and the *Wine*, I very well refreshed my self, and lying down on the Boards slept comfortably. I told the *Corporal* (who could speak *Italian*, which I also understood) that if he would get me into the *City* the next Day, I would requite him for it. He promis'd me he would, and did it accordingly. I thought there had been some *English* Merchants there, and therefore desired

[p. 254] him to conduct me to one of them; but he could find none. At length he brought me to a *French* Gentleman's House, who had a Son which lived in *England* some Time, and was lately returned home; by whom I was made very welcome: His Name was Mr. *Vander Laher*. I very well remember, when I came first before him, he asked me, Whether I was a *Roman Catholick* or *Protestant*? I replied, a *Protestant*. No matter for that, *said he*, we are bound to do good to *Strangers*. I lived, *added he*, three Years in *London*, and found *English* People very civil to me. He then enquired, what my particular Business was with him? I told him, to procure a *Pass* to go safe down the *River* (for they are so strict there, in Time of War, as to examine even their own Country-men) and, at the same Time, desired him to change a *Pistole*[397] for me, and give me such Money as would pass currant [*sic*] at the Places I was to call at on my Way; for I had sometimes changed a Piece of Gold, and before all the Exchange of it was expended in my Travels, I could not put off some of the Money without Loss. He changed my *Pistole* for me, and told me what Money would pass in *such* and *such* a Place; and what I should reserve till last to spend in *Holland*. He was, moreover, so exceedingly civil, as to go with me to the *publick Office*, where he stated my Case, and [p. 255] easily got a *Pass* for me, without any Charge. After which, he brought me to his House again, and sent one of his Servants with me to an *Inn* the next Door, where I should lodge that Night, and bid me come to him again the next Morning; when he sent his Servant to call me, and also to pay off my *Host*; but I had done that before, at which he shewed his dislike. He then conducted me to the *River-side*, where was a Boat, almost full of Passengers, ready to set out for *Mentz*.[398] This obliging Gentleman told the Master of the Boat, that he would satisfy him for my Passage; and desired an Acquaintance of his in the Boat to take care of me, and when we got to *Mentz* to direct me to a certain Merchant, for whom he gave me a Letter, and therewith a Piece of Money to *drink his Health*.

When we came to *Mentz*, every Man was to produce his *Passport*; and as they were looking over, the Person in the Boat who was desired to take care of me, sent a Boy to call the Merchant, to whom I was to deliver the Letter; who immediately came, and having perused it, invited me to his House.

This Gentleman happen'd to be a Slave in *Algier*, at the same Time I was; which made me the more welcome to him. He enquired of me about his *Patroon*, whom I knew very well; and many other Things [p. 256] we talked of, relating to *Algier*. I received much Kindness from this Gentleman; for he paid off my Quarters[399] for that Night, gave me Victuals

---

[397] *Pistole*: a valuable Spanish coin.
[398] *Mentz*: Mainz, about 25 miles west of Frankfurt.
[399] *paid off my Quarters*: paid for my accommodation.

and Money for my Passage from *Mentz* to *Cologn*; and, moreover, sent by me a Letter of *Recommendation* to a Correspondent of his there.

At Cologn I received the like Kindness, having my Passage paid for to *Rotterdam*; and, if I would, might have had a *Recommendatory* Letter to some Gentleman there too; but refus'd it (with hearty Thanks for the Offer) being unwilling to be too troublesome to my Friends.

I found great Kindness at *Rotterdam*, where, when it was known that there was one come from *Algier*, several flock'd about me; some enquiring for their Husbands, and others for their Children, to whom I gave the best Account I could. And at *Helvoetsluys*,[400] whither our *English* Paquet-Boats sail from *Harwich*, I had the same Civility shown me. But when I came into England, my own *Native* Country, I met with but *coarse* Treatment; for the very *first* Night I lay a-shore I was *Imprest*[401] into the *King's* Service (we having at that Time War with *France*.) And though I made known my Condition, acquainting them how many Years I had been in Slavery; and used many Arguments for my Liberty, with Tears, yet nothing would prevail, but away I must go, and I

[p. 257] was accordingly carried to *Colchester* Prison, where I lay some Days. While I was there, I writ two Letters, one to Sir *William Falkener*,[402] who was one of the *Smyrna* (or *Turkey*) Company in *London*, on whom I had a Bill[403] for a little Money; the other was to my *Father* in *Exeter*, to acquaint him with my *Escape* from *Turkey*: And that I had been in *England*, if I should die on the Voyage, or be lost at Sea, must have been no small Satisfaction to my *Relations*, had it so happen'd. In a few Days I was put Aboard a *Smack*, which was appointed to carry the *Imprest* Men to the *Dread-nought Man of War*. I had not been long here, before my Name was called, there being a Letter for me. I could not conceive from whence it should come, for I knew it was too soon to have an *Answer* from *Exeter*; and I was very far from expecting any from *London*; nay, I blamed my self in my own Thoughts, for writing as I did to a *Gentleman* I was a perfect Stranger to, imagining he would take no manner of Notice of me. But upon opening the Letter I found it to be from Sir *William Falkener*, who, upon the Reception of mine,

---

[400] *Helvoetsluys*: Hellevoetsluis, at that time the naval port for Rotterdam.

[401] *Imprest*: press-ganged, forced to serve in the Royal Navy.

[402] *Sir William Falkener*: William Fawkener (1642–1716) was a prosperous merchant who became one of the leading members of the Levant Company.

[403] *Bill*: credit note.

immediately went to the *Admiralty Office*, got a *Protection* for me, and sent it with all speed to me. He writ me *as follows*, "*Friend*, I am sorry, that after so long *Captivity*, and *tedious* Journey, you should meet with such an *ill Welcome* to your own

[p. 258] Country; but be of good *Cheer*, for as soon as I had yours, I went to the *Admiralty-Office*, &c." This made me rejoice exceedingly, and I could not forbear leaping upon the Deck. The *Ship's-Crew* were highly pleased with the News. I went to the *Lieutenant*, and asked him, Whether he had not a *Protection* for me? He told me, Yes; there it was; and I might go a-shore when-ever I pleased. This was not only my present Discharge, but prevented all further Trouble of that kind on the Road homeward, which otherwise I must necessarily have met with.

When I came from *Colchester* to *London*, I made it my Business, as in Duty bound, to go and pay my Thanks to that *honourable* Gentleman, for the singular Kindness he had done me. After which I made what haste I could home to dear *Exeter*, where I at last safely came, to the great Joy of my *Relations* and *Friends*, who had buried me in their Thoughts long before.

When I came to the *City*, I thought it would not be prudent to make my self known to my *Father* at *once*, lest it should quite overcome him; and therefore went to a *publick House* not far from where he lived, and inquired for some who were my *Playmates* before I went to Sea. They told me, there was one *Benjamin Chapel* lived near there, with whom I had been very intimate

[p. 259] while a Lad. I sent for him, and acquainted him who I was, desiring he would go to my *Father*, and bring it out to him *by degrees*. This he readily undertook, well knowing he should be a *most welcome* Messenger, and in a little Time brought my *Father* to me. The House was soon filled with the Neighbourhood, who came to see me. What Joy there was at such a Meeting, I leave the *Reader* to conceive of, for 'tis not easily express'd. The first Words my *Father* said to me, were, *Art thou my Son* Joseph? with Tears. *Yes*, Father, *I am*, said I. He immediately led me home to his House, many People following us; but he shut the Door against them, and would admit no one, till falling on his Knees, he had returned *hearty Thanks* to God for my *signal* Deliverance. My *Mother* died about a Year before my Return.

I was in *Algier* about fifteen Years. After we sailed from *Topsham* it was about half a Year before we were taken. And after I left *Algier* it was well nigh a Twelvemonth e'er I could reach *home*.

Thus I have given the World a *brief*, but *true* Account of my *Travels*, the

Troubles I met with, and the kind Providences of a good God towards me; which, if it be in any respect of the least Service to any individual Person, I shall reckon it a great Happiness.

[p. 260]

And, for my own part, I hope I shall never forget the *wonderful* Goodness of the Lord towards me, whose blessed Name I desire to glorify *in the Sight of all Men*.

To *Him*, therefore, *Father*, *Son*, and *Holy Spirit*, *Three Persons*, and *One God*, be all *Honour*, *Glory*, and *Praise*, World without end. *Amen*.

### FINIS

# NOTES TO PART I

1. Pitts, Joseph (1731), *A Faithful Account of the Religion and Manners of the Mahometans* (London: J. Osborn, T. Longman, R. Hett). All passages from Pitts's book, whether from the 1704 or the 1731 edition, are quoted using the original spelling, as well as Pitts's use of capital letters and italics. All quotations from Pitts's contemporaries and other primary sources are given in modernized spelling unless it was felt valuable to retain the original orthography.

2. The first published captivity narrative is by John Fox (1589): "The worthie enterprise of John Foxe, in delivering 266 Christians out of the captivitie of the Turkes at Alexandria", in Hakluyt, Richard, *The Principall Navigations, Voiages, and Discoveries of the English Nation Made by Sea or Over-land to the Most Remote and Farthest Distant Quarters of the Earth at any Time within the Compass of these 1600 Yeeres* (London: G. Bishop and R. Newberie), 131–56. Fox's narrative is reprinted with modernized spelling in Vitkus, Daniel J. (2001) (ed.), *Piracy, Slavery and Redemption: Barbary Captivity Narratives from Early Modern England* (New York: Columbia University Press), 58–70.

3. For example, Adams, Robert (1816), *The Narrative of Robert Adams, a Sailor who was Wrecked on the Western Coast of Africa, in the Year 1810, was Detained Three Years in Slavery by the Arabs of the Great Desert, and Resided Several Months in the City of Tombuctoo* (London: J. Murray). Reprinted in Boston in 1817, translated into French in 1817, Swedish in 1817 and into Dutch in 1818. A new edition by Charles Hansford Adams, was published in 2005, as *The Narrative of Robert Adams, a Barbary Captive* (Cambridge: Cambridge University Press). Captivity narratives written by Muslims are much rarer and form the main subject of Nabil Matar's (2007) "Piracy and captivity in the early modern Mediterranean", in *Pirates? The Politics of Plunder, 1550–1650,* Jowitt, Claire (ed.) (Basingstoke: Palgrave Macmillan). Matar asserts that "The Magharibi *corpus captivis* follows a paradigm that is different from its European counterparts. Arabic writers did not produce full-length accounts of their or their compatriots' captivity, nor did they offer graphic descriptions of beatings, humiliations or tortures, as in many English and French accounts. Rather the Arabic stories alluded to or briefly recounted an episode of captivity, and encounter with [Christian] corsairs, and/or an escape from slavery", (63), [chapter 56–73]. Salvatore Bono (2010) estimates that "from the sixteenth to the nineteenth centuries at least two million slaves from the Muslim Mediterranean world entered European countries", in "Slave histories and memoirs in the Mediterranean world: a study of the sources (sixteenth–eighteenth centuries)", in *Trade and Cultural Exchange in the Early Modern Mediterranean*, Fusaro, Maria (ed.) (London: Tauris Academic Studies), 105 [chapter 97–115].

4. There is a comprehensive "Bibliography of English captivity narratives from the sixteenth and seventeenth centuries" in Vitkus (2001), 371–6, giving details of twenty-seven separate works.

5. Matar, Nabil (2001), "Introduction: England and Mediterranean captivity, 1577–1704", in Vitkus (2001), 35 [introduction 1–52].

6. Vitkus (2001), 34.

7. Rose, Jonathan (2010), *The Intellectual Life of the British Working Classes*, 2nd edition (New Haven: Yale University Press), "The best-sellers of Hanoverian Britain – chapbook romances, the Bible, *Pilgrim's Progress* and *Robinson Crusoe* – all told essentially the same story. They

were all thrilling tales of adventure, about amazing journeys and terrific struggles, and memorable heroes who, with the help of God, miraculously prevail", 95.

8. For example, Pellow, Thomas (1890), *The Adventures of Thomas Pellow of Penryn, Mariner: Three and Twenty Years Captivity among the Moors*, ed. Robert Brown (London: Fisher Unwin), as part of *The Adventure Series*. For more information on Pellow see the *Oxford Dictionary of National Biography*, http://www.oxforddnb.com/ [accessed 15 April 2011].

9. For example, Devereux Spratt (d. 1688) "The capture of a Protestant divine, by an Algerine corsair, in the seventeenth century", published as an appendix to volume one of Spratt, T. A. B. (1865), *Travels and Researches in Crete* (London: J. Van Voorst), Vol. 1, 384–7 who was the author's "direct ancestor" (Vol. 1, 384).

10. For example, Hasleton, Richard (1595), *Strange and Wonderfull Things Happened to Richard Hasleton, born at Braintree in Essex, in His Ten Yeares Travailes in Many Forraine Countries*, (London: William Barley), Reprinted in Beazley, C. Raymond (1902) (ed.), *Voyages and Travels, Mainly During the 16th and 17th Centuries* (London: Constable), Vol. 2, 151–80, and with modernized spelling in Vitkus (2001), 71–95.

11. On North Africa, in general, Julien, Charles-André (1931), *Histoire de l'Afrique du Nord: Tunisie, Algérie, Maroc* (Paris: Payot). [English translation: Julien, Charles-André (1970), *History of North Africa: Tunisia, Algeria, Morocco, from the Arab Conquest to 1830* (London: Routledge)] On Algeria, Grammont, Henri de (1887), *Histoire d'Alger sous la Domination Turque (1515–1830)* (Paris: E. Leroux) and Grammont Henri de (1879), *Relations entre la France et la Régence d'Alger au XVIIe Siècle*, 4 vols. (Algiers: Adolphe Jourdan, 1879–1885). On Morocco, Castries, Henry de (1905), *Les Sources Inédites de l'Histoire du Maroc*, 22 vols. (Paris: E. Leroux, 1905–1961).

12. Haëdo, Diego de (1881), *Histoires des Rois d'Alger*, tr. by Henri de Grammont (Algiers: Jourdan; this translation originally published in parts in the *Revue Africaine*, 1880–1881). The original edition was published in Spanish as Haëdo, Diego de (1612), *Topografia e historia general de Argel* ... (Valladolid: Diego Fernandez de Cordoua y Ouiedo). Diego de Haëdo seems to have edited and published under his own name the work of the Portuguese Antonio de Sosa, who was released from captivity in Algiers in 1582; for more information on Sosa and Haëdo see Garcés, María Antonia (2002), *Cervantes in Algiers: a Captive's Tale* (Nashville: Vanderbilt University Press), 70 ff.

13. Lane-Poole, Stanley (1890), *The Barbary Corsairs* (London: Fisher Unwin) in *The Story of the Nations* series.

14. Wolf, John B. (1979), *The Barbary Coast: Algiers under the Turks, 1500 to 1830* (New York: Norton), 346.

15. Fisher, Sir Godfrey (1957), *Barbary Legend: War, Trade and Piracy in North Africa, 1415–1830* (Oxford: Clarendon Press), which rather overstates the case for the corsairs; Earle, Peter (1970), *Corsairs of Malta and Barbary* (London: Sidgwick and Jackson). An important study particularly of the janissaries (rather than the corsairs) which makes full use of the Algerian archives is Shuval, Tal (1998), *La Ville d'Alger Vers la Fin du XVIIIème Siècle: Population et Cadre Urbain* (Paris: CNRS).

16. Bono, Salvatore (1964), *I Corsari Barbareschi* (Turin: ERI–Edizioni, RAI Radiotelevisione Italiana); Clissold, Stephen (1977), *The Barbary Slaves* (London: Paul Elek); Friedman, Ellen G. (1983), *Spanish Captives in North Africa in the Early Modern Age* (Madison: University of

Wisconsin Press); Belhamissi, Mouley (1988), *Les Captifs Algériens et l'Europe Chrétienne, 1518–1831* (Algiers: Entreprise nationale du livre); Magali Morsy's critical translation of the captivity narrative of Pellow, Thomas (1983), *La Relation de Thomas Pellow: une Relation du Maroc au 18ème Siècle* (Paris: Editions recherche sur les civilisations).

17. Matar, Nabil (1998), *Islam in Britain, 1558–1685* (Cambridge: Cambridge University Press); Matar, Nabil (1999), *Turks, Moors, and Englishmen in the Age of Discovery* (New York: Columbia University Press); Matar, Nabil (2005), *Britain and Barbary, 1589–1689* (Gainesville: University Press of Florida).

18. Vitkus (2001).

19. For example, Said, Edward (1978), *Orientalism* (London: Routledge & Kegan Paul).

20. Davis, Robert C. (2003), *Christian Slaves, Muslim Masters: White Slavery in the Mediterranean, the Barbary Coast, and Italy, 1500–1800* (Basingstoke: Palgrave Macmillan), who makes extensive use of Italian archives in the way that Friedman (1983) did for Spanish archives; Colley, Linda (2003), *Captives: Britons, Empire and the World, 1600–1815* (London: Jonathan Cape), which developed Matar's linking of captivity in North Africa with captivity in North America; Ressel, Magnus (2010), "The North European way of ransoming: explorations into an unknown dimension of the early modern welfare state", *Historical Social Research/Historische Sozialforschung,* Vol. 35, no. 4, 125–47; Ostlund, Joachim (2010), "Swedes in Barbary captivity: the political culture of human security, *circa* 1660–1760", *Historical Social Research/Historische Sozialforschung,* Vol. 35, no. 4, 148–63; Kaiser, Wolfgang (2008) (ed.), *Le Commerce des Captifs: les Intermédiaires dans l'Echange et le Rachat des Prisonniers en Méditerranée, XVIe–XVIIIe* (Rome: Ecole française de Rome); Madsen, Peter (2010), "Danish Slaves in Barbary, (XVIe–XVIIIes)", in *La Guerre de Course en Récits: Terrains, Corpus, Séries,* dossier en ligne du Projet CORSO, URL http://www.oroccrlc.paris-sorbonne.fr/index.php/visiteur/ Projet-CORSO/Ressources/La-guerre-de-course-en-recits [accessed 5 May 2011].

21. Some of the chapters in Maclean, Gerald (2004), *The Rise of Oriental Travel: English Visitors to the Ottoman Empire, 1580–1720* (Basingstoke: Palgrave Macmillan) and Maclean, Gerald (2007a), *Looking East: English Writing and the Ottoman Empire before 1800* (Basingstoke: Palgrave Macmillan) deal specifically with North Africa; Voigt, Lisa (2009), *Writing Captivity in the Early Modern Atlantic: Circulations of Knowledge and Authority in Iberian and English Imperial Worlds* (Chapel Hill: University of North Carolina Press) takes some of Matar's ideas and relates them mainly to South and Central America; Norton, Claire (2009), "Lust, greed, torture and identity: narrations of conversion and the creation of the early modern renegade", *Comparative Studies of South Asia, Africa and the Middle East,* Vol. 29, no. 2, 259–68), which uses Barbary captivity narratives as its primary source material; Sayre, Gordon M. (2010), "Renegades from Barbary: the transnational turn in captivity studies", *Early American Literature,* Vol. 45, no. 2, 325–38.

22. Milton, Giles (2004), *White Gold: the Extraordinary Story of Thomas Pellow and North Africa's One Million European Slaves* (London: Hodder & Stoughton), a straightforward retelling of Pellow's story; Tinniswood, Adrian (2010), *Pirates of Barbary: Corsairs, Conquest and Captivity in the Seventeenth Century Mediterranean* (London: Jonathan Cape), an Anglocentric narrative of England's relations with the Barbary states, based on primary sources.

23. One website is called *Corso: Islam et Chrétienté devant la Modernité,* URL: http:// www.oroc-crlc.paris-sorbonne.fr/index.php/visiteur/Projet-CORSO/Ressources [accessed

5 May 2011], the associated collection of papers *La Guerre de Course en Récit: Terrains, Corpus, Séries* can be found at URL: http://www.oroc-crlc.paris-sorbonne.fr/index.php/visiteur/Projet-CORSO/Ressources/La-guerre-de-course-en-recits [accessed 5 May 2011], while an embryonic dictionary of captivity narratives (which does not include Joseph Pitts) entitled *Répertoire Nominative des Récits de Captivité en Méditerranée (XVIe–XVIIIe)* has been created at URL: http://www.oroc-crlc.paris-sorbonne.fr/index.php/visiteur/Projet-CORSO/Ressources/R.N.R.C [accessed May 5th 2011]. Bono (2010) describes the current state of research in Mediterranean slavery studies and the programme of *CORSO,* 97–115. Bono himself is the inspiration for the second website, which is mainly a biographical dictionary in Italian of most of the major figures involved in Mediterranean piracy up to the end of the 17th century. The website is entitled *Pirati, Corsari e Loro Cacciatori nel Mediterraneo (XIII Secolo–XVII Secolo): Dizionario Biografico,* and includes a glossary, maps bibliography and links: URL: http://www.corsaridelmediterraneo.it/indice/a.htm [accessed 5 May 2011].

24. Burton, Sir Richard (1855–56), *Personal Narrative of a Pilgrimage to Al Madinah and Meccah* (London: Longman, etc.), 3 vols. All references to Burton's work here are taken from the 1913 edition published in London in 2 volumes by G. Bell, which is based on the definitive Memorial Edition published in 1893 in London by Tylston & Edwards. For more information on Burton see the *Oxford Dictionary of National Biography,* http://www.oxforddnb.com/ [accessed 15 April 2011].

25. Hogarth, David G. (1905), *The Penetration of Arabia: a Record of the Development of Western Knowledge Concerning the Arabian Peninsula* (London: Alston Rivers); Ralli, Augustus (1909), *Christians at Mecca* (London: Heinemann); Kiernan, R. H. (1937), *The Unveiling of Arabia: the Story of Arabian Travel and Discovery* (London: Harrap); Bidwell, Robin (1976), *Travellers in Arabia* (London: Hamlyn); Brent, Peter (1977), *Far Arabia: Explorers of the Myth* (London: Weidenfeld & Nicolson); Freeth, Zahra and Winstone, H.V. F. (1978), *Explorers of Arabia: from the Renaissance to the End of the Victorian Era* (London: Allen & Unwin); Simmons, James C. (1987), *Passionate Pilgrims: English Travelers to the World of the Desert Arabs* (New York: Morrow).

26. Pirenne. Jacqueline (1958), *A la Découverte de l'Arabie: Cinq Siècles de Science et d'Aventure* (Paris: Le livre contemporain). There is also a translation into French of the section on Egypt by Zeinab Hamza with useful notes by Oleg Volkoff included in no. 23 of the series *Collections des Voyageurs Occidentaux en Egypte* and published as *Voyages en Egypte Pendant les Années 1678–1701* (Cairo: Institut français d'archéologie orientale) in 1981; Pfullmann, Uwe (2001), *Durch Wüste und Steppe: Entdeckerlexikon Arabische Halbinsel: Biographien und Berichte* (Berlin: Trafo).

27. Baring-Gould, Sabine (1908), *Devonshire Characters and Strange Events* (London: Bodley Head), 152–69.

28. Foster, Sir William (1949) (ed.), *The Red Sea and Adjacent Countries at the Close of the Seventeenth Century, as Described by Joseph Pitts, William Daniel and Charles Jacques Poncet* (London: Hakluyt Society), 1–49.

29. There is no mention of Pitts in Thomson, Ann (1987), *Barbary and Enlightenment: European Attitudes Towards the Maghreb in the 18th Century* (Leiden: Brill), Toomer, G. J. (1996), *Eastern Wisedome and Learning: The Study of Arabic in Seventeenth-Century England* (Oxford: Clarendon Press), or Irwin, Robert (2006), *For Lust of Knowing: the Orientalists and their Enemies* (London: Allen Lane), and only one mention in Gunny, Ahmed (1996), *Images of Islam in Eighteenth-Century Writings* (London: Grey Seal).

30. For example in al-Azmeh, Aziz (1986), *Islamic Studies and the European Imagination* (Exeter: University of Exeter, Department of Arabic and Islamic Studies), 2, and Nabil Matar (2001), 39.

1. ALGIERS: A CORSAIR STATE

1. Brummett, Palmira (1994), *Ottoman Seapower and Levantine Diplomacy in the Age of Discovery* (Albany: State University of New York Press), 95.

2. Brummett (1994), 96.

3. Bruce, Travis (2010), "Piracy as statecraft: the Mediterranean policies of the fifth/eleventh century Taifa of Denia", *Al-Masaq*, Vol. 22, No. 3, 237 [article, 235–48]. Matar (2001) also shows how in "Arabic-Islamic sources, the Barbary privateers stand out as defenders of the community and the faith", 11.

4. Hess, Andrew (1978), *The Forgotten Frontier: a History of the Sixteenth-Century Ibero-African Frontier* (Chicago: University of Chicago Press), 60.

5. Hess (1978), 61.

6. Hess (1978), 62.

7. *Encyclopaedia of Islam,* 2nd edition, article "Arudj" (on which this account of Oruç's life is based), http://brillonline.nl/ [accessed 14 April 2011].

8. Friedman (1983), xxii.

9. The Janissaries were the elite corps of professional infantrymen in the Ottoman (and by extension Algerian) army, composed exclusively of ethnic Turks, *Encyclopaedia of Islam*, 2nd edition, article "Yeni Ceri", http://brillonline.nl/ [accessed 14 April 2011].

10. The *Ocak* was among other things a unit of recruitment in the Ottoman military administration, and was composed of ethnic Turks, *Encyclopaedia of Islam*, 2nd edition, article "Odjak", http://brillonline.nl/ [accessed 14 April 2011].

11. Julien (1970), 303.

12. A *ra'īs* (Turkish *reis*) was the commander of a corsair ship, *Encyclopaedia of Islam*, 2nd edition, article "Ra'īs", http://brillonline.nl/ [accessed 14 April 2011].

13. Julien (1970), 302.

14. Knight, Francis (1640), *A Relation of Seaven Yeares Slaverie under the Turkes of Argeire, Suffered by an English Captive Merchant* ... (London: T. Cotes), 40.

15. *Encyclopaedia of Islam*, 2nd edition; the articles "dīwān" and "dīwān-i Humāyūn" do not cover the Barbary regencies, http://brillonline.nl/ [accessed 14 April 2011].

16. Julien (1970), 303.

17. For more information on Spragge see the *Oxford Dictionary of National Biography*, http://www.oxforddnb.com/ [accessed 15 April 2011].

18. The *ta'ifah* was the corporation of sea-captains composed of a number of nationalities, including renegades from Europe.

19. Abun-Nasr, Jamil M. (1987), *A History of the Maghrib in the Islamic Period,* (Cambridge: Cambridge University Press), 160; Julien (1970), 303; despite the shift in power back to the Janissaries, the title of the ruler of Algiers remained the *dey* until 1830.

20. Julien (1970), 303.

21. Although Morocco remained outside the Ottoman sphere of influence, it also pursued a strategy of corsairing and the associated ransoming of slaves, particularly during the first half of the 17th century.

22. *Encyclopaedia of Islam*, 2nd edition, article "Devshirme", http://brillonline.nl/ [accessed 14 April 2011].

23. Maclean (2004), 11–12 recounts the story of Samson Rowley, the son of English sea captain Francis Rowley, who was captured with his father and enslaved at Algiers in 1577. While the father was freed, Samson converted to Islam, was castrated and became treasurer to the *beylerbey* of Algiers, Uluç Ali. Uluç Ali himself had been born Giovanni Dionigi Galeni and was taken prisoner at the age of sixteen (see Encyclopaedia of Islam, 2nd edition, article "'Uludj 'Ali,'" http://brillonline.nl/ [accessed 14 April 2011].

24. Pitts (1731), 181–2.

25. Shuval, Tal (2000), "The Ottoman Algerian elite and its ideology", *International Journal of Middle East Studies,* Vol. 32, no. 3, 328 [article 323–44].

26. Shuval (2000), 326.

27. *Agha* (modern Turkish *ağa*) means military commander, see *Encyclopaedia of Islam*, 2nd edition, articles "Agha" and "Yeni Ceri", http://brillonline.nl/ [accessed 14 April 2011].

28. Abun-Nasr (1987), 159.

29. Shuval (2000), 330–6 for an extensive analysis of *kuloğlus* and the threat they posed to the Turkish elite.

30. For more information on Rycaut, see the *Oxford Dictionary of National Biography*, http://www.oxforddnb.com/ [accessed 15 April 2011].

31. Rycaut, Paul (1682), *The history of the Present State of the Ottoman Empire ...* (London: T. N.). There were occasional exceptions.

32. Abun-Nasr (1983), 159.

33. Bosworth, Clifford Edmund (2006), *An Intrepid Scot: William Lithgow of Lanark's Travels in the Ottoman Lands, North Africa and Central Europe, 1609–21,* (Aldershot: Ashgate) 114. For more information on Lithgow, see also the *Oxford Dictionary of National Biography*, http://www.oxforddnb.com/ [accessed 15 April 2011].

34. Matar (2005), 94; see also Barnby, Henry (1969), "The sack of Baltimore", *Journal of the Cork Historical and Archaeological Society,* Vol. 74, 101–29.

35. Pitts (1731), 3.

36. Pennell, C.R. (1989), *Piracy and Diplomacy in Seventeenth-Century North Africa: the Journal of Thomas Baker, English Consul in Tripoli, 1677–1685* (Cranbury, New Jersey: Fairleigh Dickinson University Press), 31. For more information on Thomas Baker's career see Pennell (1989), 202–6.

37. Freidman (1983), 10–11.

38. Matar (2001), 12.

39. Julien (1970), discusses the composition of the urban workforce and the trades they practised, 290.

40. Pitts (1731), 32.

41. Pitts (1731), 34.

42. Pitts (1731), 33.

43. *Encyclopaedia of Islam*, 2nd edition, article "Fatwa", http://brillonline.nl/ [accessed 14 April 2011].

44. Pennell (1989), 31.

45. Johansen, Baber (1982), "The servants of the mosques", *The Maghreb Review*, Vol. 7, nos. 1–2, 24 [article 23–31].

46. Abun-Nasr (1987), 166–7; Wolf (1979), 333.

47. Deny, Jean (1920), "Les registres de solde des Janissaires conservés à la Bibliothèque Nationale d'Alger", *Revue Africaine*, Vol. 61, 36–7 [article 19–46].

48. Pitts (1731), 169. Pitts also explained that Janissaries could not go on the pilgrimage while in service without permission from the Dey, who would allow them up to a year on full pay to undertake it, 88.

49. Quoted by Pennell (1989), 36.

50. Dan, Pierre (1637), *Histoire de la Barbarie et de ses Corsaires* (Paris: Rochelet); d'Aranda, Emanuel (1657), *Relation de la Captivité du S: Ou Sont Descriptés les Misères, les Ruses et les Finesses des Esclaves et des Corsaires d'Alger: Ensemble les Conquestes de Barberousse dans l'Afrique etc* (Paris: no pub.); translated by John Davies in 1666 as, *The History of Algiers and its Slavery with Many Remarkable Particularities of Africa* (London: John Starkey); d'Arvieux, Laurent (1735), *Mémoires du Chevalier d'Arvieux, Envoyé Extraordinaire du Roy à la Porte, Consul d'Alep, d'Alger, de Tripoli et Autres Echelles du Levant, Contenant Ses Voyages à Constantinople, dans l'Asie, la Syrie, la Palestine, l'Egypte et la Barbarie …* (Paris: no pub.); Laugier de Tassy (1725), *Histoire du Royaume d'Alger: avec l'Etat Présent de Son Gouvernement, de Ses Forces de Terre & de Mer, de Ses Revenus, Police, Justice, Politique & Commerce* (Amsterdam: Henri du Sauzet), translated into English with additions by Joseph Morgan in 1750 as, *A Compleat History of the Piratical States of Barbary, viz. Algiers, Tunis, Tripoli and Morocco: Containing the Origin, Revolutions, and Present State of These Kingdoms, Their Forces, Revenues, Policy, and Commerce* (London: R. Griffiths).

For more information on Dan, see Pauphilet, Albert, Pichard, Louis & Barroux, Robert (1996), *Dictionnaire des Lettres Françaises: le XVIIe Siècle*, nouvelle édition, (Paris: Fayard), 324; for more information on d'Aranda see Latifa Z'Rari's introduction to her recent edition of d'Aranda's *Les Captifs d'Alger*, (Paris: Jean Paul Rocher, 1997); for more information on d'Arvieux, see *Dictionnaire de Biographie Française*, Vol. 3 (1938) (Paris: Letouzet et Ané), 1230–1. I have been unable to track down any biographical information on Laurent de Tassy.

51. Wolf (179), 97.

52. Julien (1970), 290.

53. Abun-Nasr (1987), 161.

54. Davis (2003), 103.

55. Wolf (1979), 78.

56. D'Aranda, (1666) 105.

57. Four times a week according to Julien (1970), 302.

58. Knight (1640), 41.

59. *Khaznajī* was the Arabo-Turkish term used in North Africa for treasurer; the term *hazinedar* (Turkish) and *khaznadār* (Arabic) were the more common terms in other part of the Ottoman Empire.

60. The anonymous author of T. S. (1670), *The Adventures of Mr. T. S., an English Merchant taken Prisoner by the Turks of Argiers and Carried into the Inland Countries of Africa, with a Description of the Kingdom of Argiers* ... (London: Moses Pitt), though not always reliable, claims that the infantry in Algerian campaigns on land was made up of renegade Christians, 67.

61. Pitts (1731), 27–8.

62. Pitts (1731), 32.

63. Pitts (1731), 169.

64. Pitts (1731), 171.

65. Pitts (1731), 175–9.

66. Pitts (1731), 227. The Ottomans faced naval attacks by the Venetians and Maltese in the Aegean during the summer of 1694, which resulted in the Venetians capturing Chios in September 1694.

67. Morsy, Magali (1984), *North Africa, 1800–1900: a Survey from the Nile Valley to the Atlantic* (London: Longman), 43.

68. Pennell (1989), 31.

69. Pitts (1731), 216–7.

70. Baba Hasan was Dey of Algiers from January 1682 to July 1683.

71. Pitts (1731), 172–5, 209–10, 215–7. Hacı Hüseyin/Ḥajjī Ḥusayn, also known as Medio-Morto or Mezzo-Morto, was an important figure in the government of Algiers in the later 17th century, becoming Dey between July 1683 and 1686, and later taking effective power from Ibrahim in 1688. He was forced to flee to Tunis in 1689 and then moved to Istanbul, where he was appointed Chief Admiral in the Ottoman Navy. He died in 1700.

72. Pitts (1731), 175.

73. Abun-Nasr (1987), 161.

74. Pitts (1731), 10–11. The first edition spells the town Bleda (1704, 8).

75. Pitts (1731), 11.

76. Abun-Nasr (1987), 161.

77. Pitts (1731), 35.

78. Pitts (1731), 33.

79. Abun-Nasr (1987), 165, quoting Valensi, Lucette (1969), *Le Maghreb Avant la Prise d'Alger* (Paris: Flammarion), 63–4. [Translated in 1977 as: *On the Eve of Colonialism: North Africa before the French Conquest* (New York: Africana)]. For information on the commercial complexities in the Mediterranean, see Greene, Molly (2002), "Beyond the Northern Invasion: the

Mediterranean in the Seventeenth Century", *Past and Present*, Vol. 174, no. 1, 42–71 and Panzac, Daniel (2004), *La Caravane Maritime: Marins Européens et Marchands Ottomans en Méditerranée, 1680–1830* (Paris: CNRS). For the effects on commerce of the Maltese privateers, in addition to the two items cited above, see Earle (1970) and Greene, Molly (2010), "Victims of piracy? Ottoman lawsuits in Malta (1602–1687) and the changing course of Mediterranean maritime history", in *Trade and Cultural Exchange in the Early Modern Mediterranean*, Fusaro, Maria (ed.) (London: Tauris Academic Studies), 177–201. Other papers in Fusaro's collection which deal with the role of Malta are by Williams, Ann, "Sacra Militia, the Order of St John: crusade, corsairing and trade in Rhodes and Malta, 1460–1631", 139–56, and Mercieca, Simon, "Maritime caravans and the Knights of St John: aspects of Mediterranean seaborne traffic (sixteenth-eighteenth centuries)", 157–75.

80. Davis (2003), 75.

81. Abun-Nasr (1987), 165.

82. D'Aranda (1666), 105.

83. Abun-Nasr (1987), 165–6.

84. Davis (2003), claims that "at the battle of Lepanto, in 1571, when an estimated 80,000 rowers were sent into action against each other – most of them slaves, and not just on the Muslim side: in the galleys of Spain, France, Malta and some Italian states, one could find thousands of Moors, Turks, Catholic converts and not a few Protestants condemned to the oars", 75.

85. Guilmartin, John Francis (2003), *Gunpowder & Galleys: Changing Technology & Mediterranean Warfare at Sea in the 16th Century,* revised edition, (London: Conway Maritime Press), 218.

86. Guilmartin (2003), 218–23; Tinniswood (2010), 83–4.

87. Guilmartin (2003) calculates 1800 gallons of water would have been required by a typical Mediterranean galley for a twenty-day voyage, 78.

88. Guilmartin (2003), 77.

89. Julien (1970), quotes Haëdo as saying that the Muslim corsairs "made a mock of our galleys", since they were "so well tallowed and so light", 286, and that "they have such care for the order, cleanliness and fitting out of their vessels, that they think of nothing else, making a point above all of good trim, in order to be able to run and tack well", 287.

90. Davis (2003), 8.

91. Davis (2003), 35.

92. Friedman (1983), 49.

93. Friedman (1983), 7–8.

94. Hasleton, (1595), [1–2].

95. King James 1 (1603), *A Proclamation to Represse All Piracies and Depredations Vpon the Sea* (London: R. Barker), first article.

96. Manwayring, Sir Henry (1920), *The Life and Works of Sir Henry Mainwairing*, ed. G. E Manwaring (London: Navy Records Society), Vol. 2, 11.

97. For more information on Ward, Mainwaring and Verney, see the *Oxford Dictionary of*

*National Biography*, http://www.oxforddnb.com/ [accessed 15 April 2011].

98. Matar (1999), 57–63.

99. Rodger, N.A.M. (1997), *The Safeguard of the Sea: A Naval History of Britain, 660–1649* (London: HarperCollins), 349.

100. So said William Lithgow who visited Ward around 1615, see Lithgow, William (1906), *The Totall Discourse of the Rare Adventures and Painfull Peregrinations of Long Nineteen Yeares Travayles from Scotland to the Most Famous Kingdoms in Europe, Asia and Africa*, (Glasgow: James MacLehose), 315.

101. Simon Dansker is also known as Simon Danziker, Simon de Dancer, Siemen Danziger and Zymen Danseker.

102. Monson, Sir William (1913), *The Naval Tracts*, ed. M. Oppenheim, (London: Navy Records Society), Vol. 3, 83, claimed in 1617 that "it is not above twelve years since the English taught them the art of navigation in ships". Friedman (1983) is also of this view: "Large numbers of English and Dutch pirates appeared in North Africa, where they augmented the ranks of the Muslim corsairs and introduced a new naval technology, against which the traditional Mediterranean defences were inadequate." 10.

103. Hebb, David Delison (1994), *Piracy and the English Government, 1616–1642* (Aldershot: Scolar Press), 14–15, where Hebb claims that "from Seville alone, 7000 men, many of who worked in the dockyard and port, were expelled in the great purge".

104. Hebb (1994), 15.

105. De Groot, Alexander H. (1985), "Ottoman North Africa and the Dutch Republic in the seventeenth and eighteenth centuries", *Revue de l'Occident Musulman et de la Méditerranée*, Vol. 39, no. 1, 131 [article 131–47].

106. Figures taken from Davis (2003), 75.

107. Guilmartin (2003), 144–5 points out that loss of 600 experienced sailors with technical expertise during the Djerba campaign of 1560 "crippled the effective Spanish exercise of power at sea" for many years.

108. Brummett (1994), 96.

109. De Groot (1985), 132 shows that "in 1626, fifty-five of the principal corsair captains of the fleet of Algiers were Dutchmen in origin".

110. Tinniswood (2010), 76.

111. Tinniswood (2010), 150–1. For more information on Salé, see Coindreau, Roger (1948), *Les Corsaires de Salé* (Paris: Société d'éditions géographiques, maritimes et coloniales); Maziane, Leila (2007), *Salé et Ses Corsaires, 1666–1727: un Port de Course Marocain au XVIIe Siècle* (Caen: Presses universitaires de Caen); and Weiner, Jerome B. (1979), "New approaches to the study of the Barbary corsairs", *Revue d'Histoire Maghrébine*, Vols. 13–14, 205–9.

112. See Barnby (1969).

113. Lewis, Bernard (1973), "Corsairs in Iceland", *Revue de l'Occident Musulman et de la Méditerranée*, Vol. 15–16, 139–44; Thorsteinn Helgason (1997), "Historical narrative as collective therapy: the case of the Turkish raid in Iceland", *Scandinavian Journal of History*, Vol. 22, no. 4, 275–89.

114. Rodger (1997), 350.

115. Friedman (1983), 13.

116. Hebb (1994), 140.

117. Hebb (1994), 142

118. Gray, Todd (1989), "Turkish piracy and early Stuart Devon", *Report and Transactions of the Devonshire Association for the Advancement of Science, Literature and Art,* Vol. 121, 168 [article 159–71].

119. Rodger (1997), 385.

120. For more information on Eliot see the *Oxford Dictionary of National Biography,* http://www.oxforddnb.com/ [accessed 15 April 2011].

121. Jansson, Maiya and Bidwell, William B (1987) (eds.), *Proceedings in Parliament 1625* (New Haven: Yale University Press), quoted in Gray (1989), 163.

122. For more information on Monson see the *Oxford Dictionary of National Biography,* http://www.oxforddnb.com/ [accessed 15 April 2011].

123. Monson (1913), Vol. 3, 267.

124. Pitts (1731), 15.

125. Okeley, William (1676), *Eben-ezer, or, A Small Monument of Great Mercy Appearing in the Miraculous Deliverance of William Okeley, William Adams, John Anthony, John Jephs, John —— Carpenter from the Miserable Slavery of Algiers …* (London: Nat. Ponder), 4. Reprinted with modernized spelling in Vitkus (2001), 124–92.

126. Phelps, Thomas (1685), *A True Account of the Captivity of Thomas Phelps at Machaness in Barbary …,* (London: H. Hills), 2. Reprinted with modernised spelling in Vitkus (2001), 193–217. For more information on Phelps see the *Oxford Dictionary of National Biography,* http://www.oxforddnb.com/ [accessed 15 April 2011].

127. Coxere, Edward (1945), *Adventures by Sea of Edward Coxere,* ed. E.H.W. Meyerstein (Oxford: Clarendon Press), 54. For more information on Coxere see the *Oxford Dictionary of National Biography,* http://www.oxforddnb.com/ [accessed 15 April 2011].

128. Pitts (1731), 2–3.

129. Guilmartin (2003), 182–3.

130. Pitts (1731), 14, who records the name as Sir Edward Sprague.

131. Rodger (1997), explains the difficulties faced by European naval squadrons who tried to engage the Algerians: "Though the Algerians, could not match his [Sir Robert Mansell's] biggest ships, and did not attempt to fight, the coast [of Algiers] was a lee shore throughout the year, its few harbours fortified and inaccessible, and it was virtually impossible to blockade under sail, 200 miles from the nearest friendly port. Still less, could Mansell attack the formidable defences of Algiers, a city as large as London", 352. For more information on Mansell see the *Oxford Dictionary of National Biography,* http://www.oxforddnb.com/ [accessed 15 April 2011].

132. Lambert, Andrew (2008), *Admirals: the Naval Commanders who Made Britain Great* (London: Faber), 64–5. Eight Ottoman ships were sunk on the attack on Porto Farina, but "their destruction did not greatly delay Ottoman success in Crete", and "the Dey [of Tunis] was not greatly impressed". However, as a consequence of the attack, Algiers "released English and Irish slaves and opened the port for the [English] fleet to be supplied". For more

information on Blake see the *Oxford Dictionary of National Biography*, http://www.oxforddnb.com/ [accessed 15 April 2011].

133. Wolf (1979) 267, points out that the French had to return five ships to the Algerians, pay compensation for a ship they had burned, and had to "furnish the Algerians with nine thousand bombs, four mortars and a master a cannoneer for the siege of Oran", before the Algerians would consent to ransom any French slaves.

134. Le Fevre, Peter and Harding, Richard (2000) (eds.), *Precursors of Nelson: British Admirals of the Eighteenth Century*, (London: Chatham), 25. Algiers' keenness to sign a treaty with England was stimulated by the loss of one of their best ships, the 32-gun *Half Moon of Argier* in 1681 in a battle with the *James Galley* and the *Sapphire*. See the one-page broadside (1691), *An Exact and faithful account of the late bloody fight between Captain Hastings, commander of the Saphire, Captain Showel, commander of the James Galley, and Jonas Raile, captain of the Half-Moon of Algier* (London: John Gain). The lieutenant of the Turkish ship turned out to be an English renegade, whom Sir Cloudesley Shovell immediately "caused to be hanged at my yard arm". For more information on Herbert and Shovell see the *Oxford Dictionary of National Biography*, http://www.oxforddnb.com/ [accessed 15 April 2011].

135. Julien (1970), 315. Pennell (1989) shows how the same strategy was adopted by Tripoli in its dealings with the Dutch, 36–7.

136. Pitts (1731), 210–11. Maréchal Jean, comte d'Estrées, (1624–1707) bombarded Algiers in 1688. For more information on d'Estrées, see the *Dictionnaire de Biographie Française*, Vol. 13, (1975), 154–8.

137. Julien (1970), 315. Pennell (1989) demonstrates that Tripoli followed the same policy during Consul Baker's time there, p. 51.

138. Pitts (1731), 17.

139. Pennell (1989), 19, records that one ship took ten years to build in Tripoli, and required "the huge importation of timber from Anatolia, Greece, and Albania".

140. Pennell (1989), 49, calculates that of "Baker's list of thirteen ships in 1679 shows that no less than seven were built elsewhere. In other words, they were prizes that had been converted to corsairs. During Baker's stay [1677–1685] another seven prizes were added to the fleet, and one more bought out of prize money. Only one as actually built at Tripoli."

141. Wolf (1979), 142.

142. Matar (2005), 10. Matar elaborates: "If there is a date for the beginning of Britain's gunboat diplomacy in the Mediterranean, it is during the Cromwellian and the Restoration periods; and if there is a specific location, it is North Africa, where British naval power burned Barbary fleets, destroyed ports and devastated native trade, commerce and enterprise." 9.

143. Matar, Nabil (2003), "The last Moors: Maghāriba in early eighteenth-century Britain", *Journal of Islamic Studies,* Vol. 14, no. 1, 58 [article 37–58].

144. Matar, Nabil (2010) "The Maghāriba and the sea: maritime decline in North Africa in the early modern period", in *Trade and Cultural Exchange in the Early Modern Mediterranean*, Fusaro, Maria (ed.) (London: Tauris Academic Studies), 135 [article 117–37].

145. Tinniswood (2010), shows that while Great Britain only paid just over the equivalent of £1,000,000 in today's money, Spain was paying Algiers the equivalent of over 130 million pounds annually, 278.

146. Pitts (1731), 16.

147. Pennell (1989), 155.

148. Pennell (1989), 155.

149. Morgan, Joseph (1728), *A Complete History of Algiers: to which is Prefixed, an Epitome of the General History of Barbary, from the Earliest Times* ... (London: J. Bettenham. Reprinted 1970, Westport, Conn.: Negro Universities Press). iv. For more information on Morgan, see the *Oxford Dictionary of National Biography*, http://www.oxforddnb.com/ [accessed 15 April 2011].

150. Morgan (1728), iv.

151. Rodger, N.A.M. (2004), *The Command of the Ocean: A Naval History of Britain, 1649–1815* (London: Allen Lane), 88.

152. Friedman (1994), 159.

153. Davis (2003), 31.

154. Pitts (1731), 15.

155. Pitts (1731), 16; Davis agrees that the *pencik* is an eighth share (Davis (2003), 29), although the term originally mean a fifth share; see *Encyclopaedia of Islam*, 2nd edition, article "Pendjik", http://brillonline.nl/ [accessed 14 April 2011].

156. Rawlins, John (1622), *The Famous and Wonderfull Recoverie of a Ship of Bristoll, called the Exchange, from the Turkish Pirates of Argier* ... (London: Nathaniel Butter), 6. Reprinted with modernised spelling in Vitkus (2001), 96–120.

157. Okeley (1676), 8.

158. Pennell (1989), 49.

159. Davis (2003), 49.

160. Davis (2003), 49.

161. Pennell (1989), 155, quoting Consul Baker's diary entry for 11 March 1683.

162. Pennell (1989), 120, quoting Consul Baker's diary entry for 1 May 1680.

163. Pennell (1989), 123, quoting Consul Baker's diary entry for 28 August 1680.

164. Pennell (1989), 189, quoting Consul Baker's diary entry for 3 April 1685.

165. Pennell (1989), 49.

166. Barker, Andrew (1609), *A True and Certaine Report of the Beginning, Proceedings, Ouerthrowes, and now Present Estate of Captaine Ward and Danseker, the Two Late Famous Pirates,* (London: William Hall), quotes how Captain Ward in 1607 captured the *Reniera e Soderina*, "a great argosy of fourteen or fifteen hundred tunnes very richly laden with Venetian goodes and who, by computation, was esteemed to be worth two millions at the least", 14. See also Tinniswood (2010), 44.

167. Morgan (1728), 616.

168. Okeley (1676), 39. Okeley also describes a voyage of nine weeks, when they only "met with one poor Hungarian-French man-of-war", C6 verso.

169. Pennell (1989), 89, quoting Consul Baker's diary entry for 16 July 1684.

170. Hebb (1994), 267.

171. Pitts (1731), 4.

172. Davis (2003), goes on to estimate that "between 1530 and 1780 there were almost certainly a million and quite possibly as many as a million and a quarter white, European Christians enslaved by the Muslims of the Barbary Coast", 15.

173. Davis (2003), 150.

174. Davis (2003), 168.

175. Knight (1640), 7–9. It was, of course, not only the Muslims who could make negotiations difficult. Matar (2003) recounts the tale of the Moroccan ambassador to Britain, Bentura de Razy, who suffered endless humiliations in London between 1710 and 1713, see especially 45–56.

176. Davis (2003), 148.

177. Davis (2003), 223, note 35, explains that "with the founding of its congregation *De Propaganda Fide* in 1622, Rome [i.e. the Roman Catholic Church] committed itself to providing missionaries to preach all over the world, which included Catholic slave populations in Barbary. In the decades that followed, priests arrived all over the major port cities in the Maghreb, generally taking over from slave priests the running of the chapels in each *bagno*." Wolf (1979) gives more detail on the Redemptionist fathers of the Order of the Holy Trinity and the Redemption of Captives (Trinitarians) which had been founded in 1198, and the Order of Our Lacy of Mercy (Mercedarians) which had been founded in 1232: "The former, while all Western European in scope, was largely French; the latter almost entirely Italo-Spanish until the seventeenth century when Marie de Medici introduced it to France." 157. He goes on: "The redemptionist fathers were always welcomed at Algiers. The dey-pasha received them immediately on arrival, apparently to discover how much money they had brought with them for ransoms ... the first slaves to be ransomed were those belonging to the pasha and other important people, usually the old and the infirm slaves no longer useful to their patrons ... The actual redemptions took weeks of negotiation, and when it was all over, there were gratifications for the pasha, the agha, important members of the divan, and officers of the port ... The redemptionist fathers also acted as agents for private redemption of important prisoners. This service was particularly welcome, since the fathers could bring specie money into Algiers without the danger that other shipments might have and they could export the freed slaves with safe conduct to a Christian port." 158. For an exhaustive list of contemporary publications by the Redemptionist orders on North Africa, see Davis (2004 – paperback edition), 242–4.

178. Friedman (1983), 106–7.

179. Friedman (1983), 115, Table 5.

180. Friedman (1983), 147.

181. Friedman, Ellen G. (1980), "Christian captives at 'hard labor' in Algiers, 16th–18th centuries", *International Journal of Historical Studies,* Vol. 13, no. 4, 629 [article 616–31].

182. Davis (2003), 19.

183. The whole of the second part of Hebb (1994) is devoted to the Algiers Expedition.

184. Knight (1640), 51.

185. Matar (2005), 68–75.

186. Cason, Edmond (1647), *A Relation of the Whole Proceedings Concerning the Redemption of the Captives in Argier and Tunis. With the Translates and Copies of the Letters from the Bashaw, Duana, Mufty, Caddee, and Shoudes, unto Both the Honourable Houses of Parliament* ... (London: Laurence Blaikelock), 12.

187. Tinniswood (2010), 199. Rawlins (1622) recounts how he was sold for only seven pounds and ten shillings because of his lame hand, see B2 recto.

188. Tinniswood (2010), 199.

189. Gray (1989), 168, quoting David Hebb's unpublished Ph.D. thesis (1985) *The English Government and the Problem of Piracy, 1616–1642,* (London), 194, 197.

190. De Groot (1985), 133.

191. Gray (1989), 166.

192. D'Aranda (1666), 29–35; earlier d'Aranda's master had offered to release him for 2,000 patacoons at Leghorn (Livorno), 1,500 patacoons in Algiers, but d'Aranda could only raise 500, see 25. See also Davis (2003), 147.

193. Pitts (1731), 189–90.

194. (1682) *A List of Ships Taken since July, 1677 from his Majesties Subjects, by the Corsairs of Algier. With their Names, Masters Names, and Places to Which They Belong'd, and Time of Taking: with a Modest Estimate of the Loss,* (London: Richard Janeway), unpaged. Interestingly the date for the capture of the *Speedwell* is given in the list as September 1679, whereas Joseph Pitts (1731) writes that he set sail from Devon on Easter Tuesday 1678 (2).

195. As calculated by Tinniswood (2010), 239.

196. Matar (2005), 114.

197. Matar (2005), 115. For more information on the Islamic concept of slavery see the *Encyclopaedia of Islam*, 2nd edition, article "'Abd'", http://brillonline.nl/ [accessed 14 April 2011], and *Encyclopaedia of the Quran*, article "Slaves and Slavery", http://brillonline.nl/ [accessed 14 April 2011].

198. I am indebted to Davis (2003) chapters 2 (Slave Taking and Slave Breaking), 3 (Slave Labor) and 4 (Slaves' Lives) for much of the information and references in this section.

199. Pitts (1731), 5–6.

200. Pitts (1731), 8–9.

201. Rawlins (1622), B2 recto and verso.

202. Okeley (1676), C2 recto.

203. Okeley (1676), C3 recto. Elliot, Adam (1682), *A Modest Vindication of Titus Oates, the Salamanca-Doctor from Perjury, or, An Essay to Demonstrate Him only Forsworn in Several Instances,* (London: Joseph Hindmarsh) had a similar experience in Morocco, describing how a "great Black" "coursed me up and down, from one person to another, who called upon me at pleasure to examine me what trade I was of, and to see what labour my hands were accustomed to", 7. For more information on Elliot (1645/6–1700), see the *Oxford Dictionary of National Biography*, http://www.oxforddnb.com/ [accessed 15 April 2011].

204. Davis (2003), 102.

205. Also known as Bitchin, Bitchnin, and Pegelin; he is presumed to be a Venetian originally

named Piccini or Piccinino, or alternatively, according to De Groot (1985) 132, Ali (Bitchinin) Picinino was a Dutchman from Flushing/Vlissingen.

206. Davis (2003), 70, using Knight (1640) and d'Aranda (1666) as sources. Knight (1640) considered that Ali Pichilin had 800 slaves, C Recto.

207. Davis (2003), 70.

208. Wolf (1979), 98. For more general studies of plague in the Mediterranean, particularly in the 18th century, see Panzac, Daniel (1985), *La Peste Dans l'Empire Ottoman, 1700–1850* (Louvain: Peeters) and Panzac, Daniel (2010), "Plague and seafaring in the Ottoman Mediterranean in the eighteenth century", in *Trade and Cultural Exchange in the Early Modern Mediterranean*, Fusaro, Maria (ed.) (London: Tauris Academic Studies), 45–68.

209. Davis (2003), 18.

210. Pitts (1731), 162.

211. Based on the calculations of Davis (2003), 19.

212. Knight (1640), 29.

213. Webbe, Edward (1600), *The Rare and Most Wonderful Things which Edward Webbe, an Englishman Borne, Hath Seen …* (London: Ralph Blower), 7–8. For more information on Webbe, see the *Oxford Dictionary of National Biography*, http://www.oxforddnb.com/ [accessed 15 April 2011]. Pitts had the same experience when first captured: "… while the new Slaves are put into Irons in the Hold, and for a Month's time are not able to stand on their Legs, nor suffered to come upon Deck, being confin'd either to sit or lie down, without the least provision of Bedding to ease themselves … [and] the Food we had to sustain Nature … generally was only a little Vinegar (about five or six Spoonfuls) half a spoonful of Oil, and a few Olives, with a small quantity of black Bisket, and a Pint of Water a Day", (1731), 6.

214. Friedman (1980), 620.

215. Knight (1640), 14.

216. Knight (1640), 16.

217. D'Aranda (1666), 25.

218. Friedman (1980), 621.

219. D'Aranda (1666), 18.

220. Okeley (1676), E recto.

221. Cason (1647), 12. Davis (2003) confirms this by quoting that master shipbuilder Giacomo Colombin fetched "1–20 times the going rate for a common seaman or unskilled worker", 96.

222. Hasleton (1595), 27.

223. Coxere (1945), 58.

224. Coxere (1945), 59.

225. Okeley (1676), 35.

226. Okeley (1675), 35.

227. Okeley (1676), 35.

228. Pitts (1731), 47.

229. D'Aranda (1660), 157.

230. Phelps (1684), 6–7.

231. T. S., (1670) 17–21.

232. Pitts (1731), 219–21.

233. Okeley (1676), B3 verso.

234. Pitts (1731), 218. Davis (2003) asserts that light household work also "seems to have been the lot of virtually all female slaves not taken by their buyers specifically as concubines", 71.

235. Morgan (1728), 275.

236. Davis (2003), 110.

237. Clissold (1977), 56.

238. Okeley (1676), 9.

239. Quoted in Matar (2001), 18.

240. Coxere (1945), 63.

241. Pitts (1731), 184.

242. Friedman (1980), 625.

243. Friedman (1983), 85.

244. Okeley (1676), 24.

245. Friedman (1983), 88. In Morocco, Elliot (1682), describes how he had several visits from a "French fryer [friar], a very ingenious, learned man, who acquainted me that next Sunday was St Bartholomew's day, and that he intended then (having procured permission from his patron) to preach at the French Consul's house, and invited me to be his auditor", 10. However, not all priests were so well treated; Père Vacher and other French priests were fired from the mouth of a cannon in Algiers in 1683, in revenge for the French bombardment of the city, see Wolf (1979), 260.

246. Friedman (1983), 91–102.

247. Pitts (1731), 228.

248. Pitts (1731), 189.

249. Pitts (1731), 68.

250. Okeley (1676), 34.

251. Okeley (1676), 40.

252. Okeley (1676), 61–4.

253. Pitts (1731), 41.

254. Hakluyt, Richard (1589), *The Principall Nauigations, Voiages and Discoueries of the English Nation Made by Sea or Ouer Land, to the Most Remote and Farthest Distant Quarters of the Earth at any Time within the Compasse of These 1500 Yeeres: Deuided into Three Seuerall Parts, According to the Positions of the Regions Wherunto The Were Directed. … Whereunto is Added the Last Most Renowned English Nauigation, Round About the Whole Globe of the Earth* (London: George Bishop and Ralph Newberie), part, 2, 151.

255. Knight (1640), 27.

256.Voigt, Lisa (2009), *Writing Captivity in the Early Modern Atlantic: Circulations of Knowledge and Authority in the Iberian and English Worlds* (Chapel Hill: University of North Carolina Press), 53.

257. There are many works on *Lingua Franca* – see, for example, Kahane, Henry, Kahane, Renée and Tietze, Andreas (1958), *The Lingua Franca of the Levant: Turkish Nautical Terms of Italian and Greek Origin* (Urbana: University of Illinois Press); Schuchardt, Hugo (1980), "The Lingua Franca" in *Pidgin and Creole Languages: Selected Essays of Hugo Schuchard*, Glenn G. Gilbert (ed. and tr.) (Cambridge: Cambridge University Press), 65–88 (originally published in German in 1909); Corré, Alain D. (2005), *A Glossary of Lingua Franca,* 5th ed., URL: https://pantherfile.uwm.edu/corre/www/franca/go.html) [accessed 4 March 2011]; and the recent Dakhlia, Jocelyne (2008), *Lingua Franca: Histoire d'une Langue Métisse en Méditerranée* (Arles: Actes sud). Joseph Pitts (1731) clearly knew *lingua franca,* as he was able to talk to a German soldier in Frankfurt who had experience of campaigning in Italy and spoke Italian (253), but the most examples of actual usage in English captivity narratives are to found in Coxere (1945). More examples can be found in other Western languages, for example in Schuchardt (1980), who translates from the Spanish original of Diego de Haëdo's description of *Lingua Franca* on p. 78: "This *lingua franca* is so common that there is no house where it is not used. There are no houses where one or more Christians live and few houses where there is a Turk or a Moor, large or small, even children, in which it is not spoken (most people speak it quite well). It is the means by which they communicate with the Christians. The latter accommodate themselves immediately to this language. It should be added that there are very many Turks and Moors who have been captives in Spain, Italy or France, and also a large number of renegades from those and other provinces, and an additional large number of Jews who speak Spanish, Italian or French very nicely. In addition, there are all the children of the male and female renegades who suckle the natural Christian language of their parents along with their mother's milk."

258. Friedman (1980), 626, quoting a letter of Dom Manuel Joseph [sic] Nieto Martínez written in 1776.

259. Knight (1640), 3.

260. Okeley (1676), 40.

261. Pitts (1731), 226. Loualich, Fatiha (2010), "In the Regency of Algiers: the human side of the Algerine *Corso*", in *Trade and Cultural Exchange in the Early Modern Mediterranean*, Fusaro, Maria (ed.) (London: Tauris Academic Studies), points out on p. 75 that "in the absence of descendants and close relatives, freed slaves frequently stood to benefit [when their former master died]", [chapter 69–96].

262. Brooks, Francis (1693), *Barbarian Cruelty Being a True History of the Distressed Condition of the Christian Captives under the Tyranny of Mully Ishmael, Emperor of Morocco, and King of Fez and Macqueness in Barbary …* (London: J. Salusbury and H. Newman), 113–14.

263. Pitts (1731), 3.

## 2. JOSEPH PITTS: THE MAN AND HIS BACKGROUND

1. Hoskins, W. G. (1958), "Foreword", to Stephens, W.B. (1958), *Seventeenth-century Exeter: a Study of Industrial and Commercial Development, 1625–1688* (Exeter: University of Exeter), xiii.

2. Topsham is situated four miles south-east of Exeter on the Exe estuary and in the 17th century was connected to Exeter by road and by river. Although Britain's first canal linked the navigable parts of the River Exe above Topsham with the city of Exeter, the river was subject to frequent silting, so "much of Exeter's merchandise was transported by road to and from a quay built at Topsham" (Stephens, 1958), xix–xx. Topsham was administratively incorporated into the city of Exeter in 1932.

3. Stephens (1958), 8 (Table 1).

4. Serge: "A woollen fabric, the nature of which has probably differed considerably at different periods. Before the 16th c. it is mentioned chiefly as material for hangings, bed-covers, and the like; afterwards it is often referred to as worn by the poorer classes (both men and women), perh. rather on account of its durability than of its price, which seems not to have been extremely low. The name now denotes a very durable twilled cloth of worsted, or with the warp of worsted and the woof of wool, extensively used for clothing and for other purposes", *Oxford English Dictionary Online*, http://www.oed.com/ [accessed 14 April 2011].

5. Bay is a variant spelling of "Baize; originally a fabric of a finer lighter texture than now, the manufacture of which was introduced into England in the 16th c. by fugitives from France and the Netherlands", *Oxford English Dictionary Online*, http://www.oed.com/ [accessed 14 April 2011].

6. Magalotti, Lorenzo (1967), "The travels of Cosmo III, Grand Duke of Tuscany, through England", in *Early Tours in Devon and Cornwall*, Chope, R. Pearse (ed.) (Newton Abbot: David & Charles), 107. I owe this quotation and other contemporary references to Exeter to the standard articles by Fisher, Stephen (1992), "Devon's maritime trade and shipping, 1680–1780", 232–41 and Grant, Alison (1992), "Devon shipping, trade and ports, 1600–1689", 130–38, in *The New Maritime History of Devon* (1992), Vol. 1: *From Early Times to the Late Eighteenth Century*, Duffy, Michael (and others, eds.) (London: Conway Maritime Press in association with the University of Exeter). Stephen Fisher considers that "the emphasis put on the Levant trade is exaggerated", 233.

7. Fiennes, Celia (1954), *The Journeys of Celia Fiennes*, ed. with an introduction by Christopher Morris [2nd ed.], (London: Cresset Press), 245. Celia Fiennes passed through Devon on her way to Cornwall in 1698, but the diary of her travels was not published in a complete edition until 1947.

8. Perpetuana is "A durable woollen fabric widely made and used in England during the 17th and 18th centuries", *Oxford English Dictionary Online*, http://www.oed.com/ [accessed 14 April 2011].

9. Defoe, Daniel (1971), *A Tour Through the Whole Island of Great Britain;* abridged and ed. by Pat Rogers, (Harmondsworth, Middx: Penguin), 218–19. It is difficult to know exactly when Defoe visited Exeter, but the book seems to have been written from his notes between 1722 and 1725, and was published in three volumes in London, 1724–1726.

10. Stephens (1958), 107, Map 2 (overseas trade) and 119, Map 3 (coastal trade).

11. Starkey, David J., (1992) "Devonians and the Newfoundland trade", in Duffy (1992), 166 [chapter 163–171].

12. Stephens (1958), 127, Table 27.

13. Pitts (1731), 1.

14. Lympstone, spelled Lymson by Pitts, is a small port on the East side of the Exe estuary between Topsham and Exmouth.

15. Pitts (1731), 2.

16. Pitts (1731), 4.

17. Pitts (1731), xvii and 200.

18. Pitts (1731), 160; Stephens (1958), xxvi.

19. Hoskins, W.G. (2003), *Devon* (Chichester: Phillimore), 237. Hoskins's book was originally published in 1954.

20. Hoskins (2003), 237–8.

21. Brockett, Allan (1962), *Nonconformity in Exeter, 1650–1875* (Manchester: Manchester University Press), 21. In fact "the total of Nonconformist clergy in the county [of Devon] was 121, a figure higher than for any other county", 21.

22. Brockett (1962), 33.

23. Brockett (1962) 5, defines Nonconformity as "a refusal … to accept the idea of being compelled to attend services and accept religious rites with which they were not in agreement"; "The Puritans were that portion of the nation which desired to carry the English Reformation further and establish a national church of the extreme Protestant type." Presbyterians were both Puritans and Nonconformists, Calvinist in doctrine, fiercely hostile to the rites, beliefs and practices of Roman Catholicism, devoted to Bible study, and desirous of a return to what they saw as the primitive organization of the Church, where there were no bishops and Church government was in the hands of ministers together with the Elders of the Churches.

24. Pitts (1731), 203.

25. Brockett (1962), 23 and ff. on John Hopping, and 30 and ff. on Joseph Hallett the elder. For more information on Joseph Hallett I, his son Joseph Hallett II, and his grandson Joseph Hallett III, see also the *Oxford Dictionary of National Biography*, http://www.oxforddnb.com/ [accessed 15 April 2011].

26. Arianism is a theological school which believes that Jesus Christ was a created being rather than part of the eternally existing Trinity. For this reason Arians were sometimes accused of being crypto-Muslims.

27. Garcia, Humberto (2011), "Turning Turk, Turning Heretic: Joseph Pitts of Exeter and the Early Enlightenment, 1670–1740", in *Britain and the Muslim World,* Maclean, Gerald, (ed.) (Newcastle: Cambridge Scholars), 94–8 [chapter 85–101].

28. Pitts (1731), 2. Pitts says he was fourteen or fifteen when he set sail in 1678, so must have been born between 1662 and 1664, if the departure date of 1678 is accepted.

29. (1682) *A List of Ships Taken since July, 1677,* 2.

30. Pitts (1731), 183–5.

31. Pitts (1731), 187–91. Pitts refers on p. 190 to the English Consul in Tunis as Charles Baker, but in fact the consul's name was Francis and he was the brother of Thomas Baker, the English Consul Pitts came to know in Algiers. Francis Baker remained in post in Tunis until 1683 (see Pennell (1989), 55). For more information on Francis Baker's career, see Pennell (1989), 202–6.

32. Pitts (1731), 192–6.

33. Pitts (1731), 199.

34. Pitts (1731), 200.

35. Pitts (1731), describes the 1683 bombardment twice, 210 and 214.

36. Pitts (1731) 218.

37. Pitts (1731), xviii.

38. Pitts (1731), 218. Loualich (2010) has discovered through the Algerian archives that masters usually freed their slaves "at the age of around forty … before carrying out the pilgrimage. The master, anxious to perform a pious deed, a gesture of charity which will be rewarded in the afterlife, testified in favour of freeing his slave(s) following his own death, or made a declaration of freedom. In the first case, the heirs were to carry out the act; in the second the slave was freed once the act was registered", 86. See also Loualich, Fatima (2003), "Les esclaves noirs à Alger (fin du XVIIIe – début du XIXe siècles); de l'esclave à l'affranchi, vers une relation d'allégeance", *Mélanges de l'école française de Rome,* No. 115, (2003), 513–22.

39. Pitts (1731), 169.

40. Foster (1949), xi.

41. Pitts (1731), 172.

42. Beckingham, C. F. (1950), "The date of Pitts's pilgrimage to Mecca", *Journal of the Royal Asiatic Society,* Nos. 3/4, 112–13. The entry by Anita McConnell on Joseph Pitts in the *Oxford Dictionary of National Biography,* http://www.oxforddnb.com/ [accessed 15 April 2011] cites 1684 as the date of Pitts's pilgrimage.

43. Pitts (1731), 236. William Raye was British consul in Smyrna (Izmir) from 1677 to 1703. The dates of his birth and death are not known.

44. Pitts (1731), 198.

45. Pitts (1731), 227.

46. Pitts (1731), 169–72. Pitts's participation in this siege of Oran took place presumably in 1687, but 1688 is also possible.

47. Pitts (1731), 175. This appears to have been a limited engagement rather than a full-scale invasion of Morocco. Wolf (1979) puts the date of this expedition as 1688: "He [the Dey] had returned to Algiers from a punitive expedition on his western (Moroccan) frontier just when the French naval forces ended their bombardments" (270), but it possible that 1689 is intended.

48. Pitts (1731), 227–8.

49. Pitts (1731), 225–56.

50. See *Encyclopaedia of Islam,* 2nd edition, article "Funduk", http://brillonline.nl/ [accessed 14 April 2011].

51. Pitts (1731), 219.

52. Pitts (1731), 240.

53. Pitts (1731), 227.

54. Pitts (1731), 231.

55. Pitts (1731), 230.

56. Pitts (1731), 231–2.

57. Pitts (1731), 259

58. Pitts (1731), 259.

59. Pitts (1731), xvi.

60. For more information on Lowndes, see the *Oxford Dictionary of National Biography*, http://www.oxforddnb.com/ [accessed 15 April 2011].

61. For more information on King, see the *Oxford Dictionary of National Biography*, http://www.oxforddnb.com/ [accessed 15 April 2011].

62. Radford, Cecily (1920), "Joseph Pitts of Exeter (?1663–?1739)", *Transactions of the Devonshire Association for the Advancement of Science, Literature and Art,* Vol. 52, 223–38.

63. Pitts (1731), 204.

64. Radford (1920), 225.

65. Radford (1920), 236.


3. *A Faithful Account of the Religion and Manners of the Mahometans*


1.Vitkus (2001), 371–6.

2. Matar (2001), 3–52, and especially 32–40. See also Maclean, Gerald and Matar, Nabil (2011a), *Britain and the Islamic World, 1558–1713* (Oxford: Oxford University Press), chapter four, "Captives."

3. Matar (1999), 72.

4. Maclean (2007a), 21.

5. Maclean (2004), 78.

6. Brooks (1693), xv–xvi.

7. Pitts (1731), 194.

8. Hakluyt (1589), part, 2, 151.

9. Hasleton (1595), B verso.

10. Pitts (1731), 6–7.

11. Pitts (1731), 16.

12. Pitts (1731), 17.

13. Pitts (1731), 19.

14. Pitts (1731), 20.

15. Pitts (1731), 21.

16. T. S. (1670), 59.

17. T. S. (1670), 61.

18. Elliot (1682), 8.

19. Phelps (1685), 7.

20. Phelps (1685), 8–9.

21. T. S. (1670), 180–2.

22. Pitts (1731), 47–8.

23. Pitts (1731), 46–7.

24. Pitts (1731), 195–6.

25. Pitts (1704), 182–3. Archbishop Laud even created a *Laudian Rite for Returned Renegades,* in 1637 (reprinted in full in Vitkus (2001), 361–2).

26. Okeley (1676), 15.

27. Rawlins (1622), A4 verso.

28. Phelps (1685), Preface. Vitkus (2001) points out on p. 194: "Phelps expresses a patriotic nationalistic ideology and his purpose in reporting events is more practical than polemical, offering helpful information and a cautionary tale for other seamen bound for Barbary. The sort of militant, puritanical pronouncements found in Okeley's narrative are absent from Phelps's account, and this is not surprising since such an attitude would not have been welcome under the patronage of either [Samuel] Pepys [Secretary to the Admiralty] or James II, to whom Phelps says he was granted the privilege of an introduction at court. Phelps's experience did not so much lead him to thank God or invoke divine providence (although occasionally he does), as teach him to value what he terms 'the immunities and freedom of my native country and the privileges of a subject of England'."

29. Kellett, Edward (1628), *A Returne from Argier: a Sermon Preached at Minhead in the County of Somerset the 16. of March, 1627 at the Re-admission of a Relapsed Christian into our Church* (London: John Parker), 39. For more information on Kellett see the *Oxford Dictionary of National Biography*, http://www.oxforddnb.com/ [accessed 15 April 2011].

30. Rawlins (1622), B2 recto.

31. Coxere (1945), 58.

32. Knight (1640), B2 verso.

33. For more information on Blount, see the *Oxford Dictionary of National Biography*, http://www.oxforddnb.com/ [accessed 15 April 2011].

34. Blount, Henry (1638), *A Voyage into the Levant: a Brief Relation of a Journey Lately Performed by Mr. Henry Blunt Gentleman, from England by the Way of Venice, into Dalmatia, Sclavonia, Bosnia, Hungary, Macedonia, Thessaly, Thrace, Rhodes and Egypt, unto Gran Cairo: with Particular Observations concerning the Moderne Condition of the Turks, and other People under that Empire,* (London: John Legat), 112.

35. Pitts (1731), 1.

36. Pitts (1704), Preface A4, Vitkus (2001), 221.

37. Pitts (1731), xvii.

38. Pitts (1731), xvii. See also Pellow (1890), who had been forced to convert in Morocco in the early 18th century and wrote that long after his return to England, "some ill-natured people think me so [an apostate] to this day", 56.

39. Pitts (1731), 192–96.

40. Pitts (1731), 192.

41. Pitts (1731), 181. This lack of compulsion seems to have been well known in England, which would increase the difficulties encountered by returning captives; Kellett (1628) acknowledged in his sermon "that the Turks compel none to their religion", 31, while Sandys, George (1673), *Sandys Travels Containing an History of the Original and Present State of the Turkish Empire, Their Laws, Government, Policy, Military Force, Courts of Justice, and Commerce, the Mahometan Religion and Ceremonies, a Description of Constantinople, the Grand Signior's Seraglio, and his Manner of Living* ... (London: John Williams) remarked: "For they [the Turks] hold it a great grace and an act of singular piety to draw many to their religion, presenting them with money, change of raiments and freeing them from all tribute and taxes ... but they compel no man", 44.

42. Pitts (1731), 200.

43. Pitts (1731), 203.

44. Pitts (1731), 203–5.

45. Pitts (1731), 207.

46. Pitts (1731), 221.

47. Pitts (1731), 227.

48. Pitts (1731), 225.

49. Pitts (1731), 199–200.

50. Pitts (1731), 153.

51. Pitts (1731), 226.

52. Pitts (1731), 239–41.

53. Pitts (1731), 226.

54. Pitts (1731), 48.

55. Pitts (1731), 260.

56. Matar (1999), 72.

57. For more information on Shaw, see the *Oxford Dictionary of National Biography*, http://www.oxforddnb.com/ [accessed 15 April 2011].

58. Thomson (1987), 42.

59. Bosworth (2006), 127. Bosworth suggests, as does Henry de Castries, that Lithgow is indebted to Leo Africanus' *Descrittione dell'Africa* (Venice, 1550; English translation 1600) for his information, 128–9.

60. Maclean (2004), 280. *The Adventures* certainly contains many episodes which stretch the reader's credibility, such as descriptions of fabulous animals (e.g. 83 and 85), and of persons

being burnt alive in hollow brass vessels made in the shape of a lion (183–5).

61. Colley (2002), 95.

62. Colley (2002), 93. Ann Thomson (1987) is even more dismissive, complaining that captivity narratives are "of little use" as historical sources, since "they are more often than not highly romanticised", 6.

63. Colley (2002), 93.

64. Colley (2002), 13.

65. Pratt, Mary Louise (1986), "Fieldwork in common places", in *Writing Culture: the Poetics and Politics of Ethnography,* Clifford, James and Marcus, George E. (eds.) (Berkeley: University of California Press), 38.

66. Pratt (1986), 36.

67. Matar (1999), 78. However, for a sceptical view of captivity narratives as dubiously constructed narratives rather than historical sources, see Vitkus, Daniel (2010), "Barbary Captivity Narratives from Early Modern England: truth claims and the (re)construction of authority", in *La Guerre de Course en Récits (XVIe–XVIIIes: Terrains, Corpus, Séries*, dossier en ligne du Projet CORSO, 2010, URL: http://www.oroc-crlc.parissorbonne. fr/index.php/visiteur/Projet-CORSO/Ressources/La-guerre-de-course-en-recits [accessed 5 May 2011], where Vitkus states on p. 6: "Matar, caught in the grip of Foucault's author function, goes overboard in assuming that the captives are actually the unmediated authors and shapers of these narratives. But the printed captivity narratives published in England during the early modern period show extensive evidence of editorial meddling, ghost-writing, plagiarism, and embellishment. Their content cannot be taken as true tales of agony and endurance, coming straight from the heart. We should resist the notion that the story of an intense, heart-wrenching captivity in Barbary must be an accurate narration of actual events simply because its insistent claim to truth cries out to the reader with a passionate promise of veracity." However the examples Vitkus adduces to prove his contention are Webbe, Okeley and T. S., Pitts's book not being mentioned once in the chapter.

68. Snader, Joe (2000), *Caught Between Worlds: British Captivity Narratives in Fact and Fiction* (Lexington: University Press of Kentucky), 16. Later in the same book, however, Snader claims that "the captivity genre is a highly unstable, scabrous, messy genre, one that permitted wide variations in exploring the dynamic of cultural identity", 123.

69. Snader, Joe (1997), "The Oriental Captivity Narrative and Early English fiction", *Eighteenth-century Fiction,* Vol. 9, no. 3, 275 [article 267–98].

70. Snader (1997), 275.

71. Snader (1997), 276.

72. Matar (1999), 78.

73. Knolles, Richard (1603), *The Generall Historie of the Turkes* … (London: Adam Islip). For more information on Knolles, see the *Oxford Dictionary of National Biography*, http://www.oxforddnb.com/ [accessed 15 April 2011].

74. Matar (1998), 11–12.

75. Maclean (2004), 201.

76. Pitts (1731), 12.

77. Vitkus (2001) was unable to identify the location of "the Quactath", mentioned in John Rawlins's narrative, 100.

78. Pitts (1704), 38.

79. Colley (2002), 15.

80. Pitts (1731), viii.

81. Pitts (1731), 8–9.

82. Pitts (1731), 47–8, 195–6, 221–2; see also the section in the introduction entitled *The Condition of Slavery*. Snader (2000) considers that "whether set in an inquisitorial court, an Islamic state or the American wilderness, a captivity narrative's most precise register of alien tyranny was its detailed documentation of torture", 76.

83. Pitts (1731), 9–10.

84. Pitts (1731), 12–14.

85. Pitts (1731), 28–32, 223–4.

86. Pitts (1731), 30–1.

87. Pitts (1731), 32.

88. Pitts (1731) on pp. 166–8 gives a detailed account of Turkish wrestling, although he concludes his description by remarking contemptuously that none of the wrestlers have any "of our *Devonshire*, or *Cornish* skill", 168.

89. Pitts (1731), 37–9.

90. Fletcher, Giles (1597), *The Policy of the Turkish Empire: the First Booke* (London: John Windet), folio 38 and following. For more information on Fletcher see the *Oxford Dictionary of National Biography*, http://www.oxforddnb.com/ [accessed 15 April 2011].

91. Pitts (1731), 36–7.

92. La Motte, Philémon de (1736), *Several voyages to Barbary: Containing an Historical and Geographical Account of the Country. … With a Journal of the Late Siege and Surrender of Oran. To which are added, the Maps of Barbar … by Captain Henry Boyde,* 2nd edition corrected (London: Olive Payne, Joseph Duke, Samuel Baker), 33. La Motte originally travelled to North Africa in 1720 (see: La Motte, Philémon de (1721), *Voyage pour la Redemption des Captifs, aux Royaumes d'Alger et de Tunis, Fait en 1720* (Paris: Selvestre)), but I have been unable to discover any further information about him.

93. Pitts (1731), 42–3.

94. Pitts (1731), 66.

95. Pitts (1731), 64–5.

96. Pitts (1731), 65.

97. Matar (1999), 115. The whole of Matar's chapter entitled *Sodomy and Conquest* (109–27) is a valuable analysis and trenchant commentary on the English writings of the early modern period on Islam and homosexuality.

98. Murray, Stephen and Roscoe, Will (1997), *Islamic Homosexualities: Culture, History and Literature* (New York: New York University Press), especially chapters 9, 10 and 11.

99. Pitts (1731), 26.

100. *Encyclopaedia of Islam*, 2nd edition, article "Liwāṭ", http://brillonline.nl/ [accessed 14 April 2011].

101. El-Rouayheb, Khaled (2005), *Before Homosexuality in the Islamic World, 1500–1800* (Chicago: University of Chicago Press), 1.

102. Matar (1999), 121 discusses Rycaut's views in detail.

103. El-Rouayheb (2005), 3.

104. El-Rouayheb (2005), 10.

105. El-Rouayheb (2005), 139.

106. Pitts (1731), 187–91 (Tunis); 12–13, 175 (Tlemcen); 169–72 (Oran). As for errors, Pitts confuses two mosques in Tlemcen, 12–13, and mishears and thus mistranslates the name of the pre-Islamic Algerian monument Qubr al-Rūmiyyah, 10.

107. Pitts (1731), 191. Pitts is here referring to the Meskhoutine Spring (Arabic: Ḥammām al-Miskhūṭīn), which is one of the hottest in the world and lies halfway between Bône and Constantine, just off the N20 highway.

108. Pitts (1731), refers to Humphrey Prideaux (1648–1724), on p. 18, Jeremy Collier (1650–1726) and Pierre d'Avity (1573–1635) on pp. 86–7, Jeremy Collier and Jean de Thévenot (1633–1667) on p. 101, and Jean de Thévenot again on pp. 134 and 139. For more information on Prideaux see note 148 in this chapter; for more information on the other scholars mentioned see notes 195 and 196.

109. Pitts (1731), 89.

110. Pitts (1731), 90.

111. Pitts (1731), 181–2.

112. Snader's (2000) academic analysis of Pitts's book also emphasizes modesty and pride: "Especially when we recognize that travel description structures the bulk of Pitts's narrative, the combination of modesty and pride here suggests an anxious attempt to match a difficult, widely accepted and highly valued standard of discourse …" 42.

113. Pitts (1731), vi. On the other hand, Pitts is often proud of his achievements, not just in being the first Englishman to see Mecca, but in lesser matters as well, such as, for example, when Consul Baker praises him for his ability to read and write, 188.

114. Pitts (1731), vi. Bidwell (1976) considered Pitts's tale "was that of an honest Englishman, full of prejudices and distrust of foreigners, but accurate and truthful" (p. 27), a view echoed by Netton, Ian Richard, *Seek Knowledge: Thought and Travel in the House of Islam* (Richmond, Surrey: Curzon Press), p. 18.

115. Toomer, (1996), 12.

116. Toomer (1996), 14, who points out that "the capitulations [privileges accorded to foreigners to reside and trade in Ottoman lands under their own laws] which Venice and Genoa had long possessed with the Byzantine Empire were renewed by the Ottomans after they captured Constantinople in 1453".

117. Irwin, (2007), 101.

118. Quoted by Norris, H. T. (1994), "Edmund Castell (1606), and his *Lexicon Heptaglotton* (1669)", in *The "Arabick" Interest of the Natural Philosophers in Seventeenth-century England,*

Russell, G. A. (ed.) (Leiden: Brill), 78 [chapter 70–87].

119. Irwin (2007), 90.

120. For more information on Bedwell, see the *Oxford Dictionary of National Biography*, http://www.oxforddnb.com/ [accessed 15 April 2011].

121. Bedwell's source, *Muṣābaḥah rūḥāniyyah bayna al-'ālimayn*, was the work of a Catholic propagandist, rather than a Muslim; see Maclean, Gerald and Matar, Nabil (2011a), 33.

122. For more information on Wheelocke, see the *Oxford Dictionary of National Biography*, http://www.oxforddnb.com/ [accessed 15 April 2011].

123. Toomer (1996), 69, quoting the *Hartlib Papers* 33/4/2 (12 Nov. 1647).

124. For more information on du Ryer, see Hamilton, Alastair and Richard, Francis (2004), *André du Ryer and Oriental Studies in Seventeenth-century France* (Oxford: Arcadian).

125. Sergius was said to be a Nestorian monk who taught Muhammad. For more information on Sergius and other Christian legends about Muhammad's life, see Daniel, Norman (1993), *Islam and the West: the Making of an Image,* revised edition (Oxford: Oneworld), chapter 3, "The Life of Muhammad: Polemic Biography."

126. Du Ryer, André (1688), *The Alcoran of Mahomet, Translated out of Arabick into French, by the Sieur Du Ryer, Lord of Malezair, and Resident for the French King, at Alexandria. And Newly Englished, for the Satisfaction of All That Desire to Look into the Turkish Vanities. To Which is Prefixed, the Life of Mahomet, the Prophet of the Turks, and Author of the Alcoran. With A Needful Caveat, or Admonition, for Them Who Desire to Know what Use may be Made of, or if There be Danger in Reading the Alcoran,* (London: Randal Taylor), ii–xvi.

127. For more information on Ross, see the *Oxford Dictionary of National Biography*, http://www.oxforddnb.com/ [accessed 15 April 2011].

128. Du Ryer (1688), first page of Ross's postscript entitled *A Needful Caveat, or Admonition, for Them Who Desire to Know what Use may be Made of, or if There be Danger in Reading the Alcoran.*

129. For more information of Pococke, see the *Oxford Dictionary of National Biography*, http://www.oxforddnb.com/ [accessed 15 April 2011].

130. Irwin (2007), 93.

131. Irwin (2007), 94.

132. Toomer (1996), 303.

133. Irwin (2007), 126.

134. Reeland, Adrian (1712), *Four Treatises Concerning the Doctrine, Discipline and Worship of the Mahometans …,* (London: J. Darby), 82. For more information on Reeland, see Brugman, J. and Schröder, F. (1979), *Arabic Studies in the Netherlands* (Leiden: Brill), 23–5, which spells the author's surname Reland.

135. For more information on Sandys, see the *Oxford Dictionary of National Biography*, http://www.oxforddnb.com/ [accessed 15 April 2011].

136. Fletcher (1597), 1 recto.

137. Fletcher (1597), 2 recto

138. Marsh, Henry (1664), *A New Survey of the Turkish Empire Compleated,* (London: Henry Marsh), 1.

139. Sandys (1673), 41.

140. Sandys (1673), 42.

141. Bosworth (2006), 57.

142. Rycaut (1682), 185.

143. The most acute analysis of Blount as a traveller can be found in Maclean (2004), section three, "Blount's voyage: the Ottoman Levant".

144. Maclean, Gerald (2007b), "Of pirates, slaves and diplomats: Anglo-American writing about the Maghrib in the ages of empire", in *Pirates? The Politics of Plunder, 1550–1650*, Jowitt, Claire (ed.) (Basingstoke: Macmillan), 177 [chapter 169–86].

145. Wilson, Peter Lamborn (1991), *Pirate Utopias: Moorish Corsairs and European Renegadoes* (Brooklyn, NY: Autonomedia), 203.

146. Pitts (1731), xii. Also "bloody impostor", 156.

147. Pitts (1731), 43.

148. Pitts (1731), 18. Humphrey Prideaux published his *The True Nature of Imposture Fully Display'd in the Life of Mahomet, with a Discourse Annexed for the Vindication of Christianity* in London (William Rogers) in 1697, and despite much success during the author's lifetime, it is now considered "contemptible", and "an unskilful combination of Muslim tradition and Christian legend, inspired by a sour animosity towards its subject" (Toomer (1996), 292. For more information on Prideaux see the *Oxford Dictionary of National Biography*, http://www.oxforddnb.com/ [accessed 15 April 2011].

149. Pitts (1731), xi.

150. Probably the fullest 17th-century description in English of Islam as a contemporary religion can be found in Rycaut (1682), who spends around 120 pages (200–320) describing not only the Five Pillars of Islam (*Arkān al-dīn*), but also the four law schools, theological tendencies (e.g., Mu'tazilah, Murji'ah) and Sufi orders (e.g. Bektashis, Naqshabandiyyah). As Colin Heywood says, "in his prejudices, Rycaut was typical of his period … [but] on the sects and dervish orders, Rycaut is detailed, even to points of doctrine and belief", and that he "acknowledges at least Bobovius as one of his sources, together with the previously mentioned 'ulema", in Heywood, C. J. (2002), "Sir Paul Rycaut, a seventeenth-century observer of the Ottoman state: notes for a study", in *Writing Ottoman History: Documents and Interpretations* (Aldershot), Chapter 4, 53. (First published in Shaw, Ezel Kural and Heywood, C. J. (1972) (eds.), *English and Continental Views of the Ottoman Empire, 1500–1800: Papers Read at a Clark Library Seminar, January 24, 1970* (Los Angeles: William Andrews Clark Memorial Library, University of California), 33–59.)

151. Pitts (1731), 45–46, 49–63.

152. Pitts (1731) singles out "the *Hanifees*" when discussing the prayer ritual (57), and it is a reasonable presumption that he belonged to that *madhhab*, since this was the law school to which the majority, if not all, the Turks in Algiers belonged. Pitts discusses briefly the four *madhhab*s on pp. 132–3, saying that "the *Hanifees* seem to be the most *serious, devout* and *deliberate*", and that because the Ḥanbalīs "do not own *Ali* to be one of *Mahomet's* Apostles" they are "look'd on by the rest as *Heretical*".

153. Rycaut (1682), 301–5 cover ablution and prayer in reasonable detail.

154. Fletcher (1597), 12 verso to 16 recto deal very incompletely with Islamic practices.

155. Marsh (1664), 108–11 deal with the pillars of religion and other matters related to Islamic beliefs and practices. For a contemporary assessment of Marsh's views on Islam, see Matar (1999), 155–7.

156. Pitts (1731), 49.

157. Pitts (1731), 50. Rycaut (1668) was equally impressed by Muslim devotion to prayer: "It is much, in my opinion, that infidels should be possessed with that awe and sense of the divine majesty in the time of audience with him" (159). Gunny (1996) shows that some French travellers and scholars of the period also tried to understand the spirit of Muslim prayer, e.g. François Pétis de La Croix (19). For more information on Pétis de La Croix (1653–1713), see Pauphilet (1996), 658–9.

158. Pitts (1731), 71–2.

159. *Encyclopaedia of Islam,* 2nd edition, article "Hell": "Occasionally, Hell's uppermost level was seen as a temporary place of punishment reserved exclusively for Muslim sinners. In later tradition, one finds the notion that Hell has only two levels (*bābān*), an inner one (*al-jawāniyya*), from which nobody ever escapes, and an outer one (*al-barrāniyya*), in which Muslims are kept (Muttaqī, 14: 216). However, this place of temporary punishment never crystallized into a "third place" between Paradise and Hell as in the Christian tradition of purgatory", http://brillonline.nl/ [accessed 14 April 2011].

160. Pitts (1731), 72.

161. Pitts (1731), 72.

162. Pitts (1731), 197–8.

163. Pitts (1731), 198.

164. Pitts (1731), 73, 77.

165. Pitts (1731), 79–83.

166. Pitts (1731), 82.

167. Pitts (1731), 83.

168. Pitts (1731), 73, 198.

169. Pitts (1731), 78–9.

170. Pitts (1731), 55.

171. Pitts (1731), 73–4.

172. Pitts (1731), 74.

173. Pitts (1731), 198–9.

174. Pitts (1731), 43–6, 83, 146–7.

175. Pitts (1731), 44.

176. Pitts (1731), 43.

177. Pitts is quoting directly from p. two of the Preface to André du Ryer's 1688 translation of the Qur'an, entitled *The Alcoran of Mahomet* (London: Randal Taylor).

178. Pitts (1731), 147. Garcia (2011) makes much of the passage which occurs immediately after this, where Pitts remarks that Muslims "give eight or ten *Dollars* for a Copy of the

*Alcoran.* Their Dollar is about two Shillings and three Pence", claiming that "this supplementary note displaces an image of English monetary exchange (shillings and pence) onto a symbol of Muslim devotion (the Qur'an), implying that Muslims rather than Englishmen sell their faith for commercial gain" (94), which seems to be a misreading of Pitts's words. Pitts's often-expressed view was that Muslims venerated the Qur'an above all else and, as he says on pp. 45–6, "they [Muslims] think they cannot prize the *Alcoran* enough, and that there cannot be *too much* Care in preserving it". It is also possible that Pitts, who throughout the third edition made many stylistic changes to tighten the narrative, considered the second reference to the Royal Exchange redundant, and so excised it.

179. Pitts (1731), 12–13, 17–19, 63, 114–15, 215–16.

180. Pitts (1731), 19.

181. Rycaut (1682), 307–8.

182. Richard Eden (1577), *The History of Trauayle in the West and East Indies, and other Countreys Lying Eyther Way, Towardes the Fruitfull and Ryche Moluccaes As Moscouia, Persia, Arabia, Syria, AEgypte, Ethiopia, Guinea, China in Cathayo, and Giapan: With a Discourse of the Northwest Passage. Gathered in Parte, and Done into Englyshe by Richarde Eden. Newly Set in Order, Augmented, and Ffinished by Richarde Willes* (London: Richard Iugge). *The Navigation and Voyages of Lewes Vertomannus,* or Ludovico de Varthema, begins on p. 353, and the section on the Holy Cities can be found on pp. 362–70. A much abridged version was published by Samuel Purchas (1577?–1626), (1625), *Hakluytus Posthumus or Purchas his Pilgrims* (London: Henry Fetherstone). A good, annotated edition of Varthema's travels was published as Vol. 32 of Series One of the Hakluyt Society publications: Ludovico de Varthema (1863), *The Travels of Ludovico di Varthema in Egypt, Syria, Arabia Deserta and Arabia Felix, in Persia, India and Ethiopia, 1503 to 1508;* translated by John Winter Jones, and edited by George Percy Badger (London: Hakluyt Society). The section on Mecca and the pilgrimage occupies pp. 22–54. For more information on Eden and Purchas see the *Oxford Dictionary of National Biography,* http://www.oxforddnb.com/ [accessed 15 April 2011]. What little is known about Varthema's life is summed up in Badger's introduction.

183. Burton (1913), Vol. 2, 337.

184. Burton (1913), Vol. 2, 337.

185. Varthema (1863), 23.

186. Varthema (1863), 46–9. Possibly what Varthema saw was a pair of Arabian Oryx.

187. Varthema (1863), 44.

188. Varthema (1863), 45.

189. Varthema (1863), 41; Burton (1913), Vol. 2, 350, n. 1.

190. Burton (1913), Vol. 2, 358.

191. Pitts (1731), 119; Burton (1913), Vol. 2, 363.

192. Pitts (1731), 139; Burton (1913), Vol. 2, 376, where Burton says of Pitts: "This, I need scarcely say, is speaking as a Christian."

193. For example see p. 133 of William Lithgow (1906), which describes his travels in 1610–1611.

194. Pitts (1731), x–xi, 157.

195. Pitts (1731), 86–7, where he denies d'Avity's claim that Mecca had 6,000 inhabitants (Pitts makes it nearer 1,000). Pitts also states that Medina is ten days' journey from Mecca, as against d'Avity's four days, and makes it clear that d'Avity's descriptions of Muhammad's tomb have confused the decoration and lighting of the tomb in Medina with decoration found in the *Bayt Allāh* in Mecca. Pierre d'Avity (1573–1635) was the author of several geographical works in French, including a *Description Générale de l'Asie* ... (Paris: Denys Bechet et Louis Billaine, 1660), which contained articles on Mecca and Medina. These were collected and republished by Louis Moréri (1643–80) in his immensely popular *Le Grand Dictionnaire Historique, ou le Mélange Curieux de l'Histoire Sacrée et Profane* (numerous editions from 1674 onwards), and eventually translated into English and republished in *The Great Historical, Geographical, Genealogical and Practical Dictionary*, edited by Jeremy Collier (1650–1726), published without pagination in London (Henry Rhodes) in 2 volumes in 1701 (the articles on Mecca and Medina can be found in volume 2). For more information on Collier, see the *Oxford Dictionary of National Biography*, http://www.oxforddnb.com/ [accessed 15 April 2011]. For more information on d'Avity, see *Dictionnaire de Biographie Française*, Vol. 4, (1948), 887; for more information on Louis Moréri, see Pauphilet (1996), 906–7.

196. Pitts (1731), 101. Thévenot, Jean de (1687), *The Travels of Monsieur de Thevenot into the Levant* (London: H. Clark, for H. Faithorne), pt. 1, 129. For more information on Thévenot, see Pauphilet (1996), 1222, and Carré, Jean-Marie (1956*), Voyageurs et Ecrivains Français en Egypte*, deuxième éd. revue et corrigée (Cairo: Institut français d'archéologie orientale), Vol. 1, 24–9.

197. Pitts (1731), 134. Thévenot (1687), pt. 2, 152.

198. Pitts (1731), 139. Thévenot (1687), pt. 2, 153.

199. Pitts (1731), 124.

200. Pitts (1731), 145.

201. Pitts (1731), 125.

202. Pitts (1731), 138.

203. Pitts (1731), 118.

204. *Encyclopaedia of Islam*, 2nd edition, article "Subḥa", http://brillonline.nl/ [accessed 14 April 2011].

205. Pitts (1731), 144–5.

206. Pitts (1731), 144.

207. Garcia (2011) suggests that Pitts was also ambivalent in his attitude to Christianity, and that he had acquired "two fluctuating voices: a High Anglican voice that polices English 'Mahommetans' – anti-Trinitarians who threaten Church and State – and a Non-Conformist-Pelagian voice that valorises Islam as a living faith worthy of Christian respect and toleration", 86.

208. A point also emphasised by Garcia (2011), although he feels that Pitts's dislike of those Islamic practices which Pitts felt equated to Roman Catholic ritual and beliefs, "aligns him with an anti-Islamic mode of comparative religion that, by the eighteenth century, was indistinguishable from Prideaux's high-Anglican polemic" (92). However, while Prideaux had nothing good to say about Islam and was interested much more in belief than ritual, Pitts throughout his book, and especially in chapters six to eight, comments sympathetically

on Muslims' zeal and devotion and the importance to them of a direct relationship with the Word of God.

209. Pitts (1731), xv. Almost the only positive work in English on Islam published in English during Pitts's lifetime was *A Treatise by Bobovius (Sometime First Interpreter to Mahomet IV), Concerning the Liturgy of the Turks, their Pilgrimage to Mecca, their Circumcision, Visitation of the Sick etc., Translated from the Latin*, which was published in London in 1712 as part three of Adrian Reeland's *Four Treatises,* and translated by Thomas Hyde (1636–1703), Professor of Arabic at Oxford University, who added various anti-Islamic notes (for more information on Hyde, see the *Oxford Dictionary of National Biography*, http://www.oxforddnb.com/ [accessed 15 April 2011]). Wojciech Bobowski was born in 1610 probably in the Polish city of Lwow (Lwow is now in the Ukraine and called Lviv), was captured by Crimean Tatars and converted to Islam where he took the name of 'Ali Ufqī. He became one of the most important dragomans or interpreters of his time, and translated the Bible into Turkish. He died in 1675 and is often known by his Latin name of Albertus Bobovius. The section on the pilgrimage in Bobovius' book agrees almost exactly with Pitts's account, and was almost certainly written by someone who had performed the pilgrimage himself. Another pro-Islamic work written during Pitts's lifetime (but not published till 1911) was *An Account of the Rise and Progress of Mahometanism, and a Vindication of Him and His Religion from the Calumnies of the Christians* by Henry Stubbe (1632–76), in which Stubbe tried to harmonize the theology of Islam with Unitarian Christianity. For more information on Stubbe, see Holt, P. M. (1972), *A Seventeenth-century Defender of Islam: Henry Stubbe (1632–76) and His Book* (London: Dr Williams Trust); and Birchwood, Matthew (2007), "Vindicating The Prophet: Universal Monarchy and Henry Stubbe's Biography of Mohammed", *Prose Studies,* Vol. 29, No. 1, 59–72, which argues that Stubbe sought political and religious reform in England by using Islam as a model. Garcia (2011) sees Stubbe as being the first to promulgate a sympathetic approach to Islam in which "the history of monotheism [was retold] from the perspective of the Prophet Muhammad, hailed as a wise republican legislator", and as someone who "read the successful propagation of the Prophet's teachings as the recuperation of a pristine Unitarian monotheism (the unity of God) rather than marking a retrograde hybrid of Christianity and Judaism", 87.

210. Pitts (1704), folio A2

211. Pitts (1704), Preface [4]

212. Pitts (1704), Preface [1]

213. Pitts (1731), xiv–xv.

214. The 1738 edition differs from the 1731 edition mainly in minor matters of orthography, but there are some additional passages, such as on p. 36 (of the 1738 edition), where a short digression on milling and mill-stones has been introduced; p. 108 (of the 1738 edition), where Pitts comments on the taste and colour of the meat of the water buffaloes; on pp. 126, 127 and 128 (of the 1738 edition), where Pitts adds notes about the silver door of the *Bayt Allāh,* that his Patroon was given some holy water while visiting Mecca, and that in the corner of the *Bayt Allāh* an iron or brass chain can be found; pp. 187 and 190 (of the 1738 edition), where Pitts adds some minor details about his voyage to and residence in Tunis; on p. 211 (of the 1738 edition), where Pitts complains of his Patroon's believing in a "Marabbot's" prophecy; on p. 247 (of the 1738 edition) where Pitts reflects on the Armenian passenger who accompanied him to Leghorn/Livorno; and finally on p. 251 (of the 1738

edition) where Pitts describes how he was able to find lodgings in Augsburg without a passport. The fact that substantive, albeit limited, changes were made to the 1738 edition lends credence to the contention that Joseph Pitts was still alive at this date.

215. Radford (1920), 15; Foster (1949), xiii. The *British Library Integrated Catalogue* records a copy at shelfmark 10076.f.31.

216. For more information on Maundrell, see the *Oxford Dictionary of National Biography*, http://www.oxforddnb.com/ [accessed 15 April 2011].

217. Vitkus (2001).

218. Matar (2001).

219. Burton (1855–1856).

220. Foster (1949).

221. Pitts (1731), xv.

222. Pitts (1731), xvi.

223. Pitts (1731), vii.

224. Pitts (1731), xv.

225. Pitts (1731), xv–xvi.

226. Neither version is acceptable today and the preferred form is Muslims (i.e. those who submit to the Will of God). The form Moslem or Muslim was recorded in English as early as 1615 (see *Oxford English Dictionary Online*, http://www.oed.com/ [accessed 14 April 2011]), but even as late as 1953, Oxford University Press was able to issue Sir Hamilton Gibb's primer on Islam under the title of: *Mohammedanism: an Historical Survey*.

227. For example, the paragraph "And the Reason they give is, because they are not sure of living so long as to make it up again in *Fasting*, Nay, they are yet more strict, if *Ramadan* happens to be during their *Pilgrimage* to *Mecca*; for if any do *then* break their *Fast* unseasonably, they must sacrifice a Sheep for such a Default", can be found on p. 57 of the 1704 edition where, because it is out of place, it has to be introduced by the phrase "As I said before", while it fits more naturally on p. 82 of the 1731 edition (which would have been p. 56 of the 1704 edition).

228. Pitts (1704), 28.

229. Pitts (1731), 39. Loualich (2010) states that "an examination of the Ottoman records – especially the Shari'a court records of Algiers (*Maḥakim Shar'iyya*) and that of the Registers of the public treasury (*Bayt al-Māl*) reveals the almost total absence of polygamy …", 75.

230. Pitts (1704), 28, where the passage describing the wedding night is omitted from the 1731 edition, as is Sir Roger L'Estrange's fable about the inconsolable widow on p. 29 of the 1704 edition. Garcia (2011) points out the omission in the 1731 edition of the "parenthetical note comparing the Grand Mosque [of Mecca] to the [Royal] Exchange [in London]", 94, which occurs on p. 101 of the 1704 edition, and suggests that by virtue of the equation of the two "icons of international cosmopolitanism", "London's financial centre is transposed onto that of the Ka'aba …", 93. However, it is unlikely that Pitts's remarks (or their subsequent omission) can bear the weight of interpretation proposed by Garcia, and they probably merely represent Pitts's attempt to enable his readers to visualize for themselves what the Great Mosque actually looked like.

231. Pitts (1731), 22–4.

232. Pitts (1731), 40–1.

233. Pitts (1731), 64.

234. Pitts (1731), 65–6.

235. Pitts (1731), 69–70.

236. Pitts (1731), 74.

237. Pitts (1731), 91.

238. Pitts (1731), 98.

239. Pitts (1731), 109.

240. Pitts (1731), 131.

241. Pitts (1731), 150, 151, 152.

242. Pitts (1731), 158.

243. Pitts (1731), 241–2.

244. Pitts (1731), 50.

245. Pitts (1731), 68–9.

246. Pitts (1731), 88–9.

247. Pitts (1731), 90–1.

248. Pitts (1731), 95.

249. Pitts (1731), 171. A *bombagee* (modern Turkish, *bombacı*) is in Pitts's own words "one who assists in Firing the Bombs" during a siege or an assault on a fort.

250. Pitts (1731), 184–5.

251. Pitts (1731), 208–9.

252. Pitts (1731) remarks after the encounter, "I thought it a very melancholy Sight, in the Morning, to see so many Slaves and *Turks* kill'd and wounded", 212.

253. Pitts (1731), 249.

254. Pitts (1731), 257. William Fawkener (1642–1716) was a prosperous merchant who became one of the leading members of the Levant Company. See the entry on his son, Sir Everard Fawkener, in the *Oxford Dictionary of National Biography,* http://www.oxforddnb. com/ [accessed 15 April 2011].

255. Pitts (1731), 258–9.

256. Pitts (1731), 242–3.

257. Pitts (1731), xvii–xviii.

258. Pitts (1731), 236–7.

259. Pitts (1731), 226.

260. Pitts (1731), 243.

261. Pitts (1731). Pitts admits that he had lost his sense of the Christian calendar ("truly I had then forgot the Month and the Year, because the *Turks* reckon after a different manner from us", 205), which may be why there are so few dates in his book.

262. Pitts (1731), 226.

263. Garcia (2011), 97. Garcia also argues (p. 95) that the change in dedication from William Raye, the British Consul at Smyrna, in the first edition to Peter King, Lord Chancellor of Great Britain in the third edition, is theologically inspired, but it is also possible that the reason for the change is more mundane, namely that William Raye had probably died by 1731 (he ceased to be consul in 1703 after being in the post for 25 years) and that in the meantime Peter King had become the most prominent Exonian of his day, and a man whose patronage Pitts wished to secure.

264. Garcia (2011), 97–8.

265. Pitts (1731), 1.

### CONCLUSION

1. Pitts (1731), xvii.

2. Pitts (1731), vi; Pitts (1704), second page of Preface.

3. Colley (2002), 124–5.

4. Pitts (1731), xii; Pitts (1704), pp. 5–6 of the Preface with slightly different wording.

5. Pitts (1731), xiv; this sentence is omitted from the 1704 edition, which, on the other hand, on the first page of the Preface, claims that the book has been published so that Pitts may "make some manner (at least) of *Restitution* and Reparation for my past *Defection*".

6. Colley (2002), 124.

7. Pitts (1731), 21, 32–3.

8. Pitts (1731), 34, 35.

9. Pitts (1731), 98–9.

10. Pitts (1731), 107–8.

11. Pitts (1731), 145.

12. Al-Azmeh (1986), 2.

13. Matar (2001), 37.

14. Pitts (1731), xvii.

15. It is clear from the colloquial and grammatically complex phrases found in his book that Pitts had a good grasp of Turkish, although his transcriptions indicate that he may have spoken the language with a distinctly provincial accent, and are sometimes difficult to decipher. On the other hand, Pitts admitted his inability to transcribe accurately the classical Arabic used in Islamic ritual in the preface to the third edition, "And moreover, I can't pretend to a Perfection in the *Arabick* Language ...", vii, and this would seem to confirm that Pitts was much more comfortable using Turkish than Arabic.

16. Maclean and Matar (2011a), 39.

17. Colley (2002), 84.

18. Matar (2001), 39.

19. Vitkus (2001), 219.

# BIBLIOGRAPHY

# BIBLIOGRAPHY

## COMPLETE EDITIONS OF PITTS'S BOOK

PITTS, Joseph (1704), *A True and Faithful Account of the Religion and Manners of the Mohammetans. In which is a particular Relation of their Pilgrimage to Mecca, The Place of Mohammet's Birth; And a Description of Medina, and of his Tomb there. As likewise of Algier, and the Country adjacent: And of Alexandria, Grand-Cairo, &c. With an Account of the Author's being taken Captive, the Turks Cruelty to him, and of his Escape. In which are many things never Publish'd by any Historian before.* (Exon [Exeter]: printed by S. Farley for Philip Bishop and Edward Score.) 204 pages. The first edition.

PITTS, Joseph (1717), *A True and Faithful Account of the Religion & Manners of the Mohammetans. In which is a particular Relation of their Pilgrimage to Mecca, The Place of Mohammet's Birth; And a Description of Medina, and of his Tomb there. As likewise of Algier, and the Country adjacent: And of Alexandria, Grand-Cairo, &c. With an Account of the Author's being taken Captive, the Turks Cruelty to him, and of his Escape. In which are many things never Publish'd by any Historian before.* The Second Edition. (Exon [Exeter]: printed by S. Farley for Philip Bishop and Edward Score.) [10], 204 pages. The second edition, not authorized by Pitts.

PITTS, Joseph (1719), *A True and Faithful Account of the Religion & Manners of the Mahometans. In which is a particular Relation of their Pilgrimage to Mecca, The Place of Mahomet's Birth; And a Description of Medina, and of his Tomb there: As likewise of Algier and the Country adjacent; and of Alexandria, Grand-Cairo, &c. With an Account of the Author's being taken Captive, the Turks Cruelty to him and of his Escape. In which are many Things never publish'd by any Historian before.* The Second Edition. (London: printed for W. Taylor.) [10], 204 pages. A further impression of the second edition, identical to the 1717 version, and also not authorized by Pitts.

PITTS, Joseph (1731), *A Faithful Account of the Religion and Manners of the Mahometans. In which is a particular Relation of their Pilgrimage to Mecca, the Place of Mahomet's Birth; and a Description of Medina, and of his Tomb there: As likewise of Algier, and the*

*Country adjacent; and of Alexandria, Grand Cairo, &c. With an Account of the Author's being taken Captive; the Turks Cruelty to him; and of his Escape. In which are many Things never publish'd by any Historian before.* The Third Edition, Corrected, with Additions. To this Edition is added a Map of Mecca, and a Cut of the Gestures of the Mahometans in their Worship. (London: printed for J. Osborn and T. Longman, and R. Hett.) xxiv, 260 pages [excluding the publishers' list of books at the end of the volume]. The third edition, authorized by Pitts, with substantial alterations and addition to the first edition.

PITTS, Joseph (1738), *A Faithful Account of the Religion and Manners of the Mahometans. In which is a particular Relation of their Pilgrimage to Mecca, the Place of Mahomet's Birth; and a Description of Medina, and of his Tomb there: As likewise of Algier, and the Country adjacent; and of Alexandria, Grand Cairo, &c. With an Account of the Author's being taken Captive; the Turks Cruelty to him; and of his Escape. In which are many Things never publish'd by any Historian before.* The Fourth Edition, Corrected, with Additions. To this edition is added a map of Mecca, and a Cut of the Gestures of the Mahometans in their Worship. (London: printed for T. Longman and R. Hett.) xxiv, 259 pages. Republished in 1971, Farnborough: Gregg International. Includes some minor additions to the third edition as well as a few stylistic changes. Almost certainly authorized by Pitts.

MAUNDRELL, Henry (1810), *A Journey from Aleppo to Jerusalem at Easter 1697, Also a Journal from Grand Cairo and Back Again. To Which is Added a Faithful Account of the Religion and Manners of the Mahometans* By Joseph Pitts. (London: Richard Edwards.) 520 pages. Pitts's account is on pp. 281–520. Apparently a reprint of the fourth edition of 1738 with modernized spelling. [Not seen by the author.]

VITKUS, Daniel J. (2001) (ed.), *Piracy, Slavery and Redemption: Barbary Captivity Narratives from Early Modern England.* (New York: Columbia University Press.) xvi, 376 pages. Pitts's account is on pp. 218–340. An annotated reprint of the first edition of 1704 with modernized spelling.

### SIGNIFICANT PARTIAL EDITIONS AND TRANSLATIONS OF PITTS'S BOOK

BURTON, Sir Richard (1893; first published 1855–56), *Personal Narrative of a Pilgrimage to Al-Madinah and Meccah;* edited by his wife, Isabel Burton. Memorial Edition, in two volumes. (London: Tylston and Edwards, 1893.) Appendix V, pp. 358–89, contains a reprint of Pitts's narrative of his travels in Arabia while on the pilgrimage, accompanied by a short introduction and a typically erudite topographical and historical commentary. Burton originally published this account of his pilgrimage in three volumes, 1855–56. Following the Memorial Edition of 1893, subsequent reprints appeared, notably in 1898 and 1913 with an introduction by Stanley Lane-Poole (London: G. Bell, 2 vols.)

BARING-GOULD, Sabine (1908), *Devonshire Characters and Strange Events* (London: Bodley Head). The extract from Pitts's account on pp. 152–69 is a recapitulation in Pitts's own words of his time in Algiers and his escape through Europe, stripped of all his observations on Islam and his journey to Mecca and Medina.

FOSTER, Sir William (1949) (ed.), *The Red Sea and Adjacent Countries at the Close of the Seventeenth Century, as Described by Joseph Pitts, William Daniel and Charles Jacques Poncet* (London: Hakluyt Society). The extract from Pitts's account is on pp. 1-49, and covers his journey from Algiers to Mecca and back with good geographical, historical and linguistic notes.

FREETH, Zahra and Winstone, H.V. F. (1978), *Explorers of Arabia: from the Renaissance to the End of the Victorian Era* (London: Allen & Unwin). A retelling of Pitts's story, combined with extracts from the third edition of 1731, is on pp. 41–60.

VOLKOFF, Oleg V. (1981) (ed.), *Voyages en Egypte pendant les années 1678–1701 [par] E. Veryard, J. Pitts, J. Ovington, R. Huntingdon, Ch.-J. Poncet, W. Daniel; récits traduits de l'anglais par Christine Favard-Meeks [et al.]* (Cairo: Institut français d'archéologie orientale). A translation into French with good notes of Pitts's description of Egypt is on pp. 111–50.

### REFERENCE WORKS

BAYERLE, Gustav (1997), *Pashas, Begs, and Effendis: a Historical Dictionary of Titles and Terms in the Ottoman Empire* (Istanbul: Isis Press)

*DICTIONNAIRE DE BIOGRAPHIE FRANÇAISE*, (1933–) (Paris: Letouzet et Ané)

DOZY, R. P. A. (1967), *Supplément aux Dictionnaires Arabes.* 3ème edition. 2 vols. (Leiden: Brill)

*ENCYCLOPAEDIA OF ISLAM ONLINE*, 2nd edition. URL: http://brillonline.nl/

*ENCYCLOPAEDIA OF THE QURAN ONLINE*, URL: http://brillonline.nl/

KAHANE, Henry, KAHANE, Renée, and TIETZE, Andreas (1958), *The Lingua Franca of the Levant: Turkish Nautical Terms of Italian and Greek Origin* (Urbana: University of Illinois Press)

*OXFORD DICTIONARY OF NATIONAL BIOGRAPHY ONLINE.* URL: http://www.oxforddnb.com/

*OXFORD ENGLISH DICTIONARY ONLINE*, URL: http://www.oed.com/

PAUPHILET, Albert, PICHARD, Louis, and BARROUX, Robert (1996), *Dictionnaire des Lettres Françaises: le XVIIe Siècle,* nouvelle édition (Paris: Fayard)

REDHOUSE, J.W. (1968), *Redhouse yeni Türkçe–Ingilizce sözlük* (*New Redhouse Turkish–English dictionary*) (Istanbul: Ahmet Sait Matbaasi)

WEHR, Hans (1979), *A Dictionary of Modern Written Arabic: Arabic–English*, 4th edition (Wiesbaden: Harrassowitz)

## PRIMARY SOURCES

ADAMS, Robert (1816), *The Narrative of Robert Adams, a Sailor who was Wrecked on the Western Coast of Africa, in the Year 1810, was Detained Three Years in Slavery by the Arabs of the Great Desert, and Resided Several Months in the City of Tombuctoo* (London: J. Murray)

—— (2005), *The Narrative of Robert Adams, a Barbary Captive*, ed. Charles Hansford Adams, (Cambridge: Cambridge University Press)

ANON. (1682), *A List of Ships Taken since July, 1677 from his Majesties Subjects, by the Corsairs of Algier. With their Names, Masters Names, and Places to Which They Belong'd, and Time of Taking: with a Modest Estimate of the Loss* (London: Richard Janeway)

ANON. (1691) *An Exact and faithful account of the late bloody fight between Captain Hastings, commander of the Saphire, Captain Showel, commander of the James Galley, and Jonas Raile, captain of the Half-Moon of Algier* (London: John Gain)

BARKER, Andrew (1609), *A True and Certaine Report of the Beginning, Proceedings, Ouerthrowes, and now Present Estate of Captaine Ward and Danseker, the Two Late Famous Pirates* (London: William Hall)

BEDWELL, William (1615), *Mohammedis Imposturae: that is, Discovery of the Manifold Forgeries, Falsehoods and Horrible Impieties of the Blasphemous Seducer Mohammed* (London: Richard Field)

BLOUNT, Henry (1638), *A Voyage into the Levant: a Brief Relation of a Journey Lately Performed by Mr. Henry Blunt Gentleman, from England by the Way of Venice, into Dalmatia, Sclavonia, Bosnia, Hungary, Macedonia, Thessaly, Thrace, Rhodes and Egypt, unto Gran Cairo: with Particular Observations concerning the Moderne Condition of the Turks, and other People under that Empire* (London: John Legat)

BOBOVIUS, later Ali Ufki (1712), *A Treatise by Bobovius (Sometime First Interpreter to Mahomet IV), Concerning the Liturgy of the Turks, their Pilgrimage to Mecca, their Circumcision, Visitation of the Sick etc., Translated from the Latin.* Published as Part Three of Reeland, Adrian (1712), *Four Treatises Concerning the Doctrine, Discipline and Worship of the Mahometans* ... (London: J. Darby)

BROOKS, Francis (1693), *Barbarian Cruelty Being a True History of the Distressed Condition of the Christian Captives under the Tyranny of Mully Ishmael, Emperor of Morocco, and King of Fez and Macqueness in Barbary* ... (London: J. Salusbury and H. Newman)

CASON, Edmond (1647), *A Relation of the Whole Proceedings Concerning the Redemption of the Captives in Argier and Tunis. With the Translates and Copies of the Letters from the Bashaw, Duana, Mufty, Caddee, and Shoudes, unto Both the Honourable Houses of Parliament* … (London: Laurence Blaikelock)

COXERE, Edward (1945), *Adventures by Sea of Edward Coxere*, ed. E. H. W. Meyerstein (Oxford: Clarendon Press)

DAN, Pierre (1637, 1649), *Histoire de Barbarie, et de ses Corsaires, des royaumes, et des villes d'Alger, de Tunis, de Salé, et de Tripoly. Divisée en six livres, où il est traité de leur gouvernment, de leurs moeurs, de leurs cruautez, de leurs brigandages, de leurs sortilèges …. Ensemble des grandes misères et des cruels tourmens qu'endurent les chrestiens captifs parmy ces infidèles.* (Paris: Pierre Rocolet)

—— (1684), *Historie van Barbaryen en des zelfs Zee-Roovers, Behelzende een beschryving van den Koningrijken en Steden Algiers, Tunis, Salé, en Tripoli; …* (Amsterdam: Jan ten Hoorn)

D'ARANDA, Emanuel (1657) *Relation de la Captivité du S: Où Sont Descriptés les Misères, les Ruses et les Finesses des Esclaves et des Corsaires d'Alger: Ensemble les Conquestes de Barberousse dans l'Afrique etc.* (Paris: no pub.)

—— (1666), *The History of Algiers and its Slavery with Many Remarkable Particularities of Africa*, tr. John Davies (London: John Starkey)

—— (1997), *Les Captifs d'Alger*, ed. with intro. Latifa Z'Rari (Paris: Jean Paul Rocher)

D'ARVIEUX, Laurent (1735), *Mémoires du Chevalier d'Arvieux, Envoyé Extraordinaire du Roy à la Porte, Consul d'Alep, d'Alger, de Tripoli et Autres Echelles du Levant, Contenant ses Voyages à Constantinople, dans l'Asie, la Syrie, la Palestine, l'Egypte et la Barbarie* … (Paris: no pub.)

D'AVITY, Pierre (1660), *Description Générale de l'Asie* … (Paris: Denys Bechet et Louis Billaine)

DEFOE, Daniel (1971), *A Tour Through the Whole Island of Great Britain*, abridged and ed. Pat Rogers (Harmondsworth, Mx.: Penguin)

DU RYER, André (1688), *The Alcoran of Mahomet, Translated out of Arabick into French, by the Sieur Du Ryer, Lord of Malezair, and Resident for the French King, at Alexandria. And Newly Englished, for the Satisfaction of All That Desire to Look into the Turkish Vanities. To Which is Prefixed, the Life of Mahomet, the Prophet of the Turks, and Author of the Alcoran. With A Needful Caveat, or Admonition, for Them Who Desire to Know what Use may be Made of, or if There be Danger in Reading the Alcoran* (London: Randal Taylor)

EDEN, Richard (1577), *The History of Trauayle in the West and East Indies, and other Countreys Lying Eyther Way, Towardes the Fruitfull and Ryche Moluccaes As Moscouia,*

*Persia, Arabia, Syria, AEgypte, Ethiopia, Guinea, China in Cathayo, and Giapan: With a Discourse of the Northwest Passage. Gathered in Parte, and Done into Englyshe by Richarde Eden. Newly Set in Order, Augmented, and Ffinished by Richarde Willes* (London: Richard Iugge)

ELLIOT, Adam (1682), *A Modest Vindication of Titus Oates, the Salamanca-Doctor from Perjury, or, An Essay to Demonstrate Him only Forsworn in Several Instances* (London: Joseph Hindmarsh)

FIENNES, Celia (1954), *The Journeys of Celia Fiennes,* ed. with intro. Christopher Morris. 2nd edition (London: Cresset Press)

FLETCHER, Giles (1597), *The Policy of the Turkish Empire: the First Booke* (London: John Windet)

FOX, John (1589), "The worthie enterprise of John Foxe, in delivering 266 Christians out of the captivitie of the Turkes at Alexandria", in Hakluyt, Richard, *The Principall Navigations, Voiages, and Discoveries of the English Nation Made by Sea or Over-land to the Most Remote and Farthest Distant Quarters of the Earth at any Time within the Compass of these 1600 Yeeres* (London: G. Bishop and R. Newberie), 131–56

HAËDO, Diego de (1612), *Topografía e historia general de Argel* ... (Valladolid: Diego Fernandez de Cordoua y Ouiedo). Tr. into French with introduction by Jocelyne Dakhlia (1998): *Topographie et histoire générale d'Alger* (Paris; Bouchene)

—— (1881), *Histoires des Rois d'Alger,* tr. by Henri de Grammont, (Algiers: Jourdan). This translation of the first part of Haëdo's *Topografía* was originally published in parts in the *Revue Africaine,* 1880–81. Reprinted in 2002 (Paris: Bouchene)

HAKLUYT, Richard (1589), *The Principall Nauigations, Voiages and Discoueries of the English Nation Made by Sea or Ouer Land, to the Most Remote and Farthest Distant Quarters of the Earth at any Time within the Compasse of These 1500 Yeeres: Deuided into Three Seuerall Parts, According to the Positions of the Regions Wherunto They Were Directed. ... Whereunto is Added the Last Most Renowned English Nauigation, Round About the Whole Globe of the Earth* (London: George Bishop and Ralph Newberie)

HASLETON, Richard (1595), *Strange and Wonderfull Things Happened to Richard Hasleton, born at Braintree in Essex, in His Ten Yeares Travailes in Many Forraine Countries* (London: William Barley). Republished in 1902 in Vol. 2, pp. 151–80, of Beazley, C. Raymond (1902) (ed.), *Voyages and Travels, Mainly During the 16th and 17th Centuries,* 2 vols. (London: Constable)

JAMES I, King of England (1603), *A Proclamation to Represse All Piracies and Depredations Vpon the Sea* (London: R. Barker)

JANSSON, Maija, and BIDWELL, William B. (1987) (eds.), *Proceedings in Parliament 1625,* (New Haven: Yale University Press)

KELLETT, Edward (1628), *A Returne from Argier: a Sermon Preached at Minhead in the County of Somerset the 16. of March, 1627 at the Re-admission of a Relapsed Christian into our Church* (London: John Parker)

KNIGHT, Francis (1640), *A Relation of Seaven Yeares Slaverie under the Turkes of Argeire, Suffered by an English Captive Merchant ...* (London: T. Cotes)

KNOLLES, Richard (1603), *The Generall Historie of the Turkes ...* (London: Adam Islip)

LA MOTTE, Philémon de (1721), *Voyage pour la Redemption des Captifs, aux Royaumes d'Alger et de Tunis, Fait en 1720* (Paris: Selvestre)

—— (1736), *Several voyages to Barbary: Containing an Historical and Geographical Account of the Country. ... With a Journal of the Late Siege and Surrender of Oran. To which are added, the Maps of Barbary, ... by Captain Henry Boyde,* 2nd edition corrected (London: Olive Payne, Joseph Duke, Samuel Baker)

LAUD, William (1853), "A form of penance and reconciliation of a renegade or apostate from the Christian Church to Turkism" [Also known as *The Laudian Rite for Returned Renegades*], in Vol. 5, Part 2, pp. 372–6 of *The works of the Most Reverend Father in God, William Laud* (1847–1860), 9 vols. (Oxford: J. H. Parker)

LAUGIER DE TASSY (1725), *Histoire du Royaume d'Alger: avec l'Etat Présent de Son Gouvernement, de Ses Forces de Terre & de Mer, de Ses Revenus, Police, Justice, Politique & Commerce* (Amsterdam: Henri du Sauzet)

—— (1750), *A Compleat History of the Piratical States of Barbary, viz. Algiers, Tunis, Tripoli and Morocco: Containing the Origin, Revolutions, and Present State of These Kingdoms, Their Forces, Revenues, Policy, and Commerce,* tr. Joseph Morgan (London: R. Griffiths)

LITHGOW, William (1632), *The totall discourse of the rare aduentures, and painefull peregrinations of long nineteene yeares trauayles, from Scotland to the most famous kingdomes in Europe, Asia, and Affrica ...* (London: Nicholas Oakes)

—— (1906), *The Totall Discourse of the Rare Adventures and Painfull Peregrinations of Long Nineteen Yeares Travayles from Scotland to the Most Famous Kingdoms in Europe, Asia and Africa* (Glasgow: James MacLehose)

MAGALOTTI, Lorenzo (1967), "The travels of Cosmo III, Grand Duke of Tuscany, through England", in *Early Tours in Devon and Cornwall,* Chope, R. Pearse (ed.) (Newton Abbot: David & Charles)

MANWAYRING, Sir Henry (1920), *The Life and Works of Sir Henry Mainwaring,* ed. G. E Manwaring , 2 vols. (London: Navy Records Society)

MARSH, Henry (1664), *A New Survey of the Turkish Empire Compleated* (London: Henry Marsh)

MONSON, Sir William (1902–14), *The Naval Tracts*, ed. M. Oppenheim, 5 vols. (London: Navy Records Society)

MORÉRI, Louis (1674), *Le Grand Dictionnaire Historique, ou le Mélange Curieux de l'Histoire Sacrée et Profane* (Lyon: J. Girin et B. Rivière)

—— (1701), *The great historical, geographical, genealogical and poetical dictionary: being a curious miscellany of sacred and prophane history,* 2nd ed. revised, corrected and enlarged by Jeremy Collier, 2 vols. (London: Henry Rhodes)

MORGAN, Joseph (1728), *A Complete History of Algiers: to which is Prefixed, an Epitome of the General History of Barbary, from the Earliest Times* … (London: J. Bettenham). Reprinted in 1970 (Westport, Conn.: Negro Universities Press)

OKELEY, William (1676), *Eben-ezer, or, A Small Monument of Great Mercy Appearing in the Miraculous Deliverance of William Okeley, William Adams, John Anthony, John Jephs, John — Carpenter from the Miserable Slavery of Algiers* … (London: Nat. Ponder)

PELLOW, Thomas (1890), *The Adventures of Thomas Pellow of Penryn, Mariner: Three and Twenty Years Captivity among the Moors,* ed. Robert Brown (London: Fisher Unwin)

—— (1983), *La Relation de Thomas Pellow: une Relation du Maroc au 18ème Siècle,* tr. Magali Morsy (Paris: Editions recherche sur les civilisations)

PHELPS, Thomas (1685), *A True Account of the Captivity of Thomas Phelps at Machaness in Barbary* … (London: H. Hills)

PRIDEAUX, Humphrey (1697), *The True Nature of Imposture Fully Display'd in the Life of Mahomet, with a Discourse Annexed for the Vindication of Christianity* (London: William Rogers)

PURCHAS, Samuel (1625), *Hakluytus Posthumus or Purchas his Pilgrims* (London: Henry Fetherstone)

RABADAN, Muhammad (1723–25), *Mahometism Fully Explained: Containing Many Surprizing Passages, not to be found in any other author* … *Written in Spanish and Arabick, in the year 1603, for the instruction of the Moriscoes in Spain; By Mahomet Rabadan, an Arragonian Moor, Translated from the Original Manuscript, and Illustrated with Explanatory Notes by Mr.* [Joseph] *Morgan,* 2 vols. (London: W. Mears)

RAWLINS, John (1622), *The Famous and Wonderfull Recoverie of a Ship of Bristoll, called the Exchange, from the Turkish Pirates of Argier* … (London: Nathaniel Butter)

REELAND, Adrian (1712), *Four Treatises Concerning the Doctrine, Discipline and Worship of the Mahometans* … (London: J. Darby)

—— (1721), *La Religion des Mahometans, Exposée par Leurs Propres Docteurs, avec des Eclaircissements sur les Opinions qu'on leur a Faussement Attribuées, et Augmentée d'une Confession de Foi Mahometane qui n'avait point encore Paru* (The Hague: I. Vaillant). Republished in 2009 (Breinigsville, PA: Kessinger)

RYCAUT, Paul (1682), *The History of the Present State of the Ottoman Empire ...* (London: T. N.)

SANDYS, George (1673), *Sandys Travels Containing an History of the Original and Present State of the Turkish Empire, Their Laws, Government, Policy, Military Force, Courts of Justice, and Commerce, the Mahometan Religion and Ceremonies, a Description of Constantinople, the Grand Signior's Seraglio, and his Manner of Living ...* (London: John Williams)

SHAW, Thomas (1738), *Travels and Observations Relating to Several Parts of Barbary and the Levant* (Oxford: printed at the Theatre)

SPRATT, Devereux (1865) "The capture of a Protestant divine, by an Algerine corsair, in the seventeenth century", published as an appendix to Vol. 1 of Spratt, T. A. B, *Travels and Researches in Crete,* 2 vols. (London: J. Van Voorst)

STUBBE, Henry (1911), *An Account of the Rise and Progress of Mahometanism, and a Vindication of Him and His Religion from the Calumnies of the Christians* (London: Luzac)

T. S. (1670), *The Adventures of Mr. T. S., an English Merchant taken Prisoner by the Turks of Argiers and Carried into the Inland Countries of Africa, with a Description of the Kingdom of Argiers ...* (London: Moses Pitt)

THÉVENOT, Jean de (1664–84), *Relation d'un voyage fait au Levant: dans laquelle il est curieusement traité des estats sujets au Grand Seigneur ...; et des singularitez particulières de l'Archipel, Constantinople, Terre-Sainte, Égypte, ... la Meque; et de plusieurs autres lieux de l'Asie & de l'Affrique,* 3 vols. (Paris: Thomas Ioly)

—— (1687), *The Travels of Monsieur de Thevenot into the Levant* (London: H. Clark for H. Faithorne)

VARTHEMA, Ludovico de (1863), *The Travels of Ludovico di Varthema in Egypt, Syria, Arabia Deserta and Arabia Felix, in Persia, India and Ethiopia, 1503 to 1508,* tr. John Winter Jones, ed. George Percy Badger (London: Hakluyt Society)

VITKUS, Daniel J. (2001) (ed.), *Piracy, Slavery and Redemption: Barbary Captivity Narratives from Early Modern England* (New York: Columbia University Press). [Contains the annotated texts with modernized spelling of Fox, Hasleton, Rawlins, Okeley, Phelps, Pitts (1704 edition) and the *Laudian Rite for Returned Renegades.*]

VRIES, S. de (1684), *Handelingen en Geschiedenissen Voorgevallen tusschen den Staet der Vereenighde Nederlanden. En dien van de Zee-Roovers in Barbaryen; Als der Rijcken en Steeden van Algiers, Tunis, Salee en Tripoli; van't Jaer Christi 1590 tot op't Jaer 1684. ...* (Amsterdam: Jan ten Hoorn)

WEBBE, Edward (1600), *The Rare and Most Wonderful Things which Edward Webbe, an Englishman Borne, Hath Seene …* (London: Ralph Blower)


SECONDARY SOURCES

ABUN-NASR, Jamil M. (1987), *A History of the Maghrib in the Islamic Period* (Cambridge: Cambridge University Press)

AL-AZMEH, Aziz (1986), *Islamic Studies and the European Imagination* (Exeter: University of Exeter, Department of Arabic and Islamic Studies)

AUCHTERLONIE, Paul (forthcoming), "Joseph Pitts: Exeter's first orientalist?", *Oriente Moderno*

BARNBY, Henry (1969), "The sack of Baltimore", *Journal of the Cork Historical and Archaeological Society,* Vol. 74, 101–29

BECKINGHAM, C. F. (1950), "The date of Pitts's pilgrimage to Mecca", *Journal of the Royal Asiatic Society,* Nos. 3/4, 112–13

BELHAMISSI, Mouley (1988), *Les Captifs Algériens et l'Europe Chrétienne, 1518–1831* (Algiers: Entreprise nationale du livre)

BIDWELL, Robin (1976), *Travellers in Arabia* (London: Hamlyn)

BIRCHWOOD, Matthew (2007), "Vindicating The Prophet: Universal Monarchy and Henry Stubbe's Biography of Mohammed", *Prose Studies,* Vol. 29, No. 1, 59–72

BONO, Salvatore (1964), *I Corsari Barbareschi* (Turin: ERI-Edizioni, RAI Radiotelevisione Italiana)

—— (2010), "Slave histories and memoirs in the Mediterranean world: a study of the sources (sixteenth–eighteenth centuries)", in Fusaro, Maria (ed.), *Trade and Cultural Exchange in the Early Modern Mediterranean* (London: Tauris Academic Studies), 97–115.

BOSWORTH, Clifford Edmund (2006), *An Intrepid Scot: William Lithgow of Lanark's Travels in the Ottoman Lands, North Africa and Central Europe, 1609–21* (Aldershot: Ashgate)

BRENT, Peter (1977), *Far Arabia: Explorers of the Myth* (London: Weidenfeld & Nicolson)

BROCKETT, Allan (1962), *Nonconformity in Exeter, 1650–1875* (Manchester: Manchester University Press)

BRUCE, Travis (2010), "Piracy as statecraft: the Mediterranean policies of the fifth/eleventh century Taifa of Denia", *Al-Masaq,* Vol. 22, No. 3, 235–48

BRUGMAN, J. and SCHRÖDER, F. (1979), *Arabic Studies in the Netherlands* (Leiden: Brill)

BRUMMETT, Palmira (1994), *Ottoman Seapower and Levantine Diplomacy in the Age of Discovery* (Albany: State University of New York Press)

BURTON, Sir Richard (1855–1856), *Personal Narrative of a Pilgrimage to Al Madinah and Meccah,* 3 vols. (London: Longman, &c.)

—— (1893), *Personal Narrative of a Pilgrimage to Al Madinah and Meccah,* 2 vols. The Memorial Edition (London: Tylston & Edwards)

—— (1898 and 1913), *Personal Narrative of a Pilgrimage to Al Madinah and Meccah,* 2 vols. (London: Bell)

CARRÉ, Jean-Marie (1956), *Voyageurs et Ecrivains Français en Egypte,* deuxième éd. revue et corrigée, 2 vols. (Cairo: Institut français d'archéologie orientale)

CASTRIES, Henry de (1905–1961), *Les Sources Inédites de l'Histoire du Maroc,* 22 vols. (Paris: E. Leroux)

CLIFFORD, James and MARCUS, George E. (1986) (eds.), *Writing Culture: the Poetics and Politics of Ethnography* (Berkeley: University of California Press)

CLISSOLD, Stephen (1977), *The Barbary Slaves* (London: Paul Elek)

COINDREAU, Roger (1948), *Les Corsaires de Salé* (Paris: Société d'éditions géographiques, maritimes et coloniales)

COLLEY, Linda (2003), *Captives: Britons, Empire and the World, 1600–1815* (London: Jonathan Cape)

DAKHLIA, Jocelyne (2008), *Lingua Franca: Histoire d'une Langue Métisse en Méditerranée* (Arles: Actes sud)

DANIEL, Norman (1993), *Islam and the West: the Making of an Image,* revised edition (Oxford: Oneworld)

DAVIS, Robert C. (2003), *Christian Slaves, Muslim Masters: White Slavery in the Mediterranean, the Barbary Coast, and Italy, 1500–1800* (Basingstoke: Palgrave Macmillan)

—— (2004), *Christian Slaves, Muslim Masters: White Slavery in the Mediterranean, the Barbary Coast, and Italy, 1500–1800* (Basingstoke: Palgrave Macmillan) [This paperback edition contains the bibliography omitted in the 2003 hardback edition]

DE GROOT, Alexander H. (1985), "Ottoman North Africa and the Dutch Republic in the seventeenth and eighteenth centuries", *Revue de l'Occident Musulman et de la Méditerranée,* Vol. 39, no. 1, 131–47

DENY, Jean (1920), "Les registres de solde des Janissaires conservés à la Bibliothèque Nationale d'Alger", *Revue Africaine,* Vol. 61, 19–46

DUFFY, Michael (1992) (ed.), *The New Maritime History of Devon,* Vol. 1: *From Early*

*Times to the Late Eighteenth Century* (London: Conway Maritime Press in association with the University of Exeter)

EARLE, Peter (1970), *Corsairs of Malta and Barbary* (London: Sidgwick and Jackson)

EL-ROUAYHEB, Khaled (2005), *Before Homosexuality in the Islamic World, 1500–1800* (Chicago: University of Chicago Press)

FISHER, Sir Godfrey (1957), *Barbary Legend: War, Trade and Piracy in North Africa, 1415–1830* (Oxford: Clarendon Press)

FISHER, Stephen, (1992), "Devon's maritime trade and shipping, 1680–1780", in *The New Maritime History of Devon* (1992), Vol. 1, Duffy, Michael (and others, eds.), *From Early Times to the Late Eighteenth Century* (London: Conway Maritime Press in association with the University of Exeter), 232–41

FRIEDMAN, Ellen G. (1983), *Spanish Captives in North Africa in the Early Modern Age* (Madison: University of Wisconsin Press)

—— (1980), "Christian captives at 'hard labor' in Algiers, 16th–18th centuries", *International Journal of Historical Studies,* Vol. 13, no. 4, 616–31

FUSARO, Maria (2010) (ed.), *Trade and Cultural Exchange in the Early Modern Mediterranean* (London: Tauris Academic Studies)

GARCÉS, María Antonia (2002), *Cervantes in Algiers: a Captive's Tale* (Nashville: Vanderbilt University Press)

GARCIA, Humberto (2011), "Turning Turk, Turning Heretic: Joseph Pitts of Exeter and the Early Enlightenment, 1670–1740", in Maclean, Gerald, (ed.), *Britain and the Muslim World* (Newcastle: Cambridge Scholars), 85–101

GAURY, Gerald de (1951), *Rulers of Mecca* (London: Harrap)

GRAMMONT, Henri de (1879–1885), *Relations entre la France et la Régence d'Alger au XVIIe Siècle,* 4 vols. (Algiers: Adolphe Jourdan)

—— (1887), *Histoire d'Alger sous la Domination Turque (1515–1830)* (Paris: E. Leroux). Reprinted in 2002 (Paris: Bouchene)

GRANT, Alison (1992), "Devon shipping, trade and ports, 1600–1689", *The New Maritime History of Devon* (1992), Vol. 1, Duffy, Michael (and others, eds.), *From Early Times to the Late Eighteenth Century* (London: Conway Maritime Press in association with the University of Exeter) 130–8

GRAY, Todd (1989), "Turkish piracy and early Stuart Devon", *Report and Transactions of the Devonshire Association for the Advancement of Science, Literature and Art,* Vol. 121, 159–71

GREENE, Molly (2002), "Beyond the Northern Invasion: the Mediterranean in the Seventeenth Century", *Past and Present,* Vol. 174, no. 1, 42–71

—— (2010), "Victims of piracy? Ottoman lawsuits in Malta (1602–1687) and the changing course of Mediterranean maritime history", in Fusaro, Maria (ed.), *Trade and Cultural Exchange in the Early Modern Mediterranean* (London: Tauris Academic Studies), 177–201

GUILMARTIN, John Francis (2003), *Gunpowder & Galleys: Changing Technology & Mediterranean Warfare at Sea in the 16th Century.* Revised edition (London: Conway Maritime Press)

GUNNY, Ahmed (1996), *Images of Islam in Eighteenth-Century Writings* (London: Grey Seal)

HAMILTON, Alastair and RICHARD, Francis (2004), *André du Ryer and Oriental Studies in Seventeenth-Century France* (Oxford: Arcadian)

HEBB, David Delison (1985), "The English Government and the Problem of Piracy, 1616–1642", unpub. Ph.D. thesis (London)

—— (1994), *Piracy and the English Government, 1616–1642* (Aldershot: Scolar Press)

HESS, Andrew (1978), *The Forgotten Frontier: a History of the Sixteenth-Century Ibero-African Frontier* (Chicago: University of Chicago Press)

HEYWOOD, C. J. (2002), "Sir Paul Rycaut, a seventeenth-century observer of the Ottoman state: notes for a study", in *Writing Ottoman History: Documents and Interpretations* (Aldershot), Chapter 4. First published in Shaw, Ezel Kural, and Heywood, C. J. (1972) (eds.), *English and Continental Views of the Ottoman Empire, 1500–1800: Papers Read at a Clark Library Seminar January 24, 1970* (Los Angeles: William Andrews Clark Memorial Library, University of California), 33–59

HOGARTH, David G. (1905), *The Penetration of Arabia: a Record of the Development of Western Knowledge Concerning the Arabian Peninsula* (London: Alston Rivers)

HOLT, P. M. (1972), *A Seventeenth-Century Defender of Islam: Henry Stubbe (1632–76) and His Book* (London: Dr. Williams Trust)

HOSKINS, W. G. (1958), "Foreword", to Stephens, W. B., *Seventeenth-Century Exeter: a Study of Industrial and Commercial Development, 1625–1688* (Exeter: University of Exeter)

—— (2003), *Devon* (Chichester: Phillimore). Originally published in 1954

IRWIN, Robert (2006), *For Lust of Knowing: the Orientalists and their Enemies* (London: Allen Lane)

JOHANSEN, Baber (1982), "The servants of the mosques", *The Maghreb Review,* Vol. 7, nos. 1–2, 23–31

JOWITT, Claire (2007) (ed.), *Pirates? The Politics of Plunder, 1550–1650* (Basingstoke: Palgrave Macmillan)

JULIEN, Charles-André (1931), *Histoire de l'Afrique du Nord: Tunisie, Algérie, Maroc* (Paris: Payot)

—— (1970), *History of North Africa: Tunisia, Algeria, Morocco, from the Arab Conquest to 1830* (London: Routledge)

KAISER, Wolfgang (2008) (ed.), *Le Commerce des Captifs: les Intermédiaires dans l'Echange et le Rachat des Prisonniers en Méditerranée, XVIe–XVIIIe* (Rome: Ecole française de Rome)

KIERNAN, R. H. (1937), *The Unveiling of Arabia: the Story of Arabian Travel and Discovery* (London: Harrap)

LAMBERT, Andrew (2008), *Admirals: the Naval Commanders who Made Britain Great* (London: Faber)

LANE-POOLE, Stanley (1890), *The Barbary Corsairs* (London: Fisher Unwin)

LE FEVRE, Peter and HARDING, Richard (2000) (eds.), *Precursors of Nelson: British Admirals of the Eighteenth Century* (London: Chatham)

LEWIS, Bernard (1973), "Corsairs in Iceland", *Revue de l'Occident Musulman et de la Méditerranée,* Vol. 15–16, 139–44

LOUALICH, Fatima (2003), "Les esclaves noirs à Alger (fin du XVIIIe – début du XIXe siècles); de l'esclave à l'affranchi, vers une relation d'allégeance", *Mélanges de l'école française de Rome,* No. 115, (2003), 513–22

—— (2010), "In the Regency of Algiers: the human side of the Algerine *Corso*", in Fusaro, Maria (ed.), *Trade and Cultural Exchange in the Early Modern Mediterranean* (London: Tauris Academic Studies), 69–96

MACLEAN, Gerald (2004), *The Rise of Oriental Travel: English Visitors to the Ottoman Empire, 1580–1720* (Basingstoke: Palgrave Macmillan)

—— (2007a), *Looking East: English Writing and the Ottoman Empire before 1800* (Basingstoke: Palgrave Macmillan)

—— (2007b), "Of pirates, slaves and diplomats: Anglo-American writing about the Maghrib in the ages of empire", in Jowitt, Claire (ed.), *Pirates? The Politics of Plunder, 1550–1650* (Basingstoke: Macmillan), 169–86

—— and MATAR, Nabil (2011a), *Britain and the Islamic World, 1558–1713* (Oxford: Oxford University Press)

—— (2011b) (ed.), *Britain and the Muslim World* (Newcastle: Cambridge Scholars)

MADSEN, Peter (2010), "Danish Slaves in Barbary, (XVIe–XVIIIes)", in *La Guerre de Course en Récits: Terrains, Corpus, Séries*, dossier en ligne du Projet CORSO, URL: http://www.oroccrlc.paris-sorbonne.fr/index.php/visiteur/Projet-CORSO /Ressources/La-guerre-de-course-en-recits [accessed 5 May 2011]

MATAR, Nabil (1998), *Islam in Britain, 1558–1685* (Cambridge: Cambridge University Press)

—— (1999), *Turks, Moors, and Englishmen in the Age of Discovery* (New York: Columbia University Press)

—— (2001), "Introduction: England and Mediterranean captivity, 1577–1704", in Vitkus, Daniel J. (ed.), *Piracy, Slavery and Redemption: Barbary Captivity Narratives from Early Modern England* (New York: Columbia University Press), 1–52

—— (2003), "The last Moors: Maghāriba in early eighteenth-century Britain", *Journal of Islamic Studies,* Vol. 14, no. 1, 37–58

—— (2005), *Britain and Barbary, 1589–1689* (Gainesville: University Press of Florida)

—— (2007), "Piracy and captivity in the early modern Mediterranean", in Jowitt, Claire (ed.), *Pirates? The Politics of Plunder, 1550–1650* (Basingstoke: Palgrave Macmillan), 56–73

—— (2010) "The Maghāriba and the sea: maritime decline in North Africa in the early modern period", in Fusaro, Maria (ed.), *Trade and Cultural Exchange in the Early Modern Mediterranean* (London: Tauris Academic Studies), 117–37

MAZIANE, Leila (2007), *Salé et Ses Corsaires, 1666–1727: un Port de Course Marocain au XVIIe Siècle* (Caen: Presses universitaires de Caen)

MERCIECA, Simon, "Maritime caravans and the Knights of St John: aspects of Mediterranean seaborne traffic (sixteenth-eighteenth centuries)", in Fusaro, Maria (ed.), *Trade and Cultural Exchange in the Early Modern Mediterranean* (London: Tauris Academic Studies), 157–75

MILTON, Giles (2004), *White Gold: the Extraordinary Story of Thomas Pellow and North Africa's One Million European Slaves* (London: Hodder & Stoughton)

MORSY, Magali (1984), *North Africa, 1800–1900: a Survey from the Nile Valley to the Atlantic* (London: Longman)

MURRAY, Stephen and ROSCOE, Will (1997), *Islamic Homosexualities: Culture, History and Literature* (New York: New York University Press)

NETTON, Ian Richard (1996), *Seek Knowledge: Thought and Travel in the House of Islam* (Richmond, Surrey: Curzon Publishing)

NORRIS, H. T. (1994), "Edmund Castell (1606), and his *Lexicon Heptaglotton* (1669)", in Russell, G. A. (ed.), *The "Arabick" Interest of the Natural Philosophers in Seventeenth-Century England* (Leiden: Brill), 70–87

NORTON, Claire (2009), "Lust, greed, torture and identity: narrations of conversion and the creation of the early modern renegade", *Comparative Studies of South Asia, Africa and the Middle East,* Vol. 29, no. 2, 259–68

OSTLUND, Joachim (2010), "Swedes in Barbary captivity: the political culture of human security, *circa* 1660–1760", in *Historical Social Research/Historische Sozialforschung,* Vol. 35, no. 4, 148–63

PANZAC, Daniel (1985), *La Peste Dans l'Empire Ottoman, 1700–1850* (Louvain: Peeters)

—— (2004), *La Caravane Maritime: Marins Européens et Marchands Ottomans en Méditerranée, 1680–1830* (Paris: CNRS)

—— (2010), "Plague and seafaring in the Ottoman Mediterranean in the eighteenth century", in Fusaro, Maria (ed.), *Trade and Cultural Exchange in the Early Modern Mediterranean* (London: Tauris Academic Studies), 45–68

PENNELL, C. R. (1989), *Piracy and Diplomacy in Seventeenth-Century North Africa: the Journal of Thomas Baker, English Consul in Tripoli, 1677–1685* (Cranbury, New Jersey: Fairleigh Dickinson University Press)

PFULLMANN, Uwe (2001), *Durch Wüste und Steppe: Entdeckerlexikon Arabische Halbinsel: Biographien und Berichte* (Berlin: Trafo)

PIRENNE. Jacqueline (1958), *A la Découverte de l'Arabie: Cinq Siècles de Science et d'Aventure* (Paris: Le livre contemporain)

PRATT, Mary Louise (1986), "Fieldwork in common places", in Clifford, James and Marcus, George E. (eds.), *Writing Culture: the Poetics and Politics of Ethnography* (Berkeley: University of California Press)

RADFORD, Cecily (1920), "Joseph Pitts of Exeter (?1663–?1739)", *Transactions of the Devonshire Association for the Advancement of Science, Literature and Art,* Vol. 52, 223–38

RALLI, Augustus (1909), *Christians at Mecca* (London: Heinemann). Republished in 1971 (Port Washington, New York: Kennikat Press)

RESSEL, Magnus (2010), "The North European way of ransoming: explorations into an unknown dimension of the early modern welfare state", *Historical Social Research/Historische Sozialforschung,* Vol. 35, no. 4, 125–47

RODGER, N. A. M. (1997), *The Safeguard of the Sea: a Naval History of Britain, 660–1649* (London: HarperCollins)

—— (2004), *The Command of the Ocean: a Naval History of Britain, 1649–1815* (London: Allen Lane)

ROSE, Jonathan (2010), *The Intellectual Life of the British Working Classes,* 2nd edition (New Haven: Yale University Press)

ROYAL NAVY, UK (1980), *Red Sea and Gulf of Aden Pilot,* 12th edition (Taunton: Hydrographic Department)

RUSSELL, G. A. (1994) (ed.), *The "Arabick" Interest of the Natural Philosophers in Seventeenth-Century England* (Leiden: Brill)

SAID, Edward (1978), *Orientalism* (London: Routledge & Kegan Paul)

SAYRE, Gordon M. (2010), "Renegades from Barbary: the transnational turn in captivity studies", *Early American Literature,* Vol. 45, no.2, 325–38

SCHUCHARDT, Hugo (1980), "The Lingua Franca", in *Pidgin and Creole Languages: Selected Essays of Hugo Schuchard,* GILBERT, Glenn G. (ed. and tr.) (Cambridge: Cambridge University Press), 65–88. Originally published in German in 1909

SHAW, Ezel Kural, and HEYWOOD, C. J. (1972) (eds.), *English and Continental Views of the Ottoman Empire, 1500–1800: Papers Read at a Clark Library Seminar, January 24, 1970* (Los Angeles: William Andrews Clark Memorial Library, University of California)

SHUVAL, Tal (1998), *La Ville d'Alger Vers la Fin du XVIIIème Siècle: Population et Cadre Urbain* (Paris: CNRS)

—— (2000), "The Ottoman Algerian elite and its ideology", *International Journal of Middle East Studies,* Vol. 32, no. 3, 323–44

SIMMONS, James C. (1987), *Passionate Pilgrims: English Travelers to the World of the Desert Arabs* (New York: Morrow)

SNADER, Joe (1997), "The oriental captivity narrative and early English fiction", *Eighteenth-century Fiction,* Vol. 9, no. 3, 267–98

—— (2000), *Caught Between Worlds: British Captivity Narratives in Fact and Fiction* (Lexington: University Press of Kentucky)

STEPHENS, W. B. (1958), *Seventeenth-Century Exeter: a Study of Industrial and Commercial Development, 1625–1688* (Exeter: University of Exeter)

THOMSON, Ann (1987), *Barbary and Enlightenment: European Attitudes Towards the Maghreb in the 18th century* (Leiden: Brill)

THOMAS, Roger (1953), "The non–subscription controversy amongst Dissenters in 1719: the Salters' Hall debate", *Journal of Ecclesiastical History,* Vol. 4, 162–86

THORSTEINN, Helgason (1997), "Historical narrative as collective therapy: the case of the Turkish raid in Iceland", *Scandinavian Journal of History,* Vol. 22, no. 4, 275–89

TINNISWOOD, Adrian (2010), *Pirates of Barbary: Corsairs, Conquest and Captivity in the Seventeenth-century Mediterranean* (London: Jonathan Cape)

TOOMER, G. J. (1996), *Eastern Wisedome and Learning: the Study of Arabic in Seventeenth-Century England* (Oxford: Clarendon Press)

VALENSI, Lucette (1969), *Le Maghreb Avant la Prise d'Alger* (Paris: Flammarion)

—— (1977), *On the Eve of Colonialism: North Africa before the French Conquest* (New York: Africana)

VITKUS, Daniel J. (2001), "Bibliography of English captivity narratives from the sixteenth and seventeenth centuries", in Vitkus, Daniel J. (ed.), *Piracy, Slavery and Redemption: Barbary Captivity Narratives from Early Modern England* (New York: Columbia University Press), 371–6

—— (2010) "Barbary captivity narratives from early modern England: truth claims and the (re)construction of authority", in *La Guerre de Course en Récits (XVIe–XVIIIes: Terrains, Corpus, Séries,* dossier en ligne du Projet CORSO, 2010, URL: http://www.oroccrlc.paris-sorbonne.fr/index.php/visiteur/Projet-CORSO/Ressources/La-guerre-de-course-en-recits. [accessed 5 May 2011]

VOIGT, Lisa (2009), *Writing Captivity in the Early Modern Atlantic: Circulations of Knowledge and Authority in Iberian and English Imperial Worlds* (Chapel Hill: University of North Carolina Press)

WEINER, Jerome B. (1979), "New approaches to the study of the Barbary corsairs", *Revue d'Histoire Maghrébine,* Vols. 13–14, 205–9

WELLSTED, J. R. (1836). "Observations on the Coast of Arabia between Ras Mohammed and Jiddah", *London Geographical Journal,* vol. VI, pp. 51–96

WILLIAMS, Ann, "Sacra Militia, the Order of St John: crusade, corsairing and trade in Rhodes and Malta, 1460–1631", in Fusaro, Maria (ed.), *Trade and Cultural Exchange in the Early Modern Mediterranean* (London: Tauris Academic Studies), 139–56

WILSON, Peter Lamborn (1991), *Pirate Utopias: Moorish Corsairs and European Renegadoes* (Brooklyn, New York: Autonomedia)

WOLF, John B. (1979), *The Barbary Coast: Algiers under the Turks, 1500 to 1830* (New York: Norton)

## ONLINE SITES

CORRÉ, Alain D. (2005), *A Glossary of Lingua Franca,* 5th ed., URL: https://pantherfile.uwm.edu/corre/www/franca/go.html [accessed 4 March 2011]

*CORSO: Islam et Chrétienté Devant la Modernité,* URL: http://www.oroc-crlc.paris-sorbonne.fr/index.php/visiteur/Projet-CORSO/Ressources [accessed 5 May 2011]

LA GUERRE de Course en Récit: Terrains, Corpus, Séries, URL: http://www.oroc-crlc.paris-sorbonne.fr/index.php/visiteur/Projet-CORSO/Ressources/La-guerre-de-course-en-recits [accessed 5 May 2011]

PIRATI, Corsari e Loro Cacciatori nel Mediterraneo (XIII Secolo–XVII Secolo): Dizionario Biografico, URL: http://www.corsaridelmediterraneo.it/indice/a.htm [accessed 5 May 2011]

RÉPERTOIRE Nominative des Récits de Captivité en Méditerranée (XVIe–XVIIIe), URL: http://www.oroc-crlc.paris-sorbonne.fr/index.php/visiteur/Projet-CORSO/Ressources/R.N.R.C [accessed 5 May 2011]

# INDEX TO PART I

## JOSEPH PITTS: SAILOR, SLAVE, TRAVELLER, PILGRIM

# INDEX TO PART II

JOSEPH PITTS (1731), *A FAITHFUL ACCOUNT OF THE RELIGION AND MANNERS OF THE MAHOMETANS*

All references are to the pagination in Pitts's 1731 edition, which can be found in bold on the left-hand side of the text reprinted as Part II of this volume. Pitts's rendering of Arabic and Turkish words and names has been retained for this index to the text of his book. In cases where a more current or familiar style of transliteration may render the name or term more familiar to the reader, this has been included in square brackets after the entry, e.g. Beat Allah [Bayt Allāh], hawns [*khān*s], Tillimsan [Tlemcen, Ṭilimsān].